Second of Madame Mara

This Evening THURSDAY the 21st of JULY, 1796,

Will be presented the Serious Opera of

ARTAXERXES.

WITH

The original Music, Recitatives, Songs, Chorusses, &c.

Arbaces Mr. FLORIO,
(His second appearance on any Stage.)

Artabanes Mr. BOWDEN,

Rimenes Mr. STEWART,

Nobles Mr. GLENVILLE, Mr. GRACE, Mr. DOWLING, Mr. KELLY, &c.

And Artaxerxes Mrs. CHAPMAN.

Semira Miss DUNCAN,

And Mandane MADAME MARA,

(From the Opera-House, London, her second appearance here these four Years.)

The Orchestra will be augmented, and under the Direction
of Doctor Cogan.

Leader of the Band,—Mr. Fitzgerald.

The HARP SONG accompanied by Master SEYBOLD.

To which will be added a MUSICAL ENTERTAINMENT, called,

The ROMP.

Watty Cockney Mr. STEWART,

Captain Sightly Mr. GLENVILLE,

Old Cockney Mr. BARRET,

And Barnacle Mr. GRACE.

Penelope Miss DUNCAN,

Miss Le Blond Mrs. KELLY,

Quasheba Mrs. BARRET,

And Priscilla Tomboy Mrs. CHAPMAN.

§§§ Tickets and Places in the Boxes to be had of Mr. CHAPMAN, Box-keeper, at the Theatre.

THE TENTH NIGHT OF

Mr. Kemble's Engagement.

Tomorrow Evening, the Historical Tragedy of

CORIOLANUS.

Coriolanus Mr. KEMBLE.

OPERA IN DUBLIN
1705-1797

The Beggar's Wedding.

ILLUSTRATION REPRODUCED FROM THE FIRST EDITION OF THE LIBRETTO.
PRINTED DUBLIN 1729.

OPERA
IN DUBLIN
1705~1797

THE SOCIAL
SCENE
T.J.Walsh

ALLEN FIGGIS DUBLIN 1973

Illustration on Title Page

Crazy Crow.

PORTER TO THE PLAYHOUSE IN DUBLIN. HE LIVED ABOUT 1750. "CROW WAS ONE OF THOSE APPENDAGES TO THE THEATRE THAT ARE CONSTANTLY IN REQUISITION TO CARRY MESSAGES, LIGHT FIRES AND RENDER THEMSELVES USEFUL TO THE MANAGER, PROMPTER AND PERFORMERS IN GENERAL". (*Portraits, Memoirs, and Characters of Remarkable Persons.* BY JAMES CAULFIELD. LONDON 1819–20.)

© ALLEN FIGGIS & CO. LTD., 1973.

PRINTED IN THE REPUBLIC OF IRELAND BY
CAHILL & CO. LIMITED, DUBLIN.

For Ninette

CONTENTS

LIST OF ILLUSTRATIONS

INTRODUCTION

THE HISTORY OF opera in Dublin during the eighteenth century has until now been recorded only fitfully in musical or theatrical periodicals and briefly by W. H. Grattan Flood in his *History of Irish Music* and *Introductory Sketch of Irish Musical History*. Consequently it is hoped that this book will fulfil 'a long felt want'.

I have tried to relate the musical activity which then existed in Dublin's theatres to the general conditions of life in the capital during the period. Italian opera has always been prominent, with frequent presentation of works which are English either in origin or translation, and more rarely French or German opera. Ballad or comic opera and its modern counterpart, musical comedy, has had continuous popularity. In two centuries the mixture has changed little.

I have frequently quoted contemporary writers verbatim, even though original observations can be biassed or inaccurate, for this is primarily a source book.

I wish to acknowledge my debt to a number of writers whose work gave me a fuller understanding of the background of my subject. They are Professor William Smith Clark, Professor Esther K. Sheldon, Dr. La Tourette Stockwell, and that distinguished yet now virtually forgotten Irish theatrical historian, the late Dr. William J. Lawrence.

One author whom I would like to mention separately is the late W. H. Grattan Flood. It has become fashionable of late in discussions on Irish music to introduce Dr Grattan Flood as a sort of musical leprechaun from the early part of the century. As one who actually knew him perhaps I may be permitted to alter this impression.

It is true that I have had to break a lance with him over the first performance of Italian opera in Dublin; it is also true, as a distinguished English musicologist has observed, that with him patriotic zeal often proved stronger than judgement. But this tells only part of the story.

Grattan Flood spent most of his life as a church organist in an Irish provincial town. His income must have been shamefully small in relation to his abilities, his leisure time drastically curtailed by the necessity of earning a living as a music teacher. Yet he managed to find both money and time to travel to Dublin and elsewhere, to search and even more laboriously to copy down notes for his books and many articles.

His claim that Henry Purcell and John Dowland were of Irish descent is a clear example of his over-zealous patriotism. He undoubtedly wrote as a propagandist for Irish music but at a time when it was either scorned or ignored, except by a few enthusiasts. Provincial Ireland today stands in need of musicians of his stature and integrity. For the knowledge he uncovered which subsequently made my research so much easier I salute his memory.

I wish also to express my gratitude to Professor Brian Boydell for his generous assistance.

I spent pleasant hours in many libraries, especially the National Library of Ireland, the Library of Trinity College, Marsh's Library, Dublin City Library, and the Library of the Royal Irish Academy, all of Dublin; the Diocesan Library, Cashel; and the British Museum. In the larger libraries I have always found it difficult to discover the names of staff members. May I therefore thank those many people unknown to me by name who over several years gave me both their knowledge and time with such courtesy and kindness.

A few names I was able to discover, and so I can thank individually Mr. A. Hyatt King, Superintendent of the Music Room at the British Museum; and, in Dublin, Mr. Michael Breen of the National Library, Miss Mary Pollard of Trinity College Library, Miss Máirín O'Byrne of the Dublin City Library, and Mrs. McCarthy of Marsh's Library. My thanks are also due to Dean Charles W. Wolfe, who directs the excellent and too little-known seventeenth and eighteenth century Diocesan Library at Cashel, County Tipperary, and to the Misses Kathleen Lucking and Anna Drury of the Wexford County Library, who have always been so helpful in finding for me books which were otherwise unobtainable.

Finally I should like to record my indebtedness to Miss Helen Gregory, who was indefatigable in checking references and unsparing in her help.

My not very legible manuscript was neatly and accurately typed by Mrs. Phyllis Hannaford, who has not only my thanks but my admiration for such excellent work done from such poor copy.

The illustrations in the book are, with the exception of those noted later, all from the British Museum and reproduced by kind permission. The frontispiece of *The Beggar's Wedding* and the print of *Crazy Crow* are reproduced by kind permission of the Director and Trustees of the National Library of Ireland, and the play-bills by kind permission of the Board of Trinity College, Dublin. The portrait of Elizabeth Billington is from my own collection.

A friend once said to me, 'You know, you were always a theatre man.' If a little of the smell of the grease paint and size comes through these pages I shall be content.

T.J.W.

1

THAT PERPETUAL SINGING

As FAR AS is known, the word opera as commonly understood to-day was first employed in Dublin in the year 1661. On May 8 of that year, King Charles II in a royal patent 'revoked "all Graunts made to other[s] for representing anything" of a theatrical nature in Ireland, and provided that (1) John Ogilby should be granted for life the office of Master of the Revels in Ireland; (2) he should be licensed "to build upon such grounds by him to be purchased .. in Dublin .. such Theatre or Theatres as to him shall seeme most fitt .. and therein to represent Comedyes, Tragedyes and Operas" '.[1]

The revoking of 'all Graunts made to other[s]' is noteworthy since the previous holder of the patent, if only for the very short period from the previous November, and then entirely due to Ogilby's inertia, had been Sir William Davenant. Davenant had been the author and director of what has generally been considered the first English opera, *The Siege of Rhodes*. This had been presented by him in London in 1656, and on the Restoration he received a patent to set up a company of players, first housed at Lincoln's Inn Fields. There, many musical plays were performed and the theatre became known as the 'Opera'.

Ogilby, however, already held the office of Master of the Revels, which appointment he had received in February 1637/38 from the Earl of Strafford, then Lord Deputy in Ireland. Davenant's influence on the future history of opera in Ireland would in any event have been unimportant, for he was to die early in 1668.

If Ogilby had been dilatory before, he now lost no time in building his theatre. He chose for his site a piece of ground close to the Liffey Quays fronting on to 'a dirty street called Smock Alley'.[2] The Church

B

of SS. Michael and John near Essex Quay now occupies the same site. The construction of the theatre, as was then usual, included a 'music loft'. This was a gallery or room, built over the proscenium arch, in which the theatre orchestra was placed. This orchestral arrangement did not indicate an intention of presenting opera, nevertheless it was the precursor of today's opera orchestra. Professor Dent relates that it was for a performance of *The Tempest* with music by various composers at Dorset Garden Theatre, London, in 1674, that the orchestra was first placed in its now normal position. As he points out, this transference firstly permitted a much larger body of instrumentalists to take part, secondly it allowed them to be seen by the audience and so to become part of the theatre convention. It also, undoubtedly by accident rather than design, placed them where a conductor could eventually mould them with the singers on stage into one artistic whole. Meanwhile, hidden from view in their 'loft', their purpose was the entertainment of the audience with incidental music before and during the performance. There can be little doubt that they soon shared a more involved role in the productions: certainly by the 1699/1700 season when the Smock Alley Company was joined by one of London's leading composers and bass singers, Richard Leveridge.

Leveridge, then twenty-nine years old, had temporarily fled from London for this one season to escape his creditors. As a singer he was noted for his *basso profundo* voice although Hawkins records 'he had no notion of grace or elegance in singing; it was all strength and compass'.[3] He had appeared in London in Purcell's *The Indian Queen* and subsequently was to take part in the Anglo-Italian operas of *Arsinoe, Camilla* and *Thomyris*. As late as 1733 he sang in the first performance of Thomas Augustine Arne's *Rosamond*. He composed several songs, the best known today being 'The Roast-beef of Old England'. While in Dublin he composed a number of songs for the plays at Smock Alley. Professor W. S. Clark records an air, 'Marinda's Face like Cupid's Bow', and a duet, 'You, Bellamira, we admire'.[4] By coincidence he was to compose part of the music for the first opera ever to be performed in Ireland.

This was *The Island Princess, or The Generous Portuguese,* a version of Fletcher's early seventeenth-century play by the Irish author Nahum Tate,* adapted by Pierre Antoine Motteux. It was produced at Smock Alley Theatre during the 1705/06 season.** Leveridge's collaborators were Daniel Purcell, Jeremiah Clarke and William Pate. Jeremiah Clarke, a pupil of John Blow, was the most important of the four composers and still retains a tenuous foothold in musical history as the composer of 'The Prince of Denmark's March', now widely known as 'Trumpet Voluntary', and an air, 'The Bonny Grey-eyed Morn', which lives as ''Tis woman that seduces all mankind' in *The Beggar's Opera.* Daniel Purcell was a brother of the great Henry Purcell and Pate a well-known singing actor of the period.

The most interesting personality concerned is the librettist Motteux. Born in Rouen, he settled in London about 1680. There he became an auctioneer of paintings, seller of lace, and dealer in oriental goods. He next turned author. His comprehension of opera in England was both acute and prophetic, for in 1691/92 he was writing:

'Other Nations bestow the name of Opera only on such Plays whereof every word is sung. But experience hath taught us that our English genius will not rellish that perpetual Singing. I dare not accuse the Language for being over-charged with Consonants which may take off the beauties of the Recitative part, tho' in several other Countries I have seen their Opera's still Crowded every time, tho' long and almost all Recitative. It is true that their Trios, Chorus's, lively Songs and Recitatives with Accompaniments of Instruments, Symphony's,

---

*Nahum Tate was also the librettist of Purcell's opera *Dido and Aeneas.*

**The *Dublin News-Letter* of January 25/29, 1742/43, carries the following advertisement:
'For the Benefit of Mr. Philips
Being the first Time it was ever performed in this Kingdom with all the original Musick, Songs, Dances and other Decorations. At the Theatre in Smock-Alley on Monday the 14th of February will be performed a Dramatick-Opera called the Island Princess or the Generous Portuguese. Written by Beaumont and Fletcher and set to Musick by the celebrated Mr. Purcell. With the original Prologue to be sung by Mrs. Reynolds . . The whole to conclude with a grand Masque of Hymen . . with the original Epilogue to be sung by Mrs. Storer.'
Intentionally or inadvertently this ignores the production which had taken place thirty-eight years previously and another which had taken place about 1726. It should also be noted that Motteux' name is omitted and that the music is attributed to the 'celebrated' Mr. Purcell instead of his lesser known brother, and fellow composers.

Machines and excellent Dances make the rest be borne with, and the one sets off the other: But our English Gentlemen when their Ear is satisfied, are desirous to have their mind pleas'd, and Music and Dancing industriously intermixed with Comedy and Tragedy. . . what is unnatural, as are Plays altogether sung, will soon make one uneasy, which Comedy or Tragedy can never do, unless they be bad.'[5]

In this, Motteux promulgates the idea of a musical-dramatic form that was to persist in English opera almost to the end of the nineteenth century. Regretfully it must be recorded that 'he was murdered on February 17, 1718 at a brothel near St. Clements Church, London', though the article charitably, if rather naively, adds, 'The manner of his death was no criterion of his life which appears to have been sober'.[6] His place in the history of opera in Dublin is important since with one exception he was the sole librettist of the few operas which seem to have been presented there before 1727.

The Island Princess was a 'dramatick opera' in the Italian fashion, the libretto full of seventeenth-century pompous fustian, while at the same time anticipating much of the melodrama contained in the plots of nineteenth-century Italian tragic opera. There was plenty of opportunity for lavish theatrical spectacle. Stage directions such as – 'The Temple opens, an Altar is discovered, and priests near it . . Solemn Musick. Enter a Procession of Bramins as to the Sacrifice. Armusia and Quisara wreath'd and bound. Guards and Attendants', and 'The Scene Changes to the King's Palace in Tidore, thro which is discovered a Fleet of Ships of War' – the King enters 'attended with a numerous Train, Trumpets, Kettledrums and Music',[7] suggest a performance of *L'Africaine,* with which opera there is a similarity of setting.

That the opera received such extravagant staging in Dublin is extremely unlikely. In fact the only contemporary reference to the production is an announcement allowing 'the Company the sum of Twelve Pounds for making and Embellishing some Spanish shapes'.[8]*

*There was a revival of the opera at Smock Alley Theatre about 1726 with the following cast:
  'Armusia, a Noble Portuguese – Mr. Elrington.
  Ruidias, General of the Portuguese in the Spice-Islands – Mr. F. Elrington.

It did have a prologue of some originality consisting in part of a ballad composed by Leveridge. This jocularly comments on contemporary theatre-going manners and includes couplets such as:

'Ye gallery-haunters who love to lie snug

And munch apples and cakes whilst some neighbour you hug'[9]

instead of the customary rhetoric. It also had an epilogue written by George Farquhar, which sought the audience's indulgence for turning Fletcher's play into an opera. The entertainment ended with 'The Four Seasons or Love in every age. A Musical Interlude set to Musick by Mr. Jeremy Clarke',[10] which type of 'afterpiece' would appear to have been a regular part – a form of comic relief – of most English dramatic operas. This commenced with an overture. The setting was 'the four seasons on four several stages' and characters included country lasses and town sparks, an African lady with slaves and her negro lord, 'a lusty strapping middle ag'd widow' and a drunken officer – who assures her that 'One man like one nail serves to drive out another' – men and women of all ages, even including an old 'Dutch Woman with a stove warming herself' and an old miser, all making love in song and dance. Finally, 'Cupid with the four Ages, and the four Seasons mingle in a Dance' and there is a 'General Chorus of all the Voices and Instruments'.[11] The entire 'antimasque' was quite bawdy and obviously intended to be so.

Musically, *The Island Princess* was in the style, if not of the standard, of Purcell's *King Arthur*. Little of it, if any, advanced the action. The most impressive passage was probably an 'Incantation'[12] addressed to the Gods by three Bramins, followed by a short chorus. As in almost all English opera of the time, what occurred in presentation may have been relevant, it was rarely intrinsic.

Piniero, a Portuguese Officer, his friend – Mr. Rosco.

King of Tidore – Mr. Giffard.

The Governor, or Tyrant of the Island of Ternate – Mr. Vanderbank.

King of Bakam – Mr. Alcorn.

Prince of Syana – Mr. Watson.

Quisara, the King of Tidore's Sister – Mrs. Sterling.

Panura, one of her Women – Mrs. Grace.

1. Townsman – Mr. Layfield. 2. Townsman – Mr. Griffith, 3. Townsman – Mr. Sims. Bramins, Portuguese, Officers, Guards and Attendants. Scene. The Spice Islands. '(Libretto of Opera at National Library, Dublin.)

The standard of vocal performance in the Dublin production is difficult to assess. It probably bore some comparison with London, for there was a continual interchange of performers between the two capital cities. Apart from Richard Leveridge, other singing-actors mentioned by Hawkins as being 'most liberally endowed' with good voices who appeared at Smock Alley between 1675 and 1704 were Miss (or Mrs.) Cross, Mrs. Butler and John Freeman.

John Freeman was of an older generation than the others and joined the Smock Alley company about 1675, receiving his early stage training there. He later transferred to London where in 1695 he sang in Purcell's 'operatic' version of *The Indian Queen* with Mrs. Cross.

This lady, who was born about 1677, became a member of the Drury Lane company in 1694. Having injudiciously fallen in love she 'made an excursion into France with a certain Baronet'.[13] Evidently love was fleeting, for she quickly returned and, presumably to hide her embarrassment from Drury Lane audiences, late in 1698 travelled to Dublin instead. There, she was so warmly received that she did not return to London until the winter of 1704/05.

Mrs. Butler, who joined the company in 1694 was, according to Colley Cibber, 'the daughter of a decayed Knight'.[14] Undoubtedly more helpful to her career was the rumour that King Charles II had suggested her Christian name of Charlotte. 'A provident Restitution', as Cibber ironically expresses it, 'giving to the stage in kind what he had sometimes taken from it'.[15] In London she was greatly admired in Purcell's operas. Roger North describes her singing of a recitative as Cupid in *King Arthur* as 'beyond anything I ever heard upon the English stage'.[16] She is said to have come to Dublin because of a refusal to increase her salary from forty to fifty shillings a week at Drury Lane.

Another important singing-actor was Thomas Doggett.* Born in Dublin, he first joined the Smock Alley company during the 1684/85 season. He later became famous on the London stage. Congreve

*Remembered for his prize of 'Doggett's Coat and Badge' presented to the winner of a sculling race in honour of the accession of George I, still rowed by Thames watermen each year on August 1.

wrote the role of Ben in *Love for Love* for him, and he was one of the
artists to take part in *Almahide,* the first opera to be sung entirely in
Italian there. The singers in the opera were all Italian, but Doggett,
Mrs. Cross, and a Mrs. Lindsey sang in *intermezzi* in English between
the acts.

In December 1708 the Earl of Wharton, a dissolute man but a
generous patron of the arts, was appointed Lord Lieutenant of
Ireland. When he arrived in Dublin the following April he brought
Joseph Addison, the essayist, as his State Secretary, and the English
composer, Thomas Clayton, as director of Court festivities. He also
arranged for a company of actors to follow him from London.
Addison was the librettist of an opera *Rosamond* which had been set
to music by Clayton and performed at the Theatre Royal, Drury Lane,
in 1707. Clayton was also part composer (or arranger) of the opera
Arsinoe, Queen of Cyprus with libretto translated from the Italian by
Motteux. Consequently it is a reasonable assumption that these two
operas, or at least selections from them, formed part of the entertainments held throughout the year at Dublin Castle.*

Among the singing-actors who would have taken part were Anthony
Aston, the celebrated English strolling player, and his wife. Aston,
whose maternal grandfather was 'Colonel Cope of Drumally Castle in
the Co. of Armagh',[17] describes himself as 'Gentleman, Lawyer, Poet,
Actor, Soldier, Sailor, Exciseman, Publican'.[18] He relates how he
'went over into Ireland',[19] which he was again to visit in 1715 and yet
again as late as December 1732, on which occasion we learn that he
'continues every Friday in St. Patrick's Close to perform his diverting
Medley which is bespoke next Friday by Several Persons of
Distinction'.[20]

During his first visit in 1709 he presented a pastoral at Smock Alley
Theatre written by himself called *The Coy Shepherdess* which included
some singing. Two songs only are specified. The first opened Act I. –
'Scene, a Grove, discovers Melanctio sitting' – and was sung by a

---

*'Lord Wharton invited Clayton to Dublin and to produce an "opera" which must almost
certainly have been at Addison's suggestion.' (*The Life of Joseph Addison* by Peter Smithers.
Oxford. Clarendon Press. 1954. p. 180.)

Mr. Cooper who did not perform a role in the pastoral.* He can probably be identified with Mr. Coper, a singer in Betterton's company at Lincoln's Inn Field's Theatre during the 1695/96 season. The song, 'In Thought alone I can enjoy What others do Possess', was composed by Mr. Ximenes,** an almost unknown musician who is described as 'of Dublin'.[21] The second song, 'I Rove the Bleak, Cold Plain to find her, Pastora's fled away!' was sung by Mr. Champneys, as Sylvanus, to Pastora as she lay sleeping on a bank of flowers.

Later in the same year, on December 2, again at Smock Alley, a more important musical entertainment was staged. This was Pierre Motteux' celebrated masque of *Acis, Galatea and Polyphemus*. The music was by John Eccles, a well-known London theatre and opera composer. The air 'A fox may steal your hens, Sir' in *The Beggar's Opera* was originally composed by him as the song 'A soldier and a sailor', occurring in Congreve's play *Love for Love*. *Acis and Galatea* probably began, like *The Four Seasons* in *The Island Princess,* as an interlude to another opera called *The Mad Lover*. It is a short piece, the plot made familiar by Handel's later pastoral opera. But Motteux' text greatly alters the story and gives it a happy ending, where Acis, instead of being crushed with a rock by Polyphemus, is ultimately married to Galatea. An under-plot or 'antimasque' concerned with two courting lovers, Roger and Joan – a sort of Masetto-Zerlina episode – introduced a touch of comedy. This underplot seems to have been extremely popular and was to hold the stage for many years. In a Dublin theatre advertisement for May 21, 1733 we read '(not acted these ten years) the comick part of *Acis and Galatea*'.[22]

*The cast was as follows:
   Sylvanus, in Love with Pastora – Mr. Champneys.
   Melibaeus, in Love with Flora – Mr. Leigh.
   Melanctio, a Contemplative Shepherd – Mr. Aston.
   Pastora, the Coy Shepherdess – Mrs. Aston.
   Flora, a Gentle Shepherdess – Mrs. Dumene.
   Mophilda, her mother, a purblind Am'rous Old Shepherdess – Mrs. Lee.
   (Libretto in Gilbert Collection, Pearse Street Library, Dublin.)

**Dr. Grattan Flood reports a 'Charles Ximenes', very probably the same musician, drawing a salary of £40 per year in 1715 from the 'State Musick' in Dublin.
   (*Introductory Sketch of Irish Musical History*. London 1921. p. 31.)

2

THE ENIGMA OF NICOLINI

IN ALMOST EVERY modern encyclopaedia of music the reference to Dublin mentions that Italian opera was first introduced there in 1711, when Nicolini's company performed Handel's *Rinaldo*.* Nicolini, or Nicolo Grimaldi, was the reigning castrato singer of the time and was primarily responsible for the popularity of Italian opera in England. It is surprising consequently that such an important event should have gone unrecorded in eighteenth-century Irish theatrical literature.

Robert Hitchcock refers to the year 1711 at Smock Alley Theatre, but neither Nicolini nor *Rinaldo* are reported. W. R. Chetwood even suggests that Italian opera had in fact never been performed there when he states in 1749, 'Thus has this opulent City of Dublin every innocent Diversion, that may unbend the Mind, equal to any city of Europe, leaving the Italian Opera out, which can neither produce Mirth or Sorrow, Pity or Compassion'.[1] *Faulkner's Dublin Journal* of April 8/12, 1766, referring to a production of *L'Eroe Cinese,* confirms this view by announcing 'It is hoped that the Lovers of Music will patronise this first Attempt at producing a serious Italian opera on the Irish Stage'. None of these reports is of course necessarily infallible, but they are at least consistent.

On turning to the nineteenth and early twentieth century, however, we find Sir John T. Gilbert writing in 1854–59, 'That the Theatre was not badly supported in Dublin by the public in the early part of the eighteenth century appears from the performance here in 1711 by Nicolini, the distinguished singer and actor . . whether he was

*The present writer has helped to perpetuate the error in a monograph, *Opera in Old Dublin 1819–1839*. Wexford. 1952.

accompanied to Dublin by a foreign operatic Corps has not been stated'.[2]

To this Dr. W. H. Grattan-Flood in 1905 adds: 'The fame of Italian opera having spread to Dublin, Joseph Ashbury, Deputy Master of the Revels, invited over Nicolo Grimaldi Nicolini and his Italian opera company from the Haymarket in March 1711 . . Accordingly, he came over to Smock-alley Theatre at the end of March, and produced several plays, [sic] including *Rinaldo, Camilla* and *Pyrrhus and Demetrius* – Nicolini singing in Italian, whilst all the other performers sang in English. The Italian singers captured the Dubliners from April to July of the year 1711'.[3]

Again in 1921 Dr. Grattan-Flood repeats this information, now slightly modified. His reference to the other performers singing in English is now applied to singers at the Haymarket Theatre in London, and the time of Nicolini's visit is altered to 'March to June'.[4] The sentence concerning Italian singers capturing Dublin audiences, which in the above paragraph is surely ambiguous (either Nicolini was the only Italian in the company or the other Italians were singing in English), is now omitted. But he includes important information by adding, 'While in Dublin, Nicolini gave a benefit concert in aid of the Blue Coat Hospital and handed over the proceeds ($£39$ 15s. 10$\frac{1}{2}$d.) to that institution'.[5]

Gilbert's references are regrettably difficult to pinpoint, since they are compiled from a number of books listed without page attribution at the end of each chapter. Careful reading of the bibliography relevant to this particular chapter has failed to disclose any mention of Nicolini. It is more regrettable that Dr. Grattan-Flcod gives no references at all.

In order to probe the mystery, it seemed appropriate first to investigate Nicolini's appearances in 1711 at the Opera in London, with special reference to *Rinaldo*. He had first appeared there in 1708. In correspondence between Sir John Vanbrugh and the Earl of Manchester concerning his engagement, we learn that the opera season, at least for that year, would begin on September 10, and would end the following year on June 10. In 1711 Nicolini appeared in the first performance of Handel's *Rinaldo* on February 24, giving nine performances by March 24. After a break of ten days he took his benefit on April 4 in Francesco Mancini's opera *L'Idaspe Fedele* (of the renowned combat scene between Hydaspes and the lion). Further performances of *Rinaldo* followed on April 11 and 25, May 5, 9 and 26 and June 2. One must first enquire, did Nicolini take part in all these performances? It seems incredible that he would leave London until after his benefit, and since the performance on April 25 was 'at the Desire of several Ladies of Quality'[6] it can with some confidence be assumed that he did not leave until after that. It is known that in later years his role in *Rinaldo* was taken over by other singers in London – first by Mrs. Barbier on May 6, 1713, when he was quite definitely in Italy, and again in December 1714 and early in 1715 by Signora Diana Vico, when there is considerable evidence that he was still abroad. There is no record that the role was sung by anyone but Nicolini during 1711. Besides, it is unlikely that he would have relinquished his role in such a successful production during its first season or that the theatre management would have permitted him to do so.

Alternatively, could he have travelled to Dublin and returned to London between the performances listed above? It will be noted that two breaks of nine and sixteen days occur after April 25 and May 9. A factor against such a journey would be the time required to travel from London to Dublin and back to London in 1711. This would not have left sufficient time to produce and stage the three operas recorded by Dr. Grattan-Flood with a Dublin company completely inexperienced in Italian opera. Since the London season was still running it would have been impossible for him to have brought the company from the Haymarket Theatre. Nor in the time available could a 'scratch' company imported from London have staged such a difficult programme.

It is a reasonable assumption therefore that Nicolini, with or without a company, did not arrive in Dublin before mid-June. This would, of course, have permitted him to present his opera season during June or July, but this interval of time contradicts Dr. Grattan-

Flood's period of April-July or March-June, and if one cannot accept the accuracy of his period, can one accept the accuracy of his programme? Again, it must be restressed how could such an important theatrical event have occurred without any contemporary notice being taken of it?

Another aspect of the enigma which invited investigation was a peculiar similarity in all references to the subject in modern encyclopaedias and musical histories – all cited without corroborating origins. Four books were decided upon and the authors or publishers were asked if they would co-operate by giving the source of their information. From each of the four there was a generous and most helpful response.

The books chosen were the *Enciclopedia dello Spettacolo* (Rome, 1954–64), *Handel, a Documentary Biography* by Otto Erich Deutsch (London, 1955), Loewenberg's *Annals of Opera 1597–1940* (Geneva, 1955) and *Grove's Dictionary of Music and Musicians* (various editions).

The contributor to the *Enciclopedia dello Spettacolo* replied that his sources were 'Loewenberg and Deutsch'.[7] Professor Deutsch explained that research carried out some twenty years ago made it impossible to remember details, but that since he had not given any sources in his book he assumed that he had based his information on Loewenberg[8] (First edition 1943). Dr. Loewenberg's widow wrote that the information came from 'W. H. Grattan-Flood. *A History of Music,* Dublin. P. 126 f'.[9]

Grove's Dictionary presented a more complex problem. In the first two editions, a fairly detailed account of Nicolini's career contributed by Julian Marshall (1836–1903) omits any reference to his Dublin visit. In fact, the first reference to Nicolini in Julian Marshall's article occurs in the third edition of 1927, and is then inserted in a bracketed parenthesis out of chronological order as '(he sang in Dublin in March-June 1711)'. A letter addressed to the publishers of *Grove* elicited the following reply: 'We can only say that we believe the statements you quote from the third edition of Grove's *Dictionary of Music* about singers in Dublin were added to the original articles by the editor Dr. H. C. Colles, who died some time ago . . of course at this distance of time nothing remains of the original copy for the third edition, or of the corrected proofs'.[10] A further significant point concerning these additions in the third edition is that while Dr. Grattan-Flood was a contributor to the second edition of the *Dictionary,* it is in the third that he first receives the distinction of a personal reference. The contributor was again Dr. H. C. Colles.

From this, little doubt can remain that the original source of the *Grove* insertion, as of the others, is Dr. Grattan-Flood, and since the period March-June is quoted, it can even be attributed precisely to his *Irish Musical History* of 1921. Simply stated, modern knowledge on the subject rests solely and entirely on Grattan-Flood.

But what was Dr. Grattan-Flood's source? It would seem an over-simplification to attribute it to Sir John T. Gilbert, but that, as will presently be demonstrated, was his source – at least in 1905. By 1921 he had acquired the further information of Nicolini's Blue Coat Hospital concert, and with that discovery the puzzle can be solved.

But first let us review the source of Gilbert's information. It is just possible that it was identical with the above reference quoted by Dr. Grattan-Flood, but there is a reason for doubting this theory which will be mentioned later.

Instead, a most interesting broadsheet entitled 'The Signior in Fashion or The Fair Maid's Conveniency. A Poem on Nicolini's Musick-Meeting' is catalogued in the Diocesan Library at Cashel, Co. Tipperary. The date of printing is given as 1711 and while no printer's name appears on it, a printer's device does. The same printer's device on two pamphlets published in Dublin in 1711,* now in the National Library, Dublin, suggested that the printer was 'E. Waters at the New Post-office-Printing-House in Essex-street at the Corner of Sycamore-Alley'. Expert opinion that the wood-cut block of the device was the same in all the pamphlets, with the same broken titling occurring in the Nicolini pamphlet and one other, confirmed that the broadsheet was printed in Dublin by Waters. It records that Nicolini had enjoyed an ill-deserved success (in the

*See Appendix A.

opinion of the satirist)* and places beyond doubt the fact that he was in Dublin in 1711. Very likely the visit took place during the summer, since it was at that time of the year that important artists usually visited Dublin and the English provinces to augment their incomes when the London season had ended.

A second copy of the broadsheet is to be found in the British Museum. Inside the cover in which it is bound, there is recorded in fine print, 'Bound by W. Pratt for H. Stevens'.** The sometime owner of this copy was Henry Stevens, a noted American book collector and bibliographer, who travelled extensively making purchases for various important libraries and museums. He supplied many American books to the British Museum and, accompanied by the celebrated Sir Anthony Panizzi, Keeper of the Printed Book Department, undertook a 'three weeks' tour of Ireland'[11] on British Museum business in 1852. There they 'saw books, libraries, lakes',[12] Stevens 'kissed the Blarney Stone'[13] and they visited Cork and Dublin.

There can hardly be a doubt that Gilbert knew of one or other of the broadsheets. The one at Cashel seems the more likely. Almost certainly, however, Henry Stevens and Gilbert must have met while Stevens was in Dublin. Did Stevens find his copy of the broadsheet in Dublin or elsewhere in Ireland during his visit, and discuss it with Gilbert? The date, 1852, has some significance, for the first volume of Gilbert's *History of the City of Dublin* was to be published in 1854, and unquestionably he was then working on it. Whichever copy was the source of Gilbert's information, one can understand that a four-page pamphlet used merely to record the date of a singer's visit would be unlikely to be considered a reference of sufficient importance to be included in a bibliography during the mid-nineteenth century.

It should be noted that Gilbert wrote only of a 'performance here in 1711 by Nicolini',[14] the broadsheet advertises only a 'Musick Meeting', and finally, in the only original source he quotes, Grattan-Flood writes only of 'a benefit concert'.[15] Not once has the word

---

*See Appendix A.

**My attention was first drawn to this important document by Miss Helen Gregory, who, equally important, recognised the significance of the original owner's name.

'opera' been used. How then could Dr. Grattan-Flood introduce it into his *History of Irish Music* in 1905? At this remote date it is impossible to give a precise answer, but all the evidence indicates that it was an instance of *post hoc, ergo propter hoc*. Dr. Grattan-Flood knew that Nicolini had sung in *Rinaldo, Camilla* and *Pyrrhus and Demetrius* in London – he could have read it in *Grove* – and therefore, he presumably reasoned, he would perform them in Dublin. Introducing the latter two operas also permitted an anecdote about the Irish impresario, Owen MacSwiney. Obviously he did not consider the problems involved in mounting three new Italian operas for the first time in Smock Alley Theatre.

Having confirmed that Nicolini sang in Dublin in 1711, it now remains to reveal precisely where. Sir John Gilbert's reference to the visit seems ambiguous. He concludes that Smock Alley 'was not badly supported'[16] and advances as evidence 'Nicolini's performance here in 1711'.[17] But the words 'here in 1711' could apply equally well to Dublin as to Smock Alley Theatre. Again one must return to Dr. Grattan-Flood's reference to the 'Blue Coat Hospital' for the answer.

In a history of the school hospital published in 1906 one meets, as early as the year 1686, with an announcement concerning a 'great hall'.[18] Subsequently the writer continues: 'And yet at this time' (1702–1714) 'we find the sequelae of the Revolution still seriously weakening us in the general want of money. . So our Governors were obliged to look out on all sides for ways and means. A source of income had been devised by letting the great Hall for public entertainments; this was now put an end to. A rope dancer had given us one benefit night in 1703 for the use of the Hall, which yielded just £20, but the Governors decreed that . . "such diversions were very prejudicial to good government, causing the boys to be disorderly, to break the glass windows and cause scandal" . . so the rope dancing ceased, doubtless much to the disgust of our boys, and a Board Order forbade the future letting of the Hall save by special leave of the Governors. This seems to have been given some time after, when the great Italian opera singer, Nicolini, came to Dublin'.[19]

There is extant at the Blue Coat School a foolscap-sized minute book in manuscript listing, from the year 1669 'y⁰ names of y⁰ Severall benefactors with the sums by them respectively given towards y⁰ building of this Hospitall and for the support and maintenance of the children placed therein', and on page 251 under date of 1711 occurs the entry, 'Senior Nicholini one night's benefit of his Entertainm' of musick at this Hospitall £39. 15s. 10½d'. Not that the Governors received this distinguished artist more favourably than they had the simple acrobat of 1703. An entry in the minutes of '14th xber 1711' records: 'Whereas lending the Hall of this house for publick diversions of Musick meetings and other entertainments hath given great offence and found prejudiced to the interest and good Government thereof. It is therefore ordered and agreed by the authority aforesaid, that the said Hall shall be not lent for the future, or imployed for any musick meetings or public diversions whatsoever'. So, the venue of the 'Musick-Meeting' is established.

There is evidence that Nicolini used to visit Bath to give similar concerts. Thomas D'Urfey, the dramatist, in a song called 'The Bath Teazers' relates:

> 'Then comes the Eunuch* to tease them the more
> Subscribe your two Guineas to make up fourscore
> I never Perform'd at so low rate before',[20]

while Anthony Aston in his 'Bath Medley' – the type of entertainment he was performing in Dublin at St. Patrick's Close in 1732 – has a couplet:

> 'Here's half a guinea
> To hear Nicolini'.[21]

The reason for believing that Gilbert was unaware of the 'Blue Coat Hospital' source when writing his *History of the City of Dublin* is that, had he known it, it appears inconsistent that when speaking of Nicolini, he did not make known the place where his concert was held.

Further research may one day reveal exactly how many concerts

---

*In the Novello Edition of Hawkins' *A General History of the Science and Practice of Music* published in 1875, the words 'the Eunuch' are altered to 'Nicolini'.

Nicolini gave, and even what he sang. Meanwhile, unless further evidence is forthcoming, it would appear that the claim that Italian opera was introduced into Ireland as early as 1711 must be abandoned. It is not impossible that Nicolini sang arias from the operas mentioned at his 'Musick-Meeting', for it was normal procedure some twenty years later that singers coming to Dublin for concerts would include arias from operas in which they had been appearing with success in London.

Whatever he sang, Dublin audiences at least heard Nicolini's voice. This was originally soprano, but soon became contralto. Hawkins records that John Ernest Galliard (in whose opera *Calypso and Telemachus* Nicolini had sung) considered him to be both a fine actor and a good singer. In fact he appears to have been admired as much for his acting and appearance as for his singing. The Irish author Sir Richard Steele tells us how 'Every Limb, and every Finger contributes to the Part he acts, insomuch that a deaf Man might go along with him in the Sense of it'[22] and, speaking of his walking on stage, describes, 'I have seen [him] enter alone at the remotest Part of it, and advance from it with such Greatness of Air and Mien, as seemed to fill the Stage, and at the same Time commanded the Attention of the Audience with the Majesty of his Appearance'.[23] Nicolini had star quality.

He was thirty-five years of age when he first arrived in London in 1708, and undoubtedly his performance in *Rinaldo* in 1711 contributed enormously not only to the opera's success but to Handel's career in England. Joseph Addison epitomises not only the castrati, but eighteenth-century Italian opera seria, when he describes him in this opera 'exposed to a Tempest in Robes of Ermin, and sailing in an open Boat upon a Sea of Paste-Board'.[24] He was to spend the remainder of his life between London, Venice and Naples. He died in the latter city in 1732, leaving among his possessions what he credulously believed was the staff of St. Joseph, which supposed relic had been palmed off on him in London. This staff, according to Angus Heriot in *The Castrati in Opera*, may still be seen in Naples at the Church of Real Monte.[25]

B

Enigmatic references to two further singers occur in a meandering poem, 'The Progress of Musick in Ireland to Mira',[26] written in 1730 by the Reverend Matthew Pilkington, a clergyman-poet born in Dublin about 1700, who was later to marry the minor pretentious Irish authoress, Letitia Pilkington. Pilkington is chiefly known for his *Dictionary of Painters,* first published in 1770 and appearing in successive editions for almost a century.

In this poem the bard Turlough Carolan is first described:

> 'The Solemn *Harp,* beneath his Shoulder plac'd
> With both his Arms is earnestly embraced'.

Next we read:

> 'The *Muses* now from Albion's Isle retreat
> And here with kind Indulgence fix their Seat'.

There follows a complimentary reference to William Viner, a violinist and 'Master of the State Musick in Ireland' from 1703 until 1716. Matthew Dubourg, another violinist who later held the same position, is also praised. Nicolini's visit is commemorated and then we read of two singers, one of whom it seems impossible to identify.

Pilkington records:

> 'So when *Belinda's* heav'nly Beauties stand
> Wrought into Life by Kneller's magic Hand
> Her Face, her Shape, have all that *Art* can give
> Start from the animated Paint and Live;
> But, when the real Nymph, divin'ly bright
> Array'd in native Lustre, strikes our Sight
> Some nameless transport in our Bosom plays
> That Shade and Colour want the Force to raise'.

Now who was Belinda? Was this some cryptic reference to Alexander Pope's heroine of *The Rape of the Lock* or an allusion to a character in Sir John Vanbrugh's *The Provok'd Wife*? The latter, it should be noted, was a play and not an opera, and while songs were introduced, none were sung by Belinda. *The Provok'd Wife* was performed in Dublin, seemingly for the first time, in 1721,[27] but unfortunately the names of most of the cast cannot be traced. The line in the poem:

'Wrought into Life by Kneller's magic Hand'

offers an obvious clue until one discovers that the only singer or actress painted by Kneller who is known to have appeared in Dublin is Mrs. Cross.* Mrs. Cross played in *The Provok'd Wife* in London on many occasions between 1716 and 1724, but she always took the more mature role of Lady Fanciful. There is no record of her ever having performed Belinda. Her period in Dublin was 1698–1704, when she was about twenty-one to twenty-seven years old, and Kneller's portrait depicts her as a young woman. At this time Pilkington was scarcely born. Further, in 1730 he was writing from a very long memory when he described Nicolini, whom he would have heard in Dublin when he was only eleven. One begins to wonder just how much of the progress of music in Ireland Pilkington had personally experienced and how much he was merely recording from hearsay. Consequently the evidence in favour of Mrs. Cross remains ambivalent. Present knowledge permits surmise only; Belinda meanwhile retains her mask.

The second singer at first seems equally difficult to identify. We read:

'Next *Bocchi* Reigns, whom Art and Nature grace
To Smooth the roughness of the sullen *Base,*
Directs his Notes distinct to rise or fall,
Tries ev'ry Tone to charm, and charms in all'.

This appears to confirm that the singer's name was Bocchi and that he had a bass voice – until one searches in vain for a bass singer named Bocchi performing anywhere at this time. The name nonetheless looked familiar, and when the first C was replaced by an S, then, like fitting the final piece in a jig-saw puzzle, the problem was solved, for Giuseppe *Boschi* was the most celebrated bass of the eighteenth century. Extensive research having failed to disclose a

*See illustration of Mrs. Cross as St. Catherine.

bass named Bocchi,* the conclusion is compelling that this was the mis-spelling of a foreign name due to a printer's error.

Boschi, who is said to have been born in Viterbo, may have commenced his career as a member of the choir of St. Mark's in Venice. Hogarth, who incidentally also mis-spelled his name as 'Roschi', describes him as 'a singer of ability',[28] though he adds 'it does not seem that he had any reputation on the continent'.[29] Burney records that 'Boschi had a fine bass voice, for which Handel composed some of his best bass songs'.[30] Handel in fact brought him to London and he was a member of the cast of *Rinaldo* when it was produced in 1711. Burney adds that he left England after this one season, to return in 1720. In that year he was in the cast of Handel's *Radamisto* and during the following years appeared in first performances of Handel's operas, *Floridante, Ottone, Flavio, Giulio Cesare, Siroe* and *Tolomeo*. He of course also sang in operas by other composers such as, Bononcini,

---

*Professor Brian Boydell has drawn my attention to the following advertisement in the *Dublin Courant* of August 22, 1724:

'Whereas Mr. Neale in Christ Church Yard, Dublin, has with great care printed a new Opera, consisting of several Sonata's for the Violin, Violincello, Six-String Bass and Flute with a Scotch Cantata, and the Instrumental Parts thereo [sic] [thereto] after the Italian Manner, compos'd by Mr. Lorenzo Bocchi, which, (tho' the first Musical Performance that was ever printed in this Kingdom) is judg'd to be no way inferior to London Impressions, by the best Masters here: This is to acquaint all lovers of Musick, that the said Opera will be published by Subscription at the beginning of next Winter, and the Author having most of the Scotch Nobility his Subscribers, hopes to meet with the same Encouragement in this Kingdom'.

The possible coincidence of a Signor Bocchi in Dublin during the same period described by Pilkington prompts the question – Was this the artist about whom he was writing? It may or may not have been. Neither alternative, however, precludes identification with Boschi, for – however unlikely – Boschi could have been a very minor composer as well as a singer, and the conflicting christian names of Lorenzo and Giuseppe could have been an error recorded either by the *Dublin Courant* or by Hawkins in his *General History*, the apparent source of the traditional name of Giuseppe. The essential point is that amongst a group of distinguished musicians Pilkington introduces an exceptional bass singer. At that period the bass voice was not in fashion and so was a distinct rarity. Since no other important bass was then singing in London no other identification seems possible.

One other explanation remains. As already suggested, Pilkington could have taken poetic licence and have written about musicians whom he had not actually heard but of whom he had read or had been informed. He could have read of Lorenzo Bocchi in the newspapers or on theatre bills. He could then have confused the name with the more famous Boschi and written his verse with the latter artist in mind. This conclusion would at least help to solve the riddle of Mrs. Cross and Belinda.

remaining in London until 1728 when the opera company dispersed. According to Burney he then returned to Venice.

Did Boschi really perform in Dublin? The Reverend Pilkington's eulogy is convincing. Confirmatory evidence may one day emerge for, apart from this single reference, his appearance in Dublin has previously remained unrecorded. If he did sing there, at least there can be no doubt that, like Nicolini, he sang in concert only and not in opera.

3

A MASQUE AT THE CASTLE

THE NEXT ITALIAN singer whose arrival in Dublin can be recorded precisely was Signor Benedetto.* He is reputed to have 'received encouragement from the Generous Persons of Note and Distinction in this City for sixteen Concerts at half a guinea per Ticket'[1] during late October or early November 1725.

While there is no doubt about this artist's performances, there is uncertainty about his identity. Burney, writing of opera in London in 1721, mentions a 'Baldassarri sometimes called Benedetto, who had been here before in 1712',[2] and the first four editions of *Grove's Dictionary* have short articles under two names, Benedetto Baldassari and Benedetti, not for cross reference, but as if they were two different singers. The fifth edition, however, includes only Benedetti and combines the information from the earlier editions as if it had been decided that the two artists were one and the same. Under either guise he appears to have been a second-rate castrato singer who returned to London in 1720. Appearances of a 'Signor Benedetto Baldassari'[3] are chronicled in *The London Stage* for that year. He sang at the King's Theatre in the first performances of Handel's operas *Il Radamisto* and *Floridante* (with Boschi), and in an opera called *Narcisso* by Domenico Scarlatti which had some additional music by Thomas Roseingrave.

A correspondent to Steele's journal *The Theatre* relates of Benedetti how: 'It happen'd, Sir, in the casting the Parts for the new Opera, that he had been, as he conceiv'd, greatly injur'd; and, the other Day, apply'd to the Board of Directors, of which I am an unworthy Member, for Redress. He set forth, in the recitative Tone, the nearest approaching

*Reported by W. H. Grattan-Flood in an *Introductory Sketch of Irish Musical History*. London. 1921. p. 36.

ordinary Speech, that he had never acted anything, in any other Opera, below the Character of a Sovereign; or, at least a Prince of the Blood; and that now he was appointed to be a Captain of the Guard, and a Pimp'.[4]

No report of his Dublin concerts seems to be extant except a critical outburst of patriotic fervour from 'Hibernicus' in the *Dublin Weekly Journal,* who writes:

'Whilst our poor Players can scarcely get Bread among us by representing to us in an agreeable and instructive Manner, the various Passions and Humours of Mankind a wretched *Italian* songster that is no more than the Effigies of a Man shall draw from our Folly a Revenue equal to that of a Nobleman.'[5]

Opposition to the 'poor Players' continued when on December 8, 1725, 'Signiora Stradiotti, lately arriv'd from Italy'[6] – probably the first Italian prima donna ever to appear in Dublin – gave a concert at Smock Alley Theatre. It was announced, rather ambiguously, as 'A Cantata composed by Philip Percival Esq.'[7] for while Percival may have arranged the cantata, it consisted of a string of arias from Handel's operas. Philip Percival was a fashionable amateur, a viola player and composer patronised by the Prince of Wales, later George II. He was a friend of Handel and of the celebrated and loquacious Mrs. Delany who some thirty years later would write of him and his wife from Bristol: 'We found the *good couple* just as you left them— the *same* green damask gown, the *same* crimson breeches and embroidered waistcoat'.[8]

Among the Handel arias included in the programme were 'Would you gain the tender creature' from *Acis and Galatea, Dove sei dolce mia vita, Alla fama dimmi il vero* and *Benchi mi sia crudele* from *Ottone, Da tempeste il legno infranto* and *Venere bella, per un instante* from *Giulio Cesare,* and *Scacciata del suo nida* from *Rodelinda.* This was the first verifiable performance of excerpts from Handel's operas to have taken place in Dublin. A libretto of the cantata had an English translation 'by Mr. Joshua Brunel of Trinity-College'.[9] He was a Waterford youth, then only seventeen years of age, who had entered the University in 1724.

Little can be discovered of Signora Stradiotti. She had arrived in London in 1714 when she took over opera roles at the Haymarket Theatre previously sung by Mrs. Barbier, an artist who was to sing in Dublin in 1731. Her first London appearance seems to have taken place on November 16 in a *pasticcio* called *Ermelinda*. Francis Colman has recorded of this performance, 'Edelberto by Sig^ra Stradiotti. a very bad singer'.[10] No announcement of her performing in London in 1725 can be discovered.

Meanwhile, as early as 1708/09 there had arrived in Dublin an opera composer who, if he did little to influence its history there, did at least present one opera. He was Johann Sigismund Kusser who had been born in Bratislava in 1660. In Dublin he was known as Cousser, a French variation of his name which he had acquired while living in Paris, where he had come under Lully's influence. He had spent his earlier years living alternately in Stuttgart, Brunswick and Hamburg, and in the latter city made a distinctive mark as conductor, composer and opera manager between 1694 and 1696. He next proceeded to Nuremberg and Augsburg, but in 1698 he returned to Stuttgart where in 1700 he was appointed *Ober-Kapellmeister*. At this period he had composed at least fifteen operas. He visited Italy on two occasions and Hawkins credits him with introducing 'the Italian method of singing'[11] into Germany. He is first discovered in London in 1705 composing for a singer called Giuliana Celotti, who was subsequently to appear with him in Dublin.

From the year of his arrival in Dublin* until his death, he was to compose an annual birthday ode in honour of the reigning monarch. His successful *entrée* into the musical life of Dublin can also be traced from the libretti of these odes. Gaps exist in the sequence of libretti extant but while in 1709 his name is printed as composer without added title or distinction, in 1711 he is described as 'Chappel-Master of Trinity Colledge',[12] and by 1717 he had become 'Master of the

*Hawkins' *A General History of the Science and Practice of Music* gives this incorrectly as 1710. The first ode by Cousser to be discovered (at the National Library, Dublin) is dated February 6, 1709. Scrutiny of the dates of odes composed for later years confirms that this was 1708/09 according to the then existing old calendar, or 1709 according to today's Gregorian calendar.

Musick attending His Majesties State in Ireland',[13] his predecessor, William Viner, having died in 1716.

The odes were variously described as 'Serenade', 'Serenata', 'Serenata da Camera' and 'Serenata Theatrale' and had one distinguishing feature in common – all were clearly intended for performance as cantatas, perhaps in costume, but not as operas and no stage directions were given. Allegorical figures and characters from classical mythology such as Fate, Fame, Britannia, Peace, Jupiter, Minerva, Mercury and 'Heroick Virtue'[14] were introduced, all embarrassingly laudatory of their queen or king. There was also a chorus which invariably ended the ode with a climax of loyal benediction.

The performances, which were by command of the Lord Lieutenant or, due to his frequent absences abroad, more usually 'By their Excellencies the Lords Justices Special Command',[15] were held, with the exception of the first which was at Smock Alley Theatre, 'at the Castle of Dublin'.[16] They took place on the monarch's birthday at twelve noon and were preceded by a procession to the Castle and followed by a late afternoon banquet with bell ringing and cannon firing. In the evening there was a play at Smock Alley Theatre. Afterwards, fireworks over the river Liffey completed the day.

The libretti examined indicate that the standard of the odes varied from year to year. Descriptions of the performances remain undiscovered, yet certain generalisations can be inferred from the few details known. For example, one libretto which reveals some information was for the entertainment in 1712, since certain expenses of this performance were recorded by Cousser. The ode on this occasion is described both as a 'Serenata' and a 'Serenata Theatrale' and includes the following list of characters: 'Britain in a Royal Throne. The Thames [An artist representing the allegorical 'Father Thames'] encircled with Najades. Apollo with the Nine Muses. Glory and Zeal in Trionfant Carrs'.[17] Of these, Britain, Thames, Apollo, Zeal and Glory sing recitatives and arias and, very briefly, on four or five occasions, duets or trios. There is both a 'Choir of Nymphes'[18] and a second, non-designated chorus. The nymphs are members of Thames's *entourage* and he exhorts them to sing the Queen's 'deserv'd applauses'.[19] Taking part consequently was a cast of five singers, a choir of treble voices and a mixed choir.

Thames's encircling naiads and Apollo's nine muses have not been included in this list since, as will be demonstrated presently, they were not singers, but there can be little doubt that they were members of a ballet. Intimation of this occurs twice in the libretto. The more important piece of evidence is the word 'Chaconne', indicating a dance, printed in distinctive capital letters of a type face not used elsewhere in the libretto. Corroboration may be found when Thames exhorts 'ye num'rous watry Powers' to 'dance along my Banks',[20] although it should be stressed that this may have merely been a florid descriptive passage in the text and not a practical stage direction.

Next, turning to Mr. Cousser's expense account we find it set out as follows:

'For Mr. Sword's five boys	£1	3	
To John Johnson		6	
To Frank		6	
To Pierce		6	
To. Mr. Stevens, Junr.		6	
To Mr. John Adams		6	
To Mr. Webster		6	
To Mr. Crackenthorp		6	
To Mr. Marsden		6	
To. Mr. Delamain		11	6
To. Mr. Murphy		9	3
To Mr. Arnold for two Tunings ye Harpsicord		10	

Remains for my Composition and Mest⁸ Celotti's performance for each 2 pounds 13 shill 10 pence – John Sigism. Cousser'.[21]

Building history on the shifting sands of conjecture presents a hazard – it rarely stands the test of time. Yet, when a more solid foundation cannot be established, if a story is to be compiled, surmise must replace authentication. Consequently, while it could be assumed that the gentlemen named above were instrumentalists of the state band, it is extremely unlikely that this permanent body of musicians, who almost certainly were paid an annual fee, would have to be paid extra by Cousser on such a dedicated occasion. It is of course possible that he may have had to engage some extra instrumentalists, but as a chapel-master, Cousser was more likely to have been engaging singers for the performance of his composition – Celotti was one – and so, it seems probable, were most of the others with the exception of Mr. Arnold. From the list, therefore, we can deduce that Giuliana Celotti probably sang the role of Britain and that four others sang the roles of Thames, Apollo, Glory and Zeal. It should also be noted that Delamain and Murphy were paid higher fees than the other artists, excepting Cetotti. The part which Delamain may have played in the production will be discussed later.

Excluding these six, a probable group of four men (five if Mr. Swords is to be included) and five boys remained to form a chorus of trebles, altos (the line was invariably sung by men at that time), tenors and basses. The 'Choir of Nymphes' would have consisted of the five boys. Doubtless all these singers were recruited from the Cathedral choirs. Choir members taking part in performances at Smock Alley are recorded – and were frowned upon by the Church authorities – as early as 1662/63.[22] That matters were again lax in 1712 is made clear by a letter from Dean Swift in 1719. 'I have the honour to be Captain of a band of nineteen musicians (including boys)', he writes, '. . but my quire is so degenerate under the reigns of former Deans of famous memory, that the race of people called Gentlemen Lovers of Musick tell me I must be very careful in supplying two vacancies'.[23] Mr. Swords, who supplied the five boys, may perhaps be identified with Henry Swords, a lay vicar choral of St. Patrick's, who was installed in 1698.

There remain Thames's naiads, and Apollo's muses. From the foregoing it is evident that Cousser's total stipend was intended to cover the fee for his ode and payment for the singers, but payment for a temporary ballet group remains undiscovered – and unexplained. It is just possible that this is where Delamain and Murphy may have been engaged. The name of Murphy is much too common to permit identification, but a 'Mr. Delamain'[24] was performing as a dancer at Smock Alley in 1732. The span of years weakens the probability that he was the same man, but does not exclude it. If he was the same, then almost certainly his fee from Cousser was earned as *maître de ballet*, while his dancers, presumably drawn from the Smock Alley company, would have been paid, not by Cousser, but by Joseph Ashbury, the manager of the theatre.

A second theory, extravagant though it may appear, may also be considered – that the ballet was composed of a group of Court ladies. The participation of the nobility in masques at both the English and French Courts does not necessarily prove that the fashion had extended as far as Dublin. Neither does Cousser's association with Lully in Paris, when Lully was introducing the chaconne into his Court operas and ballets, necessarily mean that Cousser was to imitate Lully's formal ballets in his Dublin ode some thirty years later. Instead, evidence for the theory is to be found in two Dublin news reports – separated by a span of almost a century. First, of a performance in honour of King George the First's birthday on October 20, 1714, we read, 'a very great number of the Nobility, Clergy, Judges and Gentry, and a great many Ladies in very fine Cloathes went to the Castle' where 'a Coronation Song in honour of his Majesty was performed by the best Masters'.[25] By implication this confirms that ladies were also present in 1712. Then, eighty-two years later, in 1796, Mr. Fontaine, a dancing-master, respectfully informed the Nobility and Gentry of Dublin that his Ball had been 'fixed by Order of the Countess of Camden [the Lord Lieutenant's wife] and several other Ladies of High Rank',[26] adding the important announcement that 'The Grand Ballet performed at the Castle on St. Patrick's Night will be danced this Night by 16 Ladies and Gentlemen'.[27]

Members of the nobility dancing a 'Grand Ballet' at the Castle on a state occasion in 1796 is of course not evidence that the same form of entertainment was taking place there in 1712. Nevertheless, from the announcement a question can be summarised – In what year did the tradition of dancing formal ballets commence at Dublin Castle? Did it exist in 1712 under Delamain's direction and were the 'very fine Cloathes' which we know were worn in England and France for Court performances worn also for theatrical display in Dublin? One thing at least is certain, at an entire production cost of only £10-9-5, the Lords Justices were not unduly extravagant in the presentation of their ode to honour Queen Anne in 1712.

By 1723 things had much improved. For 'His Majesty's Birth-Day Song'[28] in that year Cousser received a fee of £20,[29] and the ode, titled 'A Contest between Marsyas and Apollo',[30] introduced an element of confrontation missing from earlier panegyrics. Yet, it remained a Serenade; there is still no suggestion of any attempt at staging.

There is however some indirect information concerning the music. In a short preface to the work Cousser explains that 'The subject was some Years ago exhibited in the Italian Tongue in a Foreign-Court'.[31] He has now had it translated into English 'yet so as the Italian Method in this kind of Performance has been duly observed'.[32] For example, 'The Character of Apollo is represented by soft and sweet Musick, and that of Marsyas by a noisy and rural one'.[33] The music was all newly composed by Cousser 'except the first and last Chorus' which were 'by the Famous Mr. Wilderer'[34] – almost certainly Johann Hugo Wilderer, a German opera composer and contemporary of Cousser and, probably, a friend. Information of different instruments accompanying the arias is given and so, for the first time, we have evidence of the style of orchestra that was engaged. Apollo has an 'Aria co'l Violino' and an 'Aria con Instrom[ti]', Marsyas an 'Aria co'l Oboe'. A Muse sings an 'Aria co'l Violino e Tamburino' and an 'Aria con Instrom[ti] Pizzicati', and a Satyr an 'Aria co'l Flauto Allemano' and an 'Aria co'l Flauto Piccolo'.[35]

Up to now the relevance of these odes in relation to opera must seem remote, until one realises that the materials for a fully staged opera are here available. In retrospect it is difficult to understand why Cousser, an opera composer with the reputation of being a successful opera director as well, from his official position as Master of the State Music, had never introduced opera performances at Dublin Castle. Eventually he did, a single performance in 1727, shortly before

he died. George II had succeeded to the throne during the same year.
His birthday occurred on October 30 and it must remain a matter of
conjecture how much his coronation, which took place on October 11,
influenced what has every appearance of being a gala birthday
celebration in this particular year. The entertainment, announced as
a 'Serenata Theatrale',[36] discontinued the cantata style of performance
and instead substituted a fully staged performance for the first time.

Conforming to the accepted allegorical style, the *dramatis personae*
are Peace, Discord, Justice and Apollo. The setting is a pastoral
scene. Peace, surrounded by cupids, rests on a flowery bank awaiting
sleep. She describes the scene:

> 'Where Liffy's Silver Current
> Runs thro' the verdent Meadows'.[37]

Discord then 'rises out of the Earth with a lighted Torch in her
Hand.'[38] At Discord's entry 'A Martial Sound of Drums and
Trumpets'[39] awakens Peace. Justice now 'descends from Heaven in a
Cloud'.[40] Again he describes the scene. The river Liffey

> 'Gliding Serenely to Neptune's Embraces
> Brightly reflecteth the covering Skies
> Flowers and Groves on its Borders that rise
> Reflecting the Glories Eblena* displays,
> Fair Palaces guilded and arduous Towers,
> Nymphs brighter than Skies, and more fragrant than Flowers
> That grace her Assemblies, and walk on her Keys'.[41]

Such descriptive singing of this highly utopian view of Dublin suggests
a classical scene in the style of Inigo Jones.

Next Apollo appears 'in a triumphant Chariot drawn by four
Steeds'.[42] Since he shortly afterwards 'descends to the Earth, and
takes Peace and Justice into his Chariot'[43] we may assume that, like
Justice, he too had entered by 'flying machine'. He instructs the
cupids to tear branches from their olive trees and to lash obstreperous
Discord. Next he decrees Discord's return to Hell, whence it seems
she has inauspiciously come on this most auspicious day. At once

---

*Sic. Eblana was the old Latin name for Dublin.

'A Dart falls from Heaven'[44] to make the decree effective. That job done, Apollo calls on 'Ye Nymphs in Woods and flowing Streams residing' to proclaim the greatness of 'George the Godlike, just, Divine'.[45] After a final Grand Chorus, 'The Chariot of Apollo ascends to Heaven, with Peace and Justice in it; and the Cupids separate, and go off the Stage on each side'.[46] This last instruction to the cupids to 'separate and go off the stage on each side' is too precise and practical to leave any doubt that this was a fully staged production.

From the stage directions recorded, one can piece together a reasonably detailed picture of the mechanics of the production. There can be little doubt that the idealised descriptions of Dublin and the river Liffey denote representational scenery in one form or another. Since the entertainment took place in a large hall, we can assume that, following the custom of Court entertainment elsewhere, the scenery was erected at the further end. The audience would have occupied the body of the hall, the more important members sitting, the majority standing about. Discord's entry and exit, rising 'out of the Earth' and plunging 'immediately into'[47] it, confirms that a raised stage was used. This would have been fitted with steps or a trap door to allow Discord to ascend from and descend again to floor level. What is not so certain is the erection of a proscenium. Nevertheless this is denoted by the use of stage machinery. The entry and departure of Justice and Apollo in their paste board cloud and chariot would lose much of their effect if the back-stage arrangements were in full view of the audience.

But was money available for such elaborate preparations for a single performance? Their Excellencies the Lords Justices were neither Medicis nor Barberinis, nor was Dublin either Florence or Rome. Presumably, when the cost of winches, ropes, pulleys and harness was added up, the additional expense of constructing a picture frame proscenium to hide these technical contrivances from the audience would not have been excessive. Special stage lighting may also have been used. Apollo on his triumphant entry declaims:

'Beamy Light around me blazing
Crowns my Head with radiant Splendor'.[48]

This description may of course have been symbolical, but, if literal, again denotes use for a proscenium behind which the source of the light would have been concealed.

Unfortunately, most important of all, nothing can be discovered about the disposition of the orchestra. We know that in seventeenth-century masques the musicians were dispersed in groups, with what must have been splendid theatrical effect when one considers the effectiveness of 'off-stage' music in modern opera. It is extremely unlikely however that Cousser had sufficient instrumentalists to deploy them in sections about the stage. Much more probably they were assembled together in front of the stage, for, apart from the lack of players, by 1727 this was the normal placing of theatre musicians.

Cousser was to die later in the same year – according to Hawkins, in Dublin. Would this single performance have led to a development of opera in Dublin had he lived longer? Almost certainly no. Cousser died at the age of sixty-seven. It is not an age at which men usually pioneer fresh artistic ventures. His staged 'Serenata Theatrale' was an isolated fortuitous event for a festive occasion.

4

FROM PRISON TO PASTORAL

WHEN DEAN SWIFT recommended to Mr. Gay 'what an odd pretty thing a Newgate Pastoral might make',[1] he can never have realised the importance of his observation to the future of English opera. The outcome was *The Beggar's Opera,* and Congreve's prophecy that 'It would either take greatly or be damned confoundedly'[2] was astute, for it was a form of entertainment that was to influence the British theatre for two centuries.

The music was derived mainly from old folk tunes, but included airs by Handel, Purcell, Bononcini and others, arranged and orchestrated by John Christopher Pepusch, a musician who had settled in London from Berlin, and who was also the composer of the overture and one of the songs. The librettist was the English poet and playwright John Gay. His play was a satire attacking contemporary political corruption, and the extravagances of Italian opera. The prologue to *The Beggar's Opera* takes the form of a dialogue spoken between a Beggar and a Player in which the former hopes that he may be forgiven for not having made his 'opera throughout unnatural like those in vogue'* for he has 'no recitative'.

So English comedy was transformed into English opera by the addition of folk tunes set to new lyrics suitable to the situation, at appropriate points in the play. In the beginning these tunes were mainly derived from old ballad airs, but as time went on and all the good airs had been adapted, composers began to write new music for the plays. This was to occur about the year 1760, when ballad opera began to be called comic opera – the music being composed rather

*The Italian operas at the King's Theatre.

33

C

than compiled – and so it was to continue down to the era of Gilbert and Sullivan.

The success of *The Beggar's Opera* in London naturally led to an early production in Dublin. This is reported to have taken place at Smock Alley on March 10, 1727/28,* just six weeks after its first London performance. This date must be accepted with caution, however, since it would place the opening performance on a Sunday, a most unlikely occurrence. A more probable date was Saturday, March 9, or perhaps Thursday, March 14.

On Saturday, March 16, it was performed for the second time 'with great Applause, his Excellency the Lord Carteret being present; the Boxes were so crowded with Ladies and the Pit and Stage with Gentlemen, that 'twas Remarked above half the people in the Gallery, were Persons of Distinction in Disguise, that Place was also so crowded that great Numbers of our Citizens were forced to Postpone the Pleasure of seeing that Performance till Thursday next, when it is Commanded to be done again'.[3]

For the following Thursday's performance the theatre was 'more Crowded with Spectators than ever, & really', we learn, 'it is now so far the Topick of General Conversation here that they who have not seen it are hardly thought worth Speaking to by their Acquaintance, and are only Admitted into Discourse on their Promise of going to see it the first Opportunity, which is so advantageous to Our Commedians, that we are told Boxes &c are bespoke for 16 or 18 Nights to come'.[4]

The names of the cast remain undiscovered with one exception,** Mrs. Sterling, who played Polly Peachum. She was a member of a well-known Smock Alley acting family called Lyddal, and so successful was her performance 'that the House called out that she might have a Benefit Night, and obliged the Players to give it her, which she had

---

*W. H. Grattan-Flood. *Introductory Sketch of Irish Musical History*. p. 36.

**W. J. Lawrence in 'Early Irish Ballad Opera and Comic Opera' (*The Musical Quarterly* New York. July 1922. p. 400) reports Lewis Layfield as being the original Captain Macheath in Dublin. He does not give the source of his information, nor has diligent research discovered it. It is almost certainly correct, for apart from Lawrence's confirmed reliability, Layfield was to perform the same role there many years later.

on Thursday [April 11] and received one hundred and five Pounds fourteen Shillings and beside thirty odd pounds thrown to her on the Stage'.[5] Two other members of the Company who probably took part, since they also received benefits, were Thomas Griffith, a Dublin man, for many years Smock Alley's leading comedian, and James Vanderbank who, having joined Smock Alley Theatre during the 1716/17 season, was still acting there in 1746.

The opera was again in the repertory during the following season and again drew full houses, being acted on December 14, 1728, 'at the Desire of several Ladies of Quality' . . 'a 40th Time'.[6]

Such theatrical success led to imitation.* Just one year later, on March 24, 1728/29, again at Smock Alley, we learn, 'at the General Desire of our Quality will be Acted the New Opera, call'd the Beggar's Wedding with Variety of Songs, Humourous Dances and other Decorations'.[7] The cast consisted of:

Alderman Quorum, a Justice of the Peace	Vanderbank
Chaunter, King of the Beggars	Fr. Elrington
Hunter, his reputed Son	Layfield
Grigg ⎤	Sheridan
Cant ⎥	Paget
Gage ⎥ Beggars	Watson
Mump ⎥	Alcorn
Scrip ⎥	Norris
Swab ⎦	Dash
Dash, Clerk to the Justice	Nelson
Phebe, the Alderman's reputed Daughter	Mrs. Sterling
Mrs. Chaunter, Queen of the Beggars	Mrs. Lyddle
Tippet, Maid to Phebe	Mrs. Vanderbank

Strumer, Mopsey, Blouze, Drab, Manchet, Tib Tatler (Beggars), Constables and Musicians. 'Scene, Dublin'.[8]

---

*W. J. Lawrence describes *Chuck, or The School Boy's Opera* performed at Smock Alley on January 27, 1728/29 as 'the first Irish-produced ballad opera'. This may have been a musical version of Colley Cibber's farce, *The School-Boy, or The Comical Rival* first produced at Drury Lane on October 24, 1702. ('Early Irish Ballad Opera and Comic Opera'. *The Musical Quarterly*. New York. July 1922. p. 400).

The prices of admission were 'Boxes a British Crown, Pit 3 British Shillings, Middle Gallery Two, Boxes in the Upper One'.[9]

Lewis Layfield was a popular Smock Alley player who had made his stage *début* as a dancer in London in 1704. He was also a musician and small-part actor and had first appeared before a Dublin audience during the 1719/20 season. In December, 1729, he 'was appointed State Kittle-Drum by his Excellency the Lord Lieutenant, in the Room of Mr. Cooper lately deceas'd'.[10] He was to serve the Dublin theatre well, for his name appears on the Smock Alley roster of artists as late as 1747/48. In May 1749, the following rather pathetic announcement appears in *Faulkner's Dublin Journal* advertising a benefit for him: 'As the Indisposition which Mr. Layfield has sometime languished under, deprives him of the pleasure of waiting on his Friends, to solicit their Favour, on this Occasion; he most humbly hopes, from their known Humanity and Benevolence, that they will give him the Honour of their Company at his approaching Benefit Play'.[11]

Although singing in ballad opera, it should be noted that none of the artists were singers as the word is understood today. During the eighteenth and much of the nineteenth century a qualification indispensable to every actor and actress was the ability to sing a simple ballad air. Of course some players had better singing voices than others and so every theatre company tried to retain a small number of singers and dancers, who also acted. The dividing line between singing and acting talents was poorly defined and the situation could frequently be expressed by the Fourth Player's lines in the Introduction to Gay's ballad opera *Polly*. 'Since the Town was last Year so good as to encourage an Opera without Singers* . . All the other Comedians upon this Emergency are willing to do their best and hope for your Favour and Indulgence'.

The librettist of *The Beggar's Wedding* was Charles Coffey, a 'native of Ireland'.[12] He may have been an actor and is said to have played Aesop in Sir John Vanbrugh's play of that name. An ironic

*The Beggar's Opera.

broadsheet dated 1729 entitled 'Dr. Anthony's* Advice to the Hibernian Aesop or An Epistle to the Author of the B———'s W———g'[13] leaves no doubt that, unlike its famous exemplar, *The Beggar's Wedding* failed to run. We read, for example:

'And your Opera three Nights flouted;
Of Pence and Praise at once debarr'd
I must confess your Fate is hard'.[14]

The second and third performances took place on March 27 and 29. Coffey complains that his play was defeated by a combination of law, sport and piety. 'I was most ungratefully us'd', he declares, 'in bringing it on, in the worst Season of the whole Year; it was acted for my Benefit on Saturday the 29th of *March* last, when almost every Body was out of Town at the Circuits, when those few Gentlemen that remain'd, either went or were preparing to go to the Curragh, which happen'd the Wednesday following; and what was as unfortunate as the rest was, that the Day immediately preceded Passion Week, a time so solemn, that people were more anxious for the preservation of their Souls than the Recreation of their Minds, and notwithstanding all the Difficulties it still liv'd and came off with Applause, tho' before a very thin Audience'.[15]

Subsequently it was to fare much better in London, for in November 1729 we learn from there, 'That the *Beggar's Wedding,* has been acted a great many Times, with applause, some Ammendments having been made thereto by Mr. Coffey, the Author, to whom the *Nobility* and *Players* have been so generous as to give very Liberal Presents in order to make amends for the bad success he had in this Kingdom'.[16] Under the title of *Phoebe, or The Beggar's Wedding,* and probably reduced to a one-act version, it received a number of performances at Smock Alley Theatre during the 1750's.

Extremely late during the same season, on June 14, 1729, we learn that 'a new Entertainment call'd Flora or Hobb's Opera is in Rehearsal at the Theatre and will be soon Exhibited to the Town, and as the Greatest Pains are taking to get up such Plays and Entertain-

*The strolling player Anthony Aston. See Chapter I. p. 7.

ments as may Delight and instruct the Audience, 'tis not doubted but our Stage which has droop'd a little on the decline of The Beggar's Opera will again Revive and meet with as much Encouragement as Ever from our Nobility and Citizens'.[17]

Further details of the production cannot be found until September 16,* when an advertisement noting the publication of the opera records, 'As it is Acted . . at the Theatre in Dublin'.[18] That it was successful is evident from an announcement of a '4th Impression'[19] printed on October 24, and as late as April 27, 1730, we again read of 'The last New Opera call'd *Flora*'[20] at the Theatre Royal. It was extremely popular and continued to be played until the end of the century. The cast of the production was:

Sir Thomas Testy	Vanderbank
Friendly	Norris
Hob	Layfield
Old Hob	Paget
Flora	Mrs. Sterling
Betty	Mrs. Hamilton
Hob's Mother	Mrs. Lyddal.[21]

The librettist of the opera was John Hippisley, an actor all his life, turned dramatist. He adapted *Flora* from an earlier play *The Country Wake* by Thomas Dogget. Hippisley is described as 'a comedian of lively humour and droll pleasantry'[22] and was the original Peachum in *The Beggar's Opera*.

Towards the end of December 1730 it was announced that Henry Carey's opera *The Contrivances* was 'now acting at the Theatre Royal in Dublin with great *Applause*'[23] and that it was 'speedily to be published'. It was, with the following cast:

Argus	Vanderbank
Hearty	Husbands
Rovewell	Layfield
Robin	Alcorn
First Mob	Dash

*Dublin newspaper files are very incomplete between June and September, 1729.

Second Mob	Hambleton
Third Mob	Norris
Woman Mob	Sheridon (sic)
Boy	Bob Layfield
Arethusa	Mrs. Hambleton
Betty	Mrs. Vanderbank.[24]

Nothing further can be discovered about the production, but the opera was successful, remaining in the repertory for sixty years. The *genre* of the work is interesting. Since the music – thirteen airs – was composed by Carey, who was also the librettist, it cannot be described as a ballad opera in the accepted sense. Rather does it presage the comic operas which were to emerge during the 1760's and it is significant that when published in Dublin it was styled, presumably by the author, a 'Comi-farcical Opera'.[25] The role of Arethusa in this opera used to be considered as 'the probationary part for female singers before they were bold enough to venture upon characters of more consequence'.[26]

Henry Carey has been described both as Anglo-Irish and as the illegitimate son of George Savile, first Marquis of Halifax. There is not much evidence to support either premise. The name is, of course, Irish and Carey described himself as a disciple of the musicians Geminiani and Thomas Roseingrave, both of whom had settled in Dublin and were to die there. His mother may have been a school mistress. Hawkins held little opinion of his abilities, recording that 'As a musician Carey seems to have been one of the first of the lowest rank'.[27] Today known solely for his ballad 'Sally in our Alley', he was nevertheless a theatre composer and dramatist of importance during the period 1729/1739, and productions of other works by him in Dublin will be noted later.

Although hardly concerned with opera, the opening of the new 'Musick Hall' in Crow Street in 1731 is of importance since many prominent singers were to perform there in oratorios and concerts. It should be emphasised that at this period Dublin had several 'Great-Rooms' in which concerts, assemblies and meetings were held. The Great Hall in the Blue Coat School is one example. Another was the Stationers' Hall on Cork Hill, while the eminent violinist Geminiani had a concert room attached to his house which was situated close to Dame Street.

A significant point is that the new music hall was opened not with a concert but with a new form of social diversion, the *ridotto* or *redoute,* which was then finding its way from Italy and France to England and Ireland. It consisted of an assembly which began with singing by well-known artists; refreshments were served during the evening, and the entertainment ended with dancing in which everybody joined. As an eighteenth-century style of entertainment it is today recalled by the *Redoutensaal* in Vienna.

The new hall was to be a renovated building standing at the end of Crow Street in what is now Cecilia Street – so named, presumably, to commemorate the patron saint of music. In 1731 this building was owned by a Mr. John Johnson who lived 'opposite to Mr. Dillons in Capel Street'.[28] At the time Johnson was also the proprietor of a 'Musick-Room'[29] close by in Dame Street where concerts were held. Then, about mid-September 1731, a Mr. White arrived 'from England with a design to open the Ridotto'.[30] There is some reason for believing that Thomas Griffith, the Smock Alley actor whom we find described the following December as 'one of the Managers of the Theatre Royal',[31] had a similar idea at the same time for 'we are informed that Mr. Griffith and he [Mr. White] by the advice of several of the subscribers have joined their Interests for the better carrying on of the same'.[32] By the end of October both gentlemen were 'upon agreement with Mr. Johnson for the Use of his new Musical Hall' and were announcing their intention 'to open the same very speedily, their subscription being almost full'.[33] By early November, they had 'actually agreed with Mr. Johnson'[34] and were 'compleating two adjacent Rooms for the more commodious Reception of the Company'.[35] The rooms were to be finished by November 13, and those gentlemen who had not paid their full subscription money were 'please to do so speedily'[36] since 'N.B. they design to open in Sixteen Days at farthest'.[37] They kept their word to the day, for on Monday, November 29, 'The Ridotto opened – about Nine o'clock where there was a very great Assembly and all persons of Distinction were very much delighted with the Diversion which did not break up till Four the Next Morning'.[38]

The Great-Room in Dame Street appears to have been used for concerts as late as May 6, 1732, for in connection with a 'Concert of Musick'[39] by Mr. Neale, the oboeist, 'at the new Musick Hall in Crow Street' on this date, it is announced that 'Tickets given out for the Great Room in Dame Street will be taken at Crow Street'.[40] It is of course possible that these tickets were issued for a benefit concert at the Dame Street room several months previously, when the house being oversold, as sometimes happened by artists promoting their own benefits, unused tickets would be accepted at later performances by the same artist.

That the 'new Musical Hall' was dependent on several non-musical events in order to survive makes disappointing, although scarcely surprising, reading. 'To be Sett', we read in May 1732, 'under the Musical Hall in Crow Street, Vaults very fitting for Wine-Cellars or any Kind of Merchandize – N.B. The said Musical Hall is very fit and commodious for any Corporation and will be Sett upon reasonable Terms. It is also very convenient for Auctions of any Kind'.[41] More than two centuries since that advertisement was printed it can be said of at least one aspect of Georgian Dublin – *Plus ça change plus c'est la même chôse.*

Concerts were of course held there. The first important one took place on Saturday, December 4, 1731, 'For the Benefit of Mrs. Barbier, lately arrived from London'.[42] She was assisted by Matthew Dubourg, and a Master Mott, presumably a boy soprano.

Mrs. Barbier was an English singer who made her first appearance in Giovanni Bononcini's *Almahide* at the Haymarket Theatre, London, in November 1711. During 1713 she was appearing in Handel's *Teseo* and, as has been related, took over Nicolini's role in *Rinaldo*. In 1717, 'being no longer able to resist the solicitations of one that pretended love for her'[43] she eloped, but by May 1724, or possibly earlier, she had returned to the stage. By 1726 she was singing in revivals of Antonio Maria Bononcini's *Camilla* and

Pepusch's *Thomyris* at Lincoln's Inn Fields Theatre, where her reputation in Italian opera attracted a following, and where she was one of the highest paid singers. Her last stage appearance is said to have taken place there in Thomas Augustine Arne's opera, *Rosamond*, in 1733. From Burney we learn that her voice was a contralto. It is Burney who also records that 'in general she performed a man's part, which, on account of the low pitch of her voice, was very convenient for the opera stage.'[44] The vocal part of her Dublin concert is announced as follows:

'In the first Act. Che gran pena.[i] Timido pelegrin.[ii] Sequell cor.[iii] Second Act. Se possono tanto.[iv] Le tigre ardi di sdegnio.[v] A Duetto between Mrs. Barbier and Mr. Motte. Third Act. Euano[vi] Chorus in Porus by Mrs. Barbier & Mr. Motte. Hor la Tromba.[vii] With the Trumpet . . and Mrs. Barbier, being very desirous of pleasing her audience, will sing an English Ballad at the end of the Consort, called "Peggy grieves me" '.[45]

The next advertisement of an opera performance at the theatre appears as follows on December 14, 1731:

'By their Graces the Duke and Dutchess of Dorsets' Special Command. For the benefit of Mr. Layfield. At the Theatre Royal on Thursday next December 16 will be acted a Tragedy call'd "Theodosius" or, "The Force of Love". All the parts dispos'd to the best Advantage, To which will be added, a Comick Opera of one Act, never performed here call'd "Damon and Phillida". With Dancing proper to the Same: Likewise Peggy grieves Me, after Mrs. Barbier's Manner and the 1st Part of the Duet of the Chorus

---

[i] ?

[ii] *Timido pellegrin* from the opera *Ormisda*. Libretto by Apostolo Zeno. Music probably by Bartolomeo Cordanus and others. Performed at the King's Theatre, London, on April 4, 1730.

[iii] *Se quel cor* from *Ormisda*.

[iv] From the opera *Poro, Re dell'Indie* by Handel.

[v] *La tigre arde di sdegno* from the opera *Admeto, Re di Tessaglia* by Handel.

[vi] ? (? *È vano*).

[vii] Possibly from Handel's opera *Tamerlano*. *The Daily Courant* of March 28, 1726 records that among a number of arias sung by Mrs. Barbier during a performance of *The Recruiting Officer* by Farquhar, there was one—*Bella Asteria et hor la Tromba*. Asteria is a soprano role in Handel's *Tamerlano*, and an aria *Bella Asteria* occurs in the opera.

in the Opera of Porus by Master Mott. And for the better convenience of the Ladies that shall sit on the Stage, the whole's to be illuminated with Wax-Candles. At the Desire of several Persons of Distinction a new Epilogue on Luxury in Dress, will be spoken by Mrs. Sterling, design'd for his Majesty's Birth-Day, and prevented by her Sickness'.[46]

The range of this book is limited to the history of opera, but, as the above advertisement makes clear, ballad opera normally formed only a very small part of an evening's theatrical entertainment. Frequently, as is shown here, it was merely the afterpiece. This should be remembered when later performances are being discussed. The operatic part of the play-bill alone will be considered. Tragedies and comedies, dancing and singing, prologues and epilogues can be assumed as forming part of the programme, but will not be included in the narrative.

With ladies seated on the stage, and the theatre illuminated by wax candles instead of common tallow or smelly oil, this was what today would be called a gala performance. The Duke of Dorset was not only a most popular Lord Lieutenant, but an ardent supporter of the theatre as well.

The opera *Damon and Phillida* was a re-arrangement by Colley Cibber, the English actor and dramatist, of his earlier 'pastoral drama' *Love in a Riddle*. This had been intended as a moral contrast to *The Beggar's Opera*. The result, however, belied W. S. Gilbert's aphorism that 'virtue is triumphant only in theatrical performances', for it was 'vilely damn'd, and hooted at'[47] on its first performance at Drury Lane, and again on the second night with the Prince of Wales present. It was then withdrawn and, considerable alterations having been made by Cibber, it was to be successfully performed under its new title for almost fifty years. It seems to have had an immediate success in Dublin for it was again performed on January 11 of the following year. Those who took part in the Dublin production were:

Arcas	R. Elrington
AEgon	Hamilton
Corydon	Alcorn
Cimon	Reynolds

Mopsus	Rob. Layfield
Damon	Layfield
Phillida	Mrs. Reynolds.[48]

On February 17, 1732, *The Island Princess* was revived, and on February 24, Charles Coffey's three act ballad opera, *The Devil to Pay, or The Wives Metamorphos'd*, was produced for the first time in Dublin. An obscure London dramatist, John Mottley, is said to have collaborated with Charles Coffey in writing the libretto. Once again the performance was 'By Command of their Graces the Duke and Dutchess of Dorset'.[49] The cast was:

Sir John Loverule	Sherridan (sic)
Butler	F. Elrington
Cook	Reynolds
Footman	Hamilton
Coachman	Alcorn
Jobson	Layfield
Doctor	Dash
Lady Loverule	Mrs. Lyddel
Lucy	Mrs. Hamilton
Lettice	Mrs. Shane
Nell	Mrs. Reynolds.[50]

and admission prices were 'Boxes 5s 5d.* Pit 3s 3d. Middle Gallery 2s 2d. Upper 1s 1d'.[51]

The music of this opera had been arranged by a Mr. Seedo, who may have been born in England and who worked in London as a theatre composer from about 1730 to 1735. His real name was probably Sidow or Sydow and he appears to have been the son of a Prussian musician.

As has frequently been noted this ballad opera influenced considerably the development of the German *singspiel,* leading directly to Mozart's *Entführung aus dem Serail* some fifty years later. One reason for this development may have been the coincidence that

---

*The odd amounts denote Irish currency which was valued one-twelfth less than English. Thus 5/5 Irish equalled a British crown, 1/1 Irish, a British shilling.

a translation of the opera was made by the sometime Prussian Ambassador to London, Caspar Wilhelm von Borcke, who was also the first German translator of Shakespeare, and with whom Sidow presumably had some contact. *The Devil to Pay* – as *Der Teufel ist los* – not only influenced *singspiel,* but was also imitated on the French and Italian stages. The last version in which it was revived seems to have been M. W. Balfe's *The Devil's in it,* in 1852.

Mrs. Sterling's sickness referred to in the advertisement for *Damon and Phillida* may have been serious for, on May 22, 1732, she took a benefit in her earlier success *The Beggar's Opera,* announced as 'being the last Time of her Performance on the Stage'.[52] The announcement adds, 'It is hop'd that her play being postponed from the 15th – will be no Disappointment to her friends, the Right Hon. the Judges, and the Honourable Society of the Kings-Inns'.[53]

Thomas Elrington, who had been manager of Smock Alley Theatre from 1720, died on July 22, 1732. As has already been noted, Thomas Griffith was being described as a joint manager of the theatre during the previous December, so Elrington may have relinquished the part management of the theatre some time previous to his death. In any event the management was now taken over by Thomas Griffith, Francis Elrington and Lewis Layfield. Their first action seems to have been the repair and redecoration of the theatre, which reopened with 'great improvements made'[54] on October 5, 1732, with *The Island Princess.*

Little of operatic interest seems to have occurred during 1733. A Florentine lutenist, composer and singer, Carlo Arrigoni, who had been engaged as opera composer to Lincoln's Inn Fields Theatre in opposition to Handel, and who produced an opera called *Fernando* without success there in 1734, 'performed a Consort of Vocal and Instrumental Musick'[55] at Crow Street Music Hall on October 20. 'The songs', we read, 'are all compos'd and to be perform'd by himself'.[56]

The absence of opera during 1733 can be traced to the lack of a serviceable theatre. The only really active theatre in Dublin that year was a small building hurriedly erected in Rainsford Street in the liberty of the Earl of Meath, outside the Lord Mayor's jurisdiction. In the same year, on May 8, the foundation stone was laid for a new Theatre Royal in Aungier Street.

Ever since the year 1670, when the galleries in Smock Alley collapsed, until 1735, when the theatre was finally razed and a new building erected, continual apprehension among the audience concerning the theatre's structural condition had to be assuaged by continual assurance from the management that it was perfectly sound. But even a certificate from Engineer and Surveyor-General Captain Thomas Burgh in 1730 testifying that the building 'was safe and would bear any Number of People who shall please to Resort thither'[57] was by then insufficient to allay audience anxiety. Cracking in the rafters presumably made a more impressive sound than the rustling of Captain Burgh's certificate.

So the new Theatre Royal in Aungier Street was opened on March 9, 1734. It was 'allow'd by all Travellers to be by much the finest in Europe. It was honour'd the first Night with the Presence of the Duke and Dutchess of Dorset, attended by most of the Nobility and Gentry of the Kingdom'.[58]

Opposition was soon to follow, however, for on May 19, 1735 (the Lord Mayor meanwhile having graciously agreed to receive the Rainsford Street company within his city walls), the foundation stone was laid for a new Theatre Royal at Smock Alley on the site of the old theatre. This theatre was opened on December 11, 1735, so that Dublin now had two theatres, both erected under royal patent.

A comparison between the theatres can be made from descriptions by two Smock Alley prompters turned theatre historians, W. R. Chetwood and Robert Hitchcock. Considered only as theatres in which operas could be mounted, Aungier Street had the advantage of a larger stage, which was fifty-four feet deep and twenty-nine feet wide from box to box. In passing it may be noted that when both theatres were under Thomas Sheridan's management in 1749 he chose to remodel and renovate the Aungier Street Theatre 'in order to have Dramatick Operas exhibited there'.[59] Chetwood confirms this impression by writing: 'I believe the Contriver had an Eye more to

Ridottos, than the *Drama,* if so, indeed his Intentions were answered, for in that Shape it may vie with that in the *Haymarket* in *London*',[60] and then referring to Smock Alley, says: 'the Stage is more cramp'd for want of Room'.[61]

Of Smock Alley Hitchcock tells us, 'the architect studiously avoided the errors and mistakes of former builders and erected a strong, elegant, commodious, well constructed theatre. The cavea, or audience part, is remarkably well constructed for the first two requisites, of seeing and hearing. In these essentials it gives place to none that I ever saw, and I think may safely say is superior to most'.[62]

In contrast he says of Aungier Street – and this is where a real problem arose, 'Experience proved that the architect failed in the two essential requisites of accommodating it for hearing and seeing. It required uncommon powers of voice to fill every part of the house, and on full nights a great part of the people in both galleries could neither hear nor see'.[63] In 1740, efforts were made to improve the acoustics. The *Dublin Newsletter* of October 21/25 relates 'they have lower'd the Sounding-Board near seven Foot, whereby the defect in the hearing will be entirely cur'd': undoubtedly an over-optimistic anticipation of the result. In brief, Aungier Street, to quote yet a third Dublin theatre historian, Benjamin Victor, was 'a very sumptuous but a very bad Theatre'.[64]

It seems appropriate at this point to consider when, in Dublin, the theatre orchestra was removed from its 'Musick loft', where we know it existed at Smock Alley certainly as late as 1698,[65] and probably much later, and placed in its present position on the ground in front of the stage. Certainly the orchestra had taken up its new position in the Aungier Street Theatre by January 10, 1743, for an announcement in connection with Arne's masque of *Comus* states: 'N.B. The Orchestra will be doubled, and there will be a Row of the Pit enclosed for the Musick'.[66] While no evidence appears to exist to mark the precise time of the transition, it seems a not unreasonable surmise that it occurred when both of the new theatres opened. Probably the arrangement existed in the old Smock Alley Theatre for some years prior to its demolition.

On May 1, 1734, Crow Street Music Hall was the venue of a most important first performance in Dublin – Handel's *Acis and Galatea*. An advertisement of April 13 reads: 'For the Benefit of Mrs. Raffa (By subscription), On Wednesday, the first of May, at the Great Room in Crow Street, will be perform'd the Masque of Acis and Galatea compos'd by Mr. Handel for his Grace, the Duke of Chandos, with all the Chorus's as it was perform'd in the Opera-house in London. Each subscriber to pay one Guinea for four Tickets and to have two printed Books of the Words of the Entertainment. Subscriptions will be taken at Mr. Gavan's in Anglesey-street'.[67] A second advertisement some weeks later adds 'Single Tickets, Three Half Crowns, British'.[68]

Mrs. Raffa was a soprano who seems to have been unknown outside Dublin. There, at Crow Street Music Hall, she made her *début* on November 28, 1733, described as 'a Scholar of Mr. Dubourg's'.[69] Her name frequently appears in concert advertisements for some years following. In this performance she undoubtedly sang the role of Galatea. Unfortunately the names of the other artists taking part have not been recorded, nor can any notice be discovered of how this significant masque, still occasionally performed in Dublin almost two hundred and fifty years later, was received.

During the following year, 1735, a unique circumstance was advertised. Mrs. Raffa took another benefit in *Acis and Galatea* on February 5. (A minor though interesting point contained in the advertisement is that tickets 'at the Door the Night of Performance' were this year reduced to 'a British Crown each'.[70]) Approximately one week later, on February 15, the following advertisement also appeared:

'At the Theatre Royal in Aungier-street on Friday the 21st of February 1734–5, will be perform'd a Pastoral Opera of *Acis and Galatea,* compos'd by Mr. Handel with an additional chorus for Trumpets. A French Horn and Kettle Drum, and an additional Song, which Mr. *Handel* compos'd for his own performance on the Harpsichord alone, to be perform'd by Mr. Davis. The Characters will be represented in proper Dresses with new Scenes of Gardens, Woods

MRS. CROSS. SINGER
(c. 1677–p. 1724)
AS ST. CATHERINE
FROM A PAINTING BY
SIR GODFREY
KNELLER.

RICHARD LEVERIDGE.
BASS AND COMPOSER
(c. 1670–1758)

HENRY CAREY.
COMPOSER AND
DRAMATIST
(c. 1690–1743)

SUSANNA MARIA
CIBBER. SOPRANO,
LATER CONTRALTO
(1714–1766)

and Fountains, as in the Opera House in the Hay-Market, where Mrs. Davis perform'd the Part of Galatea, an Entertainment of new Pastoral Dances between the Acts, the Musick for the Dances compos'd by Mr. Davis. The first Overture belongs to the Opera, the Overture of the second Act of the Opera of Ariadne. The third Act, an Overture for a French Horn, The French Horn to be perform'd by the Lord Mountjoy's Gentleman. Pit and Boxes laid together at a British Crown. Gallery, half a Crown. To begin at half an hour after six.'[71]

Dublin was in fact being treated to rival productions of *Acis and Galatea*. Did rivalry also exist between what would seem to have been Dublin's two ranking sopranos?

Dealing first with the artists taking part in the Aungier Street performance, the announcement that Mrs. Davis had sung Galatea at the King's Theatre in the Haymarket was almost certainly incorrect. A Mrs. Davis did sing the minor role of Eurilla there in June 1732 when Galatea was sung by the Italian soprano Anna Strada del Po.

The Mrs. Davis of the Aungier Street *Acis and Galatea* was Dublin-born, and was a sister of John Clegg, the distinguished Irish violinist. Evidence of this relationship comes from an announcement of a concert at Crow Street Music Hall on December 11th, 1742* 'for the benefit of Miss Davis, a Child of 6 Years old' who played the harpsichord, the 'Vocal Parts' being performed by Mrs. Davis 'and her Sister Miss Clegg who never perform'd in public before'.[72] Two years later, on May 10, 1745, a harpsichord recital was given at Hickford's Room, London, by a 'Miss Davis. A child of eight years of Age, lately arriv'd from Ireland',[73] which information confirms her identity with the child mentioned above. In this announcement Mrs. Davis is described as a 'Scholar of Bononcini's'.[74] (There was another Mrs. Davis who in 1729 had been announced in Dublin as 'a famous singer who came over with Mr. Elrington . . to entertain the town

---

Faulkner's Dublin Journal, December 4/7, 1742, reports the postponement of the concert 'till after Christmas'. It eventually took place on February 5. (*Faulkner's Dublin Journal*, January 29/February 1, 1742/43.)

D

in her way with several of the most Celebrated Italian Songs'.[75])
Burney records a 'performance of young Clegg and his sister at a
concert'[76] in Dublin on December 11, 1730, but gives an incorrect
reference – *The London Journal** – as the source of his information.
Mr. Davis, her husband, whose address is given as 'Patrick's-well
lane',[77] was a composer and harpsichordist.

Turning to the extraneous items in the programme, the interpolation of the overture to Handel's opera *Ariadne in Crete* was probably
the first performance of this overture in Dublin, since the opera had
been produced for the first time at the King's Theatre in the Haymarket in January 1734. It is at the end of this overture that the
minuet occurs, described by the 'Third Fellow' in *She Stoops to
Conquer*, as 'the very genteelest of tunes'. 'The Lord Mountjoy's
Gentleman' who played on the French horn must remain an unsolved
enigma. Presumably he was a musician in his Lordship's service. The
words 'Pit and Boxes laid together' describes an arrangement whereby
at special performances, especially at benefits, certain rows of the pit
were railed in to make extra boxes. It indicated a very full 'genteel'
audience, for at this time ladies did not enter the pit, but sat only in
the boxes.

The next advertisement for *Acis and Galatea* occurs on March 4
announcing a performance at Aungier Street for March 8. This adds
the following important information: 'N.B. The last time it was
perform'd it was not intended to be acted, but represented in
Characters sitting as in London; but now all the parts will be acted
and perform'd without Book, Acis kill'd by Polypheme, and turn'd
into a Fountain, and all the Entrances and Exits properly observ'd'.[78]

The differences in the various productions of *Acis and Galatea* in
London between 1732 and 1734, first by Thomas Arne, the father of
the composer Thomas Augustine Arne, and later by Handel, have
been the subject of thorough and scholarly research by William C.

*The following notice, discovered by Mr. Lowell Lindgren in *The Daily Post* (London) No.
3514, December 23, 1730, may have been the correct source of Burney's report. 'Dublin, Dec. 11.
a Concert of Vocal and Instrumental Musick was perform'd this Evening at Baily's Room by
Mr. Clegg, jun. and his Sister; the Instrumental part by Mr. Clegg, being his own composition,
and the Vocal Part by his Sister, who never perform'd in publick before'.

Smith.* Concerning the Dublin versions, the Aungier Street Theatre production seems quite naturally to have been the more elaborate of the two. But which of the London versions – Handel's or Arne's – was being presented?

One is inclined to assume from similarities in the Dublin and London advertisements such as 'Characters sitting as in London' which would correspond to 'There will be no Action on the Stage', that this too was the Handel version. Yet there are discrepancies which weaken the hypothesis. The Handel production was almost entirely in Italian, since Handel was then employing a large number of Italian singers. The Arne production was in English and for this reason would seem the more probable one to have been performed in Dublin. Also the Handel production is described as a 'Serenata'. Arne's production, like the one at Aungier Street, is called a 'Pastoral Opera'.

It is more difficult to determine what version was used for Mrs. Raffa's performance. Since the entertainment is called a masque and not a pastoral opera, or serenata, it may have been a yet earlier version published by John Walsh, sometime between 1725 and 1730.

The versions used, whichever they were, need not concern us unduly. Of greater importance is the description of the performance on March 8. Possibly the first performance on February 21 had not been very successful. There seems to be a note of apology in the second notice, and the announcement of the added attraction of a fully staged performance may have been considered necessary to attract an audience. The fact that no longer are pit and boxes advertised as being 'laid together' confirms this impression.

The Arne production in London was advertised as 'being the first Time it ever was performed in a Theatrical Way', which clearly indicates a stage performance. The importance of the performance 'without Book' lies in its being the first stage performance in Dublin of an opera, apart from *The Beggar's Opera,* still tenuously retained in the repertory today.

Concerning Handel by William C. Smith (Cassell and Company Ltd. 1948) to which the reader is referred.

5

THE BEST VOICES AND HANDS

THE FOLLOWING ANNOUNCEMENT appeared in the *Dublin Evening Post* for March 4/8, 1734/35: 'The Most Ancient and Rt. Worshipful Society of Free Masons, being assembled at the Grand Lodge on Tuesday last, and taking into Consideration the great and publick Affront given them by Mr. Griffith, in chusing so vile and obscene a Play for their Entertainment, as that called the Country Wife; and likewise by omitting several Entertainments, mentioned in his printed Bills, viz. a grand Piece of Musick, Dancing, the Frost Scene, &c. And they highly resenting so flagrant and palpable an Indignity done them, did (among other things) resolve, That the said Griffith ought never to have any Recommendation from the Grand Lodge; and hope the future Grand Officers will never encourage him'.

The importance of this puritanical rebuke to Brother Griffith* lies in its containing the first reference which has so far been traced of a performance in Dublin of music from one of Henry Purcell's operas, for 'the Frost Scene' is assuredly the famous scene from this composer's dramatic opera *King Arthur*. That the Worshipful Society should complain about its omission from the programme indicates that it was already popular with Dublin audiences.

A further important series of musical events is announced exactly eight months later on November 8 when 'We hear the Town is like to be diverted this Season in a far more elegant Manner than heretofore, a Society of Gentlemen having engag'd the best Voices and

---

*Thomas Griffith was a member of the Society of Freemasons. *The Dublin Weekly Journal* of June 26, 1725 records: 'After the entertainment they [Freemasons] all went to the Play . . Mr. Griffith the player, who is a Brother, Sang the Free Masons' Apprentice's Song'.

Hands in the Kingdom to perform, on every Saturday Night, Serenatas, Oritorios and Pastorellas, alternately, as Occasion shall require; and accordingly, on Saturday the 25th of October, the House in Aungier-street opened with a Serenata, which was so universally applauded by all Gentlemen of Taste that the like was repeated last Saturday Night: [November 1] As these Entertainments are conducted and managed by the Direction of Gentlemen, Lovers of Musick, which truly raises the Soul to a more than ordinary Pitch, so it is expected that these Performances will be the most entertaining of any we ever had in this Kingdom; and in order to render the Expence as easy as possible we hear the Price is confin'd to that of a common Concert'.[1]

Concerning the rather pompous 'Direction of Gentlemen, Lovers of Musick' who were organising these entertainments, it should perhaps be explained that the original subscribers to the building of Aungier Street Theatre 'were noblemen and gentlemen of the first rank and consequence in the nation'.[2] Not alone did they pay for the erection of the theatre but 'actuated by the noblest motives, agreed to superintend the concerns of the stage . . A committee was chosen from amongst them, a chairman appointed, and every Saturday they met to appoint the plays, distribute the parts, and settle the great variety of business, which unavoidably arises from so great an undertaking . . As the scheme extended, the best performers who could be procured, were to be engaged'.[3] Presumably it was this same 'committee' who, with such commendable good taste and judgement, had decided to introduce the season of weekly serenatas, oratorios and pastorellas. The comment that prices would be 'confin'd to that of a common Concert' presumes some form of staging, however limited.

The Committee also pursued their policy of procuring the best performers by engaging the Italian contralto, Maria Negri, from Handel's company in London. This singer had come to London in 1733, where she sang in twelve or more of Handel's operas between that year and 1737. Fétis says that she was born at Bologna in 1700 and that she was a pupil of the castrato singer Antonio Pasi, who in turn was a pupil of the great castrato singer and teacher Pistocchi.

In 1727 she was attached to a private opera company in Prague maintained by Count Spork, an amateur who played an important part in the development of opera in Bohemia. She next returned to Italy where she may have sung in Geminiano Giacomelli's opera *Lucio Papirio dittatore* at the Farnese Theatre in Parma in 1729.

On December 13, 1735, 'by their Graces the Duke and Dutchess of Dorset's Special command',[4] *Aminta*, 'A Pastoral Opera', was performed for Negri's benefit. 'Being a Benefit', we read, 'no Silver Tickets will be taken at the door'.[5] (These silver tickets were circular or oblong shaped transferable passes issued to subscribers and persons of importance which permitted free admission to the theatre.) It is tempting to suggest that this could have been the first performance of an Italian opera in Dublin but one must temper wishful thinking with manifest facts. The facts are that the likelihood of the performance having been sung entirely in Italian is improbable. With the exception of Negri the name of no other singer taking part has come down to us; had other Italians been engaged, their names would probably have been mentioned in the advertisements.

Extensive research has failed to identify the composer.* Settings of Tasso's pastoral drama are far too numerous to allow inference where so little evidence exists. Burney in a similar situation says of an opera *Arbaces,* 'in all probability it was an old drama with a new name and adjusted to airs selected from the works of different masters'.[6] If the Dublin *Aminta* was an opera, this description could well be applied to it. It is of course possible that it was not an opera performance but an oratorio, and it is significant that an oratorio of this name by an anonymous composer had been performed at Bologna 'nella Chiesa della Madonna di Galliera'[7] in 1733.

In the same year two insignificant lines in the *Dublin Evening Post* are the only record of a most important opera production. They read: 'On Monday next, [December 8, 1735] will be acted at the Theatre-

---

*It is just possible that the work may have been an adaptation of Colley Cibber's *Love in a Riddle* for this was a pastoral opera and the roles listed include an' Amyntas'. Another less likely possibility is an *Aminta,* music, according to Albert Schatz (cf. O. G. Sonneck's preface to *Catalogue of Opera Librettos printed before 1800.* Washington 1914), by Tommaso Albinoni, libretto by Apostolo Zeno, published in Florence in 1703.

Royal in Aungier-street, *the Prophetess, or the History of Dioclesian'.*[8]
There are no details, no author's or composer's name, although this
was almost certainly the work by the great Henry Purcell. Such brief
announcement without any comment suggests that this was not a
first performance, and it may well have been performed previously.
Nor is there any subsequent notice as to how it was received.

The libretto was an adaptation by the actor Thomas Betterton of
John Fletcher and Philip Massinger's play *The Prophetess.* Like all
Purcell's operas, with the exception of *Dido and Aeneas,* its title of
opera is mostly a courtesy one. It is a combination of opera and play
in which singers and actors take more or less equal part. The plot is
involved, as was customary, and concerns Diocles or Dioclesian, a
soldier in the Roman Army, of whom it is prophesied by Delphia
(the Prophetess) that he will become emperor. The prophecy is
fulfilled, the plot meanwhile having meandered through various
incidentals, and the opera ends with an elaborate masque.

The work presents opportunities for magnificent staging and at the
original production in London in 1690 they were splendidly taken.
We read that 'a dreadful Monster comes from the further end of the
Scenes, and moves slowly forward'[9] there to break asunder into
dancing furies. 'While a Symphony is Playing, a Machine descends . .
In it are Four several Stages, representing the Pallaces of two Gods,
and two Goddesses'.[10] The palaces, seen through a translucent haze,
were decorated with columns, brilliantly gilded and painted to
represent red, blue, green, and white marble. The scene ended 'with
a glowing Cloud, on which [was] a Chair of State, all of Gold, the
Sun breaking through the Cloud, and making a Glory about it'.[11]
To all this was added 'a Noble Garden, consisting of Fountains and
Orange Trees set in large vases' which arose from the stage like the
enchanted forest in Diaghileff's famous production of *The Sleeping
Princess.* As for ballets, besides the usual country dance and bacchanal,
there was a dance for butterflies and one in which 'Figures Grotesk'
having first danced, then sat on cane chairs about the stage, later
slipping from them to 'joyn in the Dance with 'em'.[12]

Once again the music from the work best remembered today is an air in *The Beggar's Opera,* 'Virgins are like the fair Flower,' although the chaconne from Act III and a charming air, 'What shall I do?' are also known.

The performance in Dublin has a slight political relevancy. In 1735 the penal laws were relentless and a prologue originally written by Dryden for the first performance in London in 1690 recalls, in the following lines, the Williamite Wars:

> 'Go, unkind Heroes, leave our Stage to mourn;
> 'Till rich from vanquish'd Rebels you return;
> And the fat Spoils of Teague in Triumph draw,
> His Firkin-Butter and his Usquebaugh'.

This prologue may never have been spoken in Dublin, for according to Colley Cibber it had been suppressed by the Earl of Dorset after the first performance of the opera in London for being satirical.

A concert at Crow Street Music Hall on December 10 deserves to be recorded since among the items advertised are 'some new Songs out of the Opera of Alcina'[13] which had had its first performance at Covent Garden during the previous April. On December 11 *Flora* had a revival at Aungier Street.

The year 1736 opened with a performance on January 15 at Aungier Street of 'The Wonder of the World – an honest Yorkshire man – a new Ballad Opera . . the Overture composed by Dr. Pepusch, and the songs set by Mr. Carey. It being for the benefit of Mrs. Hornby, she performing the part of Estifania'.[14] Not all the songs were set by Carey, but he did set ten. Another was by Handel, one by Nicola Porpora – the celebrated singing teacher and now forgotten composer – and two by Dr. Maurice Greene, an English musician who had tried to court favour both with Handel and Handel's rival Bononcini to the former's annoyance. Carey also wrote the play of *The Honest Yorkshireman* and this ballad opera was to remain popular right through the eighteenth century.

On February 25, a charity concert at the Music Hall in Crow Street listed, among its artists, Mrs. Davis, 'and the two Seigniora Negri's'.[15] The second Signora Negri was Maria's sister, Rosa. A less important artist, she had originally come to London with Maria and had joined Handel's company with her. She sang in a production of *Semiramis,* composed probably by Antonio Vivaldi, at the opening of the 1733 season at the King's Theatre in the Haymarket, and possibly in *Acis and Galatea* in 1734. As late as 1747 she is recorded as singing at Dresden in a performance of Hasse's opera *La Spartana generosa* to celebrate the wedding of the Elector Friedrich Christian to Maria Antonia of Bavaria.[16]

By March 6, opera was again performed at Smock Alley, when *Damon and Phillida* was played there.

In 1738, Dublin had a new Lord Lieutenant, the Duke of Devonshire, who on January 26 had 'His Majesty's Company of Comedians at the Theatre Royal in Aungier Street'[17] perform *The Dragon of Wantley* – 'a new Burlesque Operatical Dramatick Farce (never performed in Ireland)'.[18] The music was by John Frederick Lampe who had arrived in London from Saxony about 1725. There he was first employed as a bassoon player and later was engaged by John Rich, who built the first Covent Garden Theatre, as theatre composer. The play had been 'moderniz'd from the old Ballad after the Italian manner by Signor *Carini*',[19] alias Henry Carey. It was a satire on Italian opera, directed principally against Handel's *Giustino,* which had been presented in London earlier in 1737. *The Dragon of Wantley* is, nevertheless, said to have been a favourite with Handel.

According to Hogarth, 'The drama is made up of the usual elements of Italian opera of that day. There is the famous Moore of Moorehall, the redoubtable dragon-killer as well as lady-killer; there are two damsels, both in love with him, and the slighted fair one, of course, full of jealousy and rage; and there is the terrible monster who falls before the victorious hero. We have here ample room for all the tragic passions of the *opera seria*'.[20] The music he describes as 'excellent', and 'admirably adapted to the words, on the supposition that they are perfectly serious . . The melodies are spirited and graceful; and the orchestral score (consisting of the quartet of stringed instruments with the addition to two oboes) is clear and simple, yet very ingenious and full of charming effects'.[21]

The distribution of voices in the principal roles anticipates the Italian dramatic operas of the nineteenth century. Moore, the hero, is a tenor, Margery, the heroine, a soprano, the rejected Mauxalinda is a contralto and the devouring Dragon, a villainous bass. For the Dublin production the role of Moore was sung by an unidentified 'Mr. Gyles lately arrived from London'.[22]

The success of this burlesque opera led to a sequel by the same author and composer. This was *Margery, or a Worse Plague than the Dragon,* which received its first performance at Smock Alley on January 25, 1739, less than seven weeks after its production at Covent Garden. Hawkins speaks of it as being 'in no respect inferior to the Dragon of Wantley'[23] but this would appear to be contradicted by the *Biographia Dramatica,* which reports that as a sequel 'though it has some merit, it is far from being equal to the first part'.[24]

On December 15 of the same year, Peg Woffington played Polly Peachum in a performance of *The Beggar's Opera* at Aungier Street Theatre, and on December 20, a ballad opera *The Lottery* was presented for the first time in Dublin at Smock Alley. This was a benefit performance for the Smock Alley Theatre manager Lewis Duval, announced 'with a grand additional Scene which represents the manner of Drawing the State Lotteries at Guild-hall in London. The Songs being entirely new, and set to music by the ingenious Mr. Seedo'.[25] More memorable, the author was the famous English novelist and playwright, Henry Fielding.

Lewis Duval is reputed to have arrived in Dublin as a dancer. By February 1732 he was joint manager of the theatre in Rainsford Street and when the players transferred to the new theatre at Smock Alley, he accompanied them. Here he remained as manager until 1741, earning a precarious livelihood. The winter of 1739/40 did not help his financial problems. It was bitterly cold. From shortly after the date of his performance of *The Lottery* until the beginning of February, snow covered the Dublin streets, the Liffey froze and hundreds died from cold and starvation. Amidst this adversity, Duval heroically tried to keep the theatre open and, we read, 'Mr. Duval has erected in the Pit (which he designs to continue during the

Frost) a Fire Engine in which is kept a large Fire burning, the whole time of the performance, and warmed the House in such a manner as gave great Satisfaction to the Audience'.[26] By May 12, 1740, the great frost had gone and Aungier Street Theatre was again presenting Peg Woffington in *The Beggar's Opera* with Lewis Layfield as Macheath.

On August 6, 1741, the same theatre was presenting for the first time in Dublin 'a celebrated Mask (never performed in this Kingdom) called *Comus*. Written originally by the sublime Milton and performed at Ludlow Castle,* before the then Lord President, and now adapted to the Stage, and set to Musick by Mr. Henry Lawes. The Part of Comus to be performed by Mr. Quin; the Elder Brother by Mr. Ryan; Euphrosyne by Mrs. Clive. With all the original Songs to be sung by Mrs. Clive, Mrs. Reynolds, Mr. Worsdale, Mr. Layfield etc. With Dancing proper to the Mask by Mons. Lalauze and Mlle. Chateauneuf'.[27]

It should first be pointed out that the music was, of course, not by Henry Lawes** but by Thomas Augustine Arne, and Arne's name was included in later advertisements. This was a new version of John Milton's poem arranged for Drury Lane Theatre in 1738 by the Reverend John Dalton, a clergyman-poet.

The performance seems to have been a complete success, being acted 'to a crowded Audience of Persons of the best Quality now in Town; the Dresses, Machines, Flyings, and all other Decorations were entirely new, and very beautiful; the Orchestra was enlarged, several eminent Hands being added to the Band, for the Occasion, particularly Signor Pasqualino; the Musick was finely performed, having – as we hear – been a long time in Practice under the Inspection of Mr. Duburg; and the whole entertainment that Night was executed with a Decorum and Taste so elegant, as has never been attempted in this Kingdom. The Sublimity of the great Milton, the Eloquence of Mr. Quin, and the Harmony of Mrs. Clive, delighted

---

*According to Hawkins the plot was suggested to Milton by the Earl of Bridgewater from an adventure which his children had experienced, and so it was first produced at the Earl's residence, Ludlow Castle, on Michaelmas Night, 1634.

**Henry Lawes had originally composed music for Milton's masque in 1634.

and charmed everyone'.[28] This was the first performance in Dublin of an opera by Arne, who was to arrive for an extended visit there during the following June.

Comus was performed twice weekly, on Mondays and Thursdays, and seems to have drawn the town since 'by the request of the Subscribers for the Assembly, which was usually opened on Monday's, the Days for meeting will be on Wednesday's for the remainder of the Season, that it may not interfere with the Masque of *Comus*'.[29] It is a story of mythological frolic involving a lady lost in a forest and being sought by her two brothers, while Comus, the god of revelry, in an attempt to woo her, disguises himself as a shepherd by scattering magic powder.

Comus established Arne's reputation as a composer. Hogarth says: 'In *Comus*, Arne introduced a style of melody which may be said to be peculiarly his own; being neither that of the older English masters, nor of the Italian composers of the day. It is graceful, flowing, and elegant; depending for its effect neither on the resources of harmony and uncommon modulation, nor on feats of vocal execution'.[30] The statement indicated Arne's importance as a musician of his time, and his weakness in the subsequent history of English opera, for his style lacked the distinction and inspiration to bridge the span between Henry Purcell and Benjamin Britten.

A number of artists taking part in the Dublin performances had been specially engaged from London. Once more we have an example of actors and singers co-operating in the same production. Comus and the Elder Brother are acting parts, and James Quin and Lacy Ryan, both London-born but of Irish descent, were distinguished actors on the London stage who were also extremely popular in Dublin. Others engaged were Signor Pasqualino, a violoncellist celebrated amongst Handel's orchestral performers, and Monsieur Lalauze, a dancer, who had first come to Dublin with the famous Madame Violante in December 1729. In March 1731, introducing himself as a 'Dancing Master who has performed in the Opera Houses and Theatres in Paris (where he was bred) and in the City of London for several years',[31] Lalauze announced his intention of setting up as a dancing master in Dublin. Mlle. Chateauneuf, who had also been specially engaged from London for the season, was to enjoy a considerable reputation as a dancer on the Dublin stage for some years. She occasionally acted and, on March 15, 1744, took a benefit in which she played 'the part of the Virgin',[32] presumably Lucy, in Fielding's ballad opera, *The Virgin Unmasked.* She is described as 'the best of Dancers, the most agreeable Singer, and the prettiest Figure on the Stage, we have, or may see here for many years'.[33] James Worsdale, besides being a singing-actor and playwright, was also a portrait painter, having been bound apprentice to the eminent Sir Godfrey Kneller. He was said to have been a founder member of the famous Dublin Hell Fire Club. By 'artful ways' and a 'modest modish assurance' he 'gained ground and friends'[34] which in turn gained him admission to theatrical circles where he produced at least one ballad opera* based on *The Taming of the Shrew,* called *A Cure for a Scold.*

Of all these artists, Mrs. Clive was the most interesting and probably the most important. She was born in London in 1711, of Irish parents – like Quin and Ryan – her father being William Raftor, a lawyer from County Kilkenny. Having taken the Jacobite side in the war of 1690, he was dispossessed of his lands and forced to spend some years in exile in France. He eventually received a pardon from Queen Anne and returned to London. Kitty Clive was a pupil of Henry Carey and made her *début* in 1728 at Drury Lane as a page in Nathaniel Lee's tragedy of *Mithridates* 'where a Song proper to the circumstances of the Scene was introduced, which she perform'd with extraordinary Applause'.[35] In 1732 she married a barrister named Clive, but the the marriage was unhappy and they soon separated. 'Her singing', says Burney, 'which was intolerable when she meant it to be fine, in ballad farces and songs of humour was, like her comic acting, every-thing it should be',[36] while Hogarth adds, 'She was a favourite of the public as a singer as well as an actress; and we find her name in the *dramatis personae* of most of the musical pieces which appeared while

---

*Or had it 'ghosted' by the Reverend Matthew Pilkington! See *Memoirs of Mrs. Letitia Pilkington 1712–1750 Written by Herself.* London. 1928. p. 301.

she remained on the stage'.[37] She had sung in *Comus* when it was first produced with Arne's music in 1738, and she was to recreate her role of Euphrosyne successfully in Dublin. She would sing Dalila in Handel's oratorio *Samson,* when it was produced in 1743, and during the same year would also sing in his *L'Allegro* and *Messiah.*

She was Garrick's leading lady from 1746 until 1769, although, as the following story indicates, off-stage she did not always remain a lady. Tate Wilkinson tells how he was once reprimanded by Garrick for giving impersonations of a number of leading actors. 'I was exceedingly embarrassed and mortified,' he relates, 'when up came to me Dame Clive who said aloud, "Fie, young man! Fie!" and declared it was impudent and shocking for a young fellow to gain applause at the expense of the players . . "Now," added she, "I can and do myself 'take off' but then it is only the Mingottii [sic] and a set of Italian squalling devils who come over to England to get our bread from us; and I say curse them all for a parcel of Italian bitches!" – and so Madam Clive made her exit'.[38] Eventually she 'retired to a small but elegant house near Strawberry Hill, where she passed the remainder of her life in ease and independence, respected and beloved for her virtues and pleasing qualities'.[39]

We now come to one of the most important events in the history of music and opera in Dublin – Handel's arrival on November 18, 1741. *Pue's Occurrences* heralded his presence by declaring him to be 'Universally known by his excellent compositions in all kinds of Musick, he is to perform here this Winter', adding that he 'has brought over several of the best performers in the Musical Way'.[40] The first of these performers, Christina Maria Avoglio, was to arrive on November 24. She was joined shortly afterwards by Susanna Maria Cibber, *née* Arne, who was already acting in Dublin, and by a Mrs. Maclaine, a soprano, the wife of an organist whom Handel had met at Chester when on his way to Dublin, and who also became a member of the company. As is universally known, *Messiah* was to be performed for the first time during this visit, but of importance also were performances of *Acis and Galatea* and the dramatic oratorios *Esther, Hymen* and *Saul.*

It is frequently forgotten that these oratorios were written for the stage. The title page of *Samson,* which was to be presented in Dublin some years later, reads: 'Samson, an oratorio. As it is perform'd at the Theatre Royal in Covent Garden. Alter'd and adapted to the stage from the Samson Agonistes of John Milton'. As has been related concerning the first performances of *Acis and Galatea,* these oratorios were frequently performed in costume and with some attempt at *décor.* The chorus sat by the side of the stage or occasionally between the stage and the orchestra. Sometimes the principals used simple dramatic gestures, sometimes they merely followed stage directions for entrances and exits, sometimes, as with oratorios today, they remained on stage giving ordinary concert performances. It depended entirely on the place and conditions of the performance. These oratorios were considered sacred entertainments, yet they were never performed in churches or other places of worship, always in theatres or 'great-rooms'. Indirectly they were derived from the Italian *dramma sacro per musica* of the early seventeenth century. An example of their survival in the nineteenth century is Rossini's *azione tragico-sacra, Mosè in Egitto.*

The first of the entertainments listed above took place on January 20, 1742. This was *Acis and Galatea.* 'By their Graces the Duke and Dutchess of Devonshire's Special Command. At the new Musick-Hall in Fishamble-street* . . The tickets will be delivered to the Subscribers (by sending their Subscription Tickets) this Day and tomorrow, at the said Hall, from 10 of the Clock in the Morning till 3 in the Afternoon, and no Person will be admitted without a Subscriber's Ticket. To begin at 7 o'Clock. Gentlemen and Ladies are desired to order their Coaches and Chairs to come down Fishamble-street, which will prevent a great deal of Inconveniencies that happen'd the Night before; and as there is a good convenient Room hired as an Addition to a former Place for the Footmen, it is hoped the Ladies will order them to attend there till called for. Printed Books are to be had at the said Place, Price a British Sixpence. *N.B.* There is another convenient Passage for Chairs made since the last Night'.[41]

*Opened on October 2, 1741, under the management of Mr. William Neale.

The instructions contained in the advertisement indicate capacity audiences, and a newspaper notice three days later confirms that they were contented audiences as well. We learn that 'the Masque of Acis and Galatea, with one of Mr. Dryden's Odes on St. Cecilia's Day were performed . . before a very splendid Audience, so as to give infinite Satisfaction. Being both set to Musick and conducted by that great Master Mr. Handel and accompanied all along on the Organ by his own inimitable Hand'.[42] The performance was repeated a week later on January 27.

The first dramatic oratorio to be presented was *Esther*. This took place, again at Fishamble Street Music Hall, which was the venue for all of Handel's performances, on February 3, 'with Additions, and several Concertos on the Organ and other Instruments . . N.B. It is humbly hoped that no Gentlemen or Ladies will take it ill, that none but Subscribers can be admitted, and that no Single Tickets will be delivered or Money taken, at the Door'.[43] *Esther* was repeated on February 10, and again during a second subscription series on April 7.

Next came *Hymen* on March 24, repeated on March 31, having twice been postponed from March 10 and 17 owing to Mrs. Cibber's illness. *Hymen* had first been produced as the opera *Imeneo* at Lincoln's Inn Fields Theatre in 1740. There it had only two performances. In Dublin it was described as a serenata.

Lastly there was *Saul* which was performed once only on May 25. On May 12, 'the Overture . . with the Dead March'[44] had had its first performance in Dublin during a miscellaneous concert. Evidently the entire oratorio was already in rehearsal for on May 11 we read: 'As several of the Nobility and Gentry have desired to hear Mr. Handel's Grand Oratorio of Saul, it will be performed on the 25th inst. at the New Musick-hall . . Tickets will be delivered at Mr. Handel's House in Abbey-street, and at Mr. Neal's in Christchurch-yard at Half a Guinea each. A Ticket for the Rehearsal (which will be on Friday the 21st) will be given gratis with the Ticket for the Performance. Both the Rehearsal and the Performance will begin at 12 at Noon'.[45]

The performance in fact commenced at seven o'clock in the evening.

CATHERINE CLIVE
née RAFTOR. SOPRANO
(1711–1785)
AS PHILLIDA IN
Damon and Phillida.

JOHN FREDERICK
LAMPE. COMPOSER AND
INSTRUMENTALIST
(1703–1751)

THOMAS LOWE. TENOR (?–1783) AS MACHEATH IN
The Beggar's Opera.

CHARLOTTE BRENT. SOPRANO (c. 1735–
1802) AS SALLY IN *Thomas and Sally.*

That it was a success is assured from a report of the rehearsal 'at which', we learn, 'there was a most grand, polite, and numerous Audience which gave such universal Satisfaction, that it was agreed by all the Judges present, to have been the finest Performance that hath been heard in this Kingdom'.[46]

Of the singers taking part, little is known about Christina Maria Avoglio except that she was a soprano who came to London about 1740. While in Dublin she had two benefit concerts on April 5 and June 23, 1742. Returning to London, she sang in *Samson* in 1743 and in *Semele* and *Saul* in 1744. After this year her name disappears from the advertisements.

There is, however, no lack of information concerning Susanna Maria Cibber. She was a sister of Thomas Augustine Arne, who gave her her first singing lessons. One of her early stage appearances was as Galatea in her father's presentation of *Acis and Galatea* at the Little Theatre in the Haymarket in 1732. Her voice was then soprano; later it seems to have changed to mezzo-soprano. She was also famous as a tragic actress. In 1734 she married Theophilus Cibber, actor and playwright and Colley Cibber's son. The marriage was a disaster and Mrs. Cibber proceeded to have an affair with 'a young gentleman of fortune'.[47] Cibber was certainly not a gentleman for, having first condoned his wife's affair, he then brought an action for £5,000 damages against her lover. The Court is said to have awarded him £10. Nevertheless, while the case was proceeding, Mrs. Cibber was reluctant to appear on the London stage and, an engagement having been arranged with Aungier Street Theatre, she set out for Dublin. It was as an actress, consequently, that she first appeared there on December 12, 1741, as Indiana, with James Quin as Young Bevil, in Sir Richard Steele's *The Conscious Lovers*. She did not relinquish her position as a singer, however, but continued to play roles such as Polly in *The Beggar's Opera*. Her voice is said to have been small but very plaintive.

Burney states that Handel 'was very fond of Mrs. Cibber, whose voice and manners had softened his severity for her want of musical knowledge'.[48] He composed songs in *Messiah* and *Samson* specially

E

for her, but the actor-manager, Thomas Sheridan, attributed her success 'not to any extraordinary powers of voice . . but to expression only'.[49] While Handel was in Dublin she probably sang in all his oratorios and in *Acis and Galatea*. Before returning to England on August 23, 1742, she gave two concerts of his music on July 21 and 28 with her sister-in-law, Mrs. Arne.

And what of Handel during this extended visit? He lodged, as we know, in Abbey Street in a house near Liffey Street. His success, as is also known, was enormous, and his reaction to this success cannot be better portrayed than by narrating in part his frequently quoted letter to Charles Jennens, the author of *Saul*. 'The Nobility', he writes, 'did me the Honour to make amongst themselves a Subscription for 6 Nights, which did fill a Room of 600 Persons, so that I needed not to sell one single Ticket at the Door, and without Vanity the Performance was received with a general Approbation. Sig[ra] Avolio, which I brought with me from London pleases extraordinary. I have form'd another Tenor Voice which gives great Satisfaction, the Basses and Counter Tenors are very good, and the rest of the Chorus Singers (by my Direction) do exceedingly well. As for the Instruments they are really excellent, Mr. Dubourg being at the Head of them, and the Musick sounds delightfully in this charming Room, which puts me in such Spirits (and my Health being so good) that I exert myself on my Organ with more than usual Success . . I cannot sufficiently express the kind treatment I receive here, but the Politeness of this generous Nation cannot be unknown to you, so I let you judge of the satisfaction I enjoy, passing my time with honour, profit, and pleasure'.[50]

He left Dublin on August 13, 1742,[51] fully intending to come back the following year. Even as late as September 1749, 'We are assured that Mr. Handel is coming over to entertain the town this Winter'[52] but, as history can now relate, he never returned.

6

A VERY THINKING TASK

AS WAS BRIEFLY noted in the last chapter, Susanna Maria Cibber was joined by her sister-in-law, Thomas Augustine Arne's wife, in two concerts of Handel's music in Dublin during July, 1742. Mrs. Arne had arrived there with her husband on June 30. Thomas Lowe, an important English tenor from Drury Lane Theatre, seems to have travelled with them, for on July 3 all three are announced as having come 'in order to Entertain the Town with their several Performances'.[1]

On Monday, August 23, Arne left again for London. Presumably his visit had convinced him that he could successfully present a theatrical season in Dublin and it may be further presumed that his reason for returning to London was to recruit a company to carry out his plan.

He was to return to Dublin in November, for we read 'that on Friday next [December 3] (being particularly desir'd) at the great Room in Fishamble Street, Mrs. Arne will sing the Song, Sweet Bird, accompanied on the violin by Mr. Arne. And that he intends, between the Acts of his Serenatas Operas and other Musical Performances, to intermix Comic Interludes, (after the Italian Manner) amongst which, will be perform'd Tom Thumb the Original Burlesque Opera compos'd by him, the Dragon of Wantley, Miss Lucy in Town, &c. Intended to give Relief to that grave attention, necessary to be kept up in serious Performances – which he intends shall begin in January next'.[2]

His season was to take place at the Aungier Street Theatre, managed at that time by a Mr. Swan, 'a Gentleman'[3] who had been appointed to this position, when the theatre had first opened, by his fellow

67

'noblemen and gentlemen of the first rank'.[4] Chetwood considers his appointment 'a difficult Attempt for a Gentleman, almost a Stranger to the Affairs of a Theatre', adding, 'It is a very thinking Task, and a Person of Pleasure must either drop his Pursuits of that Kind, or sink in the boisterous Waves, which will require all his Time and Art, to steer his Vessel right . . However this Person by a genteel Behavior, accompany'd with Affability, joyned with good Nature, gained the Esteem of every one. He played several Parts with a delicate Decency'.[5]

The first performance of the season which took place on January 10, 1743, was, not unpredictably, a production of *Comus*. In it Mr. Swan had an opportunity to display his 'delicate Decency' as an actor, for he played the role of *Comus*. The cast list continues with: 'a pastoral Nymph, and the part of Sabrina by Mrs. Arne, the principal Bacchanal by Mrs. Baildon, from London; the Lady's Song [Sweet Echo] by Mrs. Arne, accompany'd by Mr. Neal, from England, who performed it originally; the second pastoral Nymph by Mrs. Sybilla, a Scholar of Mr. Arne's; the part of Euphrosyne to be perform'd by Miss Davis. With all the Choruses perform'd in Parts as originally in England, and never done here before. The original Prologue to be spoke by Mr. Swan and the Epilogue by Mrs. Furnival. A Row of the Pit will be taken into the Orchestra, there being an extraordinary Band of Musick provided on this Occasion. The whole conducted by Mr. Arne, who accompanies the Performance on the Harpsichord. With new Habits, Scenes, Machines, Risings, Sinkings, Flyings and other Decorations. It is hoped it will not be taken ill that none can be admitted behind the Scenes. *N.B.* This performance being exhibited at a much greater Expense than any theatrical Entertainment in this Kingdom, we are obliged to lay the Pit and Boxes together at 5s 5d. Lattaces [sic] 5s. 5d. Gallery 2s. 8d. halfp.'[6]

Evidently this revival was again successful, for it was repeated on January 13, 20 and 24, February 8 and April 21. The cast was distinguished by the presence of the actress Mrs. Furnival, although vocally the only artist of importance was Mrs. Arne. Born Cecilia Young, she was one of a family of singers whose individual identities continue to confuse musical historians. She had made her *début* in 1730 as a pupil of the violinist Francesco Geminiani. In 1734 she joined Handel's company, singing in several of his operas. Burney says of her, 'with a good natural voice and a fine shake [she] had been so well taught, that her style of singing was infinitely superior to that of any other English woman of her time'.[7] Mrs. Sybilla, *née* Gronamann, was a German soprano who married the violinist Thomas Pinto. She sang in London between 1745 and 1749, where she was Handel's second soprano during the last two years of this period. Mrs. Baildon was quite unimportant and was the wife of a singer in the company, who was to appear later in the season. Miss Davis, who sang the role of Euphrosyne, may have been the same actress who became a member of the Smock Alley company during 1745–46, where she played Lucy in *The Beggar's Opera*.

The next operas to be performed were a double bill made up of Arne's *Rosamond* set to Addison's original text, followed by his burlesque *The Opera of Operas, or Tom Thumb the Great*. This combined production, which was a benefit performance for Arne, took place on May 7. The cast was: 'King Henry, Mr. Baildon; Sir Trusty, Mr. Layfield; Page, Master Pilkington, being the first time of his Appearance on any stage; Rosamond, Mrs. Sybilla; Grideline, Miss Davis; and the part of Queen Eleanor, to be perform'd by Mrs. Arne'.[8] *Rosamond* was Arne's first opera, produced at Lincoln's Inn Fields Theatre in 1733, when he was only twenty-three.

The cast of *Tom Thumb* was as follows: 'The Part of Tom Thumb by Master Pilkington; King by Mr. Baildon; Lord Grizzel by Mr. Layfield; Queen Dollallolla by Miss Davis; Princess Huncamunca by Mrs. Sybilla. All the other Characters as Noodle, Doodle, Foodle, Giantess, Conjurer, etc. by a select Company of burlesque Opera Singers. To prevent Mistakes, Ladies are desired to take their places in Time, and on the Day of Performance to send their Servants to keep Places before five o'Clock. Tickets to be had of Mr. Arne, at his House in Aungier-street near the Theatre'.[9]

A second performance was advertised for May 27 but it 'was obliged to be put off, Mrs. Arne being taken violently ill and forbidden

by her Physician to attempt performing at the Hazard of her Life'.[10]
Ultimately, the two operas were again brought out on Saturday,
June 11, 'being positively the last Time of Mr. Arne's exhibiting any
Performance this Season'.[11] The two new artists taking part in these
performances – Baildon and Master Pilkington – are of little account.
Baildon was one of two brothers, Thomas or Joseph, who were both
singing during the same period. Joseph was a lay vicar at Westminster
Abbey, Thomas, a Gentleman of the Chapel Royal. Both were regular
members of Handel's chorus during his last years. Master Pilkington
was John Carteret Pilkington, younger son of Matthew and Letitia
Pilkington.

The Beggar's Opera seems to have been the next operatic production
conducted by Arne. 'By the Special Command of the Duke and
Dutchess of Devonshire', a performance was given on December 8,
1743. The cast included Mlle. Chateauneuf as Polly, Miss Davis as
Lucy, and Thomas Lowe, the renowned English tenor who, as was
earlier noted, had arrived with the Arnes in Dublin in June 1742, but
seemingly was only now making his first operatic appearance with
them, as Macheath.

Lowe, like most important English singers of the period, was a
sometime member of Handel's company, and Handel composed
many parts in his oratorios specially for him. Burney compares him
unfavourably, although justly, with John Beard, Handel's principal
tenor. 'Lowe', he says, 'had sometimes a subordinate part given him;
but with the finest tenor voice I ever heard in my life, for want of
diligence and cultivation, he never could be safely trusted with any
thing better than a ballad, which he constantly learned by his ear'.[12]
He evidently sang his ballads well in Dublin, for *The Beggar's Opera*
had a successful run, the eighth performance being announced for
January 5, 1744. Meanwhile *Comus* had been revived on December 17,
and again on December 22, 1743.

Lampe's *The Dragon of Wantley* was now presented on January 12,
16 and 28, 1744. The cast announced was: 'The part of Moor of
Moor-Hall to be perform'd by Mr. Lowe. The part of Margery to
be perform'd by Mrs. Arne, being her first Appearance in any comic

Character; and the part of Mauxalinda to be perform'd by Madame Chateauneuf; Gubbins by Mr. Worsdale; the Dragon by Mr. Layfield'.[13]

At these performances Arne took his customary place as conductor and accompanist at the harpsichord and, for the performance of January 28, which was a benefit for Mrs. Arne and included Shakespeare's *King Henry IV Part II,* he combined his profession of musician with that of actor, for on this occasion he also played the role of Henry, Prince of Wales, 'being his first attempt of that kind'.[14] We may presume that it was also his last.

On March 10 and 17, 1744, Arne's two masques, *The Judgement of Paris* and *Alfred,* were performed. Hogarth speaks well of *The Judgement of Paris,* praising the overture and various scenes and airs now completely forgotten, but does not mention *Alfred,* which contains the still remarkably well-known tune, 'Rule Britannia'. This was the first performance of *Alfred,* apart from its original private production on August 1, 1740, in a temporary theatre in the gardens of Cliveden, Buckinghamshire, then the residence of the Prince of Wales. Mrs. Arne had sung Venus in *The Judgement of Paris* when it was first produced in London, so we can assume that she sang the same role in Dublin. Thomas Lowe was also a member of the original cast.

The Beggar's Opera, followed by Fielding's ballad opera, *The Virgin Unmasked,* was performed on March 15. On the same evening at 'the Taylors' Hall in Back Lane', a concert of vocal and instrumental music was announced with 'Hush ye little warbling quire [from *Acis and Galatea*] and Tell me lovely Shepherd [from Boyce's serenata, *Solomon*] to be sung by Miss Young who never performed before in Publick'.[15] It is impossible to decide with certainty which member of the Young family this was – if she was not just a singer with the same name. A *début* in such modest circumstances would suggest that if she were one of the family, which seems likely, then she must have been little more than a child. Her age would therefore tend to identify her as Isabella Young, a niece of Mrs. Arne, and a pupil of the bass singer Gustavus Waltz; she was subsequently announced as making her first appearance at a concert in the New Theatre in the Haymarket on March 18, 1751.

Between March 29 and June 6, the season continued with five performances of *Rosamond*, two performances of a double bill composed of *Alfred* and *The Judgement of Paris*, and one performance each of *Comus, The Dragon of Wantley* and *The Beggar's Opera*.

From April 2 onwards all these performances took place, not at the Aungier Street Theatre, but at Smock Alley. This arose from a merger which took place between the companies of both theatres in October 1743 whereby one united company had transferred to the Aungier Street Theatre. A new arrangement now brought the united company back to Smock Alley. Probably the Aungier Street Theatre was closed at the end of March and so the Arne engagement continued at the other theatre.

For the next four seasons no new operas or masques seem to have been produced in Dublin. The principal and virtually the only ballad operas performed between 1745 and the end of the 1747/48 season were *The Devil To Pay, Comus, The Beggar's Opera* (advertised in April 1746 as 'not acted here these two years'[16]), *Damon and Phillida, Flora,* and *The Dragon of Wantley,* and in all that time the number of performances of all ballad operas produced hardly exceeded twenty.

This musical drought was alleviated on February 4, 1748, when *Samson* was announced for performance at Fishamble Street Music Hall, being described as 'the Masterpiece of that great Man, Mr. Handel; and as it is the first time of its being performed in Ireland, will be honour'd by great Numbers of the first Rank, and all true Lovers of Musick'.[17] Exactly one week later, on February 11, again at Fishamble Street, 'the celebrated Oratorio of Judas Maccabaeus . . was performed to a most grand and polite Audience . . under the conduct of Mr. Dubourg to the entire Satisfaction of all the Company'.[18]

From the lack of operas produced, it might seem that Thomas Sheridan (Richard Brinsley Sheridan's father), who in the spring of 1745 had returned from London to take over control of both Dublin theatres, was indifferent to music. On the contrary, from the beginning, Sheridan took an energetic interest in the music performed in his theatres, not that his efforts were appreciated by all the members of his audiences. For example, we find him complaining that the instrumentalists in the orchestra were being saluted 'with a Volley of Apples, and Oranges'[19] – this had occurred in December 1746. Such abuse had ultimately got completely out of control when bottles and stones were thrown, until 'there was no Resource found, but ordering the Band never to go into the Box, but to play behind the Scenes at least till the Pit was so full that they might be protected'.[20]

Not that this resolved the problem, for the following November he was obliged to issue the following manifesto:

'The Manager of the Theatre Royal having at an Extraordinary Expense provided the best Band of Musick which he could procure, was in hopes that he had done a Thing which would be very agreeable to the Town in general, but more particularly so to that Part of the Audience who came early to the Galleries to procure good Places, and that it would make the time before the drawing up of the Curtain pass less heavily if they were to hear some of the best Pieces performed by the best Hands. But to his great Surprise, he finds for some nights past that the Band has been treated in such a Manner as renders it impossible for them to stay in the Box; for besides the Danger to their Persons, in one Night they sustained at least ten pounds worth of Damage by having some of their most valuable Instruments broke. He therefore thinks it his Duty to acquaint the Public that his Musician performers are such as will not Submit to Treatment of this Kind and if it should be continued hereafter, he fears the Audience must be content with worse Hands or having no Musick at all before the Play begins.'[21]

(Were the 'worse Hands' to be a just retribution on audiences which would not appreciate better ones, or the sort of 'Musician performers' at whom it was considered artistically justifiable to throw bottles?)

Sheridan's phrase, 'at least till the Pit was so full that they might be protected' is novel in its idea of having the instrumentalists protected by a timely bodyguard of pit-goers. It also raises a nice moral issue.

At what time was the pit considered to be 'so full' that the audience there would be endangered? There seems to have been an *esprit de corps* in the galleries to ensure that these non-combatants would at least escape physical injury, for a notice in October 1749 directed at 'Evil minded Persons [who] have of late frequented the Galleries, and have thrown Stones and other Things at the Band of Musick during the Time of Performance' distinguishes between 'the great Disturbance of the Audience' and 'the Peril of the Musicians'.[22] Withal like a general showing a classical disregard for his men's lives, Sheridan continued to send greater and greater numbers of musicians into the 'Box' and for the forthcoming season of 1748/49 announced: 'The Orchestra is much enlarged, in order to render it capable of containing the extraordinary Number of Hands who are engaged this Season. The Band is to consist of 10 Violins, a Harpsichord, two double Bases, a Tenor, (viola) a Violenchello, two Hautboys, two Bassoons, two French Horns, and a Trumpet. The Musical Performances will be conducted by Signior Pasquali, (who played the first Violin at the Opera in London) who will also lead the Band. Mr. Lampe, the celebrated Composer, from the Theatre-Royal in Covent-Garden, will accompany all his own Performances on the Harpsicord.'[23]

He was also prodigal in his engagement of singers, for he brought from London for the season, Mrs. Lampe, Mrs. Storer, Mrs. Mozeen and Mr. Sullivan. The most important of these artists was Mrs. Lampe, wife of John Frederick Lampe, the composer of *The Dragon of Wantley*. Lampe had been engaged as composer and harpsichordist to the theatre for the same season. Mrs. Lampe, *née* Isabella Young, was a sister of Mrs. Arne. She is not to be confused with the singer of the same name who had made her *début* at the Taylors' Hall in 1744 and who, it is presumed, would have been her niece. While by no means as distinguished an artist as her sister, Mrs. Lampe was well known in London and the provincial cities. Both Mrs. Storer and Mrs. Mozeen were married to actors in the Smock Alley company. The former had been engaged originally by Sheridan for the 1745/46 season and soon became a favourite with Dublin audiences. Daniel

Sullivan is said to have been a boy vocalist in Dublin in 1737. Later his voice turned counter-tenor and in 1744 he became a member of Handel's company, but was not a success. In 1745 he was singing at Bath and in 1746 returned to Dublin, where Garrick described him as looking 'gay and sensible as usual'.[24] On March 13 of the same year he made his first appearance as Moore in *The Dragon of Wantley* 'at the Request of several Persons of Quality'.[25] He visited Dublin for several seasons where his singing seems to have been popular, and died there at his lodgings in the Cornmarket on October 13, 1764.

Even with this nucleus of singers among his singing actors and actresses, Sheridan presented comparatively little opera, ballad or dramatic, from the commencement of his 1748/49 season up to February, 1750. There were, of course, revivals of *Comus, The Beggar's Opera, Damon and Phillida, The Dragon of Wantley,* and the rest but, apart from one performance of 'an operatical play', *Jack The Giant Queller,* by the Irish author Henry Brooke on March 27, 1749, almost no new works.

Sheridan cannot be blamed for this, for by 1748 the old style of English ballad opera was languishing, and there simply were no new works available for production. The second period of English opera (that is, comic, as distinct from ballad opera) was not to begin in Dublin until 1763. Sheridan did, however, on January 13, 1749, present at Smock Alley a dramatic opera, *The Tempest, or the Enchanted Island,* Thomas Shadwell's version of Davenant and Dryden's arrangement of Shakespeare's play 'in which', it was announced, 'all the Songs and original Musick, compos'd by Mr. Purcell will be carefully revived'.[26] There had been previous productions of *The Tempest* in Dublin; one took place in 1738, but it seems basically to have been Shakespeare's play with music added.*

---

*A production which was staged on December 9, 1742 probably used Purcell's music although this is not specifically stated. *Faulkner's Dublin Journal* of November 30/December 4, records: 'The Company of Comedians at the Theatre in Smock-alley, having procured the original Musick of The Tempest or the Inchanted Island, from London, intend to perform the same on Thursday next . . And in order to have the same done in the regular manner they do not perform there on Monday next, being obliged to make great Alterations to the Stage'. On this occasion the roles of Dorinda and Amphitrite were taken by Mrs. Storer.

The present production was an authentic revival of Purcell's original work of 1695, concluding with the masque of *Neptune and Amphitrite*. It was carefully presented, 'the Scenes, Machines and other Decorations proper to the Play being entirely new'.[27] There were the usual 'Sinkings' and 'Flyings' and 'an extraordinary Piece of Machinery representing the rising Sun, never but once exhibited in this Kingdom'.[28] The opera is remembered today by the songs, 'Arise, ye subterranean winds', 'Come unto these yellow sands', 'Full fathoms five' and the soprano air 'Halcyon days'. The singing roles were taken by Mrs. Storer, as Ariel, 'with the songs in Character'; Mrs. Mozeen was Dorinda, '(who never saw a Man) with the Song of Dear pretty Youth'.[29] Sullivan was Neptune and Mrs. Lampe was Amphitrite.*There were four other performances during this first season, on January 19 and 25, February 17, and March 6, and it was to be revived annually for many years.

Neither Fishamble Street nor Crow Street Music Halls produced any novelties in the 1748/49 season. There were at least eight revivals of *Acis and Galatea* during the period. The five most important took place at Fishamble Street on November 18 and 25, 1748, when Mrs. Arne sang and '(tho' but just recovered out of a violent Fever) gave entire satisfaction',[30] a performance on February 7, 1749, in which she also sang, and two performances on October 24 and November 7 during the same year. The cast announced for these performances included Mrs. Lampe, Mrs. Storer, Mrs. Mozeen, Daniel Sullivan, and Samuel Howard, a tenor of little importance – but later known as an organist and composer – whom Sheridan had also engaged from London. The conductor was Nicolò Pasquali, a violinist and composer, whom Sheridan brought to Dublin at the beginning of the season as leader of the orchestra. While there, he composed and arranged a number of masques and entertainments which were successfully performed at Smock Alley. These included *Apollo and Daphne, The Triumphs of Hibernia* and *The Temple of Peace*. He also composed incidental music for *Hamlet* and *Romeo and Juliet*.[31]

---

*The last three characters are of course extraneous to Shakespeare's play.

Another performance of *Acis and Galatea* was given at the Philharmonic Room (also situated in Fishamble Street) on November 23 'by particular desire of several Ladies of Quality'[32] and introduced Miss Oldmixon, a new English soprano, as Galatea. She was the daughter of John Oldmixon, a forgotten English historian and pamphleteer. In 1749 she had had a benefit performance of *Acis and Galatea,* at Hickford's Concert Room in London, the other singers being the celebrated Caterina Galli, John Beard, and Thomas Rheinhold. The performance was conducted by Matthew Dubourg.

So, operatically, it was a dull period in Dublin, the only announcement of better music to come being an advertisement for a performance of Handel's *Joshua*, 'never done here before',[33] to take place at Fishamble Street Music Hall on January 25, 1750. The vagaries of winter weather were, however, to cause not alone one but two postponements of the work, for we read: '*N.B.* Part of the Musick for the above Oratorio being delayed in England by contrary Winds, the Rehearsal has been put off to Monday the 29th Inst . . and the principal performance is also put off to Thursday the 1st of February'[34]; and again: 'The Musick for the Oratorio of Joshua being still detained in England, the Governors of the Hospital for Incurables [in whose aid the performance was being given] find themselves under a Necessity either of performing some other Oratorio, or postponing Joshua to a farther day, but in Regard to the Expectations the Publick may have of that celebrated new Piece, the procuring of which has been attended with considerable Expense, they think fit to postpone it rather than disappoint them; and Notice shall be given of the Time of the Performance upon the Arrival of the said Musick'.[35]

Ultimately the public rehearsal was deferred until March 12 (which suggests that the music had been delayed by something other than 'contrary Winds') when it was performed 'to a most polite and numerous Audience'.[36] We learn that 'the Whole was so well conducted as to give general Satisfaction and 'tis thought the House will be so very full on Thursday Night next, that the Ladies, for their own

Convenience, are requested to come without Hoops'.[37] On Thursday, March 15, the first performance took place before 'a crowded Audience of the Nobility and Gentry' when it 'was executed with the greatest Accuracy by the Performers, and conducted with much Satisfaction and judgement'.[38]

7

THE ENGLISH TASTE IN GENERAL

THE DECADE FROM 1750 to 1760, which was to introduce only two episodes of operatic importance, commenced timidly at Smock Alley on February 16 of the former year with a performance of Dr. William Boyce's one-act musical entertainment, *The Chaplet*. Slight though this entertainment was, it must be distinguished from ballad opera, since the dialogue is set to recitative. The libretto was by Moses Mendes, a gentleman who combined the professions of poet, dramatist and stockbroker. More singularly, his grandfather, who had been physician to King John IV of Portugal, had accompanied Catherine of Braganza when she set out on her voyage to England to marry King Charles II. While travelling, she is reputed to have contracted erysipelas, which Mendes treated so effectively that the future Queen made him a member of her household, thereby establishing the family in England. There were five performances of *The Chaplet* during the season and the cast included Mrs. Storer, Mrs. Lampe, Mrs. Mozeen and Daniel Sullivan.

Much more significant was an announcement made in November 1749, that the Aungier Street Theatre, which had closed in March 1744 and reopened in October 1748 to accommodate 'Grand Festinos',[1] a *ridotto* type of entertainment, was once again to be reconstructed 'in order to have Dramatick Operas exhibited there'.[2] This occurred on February 10, 1749/50, when the perennially popular *Comus* was performed.

Thomas Sheridan was then manager of both Dublin theatres and to him credit is due, not alone for re-introducing opera to the city, but for introducing what was probably the most important opera yet to be heard there. This was Purcell and Dryden's *King Arthur* which was produced on March 17. Exceptionally and unfortunately no cast list is given, but the production was undoubtedly successful, for it was subsequently performed on March 24 and 29, April 7 and 21 and May 5, 19 and 26. It seems to have received little comment from the press. A preliminary notice refers to 'the Opera-House in Aungier Street'[3] and an advertisement for the second performance announces that 'The Stage will be illuminated with Wax'.[4]

After *Dido and Aeneas, King Arthur* was Henry Purcell's most celebrated opera. It differs from both *Dioclesian* and *The Tempest* in that the text was originally written as an opera libretto and was not an adaptation of an earlier play. John Dryden, in a frequently quoted phrase from his preface to the work, describes Purcell as having composed it 'with so great a Genius that he has nothing to fear but an ignorant, ill-judging Audience'.[5] As with *Dioclesian,* the story of *King Arthur* combines legend with fantasy, the scene changing from Rome to England. King Arthur of the Britons is at war with King Oswald of the Saxons. Oswald has recruited a wizard, Osmond, as his chief-of-staff, who in turn is assisted by two spirits. Merlin, that popular wizard of Arthurian legend, is naturally on King Arthur's side and he persuades Philidel, one of Osmond's spirits, to desert to the Britons. There is also Emmeline, Arthur's betrothed, who has to fight off the advances not only of Oswald but of Osmond as well. However, all ends happily. Arthur meets Oswald in hand-to-hand combat and having beaten him offers him his freedom.

Conforming to contemporary taste, the opera ended with a masque which introduced mythological figures such as Aeolus, Pan and Venus. It is Venus who sings the charming and best known air in the opera, 'Fairest Isle all Isles Excelling'. This air and the renowned 'Frost Scene' in Act 3 are the only two wellknown vocal pieces from the opera. The latter scene is conjured up by Cupid waving his wand and disclosing a vast space of snow and ice. Professor Sir Jack Westrup has pointed out that the idea of the *tremolando* for chorus and strings which so imaginatively depicts this wasteland of ice and cold originated

Thomas Augustine Arne. Composer (1710–1778)

Kane O'Hara.
Composer and Dramatist (1711–1782)

HENRY WOODWARD. MANAGER AND ACTOR (1714–1777)

HENRY MOSSOP. MANAGER AND ACTOR
(1729–1774)

in one of Lully's operas fourteen years before *King Arthur* was produced.* Nevertheless the novelty and effectiveness of the music must have been a revelation to a seventeenth or early eighteenth century audience hearing it for the first time.

The next new opera to be performed was Henry Carey's *Nancy, or The Parting Lovers*. This took place at Smock Alley on May 4, the cast including Mrs. Storer, Daniel Sullivan and Samuel Howard.

In July of the following year, 1751, the lease of the Crow Street Music Hall changed hands. The 'new' music hall at Fishamble Street had presented opposition to the older hall and the then lessee, Peter Bardin, a Smock Alley actor, let Crow Street at an annual rent of £133 15s. od. with the added covenant that he was to receive two free tickets to any part of the house for all performances. The new lease holders were Daniel Sullivan, the tenor, Joseph de Boeck, a violoncellist, Stefano Storace, double bass player and father of Nancy Storace (the original Susanna in *Le Nozze di Figaro*), Samuel Lee, violinist and musical director, and a second violinist and conductor, Gian Battista Marella. Marella's name appears frequently in concert advertisements at this time. In the *Dictionary of National Biography* the reference to John Oldmixon records that 'one daughter presumably Mrs. Eleanora Marella sang at Hickford's Rooms in 1746'. This, and an abstract of a will made by her brother George, identify Eleanora Marella with the Miss Oldmixon who was singing in Dublin in 1750. *Faulkner's Dublin Journal* of October 1/5, 1754, records her marriage to Marella, so presumably they had found romance in Dublin. Certainly there was little romance attached to the new Crow Street Music Hall venture, for by 1753 the syndicate had quarrelled. Reinforcing the management obviously had not reinforced the box-office receipts.

Sheridan's continued interest in opera was again apparent by a visit which he made to London during October 1751. He was then trying to engage Italian singers to present opera in Dublin during the following season. Benjamin Victor (Sheridan's Dublin theatre

*Purcell by J. A. Westrup. (J. M. Dent and Sons Ltd. 1937.)

F

manager), in a letter dated October 21, 1751, addressed to his patroness, the Countess of Orrery, informs her: 'The brilliant *Mrs. Woffington* is the only theme in or out of the Theatre; your ladyship may remember in a former letter, it was my private opinion that she would perform here, though Mr. *Sheridan* so strongly opposed it. His endeavours were for the Italian singers, and operas – but his good genius prevailed – She came like his better angel to save him from the gulph that was opened for him!'[6] Victor was, of course, prejudiced. He later recorded, 'I will venture to make this Observation upon serious Operas – that notwithstanding the great success some have met with, and the Encouragement given by People of Fashion to that exotic Entertainment (whether exhibited in *Italian or English*) they are not, or ever can be adapted to the *English* Taste in general'.[7]

Consequently it was not till some months later that a hybrid form of Italian opera was heard in Dublin, though not at Smock Alley, with the arrival of the castrato singer, Gaetano Guadagni. The first announcement of his visit which can be found comes appropriately from that Elsa Maxwell of the eighteenth century, Mrs. Delany. In a letter dated January 26, 1752, she writes: 'Last Saturday we were invited to the Primate's to hear music . . chiefly Italian – the Stabat Mater, sung by Guadagni (whom you heard sing in Mr. Handel's oratorios) and Mrs. Oldmixon; Dubourg the principal violin.'[8] This letter, coupled with the fact that his first advertised performance to be discovered so far was announced as a benefit, suggests that Guadagni had arrived in Dublin an appreciable time earlier, possibly during 1751. Although no evidence to support this assumption can be discovered, we read, surprisingly, in a racing announcement of August 31/September 3, 1751, 'On Monday the 26th past, began the Races of Bellewstown near Drogheda . . on Wednesday the 28th, the Thirty Pounds Plate was run for by Mr. Burrass's Mare Sprightly Peggy, Mr. Walpole's Horse Signior Guadani, Mr. Fitzgerald's Gelding Welcome, and Mr. Langan's Horse Irish Beau, which was won by the former'.[9] One wonders who was Mr. Walpole, sporting gentleman and connoisseur of singing.

Gaetano Guadagni was born at Lodi near Milan about 1725,

making his first appearance at Parma in 1747 and coming to England in the following year. He was handsome and had a good contralto voice but at that time no vocal technique. In London he was taken up both by Handel and by Garrick, the former giving him parts in some of his oratorios, the latter, lessons in acting. According to Burney, during this period 'he was more noticed in singing English than Italian'.[10] The anomaly of Guadagni as a castrato singer was that he did not dazzle his audience with *cadenze* and *fioriture*. This is difficult to understand. Being a castrato would seem to presuppose not only an ostentatious florid style, but intensive training in the art of singing as well. Yet all authorities are agreed that his schooling was rudimentary, and in fact he had spent his first years as an *amoroso* or 'juvenile lead' with a *buffo* company.

'The Music he sung,' explains Burney, 'was the most simple imaginable; a few notes with frequent pauses, and opportunities of being liberated from the composer and the band, were all he wanted. And in these seemingly extemporaneous effusions, he proved the inherent power of melody totally divorced from harmony and un-assisted even by unisonous accompaniment. Surprised at such great effects from causes apparently so small, I frequently tried to analise the pleasure he communicated to the audience, and found it chiefly arose from his artful manner of diminishing the tones of his voice, like the dying notes of the Aeolian harp. Most other singers captivate by a swell or *messa di voce*; but Guadagni, after beginning a note or passage with all the force he could safely exert, fined it off to a thread, and gave it all the effect of extreme distance'.[11]

Describing his return to England in 1769, Burney writes: 'His figure was uncommonly elegant and noble; his countenance replete with beauty, intelligence, and dignity; and his attitudes and gestures were so full of grace and propriety, that they would have been excellent studies for a statuary'.[12] With this advantage of appearance and with a voice elegant in its simplicity of style and line, he was a natural performer for the music of the classicist, Gluck, and he was the first Orpheus when *Orfeo ed Euridice* was performed at Vienna in 1762. To quote Burney once again: 'In this last drama, his attitudes, action, and impassioned and exquisite manner of singing the simple and ballad-like air; *Che farò*, acquired him very great and just applause'.[13]

Guadagni's appearances in Dublin included the benefit concert mentioned earlier 'By Command of their Graces the Duke and Dutchess of Dorset' (who had returned to Dublin in December 1750), which took place on February 8, 1752, 'At the Great Musick-hall in Crow street'.[14] He was assisted at this concert by Miss Oldmixon and the tickets were priced at half a guinea. On March 11, he gave a further concert at Fishamble Street, again with Miss Oldmixon, under the auspices of 'the Gentlemen of the Morning Concert . . For the Enlargement and Relief of the poor Prisoners confined for Debt in the several Marshalseas in this City', when breakfast was announced for 11 o'clock, 'and the Musick at 12'.[15] That evening he sang at Crow Street when a ball was announced to take place after the concert. On March 19 he sang with Daniel Sullivan at Crow Street, 'After which', it was announced, 'there will be an Assembly, with Tea, Coffee, Cards etc. Mr. Storace [whose benefit it was] will take care to have a good Band of Musick for Country Dances'.[16] He was performing at Fishamble Street Music Hall on April 16, singing 'several favourite Italian and English Songs which will be expressed in his Bills'. Tickets cost 5s. 5d. each and were 'to be had at his lodgings in College-street'.[17] Finally, for the benefit of Miss Oldmixon, at Fishamble Street Music Hall on April 27, he was advertised to sing in *Samson*: 'Composed by Mr. Handel. With the Dead March, Lamentation and Chorus of Virgins, never performed here before.'[18]*

Guadagni ended his days at Padua where he was attached to the Church of St. Anthony at a fee of four hundred ducats a year. Here Burney heard him sing in 1770. Lord Mount Edgcumbe, while on his Grand Tour, was to hear him there in 1784 and was disappointed when Guadagni, having invited him to his home to take coffee, entertained him not by singing, but by exhibiting puppets 'in which he took great delight'.[19] Michael Kelly, the Irish tenor, who had

---

*The first performance in Dublin is reported to have taken place on February 4, 1748. See p. 72.

visited Guadagni some years earlier, had the same story to tell. 'He had built a house, or rather a palace,' he relates, 'in which he had a very neat theatre, and a company of puppets, which represented L'Orpheo e Euridice; himself singing the part of Orpheo behind the scenes . . His puppet-show was his hobby-horse, and as he received no money, he had always crowded houses. He had a good fortune, with which he was very liberal, and was the handsomest man of his kind I ever saw'.[20] By about 1785 his 'good fortune' had been dissipated and, ending his days in great poverty, he died in 1792.

On March 6, 1753, Thomas Roseingrave, a member of a wellknown Dublin family of musicians, presented his opera *Phaedra and Hippolitus,* for one performance, in concert form, at Fishamble Street Music Hall. The vocal parts were sung 'by the best Performers',[21] and Roseingrave conducted. We learn that the public rehearsal was performed 'to a numerous Audience, which met with the highest Applause, the Connoisseurs allowing it to exceed any musical Performance ever exhibited here, in Variety, Taste, and Number of good Songs, so it is not doubted but there will be a crowded Audience, at the Performance next Tuesday Night'.[22] Roseingrave was mentally unstable. About the same time that he was presenting his opera in Dublin, Mrs. Delany was writing: 'Mr. Roseingrave (who was sent away from St. George's Church [at Hanover Square, London, where he had been appointed organist in 1725] on account of mad fits) is now in Ireland, and at times can play very well on the harpsichord.'[23] His father willed him only five shillings. Insanity was then considered not an illness but a misdemeanour.

Up to the beginning of March 1754, when Thomas Sheridan left Dublin for London, no new opera had been produced either at Smock Alley or Aungier Street since the performances of *King Arthur* and *Nancy, or The Parting Lovers* in 1750, and almost two years had still to pass before the situation altered.

Meanwhile, on October 25, 1755, it was announced that 'Mr. Arne, who is arrived in this Kingdom, with several vocal performers, having agreed with the Managers of the Theatre Royal, Proposes, to entertain the Public Three Nights with a New Opera in the English Language, called, Eliza. The first Performance will be in the Beginning of November. The Subscription is opened at the Office of the Theatre in Smock-alley, where Attendance will be given every Day from Twelve to Three. Five Box Tickets for the said Opera will be delivered to each Subscriber for One Guinea. The Orchestra will be considerably enlarged, a fine Organ put up, an Additional Number of the best Instrumental Performers engaged, and Mr. Arne will accompany the Operas on the Harpsichord'.[24]

The vocal performers whom Arne had brought with him were his wife, her sister, Miss Esther Young, a niece, Miss Polly Young, Miss Charlotte Brent, Miss Spencer, and a Mr. Sadler. Esther Young was a contralto who had been a member of Handel's company in 1744, and was one of the Covent Garden company for whom he composed his unproduced work *Alceste*. Polly Young was to enjoy a considerable success during this season. She returned to Smock Alley in 1757, 1761, and 1762, and in 1766 married the famous violinist, François Barthélemon. John O'Keeffe, the Irish dramatist, who describes her as a 'beautiful little creature', relates that 'she was a fine singer, and played and sung Ariel, in Shakespeare's Tempest to great and pleasing effect: from her charming face and small figure, she appeared a bewitching sprite'.[25] Charlotte Brent was a pupil of Arne. Her father was a fencing master and counter-tenor who had sung Hamor in the original production of *Jephtha* in 1752. She was making her *début* in Dublin and later was to have an extremely successful career, Arne composing the formidable role of Mandane in his opera *Artaxerxes* for her. Charles Dibdin writes of her 'possessing an exquisite voice and being under a master, the great characteristics of whose musical abilities were natural ease and unaffected simplicity . . Her power,' he continues, 'was resistless, her neatness was truly interesting and her variety was incessant. Though she owed a great deal to nature, she owed a great deal to Arne.'[26] Miss Spencer remained at Smock Alley during the following season of 1756/57, playing Catherine 'with Songs in Character'[27] in *Catherine and Petruchio,* Garrick's adaptation of *The Taming of the Shrew*. This was announced as the first time 'of her attempting a Character on the Stage'.[28] She was also to attempt Euphrosyne in *Comus,* a singing witch in *Macbeth,* Tippet in *The Beggar's Wedding,* and Amphitrite in an Arne/Purcell version of *The Tempest.* Mr. Sadler remains unidentified.

The first performance of *Eliza* eventually had to be postponed from the beginning of November until November 29 'on account of the Indisposition of a principal Performer'.[29] The indisposed performer was Mrs. Arne who seems to have suffered from chronic ill health and was continually cancelling her appearances. Also, her relationship with her husband had at this time reached an unhappy stage and they were to separate during the following year.

The postponed performance was well received. We read, 'On Saturday last at the Theatre Royal in Smock-alley, was perform'd, Mr. Arne's new Opera, call'd Eliza: The noble and splendid Appearance, and the great and just Applause throughout the whole Performance, were strong Indications of the good Taste reigning in this Kingdom, and a generous, though proper Compliment to that great Master of his Science, Mr. Arne. Mrs. Arne, whose Excellence is well known, had the Misfortune of a violent Hoarseness, and rose from her Bed in a Fever to perform; Mr. Sadler and Miss Brent were greatly approv'd; but Miss Polly Young, a child of six years of Age, pleased and astonished the whole Company, having a sweet melodious Voice, accenting her Words with great Propriety, and Singing perfectly in Time and Tune. The Poem is, by all judges of good Writing, thought excellent; the Orchestra was full, and perform'd without a Fault; but the Judgement, Taste, Expression, and Variety of the Music would be injur'd in an Attempt to commend it.'[30]

Hogarth certainly had no great opinion of the opera, describing it as 'a long and (to judge from the words of the music) a dull piece, on the subject of the Spanish Armada.* The principal character was Eliza (or queen Elizabeth) . . and the chief songs are loyal and patriotic effusions suited to the occasion'.[31] His choice of critical words may have been apt, for the libretto was by a hack English

*Was it from this that Richard Brinsley Sheridan got his idea for the play 'The Spanish Armada' in *The Critic*?

writer named Richard Rolt, who having taken the Jacobite side in 1745, came to Dublin shortly afterwards in the hope of finding employment there. He has been chronicled as 'Dull Rolt, long steep'd in Sedgeley's nut-brown beer'.[32] There were two further performances of the opera on December 4 and December 20.

During the remainder of the season there were revivals of Arne's operas *Rosamond* and *Comus,* and then a revival of Purcell's *The Tempest,* in which the music was announced as being 'new composed'[33] by Mr. Arne. This reads like *lèse-majesté,* yet Hogarth has confirmed that Arne always regarded Purcell's genius with reverence and justifies his new arrangement of the music by reminding us that for *The Tempest* he composed Ariel's charming air, 'Where the bee sucks'. Next, on March 20, 1756, in a double bill with *Comus,* was announced 'a Farce (never acted before) called, The Pincushion: Being a Manuscript of the celebrated Mr. Gay's, Author of The Beggar's Opera. The Songs adapted to favourite Ballad Airs of Mr. Arne's. The characters by Mr. Sadler, Mrs. Pye, Miss E. Young and Miss Brent'.[34] Mrs. Pye was a minor member of the Smock Alley company for several years, who occasionally took singing roles. The season ended with further revivals of *The Chaplet, The Beggar's Opera,* and *Damon and Phillida,* concluding with *Alfred,* 'in the manner of an Oratorio'[35] at Fishamble Street Music Hall.

Mrs. Arne was to return to Dublin in December 1756, having by then left her husband; Polly Young seems to have remained there after the 1755/56 season. We again find Mrs. Arne in Dublin in April 1758, but by this time her career was in decline (she was then forty-seven) and the communicative Mrs. Delany was able to write with sanctimonious malice on August 8 from Mount Panther near Dundrum in County Down:

'We dined at Mr. Bayly's. . . I was surprised there at meeting Mrs. Arne (Miss Young that was); they have her in the house to teach Miss Bayly to sing; she was recommended to Mr. Bayly by Mrs. Berkeley as an object of compassion. She looks indeed much humbled, and I hope is as deserving as they think her to be; great allowances are to be made for the temptations those poor people fall under. She has been severely used by a bad husband, and suffered to starve, if she had not met with charitable people. She behaves herself very well, and though her voice has lost its bloom as well as her face, she sings well, and was well taught by Geminiani and Handel, and had she not been idle would have been a charming singer. Mr. Bayly plays on the violin, his curate on the German flute; Mrs. Arne and Miss Bayly sing, and a girl of nine years old accompanies them on the harpsichord most surprisingly – she is a niece of Mrs. Arne's; the race of Youngs are *born* songsters and musicians.'[36]

If one accepts Polly Young's published age of six in 1755, Mrs. Delany's announcement of 'a girl of nine years old' in 1758 leaves little doubt that this was the same niece. Mrs. Arne's name disappears from newspaper advertisements after 1760, when age had undoubtedly ended her career. She seems to have become reconciled with her husband before his death, for in his will he divided his estate between her and their son Michael.

On April 6, 1758, a serenata called *L'Endimione* by the forgotten Italian or French opera composer, Andrea Bernasconi, was given at Fishamble Street Music Hall. It was presented 'by the Ladies and Gentlemen of the Musical Academy'[37] and since one of the singers taking part was Lady Caroline Russell, a daughter of the Duke of Bedford, then Lord Lieutenant, a social success at least was assured. A press notice confirms this. 'As there is Reason to believe that the Audience will be very numerous', we read, 'it is humbly requested that the Ladies will be pleased to come without Hoops, and order their Coaches down Fishamble-street'.[38]

From October 1756, when he returned from London to become manager of Smock Alley Theatre again, until his career as a Dublin manager ended in 1758, Thomas Sheridan had produced no new operas. The reason for this has already been given – there simply were no new English operas to be produced. Yet his interest in opera persisted, and he travelled to London during the summer of 1758 to engage artists for Smock Alley '(especially, by request, a company of singers for operas and burlettas)'.[39] However, by November 1758 Sheridan was contemplating the advantages of remaining in London, and by the following February had finally decided to sell his Irish properties and 'return no more'.[40] So the advent of Italian opera was once more postponed.

The next performance of a new opera does not appear to have taken place until 1761 when, for April 27, was announced 'a new Musical Entertainment, call'd, Thomas and Sally, as performed at the Theatre Royal in Covent Garden. The Musick Composed by Doctor Arne. The principal characters by Mr. Digges, Mr. Shaw, Miss Green and Miss Young'.[41] The members of the cast were all Smock Alley players. West Digges was replaced by a Mr. Brown in the role of Thomas when the opera was eventually produced. Tate Wilkinson records that Brown was held 'in much esteem as an actor and a gentleman at Bath and Edinburgh – once attempted Richard at Drury Lane, but was barely permitted to finish the part'.[42] To this John O'Keeffe adds, 'he played by the nights on half profit, and did well; but turned manager [at Smock Alley] and broke. In his own character he was a misanthrope, and was never seen but on the stage. It was said his real name was Doyle.'[43] Shaw, who played the Squire, was not an important artist; Miss Green, who sang Dorcas, has not been identified. She should not be confused with Mrs. Henry Green, a favourite actress with Dublin audiences during the early 1750's, for this artist was appearing at Covent Garden Theatre in April 1761. The role of Sally was taken by Miss Young, and once again it must be assumed that it was Miss Polly.

Thomas and Sally is still occasionally performed. The plot concerns the attempts of a wicked squire on the virtue of Sally, who is rescued from her demoralising fate by her sweetheart, Thomas, an honest sailor. Two items concerning the opera are worthy of note. It was an early example of English opera with sung recitative instead of spoken dialogue, and the first example in which clarinets were introduced into the orchestra. The libretto is the earliest extant work by the wellknown Irish dramatist, Isaac Bickerstaffe. As will be evident, Bickerstaffe was one of the most prolific English librettists of the eighteenth century. Little is recorded of him except that he was born in 1735 and that in 1746 he became page to Lord Chesterfield when the latter was appointed Lord Lieutenant. That his name – Isaac Bickerstaffe – was assumed cannot be entirely outruled for the same name had earlier been used as a pseudonym both by Sir Richard Steele and Dean Swift. Later he is said to have become an officer of Marines, but in 1772, being suspected of what has euphemistically been described as 'a deed without a name',[44] he fled to the Continent. He died about 1812.

Thomas and Sally was produced as an after-piece with the tragedy of *Tancred and Sigismunda*. Consequently it is difficult to decide how much the evening's entertainment owed its success to the opera rather than to the play. Contemporary newspaper reports indicate that the play was the attraction. Some significance may however be attached to the continued existence, however frail, of *Thomas and Sally,* while *Tancred and Sigismunda,* like another well-known royal personage, are now a long time dead. Even before the first performance, it was announced, 'In Order the better to accomodate the Ladies, Part of the Pit will be railed into the Boxes',[45] and after the performance we read of 'There having been an extraordinary Overflow of Company'.[46] The opera was repeated on May 8 and 13.

8

A KIND OF POOR RELATION
TO AN OPERA

SEVENTEEN SIXTY-ONE was the year when at last it can be stated unequivocally that Italian opera was performed in Dublin. True, the operas produced were musically and dramatically second-rate. They were burlettas, described by one of the characters in an English burlesque of about 1750, as 'a kind of poor Relation to an Opera'.[1] Burlettas were in fact an early form of *opera buffa* which differed from *opera seria* in introducing fewer castrato voices and in giving greater opportunities to the basses and, of course, in having a comic plot instead of a dramatic one.

The group of Italian artists which arrived in Dublin was a company of strolling players, although one of them was later to become famous. They were Antonio Minelli, Giovanni Battista Zingoni, and four members of a family called de Amicis. We find Zingoni and the de Amicis, who were the back-bone of the company, performing at Brussels and Antwerp in 1759, and after their season in Dublin they were engaged for the King's Theatre in London. The following ballet troupe was also engaged for Dublin: Giovanni Battista Tioli (who was also the choreographer), Giuseppe Genovini, Vicenza Lucchi, Robert Aldridge and Master Jemmy Godwin. There was also a small *corps de ballet* of figure dancers.* Almost all Italian opera companies visiting Dublin during the eighteenth century included ballet dancers. These do not appear to have taken an integral part in the operas, however, but merely to have performed short ballets between the acts and at the end of the performances.

*The story of the formation of the company for Dublin is described in detail by Antonio Minelli in Appendix B.

Antonio Minelli was a singer and, for the first month of the season, the impresario of the company. Zingoni combined the talents of *maestro* and tenor singer. He was to sing the tenor roles in Johann Christian Bach's operas *Orione* and *Zanaida* at the King's Theatre in London during the following season. Another artist, Anna Dunlap, was a member of the Smock Alley company, playing Polly in *The Beggar's Opera* in 1765. The de Amicis family included the father, Domenico, a bass, Maria Anna, his daughter and Gaetano, his son, both of whom sang small roles. The star of the company was a second daughter, Anna Lucia, a soprano, who was born about 1740. In 1761 she was at the onset of a career which was to bring her the principal role of Giunia in the first performance of Mozart's *Lucio Silla* in 1773.

Leopold Mozart, writing to his wife while the opera was in rehearsal, told her, 'de Amicis is our best friend; she sings and acts like an angel, and is extremely pleased because Wolfgang has served her extraordinarily well. Both you and the whole of Salzburg would be amazed if you could hear her!'[2] Burney says, 'De Amicis was not only the first who introduced *staccato divisions* in singing on our stage, but the first singer that I had ever heard go up to E flat in altissimo, with true, clear, and powerful *real* voice'.[3] Speaking of her performances in London he continues, 'Her figure and gestures were in the highest degree elegant and graceful; her countenance, though not perfectly beautiful, was extremely high-bred and interesting; and her voice and manner of singing, exquisitely polished and sweet. She had not a motion that did not charm the eye, or a tone but what delighted the ear. Indeed, she acted and sung for the whole family; for by her merits and good works, she covered the multitude of their sins, which would otherwise have had no remission'.[4]

John O'Keeffe, who as a boy had attended the Dublin performances, agrees with Burney in his appraisal of Anna Lucia, describing her as 'one of the most charming actresses',[5] but contradicts his severe judgement of the remainder of the family. Domenico, for example, he flatly declares to have been 'the best comedian I had ever seen before, or since. His acting in a burletta where he personated a physician, a beau, and a terrified blacksmith,* the latter in a night scene, with a lantern, was wonderfully fine in the diversity of character'.[6]

The dancer and choreographer, Tioli, had first arrived at Smock Alley from Italy during the 1757/58 season, later travelling with the company to Cork. Signora Lucchi had been a member of Garrick's company at Drury Lane from 1757 to 1761. Tioli joined the Drury Lane company for the 1760/61 season and it was from here that Minelli probably engaged both artists. Since there was a Mrs. Godwin playing at Smock Alley in 1758, it is a reasonable assumption that Master Jemmy was her son. Robert Aldridge, who was born about 1739, has been styled 'the finest Irish-born dancer of the day'.[7]

The casts for burlettas were divided into two groups. The principal or *buffo* group was made up of two women, the *prima* and *seconda buffa*, and three men, the *primo buffo*, the *buffo caricato* and the *ultima parte*. The first of these men was a tenor, the second usually a bass, the third always a bass. The secondary or romantic group consisted of two lovers, the *uomo serio* (or *amoroso*) and the *donna seria*. This formal arrangement, originally strictly enforced, became lax as time went on and was not always observed in Dublin. Most of the Dublin productions were, in fact, *pasticcios* – operas into which arias, duets, trios and concerted numbers from other operas were introduced indiscriminately, the intention being to let the audience hear as many of their favourite airs as possible. As a form of entertainment it was enormously popular during most of the eighteenth century and was practised by even the best composers. In 1789 a *pasticcio* called *L'Ape* was produced at Vienna with music by twelve composers, and a performance of Gluck's *Orfeo ed Euridice* at Covent Garden in 1792 included music by J. C. Bach, Handel, Sacchini, Reeve, Mazzinghi – and Gluck.

The first burletta performance in Dublin took place at Smock Alley Theatre, then under the management of Henry Mossop, an Irishman, excellent tragedian and Trinity scholar, on December 19, 1761, when Giuseppe Scolari's 'drama giocoso'[8], *La Cascina*, was

*Probably *Gl'Intrighi per Amore*.

produced. The *pasticcio* situation is immediately evident since the composer's name announced in the press advertisements and in the printed libretto is not Scolari, but Baldassare Galuppi. Undoubtedly this merely meant that music taken from some of Galuppi's operas was included for, due to the success of his *Il Filosofo di Campagna,* Galuppi's name was much better known than Scolari's, and so was more likely to attract an audience. The cast was:

Lavinia, the Mistress of the Dairy-House	Anna Dunlap
Lena, a Shepherdess	Anna Lucia de Amicis
Pippo, an husbandman	Domenico de Amicis
Conte Ripoli, an affected Lover	Antonio Minelli
Berto, a Countryman	Giovan-Battista Zingoni
Cecca, a Country-girl	Maria Anna de Amicis.[9]

The evening's performance also included at 'End of the first act, a grand Ballet Dance, call'd, The Hungarian Camp. Hussars by Master Godwin, and Signior Genovini, Officers of the Pandours by Signior Tioli, and, Signiora Lucchi, End of the second act, a Dance, called The Furnace [sic] of Vulcan, with the arrival of Venus and her attendants, in which will be introduced a Song in praise of the City of Dublin. Venus by Signiora de Amicis, Mercury Master Godwin, Jove, Signior Tioli, Juno by Signiora Lucchi. The Books of the Opera with an English translation, to be had at Sig. Minelli's lodgings at Mr. Rhames's Musick shop on the Blind quay, and at the Theatre. Boxes, Pit and Lattices 5s 5d – Middle Gallery 2s 2d. Upper Gallery 1s 1d. The Burletta will begin precisely at Seven o'Clock. No person whatsoever will be admitted behind the Scenes. Gentlemen and Ladies are requested, by Mr. Minelli, director of the Burlettas, to leave their Subscription Tickets at the door of the theatre and they shall be sent to them in the morning'.[10]

These details illustrate the style of entertainment which took place on the evenings when the burlettas were performed. According to Hitchcock, *La Cascina* had been produced 'after much preparation' and 'pleased much'.[11] It was in this opera that O'Keeffe describes Anna Lucia de Amicis as being 'most captivating in the song where the ring is held over her head by the Squire',[12] Count Ripoli. The opera had nine performances during the season: on December 19, 21,* 26 and 29 and in 1762, on January 16 and 19, April 3 and May 3** and 15.

The second 'drama giocoso',[13] *La Finta Sposa,* was performed on January 5, 1762. The libretto announces 'Music is by Mr. John Baptist Zingoni except the songs thus marked (*)'.[14] Out of approximately twenty-eight musical items, only five are so marked, so at first it would appear that Zingoni was the principal composer of this *pasticcio.* But one must not accept this unreservedly. In 1755 an opera of the same name, composed by a now almost forgotten composer named Gaetano Latilla, was performed at the Teatro Formagliari, Bologna, with the de Amicis family in the cast. Zingoni, according to Minelli, was employed 'for correcting two Operas *La Cascina* & *Finta Sposa*'.[15] The word 'correcting' could, of course, be interpreted as composing, but none of the music in *La Cascina* is attributed to him, which suggests that his work on these operas consisted of orchestrating, arranging the music, or introducing a number of arias by different composers. A greater or lesser amount of Latilla's music could have been 'borrowed' by Zingoni. Latilla, who was then in Venice, was not in a position to know what was going on in Dublin.

The cast was:

Lisetta, Eugenia's Chamber-maid, who in disguise, takes up both the Name and Dress of Eugenia to deceive Piombone	Anna Lucia de Amicis
Eugenia, in love with Camillo	Anna Dunlap
Camillo, a Roman Nobleman to whom was promised to marry Eugenia† [sic]	Giovan-Battista Zingoni
Ridolfo, a friend of Camillo, who feigns to pass as a Master of Ceremonies	Antonio Minelli

*An extra performance may have taken place on December 22. See Appendix B.

**Performed 'after Cymbeline' with 'Several recitatives omitted, to contract this performance into a moderate length'.

†Printing errors or hasty translation makes amusing nonsense of some of the descriptions of the characters. These errors do not occur in the original Italian on the opposite page in the libretto.

SPRANGER BARRY.
MANAGER AND ACTOR
(1719–1777)

NICOLINA GIORDANI.
SOPRANO (c. 1740–p. 1775)
AS SPILETTA IN
Gli Amanti Gelosi.

ANN CATLEY. SOPR
(1745–1789) AS
EUPHROSYNE IN *Co*

FOR THE BENEFIT OF M˜ TENDUCCI

TICKET FOR A BEN
PERFORMANCE FOR
TENDUCCI.

Ottavia, Sister to Eugenia, in disguise, she acts as Eugenia's Chamber-maid	Maria Anna de Amicis
Piombone Serravalle, Heir of Baron Pascuccio, came to Rome to marry Eugenia	Domenico de Amicis.[16]

There were four performances on January 5, 9, 12 and 23. Immediately afterwards a dispute over their contract arose between Minelli and Domenico de Amicis.* Minelli, according to Hitchcock, then 'settled in Dublin, in the wine and spirit trade', where in 1794 he was 'still living on the Bachelor's-walk, a gentleman of worth and character'.[17]

Meanwhile de Amicis, who, since his family made up four-sevenths of the company, naturally controlled it, decided to continue the season under his own direction. In a letter to *Faulkner's Dublin Journal* in which he expressed 'the utmost Gratitude for the Favour and Encouragement' which he and his family had received in Dublin, he declared his intention of remaining there in preference to offers which he had received from London, and announced 'a new Comic Opera, called, *Gl'Intrighi per Amore,* ready to be performed'.[18] This was presented on January 29 and subsequently on February 3, 6, 10, 13 and 17 (the last performance by command of the Lord Lieutenant, the Earl of Halifax), March 24, April 14 and 28, and, in a shortened one-act version, on May 15.

The intriguing part of this burletta lies not only in its title but in its music as well, for unaccountably no composer's name is given in the libretto, although in all the other libretti a composer's name (correct or incorrect) is printed. Nor can a performance elsewhere be traced, although its success in Dublin suggests that it merited production in other theatres. Was it performed subsequently under a different title, or was it a wellknown burletta performed in Dublin under an assumed title?** The cast was:

---

*See Appendix B.

**An opera with the very similar title of *Gli intrighi amorosi* composed by Galuppi to a libretto by Petrosellini was produced at Venice in 1772 (*Grove*) and at Vienna in 1776 (Bauer. *Opern und Operetten in Wien*).

Timitilla, Pascasio's Ward	Anna Lucia de Amicis
Rosmira, Daughter to Pascasio	Anna Dunlap
Don Sabione, betrothed to Rosmira	Domenico de Amicis
Pascasio, Timitilla's Guardian	Giovan-Battista Zingoni
Giacintina, a Waiting Maid	Maria Anna de Amicis.[19]

From January onwards the burlettas were performed regularly twice weekly on Tuesdays and Saturdays, but on January 30 we read, 'In Order to prevent as much as possible, the Burlettas from interfering with the Engagements of the Ladies and Gentlemen at the Castle on Tuesday Nights, Mr. Mossop has changed the Burletta Night from Tuesday to Wednesday',[20] and so they continued on Wednesday and Saturday until the season ended in May.

The next burletta performed on February 20 should have been the most important of the season, for it was Baldassare Galuppi's* 'drama giocoso',[21] *Il Filosofo di Campagna*. It was played, however, with a secondary title of *Il Tutore burlato*,** so altered and simplified that it was almost another opera. One of the principal characters, Nardo, the rich middle-aged country philosopher, was deleted entirely. This was undoubtedly due to the forced defection of Antonio Minelli from the company, for Nardo would have been his role. When produced in London in January 1761, Burney wrote that it 'surpassed in musical merit all the comic operas that were performed in England, till the Buona Figliuola'.[22] In Dublin it had seven performances, on February 20 and 23, March 3, 10 and 13, April 21 and May 12. After this last performance, 'it was announced, Signiora de Amicis, Signior Zingoni and Signior de Amicis will sing the favourite Song God Save the King.'[23] The cast was:

Eugenia, Daughter of Don Tritemio	Anna Dunlap

*Sometimes named 'il Buranello', having been born on the island of Burano near Venice. He would seem to have been the only internationally famous man ever to have been born there for both the island's principal square and street are named after him. The precise place of his birth on the island is no longer known, but is commemorated by a plaque on a house-front in the square.

**Loewenberg is not quite correct in stating 'this production is always quoted as *The Guardian tricked* for the simple reason that the British Museum copy of the libretto lacks the first, Italian title page'. There are two copies of the libretto at the British Museum, one of which is complete.

Lesbina, Tritemio's Ward	Anna Lucia de Amicis
Don Tritemio, Eugenia's Father, and Lesbina's Guardian	Domenico de Amicis
Rinaldo, in love with Lesbina	Giovan-Battista Zingoni
Lisetta, Waiting Maid to Lesbina	Maria Anna de Amicis
Capocchio, a Publick Notary	Gaetano de Amicis.[24]

On February 27, Anna Lucia de Amicis took a benefit in another *pasticcio* by Zingoni called *La Creanza*.* This was by command of the Lord Lieutenant, to whom Signorina de Amicis dedicated a grandiloquent preface in the libretto of the opera. Zingoni assumed responsibility for seventeen out of the twenty-five musical numbers in this 'drama per musica'.[25] One to which he did not lay claim is the well known *Tre giorni son che Nina,* a popular air attributed both to Ciampi and Pergolesi, which seems to have been interpolated into several operas at this period. Sung variously by either hero or heroine, in *La Creanza* it was sung by the heroine, Fiammetta.

The cast was as follows:

Sinfronio, in love with Fiammetta	Domenico de Amicis
Fiammetta	Anna Lucia de Amicis
Lisaura, the Marchioness of Poggio	Anna Dunlap
Lindoro, the Captain	Giovan-Battista Zingoni
Serpina, a Waiting-Maid	Maria Anna de Amicis.[26]

It cannot have been very successful, for there were only three performances during the season, on February 27, March 6 and April 17.

An 'Opera comica'[27] by the Neapolitan composer Domenico Fischietti, *Il Mercato di Malmantile,* was performed on March 17

---

*In a card-index at the British Museum compiled by the late Dr. Alfred Loewenberg, for what he presumably intended to be a catalogue of libretti, the following reference to this production of *La Creanza* occurs: 'an opera of this title presumably the same text was performed at Brussels in 1759 (copy of the libretto Cat. Bibl. Soleinne No. ..) with music by Lorenzo da Bologna; for his setting the six airs referred to in the title may have been retained. (see Liebrecht pp. 193–194) and also at Antwerp December 8, 1759. (Grégoire Panthéon Vol. VI)'

Lorenzo da Bologna may have been Luigi da Bologna, a composer mentioned in Eitner's *Quellen-Lexikon der Musiker und Musikgelehrten.* He is described as the composer of three symphonies and of an opera, *L'Isola di Calipso,* performed at Esterhazy under Haydn's direction in 1786. Bauer *(Opern und Operetten in Wien)* records the production of his opera *Calipso abbandonata* at Vienna in 1783.

and had further performances on March 20, 27, and 31 and May 19. Burney, speaking of its London production* which included a number of airs by Galuppi, having praised Galuppi's music, pays Fischietti an equivocal compliment by stating that his 'songs have likewise considerable merit of the same kind'.[28] It was a popular opera and after its original production in Venice was performed at Bologna, Florence and Milan during the same year. The Dublin cast was:

Lampridio, the Governor of Malmantile	Domenico de Amicis
Brigida, Daughter of Lampridio	Maria Anna de Amicis
Rubicone, a Mountebank	Gaetano de Amicis
Berto, a Country Man, Syndic of the Village	Giovan-Battista Zingoni
The Marchioness, a Widow	Anna Dunlap
Lena, a Country-Girl	Anna Lucia de Amicis.[29]

The dancers were Aldridge and Lucchi.

Next, Giovanni Battista Pergolesi's most famous and still performed 'opera giocosa'[30] *La Serva Padrona,* was presented in a double bill with *Gl'Intrighi per Amore* on March 24, and with *La Creanza* on April 17. The cast was:

Uberto, an old Gentleman, doatingly fond of his Servant Maid Serpina	Domenico de Amicis
Serpina, a Servant Maid to Uberto, an artful saucy girl	Anna Lucia de Amicis.[31]

The name of the actor who mimed Vespone is not given but the dancers were again Aldridge and Lucchi. The libretto attributes the text, correctly, to Gennaro Antonio Federico.

A 'drama in musica',[32] *Li Due Rivali,* was performed on May 1, 5 and 8. The libretto gives the composer's name as Nicolo Tommelli,

---

*A note on the English title-page of the Dublin libretto at the British Museum, seemingly in contemporary handwriting, states: 'The Music by Sigr. Fischetti [sic] but the same piece was produced in London Novbr. 7, 1761, the music by Galuppi and Fischetti'. Burney confirms both the November 7 date and the collaboration of Fischietti and Galuppi on this occasion. Loewenberg, however, gives a somewhat different version, recording the first London production on November 10, 1761, and announcing the introduction of extra airs by Galuppi at a revival on April 14, 1762.

presumably a misprint for Niccolò Jommelli. This, however, does not help to identify the opera unless it should have been Jommelli's *intermezzo*, *I Rivali Delusi*. The cast was:

Bella Rosa	Anna Lucia de Amicis
Ginevra, in love with Saraca	Anna Dunlap
Giacinto, in love with Bella Rosa	Domenico de Amicis
Saraca, in love with Bella Rosa	Giovan-Battista Zingoni
Lisetta, waiting-maid to Bella Rosa	Maria Anna de Amicis
Leandro, Knight of the Sun	Gaetano de Amicis.[33]

The 'cuts' pencilled into the libretto of the opera at the British Museum exclude entirely this last exotic character from the production.

Finally the de Amicis company on May 22 and 26 gave performances of what they described as a 'new Burletta, called La Partenza: or, The Farewell. Composed of all the favourite Airs contained in the foregoing Burlettas, being the last Burletta that will be performed'.[34] Obviously, these were nothing more than two concerts in costume of the most popular musical numbers of the season. With the intention presumably of promoting an Irish-British-Italian *entente cordiale*, the last performance ended 'with the favourite Song of God save great George our King'.[35]

One may now enquire what, dramatically and musically, these burlettas were like. It was not just coincidence that the text of at least three out of the eight produced, *La Cascina, Il Filosofo di Campagna* and *Il Mercato di Malmantile*, were by the renowned Venetian playwright Carlo Goldoni, for his output of comic plays and comic opera libretti almost exceeded his fame. During the eighteenth century, Venice was the most pleasure-loving and liberal of cities. Unlike other Italian states, the Venetian state was ruled not by a Grand Duke but by an oligarchy of merchant princes. Among Italian cities it was the first to have an opera house open to the public – in 1637. Goldoni, who was the founder of modern Italian comedy, began writing about 1730. Today we can see his Venice depicted in the paintings of Canaletto, Tiepolo and Pietro Longhi, and while there were other librettists and other cities, he and Venice exemplify the dramatic form of these simple operas. They were stylised comedies of individuals set mainly against the background of Venetian social life. No more appropriate setting could have existed for them and, with occasion and environment coinciding, Italian *opera buffa* composers happily found their ideal librettist just as Sullivan was later to discover Gilbert.

Descriptive details of the characters have been given with the cast lists of the burlettas to illustrate their stylised form: elderly bachelors and elderly guardians with wards, love-lorn mistresses and pert servant maids, elegant counts and intrepid captains. Today we know them all as Don Pasquale and Doctor Bartolo, Rosina and Norina, Susanna and Despina, Ernesto and Count Almaviva.*

The opportunity has occurred within recent years to hear two of these burlettas, *La Serva Padrona* and *Il Filosofo di Campagna,* on the stage. *La Serva Padrona* has, of course, always remained in the repertory and retains its celebrity by having contributed to the famous *Guerre des Bouffons* in Paris in 1752. Originally performed in two parts as *intermezzi* between the acts of a forgotten *opera seria –* *Il Prigioniero Superbo –* by Pergolesi, today, as has frequently been asserted, it is often produced for no better reason than that it requires only a *basso buffo,* a soprano, a mute actor, a string quartet and a harpsichord. The plot is trifling. Uberto, an old bachelor, berates his servant-maid, Serpina, for not bringing his chocolate. But Serpina has ideas of her own. She disguises Vespone, Uberto's valet, as a Bulgarian officer and introduces him to Uberto as her *fiancé,* whereupon the gullible old man falls for the ruse and offers to marry her himself.

The plot of *Il Filosofo di Campagna,* while just as predictable, is at least more complex. Don Tritemio wishes his daughter Eugenia to marry Nardo, a rich middle-aged country philosopher, but Eugenia loves Rinaldo. Lesbina (again the servant-maid) passes herself off as Eugenia to Nardo so captivatingly that, when the truth becomes known, he is content to marry her instead.

*Although, as the eighteenth century progressed, Venice was to lose its operatic supremacy to Naples, yet as late as 1810 its tradition of *opera buffa* was being continued by Rossini with *La Cambiale di Matrimonio,* his first opera, to be followed by four others during the next three years, ending with *L'Italiana in Algeri.*

Musically these naive entertainments have a limited interest for a modern audience. Although overloaded with *recitativo secco,* they still retain their period charm when performed with style and artistry. Performed badly, as they undoubtedly were in Dublin, the music becomes boring. Yet one must consider them in the musical context of their own time and hear them through the ears of a Dublin audience of two hundred years ago. There is little point in seeking pre-echoes of the youthful Mozart, although they occur fitfully in Galuppi's music. Mozart was as far removed from the scene then as a musical message from Mars is today. The audiences that attended Smock Alley were not assemblies of musical connoisseurs. They were ordinary theatre-goers in search of entertainment and, after a lifetime of conventional play-going, here was entertainment as novel and diverting as the spectacle of 'the wonderful Scene of Harlequin's Escape into a Quart Bottle'.[36] Without doubt they were entertained, for the burletta season lasted just over five months, during which time forty-three performances are recorded as having been given.

Since a rival theatre had been built on the site of the Crow Street Music Hall and opened in October 1758 under the management of the Irish actor Spranger Barry in association with the comedian Henry Woodward, such success was bound to create jealousy. As early as January 19, 1762, *Faulkner's Dublin Journal* had rebuked Woodward, for derisively interpolating the word 'burletta' into his role in the play of *Leth, or Aesop in the Shades.*

A riposte to the situation was delivered by Kane O'Hara, a talented author-musician and Irishman-about-town, who wrote 'a new English Burletta, called, Midas',[37] which was produced at Crow Street Theatre on January 22, 1762. John O'Keeffe relates that he 'was at O'Hara's house in King-street, Stephen's-green, one morning, at a meeting with Lord Mornington, Mr. Brownlow, M.P. a musical amateur and fine player on the harpsichord, when they were settling the music for Midas'.[38] He gives the cast as Sileno by Corry, 'Apollo, Vernon; Midas, Robert Mahon; Dametus, Oliver; Pan, Morris; Daphne, Miss Elliot; Nysa, Miss Polly Young . . and Mysis, Miss Macneil (afterwards Mrs. Hawtrey)'.[39] *Faulkner's Dublin Journal* of

January 13/16 and *The Dublin Courier* of January 15/18 announce,
'The principal characters by Mr. Vernon, Mr. Corry, Mr. Mahon,
Mr. Oliver, Mr. Adcock, Mr. Messink, Mr. Ellard, Mrs. Bridges,
Mrs. Glover, Mrs. Knipe, Miss Young and Miss Elliot. With new
Dances and Decorations'.

Either the advertisements have erred or O'Keeffe's memory was
at fault concerning Miss Macneil. Of the principals mentioned
who seem certain to have taken part, Joseph Vernon was the most
widely known. He began his career as a boy soprano at Drury
Lane, but by 1754 he was singing as a tenor. From 1765 onwards
he became an established favourite. This was due to the excellence
of his style of singing rather than to the quality of his voice, which
was poor. O'Keeffe recalls meeting him at Vauxhall, where he
sang for almost twenty years, and relates that had he 'not been
a capital singer, he would have been thought a first-rate actor'.[40]
All this is confirmed in an article concerning him written about 1770.
'It is so seldom found that it is now scarcely expected', we read, 'to
meet a good actor united to a good singer: – Vernon stands an
exception to this rule; for though now he only lives in point of voice,
upon the echo of his former reputation, he *was* excellent in both, and
did not too apparent a coxcombry eternally settle itself on his features,
there are many parts in comedy that would receive force from his
abilities.'[41] As a singing actor, he specialised in roles such as the Clown
in *Twelfth Night* and Autolycus in *A Winter's Tale*.

The most important actor in the cast was John Morris, a favourite
with Dublin audiences for many years. His roles included Ben in
Congreve's *Love for Love,* Gubbins in *The Dragon of Wantley* and
Falstaff both in *King Henry IV Part I* and *The Merry Wives of
Windsor*. Robert Corry who, again according to O'Keeffe, took over
the role of Sileno from Spranger Barry when Barry found that he
could not sing it, was a popular Dublin theatre singer. He first
appeared at Smock Alley during the 1756/57 season and there his roles
included Amiens 'with Songs in Character'[42] in *As You Like it,* a
singing witch in *Macbeth* and Sir John Loverule in *The Devil to Pay*.
Of the remaining two men, Robert Mahon was a character actor

and singer who had made his first appearance at Smock Alley in 1750 as a dancer. He was a member of the Covent Garden company in 1769. Lewis Oliver joined Smock Alley in 1757. He played such roles as Corin in *As You like it,* Second Bacchanal in *Comus,* and Roderigo in *Othello.* Ann Elliot, who played Daphne, was coached by Arthur Murphy, the Irish dramatist, for various parts in his plays. Her speaking voice is said to have been clear and sweet and she was 'successful in pert and sprightly comic roles'.[43] Polly Young has already been discussed.

Although presented as an English burletta, *Midas* is a burlesque, not of *opera buffa,* but of *opera seria,* for its characters are mythological gods and mortals. In an introduction to the libretto published in London in 1764, the editor, referring to 'the stile which prevails in the following scenes', explains that 'They are written in the true spirit of the mock-heroic'. The music consisted of popular melodies. Some were taken from Italian operas. Some were folk-tunes of various countries such as the French *A la Santé du Père d'Oleron* and the Irish *Sheelagh na Guiragh.* Sometimes a song is described as set 'To its own Tune', presumably the introduction into the burletta of a popular song of the period. W. J. Lawrence has recorded that 'in its frequent resort to concerted music [it] bridged the gap between ballad opera and comic opera'.[44] The gap between ballad opera and *opera buffa* was similarly bridged by having the dialogue 'given in Recitative accompanied by Music'.[45] The work had frequent revivals until well into the nineteenth century.

The following notice which appeared in *Faulkner's Dublin Journal* of February 9/13, 1762 is recorded as a vignette to the end of this chapter. 'For the Benefit of Miss Schmeling from Hesse-Cassel in Germany, at the Great Musick-Hall in Fishamble-street. – on Monday the 15th of February 1762, will be performed a grand Concert of Vocal and Instrumental Music, in which Miss Schmeling will sing some select Italian and English Songs, and perform on the Violin and Guitar. After the Concert a Ball. To begin exactly at Seven o'Clock. Price 5s 5d. Tickets to be had at her Lodgings at the Knave of Clubs in Eustace-street. N.B. She purposes teaching Ladies to play on the

Guitar.'[46] Miss Schmeling was then a young lady not quite thirteen years old. Dublin was to hear her again thirty years later when she returned in much more widely advertised circumstances under her famous married name of Madame Mara.

9

MORE POOR RELATIONS

ALTHOUGH THEY WERE never to know the phrase, Henry Mossop at Smock Alley and Spranger Barry at Crow Street were now to learn that there's no business like show business, for rivalry between their theatres would ultimately ruin both of them.

On February 2, 1763, Barry presented a revival of Purcell's *King Arthur* with the announcement that 'he flatters himself that the particular Excellence of the Paintings, the Magnificence and Variety of the Scenery, Machinery and other Decorations will merit the Approbation of the Public'.[1] Among the large cast Philadel '(with the songs)'[2] was performed by Mrs. Mahon. Mrs. Dancer, who later became Spranger Barry's wife, acted Emmeline. Barry played King Arthur and 'the vocal parts' were taken by Wilder, Mahon, Eals, Hoffman, Sadler, Corry, Hamilton, Mrs. Glover, Miss McNeil and Signora and Master Passerini. Dances were performed 'by Mr. Slingsby &c.'[3] The result seems to have been highly successful and we learn that 'The sudden Changes of the beautiful Variety of Scenery seemed to surprise and alarm the Audience, as the Effect of real Magic (on which the Fable turns) and not as the Invention of theatrical Art'.[4]

Performances followed on Monday evenings for six succeeding weeks, and there were a further seven performances between the end of March and early June. The production was again revived, with some slight changes in the cast, on the following November 25, continuing with occasional performances until January, 1764.

Virtually all the artists taking part were members of the Crow Street Theatre's stock company. Simon Slingsby, the dancer, was a pupil of Robert Aldridge – mentioned in the previous chapter. By 1766 his career had taken him to Paris. Apparently he had broken an agreement

with the Haymarket Theatre in London, for David Garrick in a letter
to the elder George Colman, who was then living in Paris, requests, 'If
you were well enough to see the Dancer, Slingsby, hint to him from
yourself that he did wrong to send his brother to make an engagement
with us, and then fly off'.[5] As late as 1781 he was being hailed in
London, where he had returned as first dancer to Drury Lane
Theatre as 'the nimble footed son of Hibernia'.[6]

Describing the Passerini family, who had arrived in Dublin a short
time previously, John O'Keeffe speaks of Passerini (a violinist), his
wife (a soprano) and 'two nephews, little brown Italian boys, Tenino
and Ceccino whom he brought up with musical rigour',[7] but all
contemporary accounts mention only *one* Master Passerini, and it
seems probable that he was a son rather than a nephew. Passerini,
who is described wearing 'a black velvet coat, tissue waistcoat, and
large flowing powdered wig',[8] was one of Michael Kelly's first singing
teachers, and in his *Reminiscences* Kelly relates how during his
travels in Italy he met Passerini's father in Bologna.

We first learn of Giuseppe and Christina Passerini in a letter
written by Handel to Telemann in December 1750. In it Handel
records: 'I was on the point of leaving the Hague for London when
your most agreeable letter was delivered to me by Mr. Passerini. I had
just enough time to be able to hear his wife sing. Your patronage and
approval were enough not only to excite my curiosity but also to
serve her as a sufficient recommendation; however I was soon
convinced myself of her rare quality. They are leaving for Scotland to
fulfil concert engagements there for a season of six months. There she
will be able to perfect herself in the English language; after that (as
they intend to remain some time in London) I shall not fail to be of
service to them in all ways that may depend on me.'[9] Christina's
name is among the list of singers appearing in London between 1753
and 1760 where she performed in various theatres ranging from the
King's and Drury Lane down to minor playhouses and common
booths. During the same period she and her husband are credited
with popularising Handel's oratorios in the English provinces.

Saunders' News-letter of February 14, 1809, announces that a

'Mr. Passerini, a gentleman well-known in the musical world on returning from Booterstown-avenue on Wednesday night last [February 8] missed his way and was unfortunately drowned'.[10]* This was not Giuseppe (as has been assumed), for his Christian name is recorded as Francis[11] and, as will be confirmed later, his correct identification is Master Passerini.

On April 22, 1763, 'Signiora Passerini and others' performed 'The Musical Pastoral Entertainment of Nysa and Thyrsis'[12] at Crow Street Theatre. The title suggests some resemblance to Kane O'Hara's successful *Midas* of the previous year.

The English comic opera *Love in a Village,* libretto by Isaac Bickerstaffe, was performed at Crow Street on July 8, 1763. Almost half of the music had been composed by Thomas Augustine Arne; the remainder was a *pasticcio* by sixteen different composers as diverse as Baildon, Handel, Carey and Galuppi. Two Irish ballad tunes, 'St. Patrick's Day' and 'Larry Grogan' were also introduced and this has led to the inclusion in at least one libretto[13] of Larry Grogan's name among the list of composers. So a famous gentleman Irish piper from the County Wexford, after whom the tune is named, is commemorated in the annals of English opera. *Love in a Village* has been described as a 'Production of Bickstaff's juvenile Fancy. It was written when he was only Eighteen, at a beautiful situation in the County of Carlow in Ireland, on the Banks of the River Slaney, and afterwards amended with some new Situations, particularly a Statute Fair, the Dance and some other Appendages, after he came to London.'[14] It was in fact a revision of a much earlier ballad opera by Charles Johnson called *The Village Opera.*

*Whatever their connection with the district, the Passerini family's association with Booterstown was persistently unfortunate. The following report appears in *Saunders' News-letter* on Monday, September 30, 1776.

'As Mr. and Mrs. Passerini were returning from Booterstown, about 7 o'c on Friday evening last, in their Chair, they were attacked by two Footpads (young men) at Bagatroth Castle, between Ball's Bridge and the New Road; one of them seized the Horse, while the other presented a Pistol in the chair, and robbed Mr. Passerini of his Cash and a Pinchbeck Skeleton Watch, engraved with a Rose in the Middle, made by John Faucett, Dublin. It is requested if the said Watch is offered for Sale or Pawn it may be stopped and Notice given to Mr. Faucett, Watchmaker, Dame-street, who will give 1 guinea reward and no questions asked – or three guineas for the thief and watch.'

Those who took part in the first Dublin performance were:

Justice Woodcock	Shuter
Eustace	Dyer
Hawthorn	Wilder
Young Meadows	Mahon
Sir William Meadows	Morris
Hodge	Glover
Lucinda	Mrs. Mahon
Mrs. Woodcock	Miss Mason
Margery	Miss Willis
Cook	Messink
Footman	Oliver
Carter	Ellard
Laundry-maid	Mrs. Packenham
Lads	Lee, Stewart, Osmond, Stagaldoir
Lasses	Mrs. Ellard and Mrs. Stagaldoir
Rosetta	Mrs. Lessingham.[15]

Slingsby and Miss Dawson obliged with a country-dance and a double hornpipe in the first act.

Mrs. Jane Lessingham, *née* Hemet, formerly Mrs. Stott 'from the Theatre-Royal in Covent Garden',[16] was primarily an actress, and not a particularly brilliant one at that, hence it is not easy to understand the reason for her engagement as Rosetta, a role taken in the original production of the opera by Charlotte Brent. George Anne Bellamy in her *Memoirs* 'allows' that Mrs. Lessingham's beauty and figure were 'greatly in her favour',[17] a generous compliment from a rival actress which may also explain this apparent mis-casting.

The announcement that 'Miss Davies from London will perform Airs with Variations on the Armonica a compleat Instrument of Musical Glasses with Singing',[18] at Crow Street Theatre on November 7, 1763, presents a problem similar to the one which arose over Nicolini – that of proving that Miss Davies was in fact not there.

The ambiguity arises from an entry in *Grove's Dictionary* which records that Cecilia Davies 'appeared at the Theatre Royal, Dublin in

Nov. 1763 and in 1764 (*Dublin Journal*, No. 3811).[19] What *Faulkner's Dublin Journal*, No. 3811 (November 1/5 1763) does state is, 'We hear that the celebrated Miss Davies who perform'd last Winter in London with universal Applause on the Armonica, is engaged for a few nights at the Theatre Royal and will make her first Appearance on Monday next'.[20] Neither in this nor in subsequent reports is Miss Davies' Christian name given, an omission which causes the confusion, since Cecilia had a younger sister named Marianne, also a singer but, again to quote *Grove*, a singer who 'About 1762 . . achieved much more repute for her skill on the armonica'.[21]

The question arises, consequently, was it Cecilia or Marianne who appeared in Dublin? Cecilia was by far the more important artist, and had a highly successful career on the Continent where she was known as 'L'Inglesina'. Unfortunately all the evidence indicates that it was the less important Marianne who sang in Dublin. This can be assumed with some certainty from announcements of the performances which state that 'Miss Davies' played both the German flute and the harmonica; of the two sisters Marianne alone played these instruments. The matter is further confirmed by correspondence in connection with some oratorio performances which Passerini was presenting and in which Miss Davies sang. A critical letter addressed to Passerini by 'an English Gentleman whom Affairs of Consequence brought over'[22] states that 'Miss Davis's [sic] excellence is well known to lye in the instrumental way',[23] which manifestly describes Marianne, and not Cecilia, who was a singer only.

A performance on December 19, again at Crow Street, of 'A Mock Italian Burletta La Pastorella, &c in the manner of Sig. D'Amicis, Zingoni &c. Dancing by Signor Giorgi and Signiora Giorgi'[24] is obviously an attempt to capitalise on the success of the Italian burlettas at Smock Alley Theatre, two years previously. Signor Giorgi is first discovered as one of eleven dancers in David Garrick's company at Drury Lane during the 1757/58 season. Here, partnered by Signora Lucchi (of the 1761 Smock Alley burletta company), he made his first appearance after a performance of Macbeth on October 4, 1757, in a dance called 'The Italian Peasant'. Signora

Giorgi appeared at Drury Lane for the first time on December 31, 1759, and both their names are to be found among Garrick's company until 1774. Both were well-known dancers in their time and Giorgi was appointed *maître de ballet* at the 'little' theatre in the Haymarket, London, when the elder George Colman became lessee in 1777. They had been engaged for Dublin in the autumn of 1763, for we read that 'Yesterday [September 28] Mr. Barry Patentee of the Theatre Royal at Dublin, set out for Ireland. He has engaged the dancers, Vincent [who will be noticed later] Georgi [sic] and his wife, with whom Mossop had been for a considerable time in treaty, but had not absolutely engaged them'.[25] Hostilities between the rival managers were beginning.

Barry continued to press his advantage when in April 1764 he begged 'leave to acquaint the Publick that ever studious of its Entertainment, he [had] at great Expense, engaged a Company of Italian Burletta Performers lately landed in this Kingdom, to exhibit their Talents on his Stage during the Remainder of this Season'.[26]

The first burletta, which was performed on April 28 'by Command of his Excellency the Lord Lieutenant and the Countess of Northumberland'[27] was Pergolesi's *La Serva Padrona*. The cast was 'Hubert (an Old Man) – Signior Mauro Guirini, Serpina (his Governante) – Signiora Rosa Guirini'.[28] Three artists, or possibly four in all, made up the entire burletta company.

The Guirinis – a more correct spelling of the name is Guerini, although Gurrini is also found – were a family of 'strollers' who in October and November 1763 were performing 'at the Theatre in the Mint-Yard'[29] at York the same programme of burlettas that they were to perform in Dublin. A Monsieur Guerin had made his first appearance on the English stage at Covent Garden on November 1, 1755, and as dancers, the Guerini's names appear among Garrick's company at Drury Lane during the 1762/63 season. As eighteenth-century strolling players they had of course not only to act and dance, but also sing, though such versatility cannot have helped the vocal standard of their burletta performances.

The second burletta, presented on May 3, was 'La Zingara, or The

Fortune Teller'[30] by Rinaldo di Capua. Dr. Burney once met Rinaldo di Capua who, he relates, 'was then living or rather starving in 1770 at Rome, the chief scene of his former glory!'[31] 'Diogenes the Cynic', he declares, 'was never more meanly clad through choice, than Rinaldo through necessity: a patched coat, and stockings that wanted to be patched or darned!'[32] Much of Rinaldo's music consisted of *opera buffa* and *intermezzi,* like *La Zingara,* which had had its first known performance at Paris in 1753, although it was probably composed as early as 1739. While maintaining the convention of clever servant girl marrying an old dotard, *La Zingara* introduced the novel role of a man disguised as a bear to augment the stock characters of burletta. This undoubtedly ensured its success in Dublin as it had in Paris where it was paid the ultimate compliment of a parody by C. S. Favart in his famous *La Bohémienne.*

The cast at Dublin was Nisa, a pretty gipsy girl, Rosa Guerini; Calcante, an infatuated old miser, Mauro Guerini; and Tagliaborse, Nisa's brother (who disguises himself both as bear and magician in order to defraud the old man and trick him into marriage), Antonio Minelli. Minelli's name among the company throws doubt on Hitchcock's statement that having left the Smock Alley burletta company in 1762 he had 'settled in Dublin in the wine and spirit trade'; certainly not as early as 1764, for instead of closing his shop and stepping across Essex Bridge to return to his old *métier* as Hitchcock would have us believe, the address of his lodgings is given as 'at Mr. Roe's in Drogheda-street near Abbey-street'.[33]

The first performance of *La Zingara* was received 'with uncommon Applause, all the Performers exerted themselves in a masterly Manner . . and gave infinite Satisfaction'.[34] There were two further performances, the second on May 5, the third, a double-bill with a performance of *La Serva Padrona,* on June 14. The latter was a benefit performance for the Guerinis. Their newspaper appeal for support explains that 'they being intire strangers in this City, take this Method of begging the Favour, Protection and Assistance of the Nobility and Gentry, to raise a little Money, to enable them to undertake their Voyage and Journey; the Favour and Interest upon this

H

Occasion shall always be acknowledged with the most profound Gratitude . . Tickets [were] to be had of Signor Gurini at Mr. Hogan's Shoe Warehouse on Essex Bridge'.[35]

Pergolesi's 'Tracollo, or The Amorous Robber'[36] was given one performance on May 12. Like *La Serva Padrona,* this burletta had originally formed two *intermezzi* – performed between the acts of his *opera seria Adriano in Siria.* It received various titles over the years, the most common being *Livietta e Tracollo* or *La Contadina astuta.* There were different versions both of libretto and score. The Dublin production from its secondary title *The Amorous Robber* would appear to coincide with a version performed at Venice in 1750 under the title of *Il ladro convertito per amore.* Two roles only were announced in Dublin advertisements – Tracollo, Mauro Guerini, and Livietta, Rosa Guerini. The cast is completed by a mute character, Fulvia, which stresses the similarity of the work with *La Serva Padrona.* During the first act of the burletta Mr. Slingsby danced 'The Medley, Loughlin Prossough' and, during act two, 'a new Pantomimical Dance, call'd The Lover Restor'd'.[37]

On May 19 'Il Maestro di Musica or The Music Master'[38] was performed. No composer's name is ascribed, although without doubt it was the wellknown burletta attributed for many years to Pergolesi which modern scholarship has identified as being based on Pietro Auletta's opera, *Orazio.*[39] First presented under the title of *Il Maestro di Musica* at Paris in 1752, the score was published there during the following year under Pergolesi's name. This version was in fact a *pasticcio* with music by Pergolesi, G. M. Capelli, Auletta, Latilla and possibly Galuppi. No cast is given for the Dublin performance, but it was announced that 'Signor Gurrini will introduce an Italian song set to English Music'.[40] A comic ballet at the end of the first act was also announced, 'called The Lover Restor'd or The Old Man Metamorphos'd. The principal Characters by Mr. Vincent, Signiora Lucchi'.[41] Lucchi had evidently returned to Dublin for another season and Vincent, as earlier noted, had been engaged by Barry with the Giorgis. He had first appeared at Drury Lane on September 25, 1761, and from his name, and the information that this was his 'first appearance on the English stage',[42] was probably French.

A performance of what was described only as 'a new Italian Burletta',[43] sharing the bill with the popular tragedy of *The Fair Penitent,* was announced for May 30, 'For the benefit of Signior and Signiora Minelli'.[44] This is the only occasion on which Signora Minelli's name appears during the engagement. It is possible that she had been singing minor roles, or was a dancer.

The last 'new' burletta to be performed during the season took place on June 2 and was advertised as *Li Are Cicisbei Rivali.* The second word is undoubtedly misspelled and since no composer's name is given one can only guess the correct title. It is just possible that it was the same as 'a new Burletta in three Acts call'd The Gamester',[45]* performed by the Guerinis at York the previous year, where all the burlettas were advertised with English titles only. A more precise identification may be discerned by altering the first letter of the word *Are* (almost certainly a printer's error), to *T*. We then have the title *Li Tre Cicisbei Rivali* which could correspond with *Li Tre Cicisbei Ridicoli*, a burletta by the Milanese composer Natale Resta, first performed at Venice in 1748. It was introduced into London in March 1748/49 with incidental airs added by Vincenzo Ciampi, the conductor of the Italian company performing it. The cast of the Dublin performance was given without details as: 'The principal characters by Signor Mauro Gurrini, Signor Minelli and Signora Rosa Gurrini etc.'[46]

It is obvious that this was a much shorter and far less important burletta season than had taken place at Smock Alley Theatre during 1761/62. In all only nine performances of five or possibly six burlettas were given at irregular weekly intervals, usually on Saturday evenings. The company too seems to have been lamentably small. Three singers only are announced, although Minelli's wife may also have taken part,

---

Prima facie The Gamester is the celebrated *intermezzo Il Giocatore.* It must be remembered, however, that during the eighteenth century radical changes were made not only to the text and music of Italian burlettas but to their titles as well. Loewenberg records that *Il Giocatore* was performed in Edinburgh on June 27, 1763. This was probably by the Guerini troupe. Since *Il Giocatore* was in their repertory it may instead have been the unnamed Italian burletta performed by them on May, 30.

so that the standard of performance must have been rudimentary. Nevertheless, the following newspaper correspondence which appeared in May suggests that the season had been successful. It also emphasises the jealousy existing between Barry and Mossop.

We are informed that 'Mr. Barry having seen with great surprise a paragraph in one of the English News-papers importing that he had disposed of the Theatre-Royal in Crow-street, with all his interest therein to Mr. Mossop, for one thousand pounds, per Annum, and that Mr. Mossop intended to shut up his Theatre in Smock-alley and to perform in the said Theatre-Royal during the next and the following Winters etc. Circumstances manifestly intended, and artfully calculated to hurt Mr. Barry's Credit, and to withdraw from him, the Patronage of his Friends and the Public; thinks himself indispensably obliged, thus publickly to assure them in the most solemn manner that this injurious Report has been propagated maliciously without the least Foundation; he, not only never having disposed of his said Interest to Mr. Mossop, on those or any other Terms. On the contrary, he has sent a Person to England to endeavour to engage there, at the greatest Salaries, the best Theatrical Performers of every kind, and purposes, if he can hope for any reasonable public Encouragement to establish a compleat Burletta in the Theatre-Royal, to be performed by the most skilful Singers, whom he will send for on Purpose, this Summer from Italy'.[47]

Three weeks later this announcement was followed by a confident manifesto, captioned with the resounding title of: 'Proposals for a Subscription towards establishing a compleat Burletta in this Kingdom, for the ensuing Winter, at the Theatre Royal in Crow-street, humbly offered to the Consideration of the Nobility and Gentry, by the Manager of the said Theatre'.[48] The proposals, which were eminently practical, were as follows:

'1. Every Person subscribing five Guineas shall, before the opening of the Burletta, receive 24 transferrable Tickets; these Tickets to be made use of on all Theatrical Performances as well Burlettas as others, during the Winter, as the Subscribers may chuse, Benefit Nights excepted.

2. Every Person subscribing two Guineas and a half, shall receive 12 Tickets as above; and

3. Every Person subscribing two Guineas shall receive nine Tickets.

4. As soon as the Subscription shall amount to 600 Guineas the Manager will dispatch an experienced Undertaker to Italy, to engage at any Price the most capital Performers, and to collect the greatest Variety of new and approved Burlesque Pieces; These Performers, with all their Requisites, to be landed in Ireland before the beginning of next November.

5. The Manager will exhibit two Burlettas in each Week during the season, on such particular Nights, as shall be previously appointed by the Majority of the principal Subscribers.

6. The Company shall consist of six, and occasionally of seven Performers, according as the Number of Characters in the several Dramatic Pieces may require.

7. The Manager shall furnish their Performances with a compleat Band of the best Instrumental Musicians and Dancers, with new Habits and Decorations, and also with Scenery entirely new, to be painted by the eminent Mr. Carver.*

8. Lastly, the Subscribers are requested to advance the Money at the Time of subscribing, in order that (being immediately lodged in Mr. Latouche's Bank) its Credit may the sooner be transmitted to Italy, as a Security to the Performers, for the punctual Execution of the Contracts to be entered into with them, and in order that it may be refunded to the Subscribers, in case of any Failure of this proposed Scheme.'[49]

Regretfully it must be explained that, reassuring as the proposals were, the scheme failed. However, during the 'ensuing Winter' Henry Mossop mounted a counter-offensive of burlettas at Smock Alley Theatre and with considerably more fire power, for, added to the

---

*Carver was a Dublin-born scene painter who subsequently migrated to Covent Garden. O'Keeffe records that 'An old scene of his painting remained in the Dublin theatre (Crow Street), which the carpenters preserved as a relic; so that, while they could wield a hatchet or handsaw, no painter dared touch it with his brush'. (*Recollections of the Life of John O'Keeffe, Written by Himself*. London. 1826. Vol. II. pp. 38/39.)

Guerinis, he had been able to engage a far more distinguished burletta family. As a showman, Mossop knew when he had acquired star quality for his theatre, and his 'puff preliminary' announcing the event is suitably grandiloquent.

In it he 'begs leave to acquaint the Public that he has engaged, for their Entertainment this Season, a Set of Burletta Performers, consisting of the celebrated Signiora Spiletta, her Father, her Sister, and the rest of that Family, who appeared some Years ago at the Theatre in Covent Garden, and engaged the Attention of the Public for an entire Season, with universal Applause. He proposes to exhibit the Burlettas in most extensive Manner that these Entertainments will admit of, and has for that Purpose engaged some other Performers to join Signiora Spiletta's Family in order to make the Number entirely complete. The Burletta will consist of seven Performers, besides Dancers, which, with an additional Number of Instrumental Performers, who are now at Chester, on their way to Dublin, will make the entire Expence of this Entertainment amount to a very considerable Sum. Mr. Mossop therefore, most humbly hopes for the Favour and Patronage of the Public in general and of all Lovers of Music, in particular, in Support of this Undertaking, which he is the more particularly encouraged to hope for, as he flatters himself it has appeared evident, that he has, for a considerable Time past, been at very great Expence and Trouble, and used every Endeavour within his Power, in order to bring Musical Entertainments in this Kingdom to as much Perfection as possible. He returns the most sincere Thanks to those Ladies and Gentlemen who were pleased to offer Subscriptions for the Support of the Burlettas which he will beg leave to decline troubling them for, as he is well assured that the Entertainments, in Proportion to their Merit, will meet a suitable Encouragement from the candid Public. [A nice touch of upmanship this. Unlike poor old Barry, Mossop has no need of subscribers' money to finance his undertakings.] He begs leave further to inform them, that notwithstanding the extraordinary Expence attending the Burlettas, there shall be no additional Expence to the Public but the Prices shall remain the same as on the ordinary Nights'.[50]

A week later there was further stimulating news with the arrival 'from England of Signior Peretti a celebrated Italian Performer'.[51] There had also arrived 'from England a number of Instrumental Musicians who are engaged to perform this Season at the Theatre in Smock-alley'.[52] Dublin was indeed enjoying musical activity of unusual intensity.

'Signiora Spiletta' was a *nom de théâtre* acquired by the singer Nicolina Giordani because of her successful performance in this role in the burletta *Gli Amanti Gelosi* at Covent Garden. The Giordanis were a Neapolitan family. Today they are remembered – if at all – by one *canzonetta*, *Caro mio ben*, which, ironically, was not composed by a member of this family, but probably by another Neapolitan composer bearing the same surname, who may or may not have been a relative. They had appeared in London at Covent Garden as early as December 1753 and had continued to perform there during succeeding years. The family group engaged for Dublin consisted of the father, Giuseppe, a *buffo* singer, librettist, and the impresario of the company; Antonia, his wife; his sons, Tommaso, a composer, and Francesco, a dancer; and his daughters, Nicolina (La Spiletta) and Marina, both singers.* Tragedy then struck the family. *Faulkner's Dublin Journal* of October 30 records the death 'In Capel-street, Madame Giordani, Mother to the celebrated Signiora Spiletta'.[53]

Giuseppe, Marina and Francesco would seem to have been routine artists although John O'Keeffe describes Francesco as 'a first-rate dancer'.[54] Tommaso, born at Naples about 1733, was intermittently to spend many years as a theatre composer in Dublin and his name frequently appears in later operatic history there. Nicolina was the

---

*The genealogy of the Giordani family is complex. An earlier theory that a composer, Carmine Giordani (c. 1685/1758) was the father both of Tommaso, mentioned above, and a Giuseppe Giordani (c. 1753/1798) called Giordanello has now been justly discredited. Nevertheless the Giuseppe Giordani who visited Dublin could have been Carmine Giordani's son – he could have been born about 1705/1710 – and Giordanello could have been this Giuseppe Giordani's youngest son. *Grove's Dictionary* (Fifth Edition. Vol. III. p. 647) is perfectly correct in stating 'if Giuseppe was the son of Carmine, he cannot have been the brother of Tommaso and *vice versa*' but this does not rule out Tommaso and the younger Giuseppe being brothers. The lengthy period between Tommaso's birth (circa 1730) and that of the younger Giuseppe (circa 1753) is not more difficult to accept than that Carmine, born circa 1685, had a son, Giordanello, born sixty-eight years later.

outstanding member of the family and in Dublin she achieved a success comparable with her reception in London eleven years earlier. At that time Sir Horace Walpole wrote, 'there is started up a burletta at Covent Garden, that has half the vogue of the old Beggar's Opera: indeed there is a soubrette, called the Niccolina, who besides being pretty has more vivacity and variety of humour than ever existed in any creature'.[55] Arthur Murphy relates that Nicolina 'displayed such lively traces of Humour in her countenance, and such pleasing variety of action, and such variety of graceful deportment, that she is generally acknowledged to be in that Cast of playing, an excellent comic actress'.[56] She was still singing in London as late as 1775 but by that time her voice must have greatly deteriorated for we are informed of 'the jarring notes of the spleen-provoking Signora Spiletta'.[57]

The other singer who joined the company, the castrato, Nicolo Peretti, seems to have come to London early in 1762, for he sang the title role when Thomas Augustine Arne's opera *Artaxerxes* was first performed at Covent Garden, on February 2 of that year. On that occasion, it was reported, 'but Signior Peretti from being so little master of the English language was unfortunately almost unintelligible'.[58] During the following season he was a member of the Italian opera company at the King's Theatre. Subsequently he was to become a music teacher in Dublin, where his name is to be found as late as 1782. In that year, 'with the greatest Respect [he] begs leave to acquaint his Patrons, Protectors and Friends that his Benefit . . is at the request of several Ladies of Distinction postponed till Monday May the 20th, when there will be a Grand Ball at the Exhibition Room, William-street, conducted in the genteelest Manner by Mr. Hanlon, with Tea, Coffee, Negus &c.'[59] He gives his address as 'No. 40 Upper Jervais-street'.[60] He was one of Michael Kelly's teachers and Kelly relates that 'He had a fine contre altro [sic] voice and possessed the true portamento so little known in the present day'.[61]

A second dancer, Signora Marcutii, had also travelled to Dublin. This may have been Signora Felice Marcucci, who in August 1763 had been engaged at Venice as 'first comic dancer'[62] for the King's

Theatre in the Haymarket. Her contract there was for a period of seven months at a fee of 400 sequins, plus her expenses, 'and also those of another person with her to London free of all charges'.[63] Altogether, it was without doubt the finest Italian opera company yet assembled for a Dublin theatre.

Meanwhile Mossop was not without his problems. In mid-October 1764 he had 'purchased the two houses in the old Post-Office Yard in Fishamble-street . . in order to open a new Passage into the Theatre',[64] but then on October 20 it was announced: 'This day at twelve o'clock, Smock-Alley Theatre took fire while they were in rehearsal occasioned by a chimney of the King's Arms tavern taking fire, which communicated itself to the Play-house and greatly alarmed the town. They were obliged to pull down a great part of the side-wall of the play-house to prevent the fire spreading, which luckily had the desired effect.'[65] Repairs to the side-wall must have been effected without delay, for the first burletta of the season was announced for performance on November 23, 1764. With La Spiletta available, the choice of *Gli Amanti Gelosi* was inevitable.

Giuseppe Giordani was the librettist of this 'dramma comico per musica'. When first produced in London the music, according to Burney, was by Gioacchino Cocchi, composer to the King's Theatre, but for the Dublin performances music by Baldassare Galuppi was used, with the exception of the overture and three airs which had been composed by Tommaso Giordani.[66] These airs were introduced for Peretti in the first and second acts and appear to have been first sung during the third and fourth performances. The cast was as follows:

'*Spilletta* [sic] a young sprightly girl, Signora Nicolina Giordani, called by the name of *Spiletta,* from the Excellence of her Performance in this Character'.[67]

Balanzone	Mauro Guerini
Camilla	Marina Giordani
Errico	Nicolo Peretti
Armonica	Rosa Guerini
Copellone	Giuseppe Giordani
Lucinda	Anna Dunlap

who, as in the 1761/62 season, had joined the burlettas from the Smock Alley Theatre stock company. There were new dances by 'Signior Francisco Giordani and Signora Marcutii – and an entire set of new Dresses'.[68] Mossop also kept his promise about the prices of seats, for Boxes, Lattices and Green Box remained at 5/5, pit seats were 3/3 and seats in the galleries were 2/2 and 1/1. Finally, it was announced that 'The Overture will begin at a Quarter Before Seven precisely'.[69]

Further performances of *Gli Amanti Gelosi* followed on November 28 and on December 3, 10, 17, 26 and 31. It next shared the bill with Shakespeare's *King Lear* on January 19 and with *King Henry IV, Part I* on January 24, 1765. To arrange this it was necessary that the burletta should be 'contracted into two short Acts', so the recitatives were shortened and some of the 'unnecessary Characters' were omitted and 'none but the principal Characters and the favourite Airs'[70] were retained. During December the performances had been announced for Monday evenings. This made it necessary to postpone one until Wednesday December 26, since, we learn, 'Monday next happens to be Christmas Eve, on which Night it would be improper to have any Theatrical Performance'.[71]

A second burletta, *Don Fulminone, or The Lover with two Mistresses,* by Tommaso Giordani was performed on January 7, 1765. The cast again included Giuseppe, Nicolina and Marina Giordani, Mauro and Rosa Guerini, Peretti and Anna Dunlap, and dances were again arranged by Francesco Giordani and Felice Marcutii, 'particularly a new Dance called The Barber's Shop'.[72] We read that 'the Audience were pleased to express very great Satisfaction' and that 'The same Burletta by particular Desire, will be performed again on Saturday next; for the future it will be continued on the Saturday in each Week'.[73] But it was not. The performance announced did take place on Saturday, January 12, but, as has already been noted, shortened versions of *Gli Amanti Gelosi* were performed on January 19 and 24, and the only other advertised performance of *Don Fulminone* took place on Thursday, January 31.

Consequently, the burletta season inaugurated with such a journalistic flourish was precipitously to come to an end. It had lasted just ten weeks, during which time only twelve performances of two operas had been given. As we know, at least two of these performances were abridged versions and the intimation that 'none but the principal Characters and the favourite Airs will be continued'[74] suggests either the forced dismissal by Mossop of artists performing 'unnecessary characters'[75] in order to economise on their salaries, or a lack of interest in the burlettas by the audiences. Even sharing the bill with Shakespeare's dramas is a clear indication that the burlettas were failing to attract.

But where had Mossop gone wrong? This was, after all, the best burletta company to have foregathered in Dublin up to that time, and the 1761/62 season at Smock Alley under Mossop's management had successfully run its advertised season of forty performances in five months. What had now turned success into failure? The answer remains unresolved, for let a theatrical production be ever so good, the finest artists engaged, the critics employing all their superlatives, yet if for some obscure reason the public decides against it, then nothing will attract an audience. This, at least in part, may explain Mossop's failure.

There was, however, one other factor which should not be overlooked for in its relation to Italian opera it was to exist in Dublin right through the eighteenth century. This was a prejudice against foreign singers, already observed as early as 1725 with the engagement of Benedetto Baldassari, and now occurring once again. The reason for this prejudice is never completely obvious. Undoubtedly professional jealousy was a basic cause, but why it should flare up at certain times, and at others pass without provoking a disapproving flicker, is not always clear.

During this period rivalry between Mossop and Barry was at its peak and libellous hack-writers were easy to recruit. Whatever the reason, a letter signed 'R.F.' attacking the operas now appeared in the *Dublin Courier*. Since it was published on November 23, the same day as the first performance of *Gli Amanti Gelosi*, enmity was the obvious motive; the burlettas were being condemned before they could be judged. The letter is obtuse and verbose. It postulates that the purpose of the theatre is not only to amuse *and* instruct but also 'to improve the morals of the People'.[76] This latter sentiment must have come as quite a surprise to eighteenth-century Dublin theatre-goers who up to then had hardly realised that a visit to the theatre was expected to correspond with a visit to church. The writer then proceeds to admonish theatre managers who ingenuously believe that 'if the town is desirous of having Operas, 'tis their business to have them'.[77] Such men 'who are weak enough to talk in this manner'[78] should have their patents withdrawn by the Government. To those who would equivocally try to defend their position by introducing the quibble of English opera he utters the following stern rebuke: 'I would have everything unnatural banished from amongst us; and I think it scarcely a greater infamy to the English nation, to countenance the unpardonable vices of Italy in their persons, than to adopt them in their undertakings. The present rage for Operas is more than a prostitution of our good sense. 'Tis in fact a Pathicism of the judgement, and what must throw an everlasting stigma on our reason if we do not instantly cast it off.'[79] Lastly, there is an exhortation to 'banish the Opera, if it must still exist, to the senseless walls of the Haymarket House, and confine it to the effeminate squallers of Italy and the few admirers which ignorance and novelty may have raised it in this Kingdom'.[80]

To this criticism 'Harmonicus', a 'constant reader',[81] replied with masterly restraint in *Faulkner's Dublin Journal*. He introduces his letter with the assurance that he will not 'assume the Character of a Dictator, nor presume to Prescribe Opinions for others';[82] he will merely relate the facts of the situation which his readers can then 'disapprove or commend according as they appear reasonable'.[83] The facts – viewed, of course, with complete impartiality, were as follows. He admits that he went to the theatre 'with very little Expectation of Entertainment'[84] for it had been his constant experience, whether in Holland, Italy or London that 'Troops of these Sort of Comedians were generally made up of the most wretched Performers . . [where] the Strength of each Entertainment consisted in One Woman'.[85] Of the rest, it was just 'Pain and Torture in being compelled to see and hear them'.[86] One did not have to travel abroad to encounter this sort of thing. One had only to recall the visit of the de Amicis company a few years previously. 'Signora de Amicis was allowed by all to have great merit . . but then the rest were of so wretched a kind, that nothing could account for the Indulgence of the Audience, during the Performance, except their Inclination to show Encouragement'.[87] Nor was that all, for 'the best and most Capital Pieces in Italian Music, were obliged to be, either entirely omitted, or else to be cut and mangled so as to be wrought down to the Meanness and Poverty of the Performers'.[88] He explains that he has recounted this earlier engagement at some length because 'Things are never so well illustrated as by Comparison'.[89]

And *what* a comparison can there now be made! It is quite incredible, 'a Matter of Wonder how the Manager of the Theatre could contrive to collect together from different Nations, such a Number of People of Merit'.[90] Even 'the meanest Individuals . . have considerable Merit, suited to their particular Station and the Characters they perform'.[91] 'Signior Giordani's Merit is of the first and most eminent Kind in the Character of the Buffo, Signora Giordani and Signora Dunlap are very excellent singers in the Serious Style; and Signior Peretti is (without any Exception) the most Capital Singer that has been yet heard in this Kingdom.'[92] And what can one say of Signora Spiletta? Nothing! – for 'it is not in the Power of any Words to give an adequate Idea of her Merit'.[93] However, since he cannot leave his subject unfinished, he must try to find some words, inadequate as they may be, to describe her performance. On consideration he can arrive at but one conclusion, that Signora Spiletta – 'besides her great musical Excellence',[94] of course, – is 'without any Exception whatever, THE GREATEST ACTRESS THAT HAS BEEN EVER YET SEEN UPON ANY STAGE'.[95]

So much for the impartiality and credibility of eighteenth-century Dublin theatre reviews. Alas for opera, 'R.F.'s' pedantry was to outwit 'Harmonicus'' puff; for not alone was the burletta season a failure, but while Italian operas were to be very infrequently performed during succeeding years, no organised Italian company was to appear again in Dublin until 1777.

'Harmonicus' did include one item of historical importance in his letter. In speaking of the de Amicis company he recorded, 'We had a remarkable Instance of this Kind a few Years ago in this City, when the Manager of Smock Alley Theatre first introduced the Italian Music upon our Stage',[96] which helps to confirm that 1761 was the year when Italian opera was first performed in Dublin.

10

DIVISIONS AND DIFFICULTIES

A NEW AND CAPRICIOUS star was meanwhile blazing a fiery trail across the Dublin stage. This was Ann Catley, the daughter of a hackney coachman and a washer-woman, born in a London slum in 1745. Courtesan or whore from the age of thirteen (according to whether one wishes to describe her indulgently or with frankness) she was, above all, an actress of natural talents and intelligence, with a pretty voice – an eighteenth-century counterpart of Nell Gwynn. She made her first appearance as a singer at Vauxhall Gardens in 1762 while she was a pupil of William Bates. She was to remain a favourite with Dublin audiences for many years, due perhaps as much to her ready wit as to her ability on the stage. It is related that the distinguished Reverend Dean Bailey who, as a prominent governor of the Rotunda Hospital, was much concerned in the organising of concerts for its upkeep, addressed a card to her as follows: 'Dean Bailey's compliments to Miss Catley, and requests to know when she can give him a night at the lying-in hospital and her terms'; to which she replied: 'Miss Catley presents her compliments to the reverend Dean Bailey, for three nights to come she is engaged to particular friends, but on the fourth will be at his service'.[1]

In appearance, she was a brunette, 'not beautiful but pleasing. Her face was oval, her features petite, and her eyes small'.[2] Her hair, which was thin and lank, she always wore in a fringe 'in an even line almost to her eyebrows', so setting a fashion in hair style which was imitated by the fashionable ladies of Dublin and called 'Catley-fied'.[3] A brief appraisal of her career records that she 'has been many years a popular artist with a moderate share of genius, taste, and industry;

but with a voice, which has hardly ever been exceeded in melody or compass; and with a hoydening kind of assurance and familiarity with the audience, which have often exhorted a laugh from those who have thoroughly disapproved of her'.[4] This career did not last long for in 1780 we read that, as Deborah Woodcock in *Love in a Village,* 'Miss Catley was a complete old maiden aunt. We are sorry that her ill health enabled her, in the stage phrase, to "look the part so well"'.[5] Nine years later she was to die of pulmonary tuberculosis, which had afflicted her most of her life.

Although she had been appearing in Dublin for some time (her roles included Macheath* in *The Beggar's Opera*), her first important operatic role there was Mandane in Thomas Augustine Arne's *Artaxerxes*. This was the first production of *Artaxerxes* in Dublin and it took place at Smock Alley Theatre on Friday, February 22, 1765, having been postponed from the previous Monday, February 18.** The cast was: Arbaces – Signora Passerini '(being her 1st Appearance on this Stage)',[6] Artaxerxes – Peretti (his role in the original production of the opera at Covent Garden), Artabanes – Wilder, Rimenes – Ryder, Semira – Mrs. Hawtrey, and Mandane – Ann Catley. There were 'entire new Dresses',[7] scenery and decorations, and dances were by Francesco Giordani and Signora Marcutii.

Artaxerxes was Arne's most famous opera. It has been described as 'virtually the last of the eighteenth century English operas after the Italian manner'.[8] As such, it had a considerable vogue until the early nineteenth century, and as such it is now a museum piece, occasionally taken out and dusted off for an esoteric festival performance. The text of the opera, which Arne himself had translated from

---

*This was not an uncommon conceit of the eighteenth and nineteenth century theatre. It permitted a star performer to play a favourite role in a bizarre style while displaying her figure in breeches - a most daring impropriety at the time. Ann Catley was the first 'lady' Macheath. She was followed a decade or so later by another Irish singing actress, Mrs. Kennedy. Then came Mrs. Cargill and several others and, about 1820, the renowned Madame Vestris.

**Faulkner's Dublin Journal* of February 16/19 states: 'The celebrated English Opera, called *Artaxerxes* has been in rehearsal for a considerable time at the Theatre in Smock Alley, and being now near ready for Performance, it will be exhibited in a few Days.' The first review of any performance appears in the edition of February 19/23, which refers to the performance taking place 'Last Night', that is, Friday, February 22.

Metastasio, had been used many times previously by other composers, among them Hasse, Jommelli and Gluck – his first opera.

Burney gives his opinion that 'in setting *Artaxerxes*, though the melody is less original than that of *Comus,* Arne had the merit of first adapting many of the best passages of Italy, which all Europe admired, to our own language, and of incorporating them with his own property, and with what was still in favour of former English composers'[9] – which seems to be a polite way of saying that Arne had indulged in a form of plagiarism common in English operatic productions of this period. This impression Burney endorses, when he adds that Arne 'crouded the airs, particularly in the part of Mandane for Miss Brent, with most of the Italian divisions and difficulties which had ever been heard at the opera'.[10] It also proves that Catley was a singer of ability for at least one of Mandane's airs, 'The soldier tir'd of war's alarms', bristles with technical difficulties and was a recognised *aria di bravura* in the repertoire of every leading English soprano during the eighteenth and early nineteenth century.

Of the first Dublin performance, we learn that 'the Audience was very numerous and brilliant, and the Applause given to the Opera was uncommonly great. It was the opinion of many People that the Opera is exhibited in a higher Degree of Perfection than it is in London, both with respect to the Merit of the Performers, and likewise the Richness and Magnificence of the Dresses, Scenes and Decorations'.[11] Whatever about the 'Richness and Magnificence of the Dresses', etc., one must dismiss as presumptuous the extolling of the Dublin performers over their London counterparts, for the Covent Garden cast included, besides Charlotte Brent, Tenducci as Arbaces (he would later sing this role in Dublin) and John Beard as Artabanes. A more interesting comparison can be found in the singing of the part of Arbaces, originally a castrato role, by a soprano, as it would be sung in a production of the opera taking place to-day.

A likely reason for the production of the opera at Smock Alley, apart from its novelty, was the availability of Peretti for the role of Artaxerxes. Following the first performance on February 22, there were further performances on February 27, and on March 4, 8, 13,

I

20 and 28. A break in the performances then occurred, due to the termination of Signora Passerini's engagement with Mossop. Her engagement was renewed in April, which resulted in performances with the same cast taking place on April 13, 20, 26 and 29.

Rivalry between Smock Alley and Crow Street now reached a peak, when both theatres announced in March that they had Bickerstaffe's comic opera *The Maid of the Mill* in rehearsal. Hitchcock recounts how this came about. 'Both managers', he explains, 'thought it an object worth their utmost attention. The words of the opera were published and equally free for both. But the music was in manuscript and the sole property of the Covent-garden manager. From him Mr. Barry purchased it and consequently imagined that he had in this instance securely triumphed over his antagonist. In this dilemma Mr. Mossop found an unexpected resource, in the great abilities of Signior Giordani. It is a fact well established, that though the parts were writing out in Dublin for Mr. Barry, yet did Signior Giordani sit down and new compose the entire opera of the *Maid of the Mill* in full score, with all the accompaniments in less than a fortnight'.[12]

Tommaso Giordani had evidently been appointed 'composer in residence' to Smock Alley Theatre. Earlier in January he had 'arranged' *The Beggar's Opera* with none too happy results, for the Italian embellishments of his settings were considered inartistic when used for simple ballad airs. Giordani was to remain in Dublin composing and arranging operas and musical entertainments for Smock Alley and Crow Street theatres until 1769. He was later to return in 1783 and intermittently he lived and worked there for over twenty years.

His musical output both for the Dublin and London theatres was prolific. Concerning his compositions, an interesting announcement was to appear in 1784. This recorded that 'The Opera on the "Marriage of Figaro" preparing by Mr. Daly for the Dublin Theatre is composing by Mr. Giordani'.[13] If it was ever performed – and further research over the period may reveal that it was – it would have placed his operatic version of Beaumarchais' play on the stage prior to Mozart. He was essentially an ephemeral composer. A contemporary criticism that 'We have so often detected the shameless plagiarisms of this Signor Giordani, that we can not but wonder at the matchless intrepidity of his face'[14] reads harshly, but is probably a fair assessment of his indifferent musical talents.

Samuel Arnold, the original musical arranger of the airs set to Bickerstaffe's lyrics, was born in London in 1740 and died there in 1802. *The Maid of the Mill* was his first composition for the opera stage. Like *Love in a Village,* it was a *pasticcio,* containing airs by twenty different composers. Two solos and two quartets only were composed by Arnold, but his arrangement of music by the other composers was accomplished, and the opera was to remain in the repertory until the early part of the nineteenth century.

To return to its first Dublin productions, the following notices concerning the two theatres appeared on March 23, 1765:

'The Comic Opera of *The Maid of the Mill* which has been so universally approved (with the several Alterations and Improvements made since it was first performed) is now in Rehearsal at the Theatre Royal in Crow-street, and will be performed there in a few Days . . with entire new Scenery by Mr. Carver, new Dresses – and the original Music which has been collected from the most favourite Operas now in Vogue in France and Italy'.[15]

'The new Comic Opera called The Maid of the Mill written by the Author of *Love in a Village,* has been in Rehearsal for a considerable Time at the Theatre in Smock Alley, and being now ready for Representation, it will be exhibited in a few Days . . The Music is entirely new and designedly composed for the particular Words of this Opera, with Dances incident to the Piece; new Dresses and new Scenes. The Paintings by Mr. Jolly; the Music by Signior Tommaso Giordani'.[16]

The relative casts from the two theatres were as follows: the Crow Street cast is noted first.

Lord Aimworth	Barry/Ryder
Sir Harry Sycamore	Mahon/Collins
Mervin	Palmer/Jagger
Lady Sycamore	Mrs. Kennedy/Mrs. Kelf

Theodosia	Mrs. Mahon/Mrs. Wilder
Fanny	Mrs Glover/Signora Spiletta
Fairfield	Glover/Dawson
Giles	Morris/Wilder
Ralph	Hamilton/Walker
Patty	Mrs. Dancer/Miss Catley.

There is little to choose between them. If Smock Alley had Catley and La Spiletta, Crow Street had Spranger Barry.

As Hitchcock has suggested, the race between the two theatres to achieve the first performance was neck and neck, which Mossop and Smock Alley were to win by a head, for the first performance in Dublin took place there on March 26, while Crow Street was obliged to postpone its *première* until March 30. We read that at Crow Street the opera was performed 'to a polite and crowded Audience with universal Applause'.[17] Concerning the Smock Alley performance, there is a letter from one 'Benevolus' which from its style and content strongly suggests a 'Harmonicus' of 1764. Naturally, this performance too met with 'extraordinary Applause'.[18]

Indeed all notices in connection with these and other productions in Dublin during this time are summarized in a prototype review ironically published about the Haymarket Theatre, London, in 1783. This states: 'In order to avoid unnecessary repetitions during the season, the public are desired, once for all, to take notice, that every performance at this theatre will be exhibited to the most brilliant *crouded*, and Overflowing audiences, and received with loud and universal *bursts* of most Unbounded and Uncommon applause'.[19]

'Benevolus' introduces one point of some significance when he explains that Giordani had 'the favourable Circumstances (so very seldom* the good Fortune of Composers) of having the Actors before his Eyes, for whom he had to compose',[20] for this permitted him to adapt and suit 'the songs of each Character to the peculiar Powers of the respective Performers'.[21]

---

*Not *very!* Mozart had his resident company of singers at Vienna, Haydn his company at Esterhazy. In fact it was then the custom for composers to write the music of their operas with certain singers in mind and, on occasion, to defer to their wishes.

The Maid of the Mill does not appear to have been a complete success in Dublin. This may have been due to its simultaneous production at both theatres. Between them fourteen performances were presented from March 26 until May 13 – a good run for one theatre, a moderate run for two. The rivalry of Mossop and Barry was beginning to assume the aspect of the legend of the Kilkenny cats.

On April 9, 1765, Peretti, who was then lodging at 'Mr. Murphy's, the Corner of Stable Lane, Abbey-street',[22] took a benefit at Smock Alley. The programme was a double bill consisting of *Gli Amanti Gelosi* and 'the Comic Opera of The Jovial Crew with Miss Catley'.[23] *The Jovial Crew* had begun its existence as a play by the Caroline dramatist, Richard Brome. In 1731 it was adapted to a comic opera by Edward Roome, Matthew Concanen and Sir William Yonge. There were various editions and it is probable that the music for the Dublin version had been arranged by William Bates, Ann Catley's rather unsavoury singing teacher, with some additional airs by T. A. Arne. Of Bates' talent as a composer it was said, he 'had bluster, and bustle, and could compose songs as fast as a blacksmith can make hobnails all of the same size and quality'.[24]

On April 19 there was a Smock Alley revival of Boyce's *The Chaplet* with Spiletta as Pastora and Catley as Laura, 'being their first appearance in those Characters',[25] and on May 8 the same theatre presented 'a new Comic Opera, never performed in this Kingdom, called The Capricious Lovers. The Music entirely new. Composed by Mr. Rush'.[26] This was an English version by Robert Lloyd of C. S. Favart's *Le Caprice amoureux ou Ninette à la Cour,* with music by the English composer, George Rush.

Another version of the same work entitled *Phyllis at Court* with music composed by Tommaso Giordani was to be performed at the Crow Street Theatre on February 25, 1767. The libretto of this production records that 'In order to make the piece entertaining (and in conformity with the Italian burletta) musical dialogues have been added towards the end of each act; these are known among the Italians by the word *finale,* and are deemed indispensibly necessary in an entertainment of this sort'.[27]

An announcement of considerable importance was made by Mossop on May 18, 1765, when he begged leave 'to acquaint his Friends and the Public' that he had engaged 'at vast Expense, some of the most capital Singers in England'.[28] His plan was to produce English operas on three evenings each week and the season was advertised to commence about June 15. For once, Mossop was not over-rating the quality of his programme, for his roster of artists included the distinguished castrato singer, Giusto Ferdinando Tenducci.

The outline of Tenducci's life has been recorded so frequently that essential facts only will be given here. He was born at Siena about 1736, and made his first stage appearances in Italy some twenty years later. He arrived in London in 1758, and there in 1762 his fame was crowned by his performance of Arbaces in Arne's *Artaxerxes*. He was never among the first rank of castrato singers such as Farinelli, Nicolini or Caffarelli, but the pre-eminent distinction which his voice may have lacked was to adorn his life with an affair in its way as sensational as the adventures of Farinelli at the Royal Court of Madrid.

This occurred in Ireland where Tenducci arrived on June 9, 1765, having sailed from Holyhead to Dublin.[29] While pursuing his operatic engagement there, Tenducci spent much of his time at a gentleman's house a few miles outside the city. There he met a young lady, a visitor from Limerick, obviously stage-struck, to whom he gave singing lessons but, and the importance of the point will be understood as the story evolves, 'without reward or fee'.[30] Inevitably she became infatuated with him, and ultimately they were married in August 1766 at Cork where Tenducci was then performing at the Theatre Royal.

So a young Irish lady had married an Italian castrato almost twice her age. Well might *Faulkner's Dublin Journal* gravely announce from Limerick on August 28, 'An amiable young lady has deserted her Parents and thrown herself away upon an Italian Singer; a most extraordinary Matter of Amazement, and no doubt a great distress to a very respectable Family'.[31]

A great distress it was indeed, for the young lady happened to be

Dorothea, daughter of Thomas Maunsell of Limerick, LL.D., Barrister-at-Law, King's Counsel, Counsel to the Commissioners of Customs and Member of Parliament for Kilmallock, and his wife, Dorothea, youngest daughter of Richard Waller of Castle Waller, County Tipperary.[32] It is impossible to imagine greater catastrophe, yet more must be described – for the couple had been married by a 'Popish Priest'.[33] As Bernard Shaw was to exclaim approximately a century and a quarter later, 'If you have never been in Ireland you do not know what Protestantism is',[34] so one can envisage the situation only by relating it – at the time of Shaw's apophthegm – to that perdurable English family, the Forsytes, and – completely aghast at the thought – ask oneself, what would old James have said? Counsellor Maunsell said little; he acted instead. The marriage had of course been celebrated in secret but in Ireland, even with the lack of communication that existed in the eighteenth century, secrecy merely meant that not more than a hundred people knew of it within the first twelve hours.

Leaving Tenducci to continue his engagement in Cork, his wife set off the following morning to return home, but on reaching Mallow discovered that the story of the marriage had arrived there before her. Realising that her father must soon learn of the affair and comprehending the amplitude of his wrath when he did, she decided that it was now necessary for Tenducci to abduct her. With this intention she arranged to visit her sister Elizabeth who was married to a landlord's agent* named Henry White and lived in County Tipperary about twelve miles** from Limerick city.

The story of her adventures which she tells in a 'Letter to a Friend at Bath' reads like a novel by Maria Edgeworth or Lady Morgan. All the stock Irish characters are present including a faithful retainer named Jerry. The elopement took place on the night she arrived at her sister's house† and with extraordinary naiveté the re-united

---

*'To Lord C—' who cannot be identified with certainty. He may have been Lord Clanricarde.
**Whether the distance was measured in Irish or English miles is not recorded. Twelve Irish miles would equal about sixteen English.
†The address is given as 'G—n h—ll.'

couple set out for Cork, where almost immediately they were seized by a party of Maunsell and Waller relatives and friends, with an attendant bodyguard of servants, Dorothea to be returned to the frigid bosom of her family, Tenducci to be lodged in Cork jail.

'There he was thrust into what is called the common hall, a dungeon intended only for felons and murderers, cold, damp, highly offensive to the smell, and without a glimmering of light. Here he lay surrounded by malefactors; some of whom were screaming with the agonies of a galling yoke, with which they were chained by the neck to the ground, and others still more wretched with the dreadful expectation of suffering in a few days that death to which they were already doomed'.[35] A report from Cork on September 1 confirms his unhappy plight. 'Last Thursday night,' we learn, 'Mr. Tenducci, an Italian singer belonging to our Theatre, was Arrested on an Action of Damages, for having seduced and married a young Lady of good Family and Fortune who had been lately his Pupil. He was enlarged on Saturday, but was this Morning arrested again, and now remains in Confinement'.[36]

For poor Tenducci there now ensued a Kafkaesque episode in which he was dragged from the Pilate of the Master of Chancery to the Herod of a number of Justices of the Peace. Of course it cannot be said that the circumstances were entirely legal; Counsellor Maunsell had sufficient influence in law affairs to see to that. In the background there was also Uncle Eaton Maunsell who had been Sheriff of Limerick in 1760, and Uncle Richard who, according to Dorothea, 'with a malicious smile' observed, 'Tenducci is now in gaol, and there he must stay till his flesh rots from his bones and they shall moulder away with a variety of wretchedness'.[37] Ah well, such is the temerity of youth and love! It must be admitted that however much he was in love, Tenducci was no longer young, nor can he have been so ingenuous as to misjudge the dilemma in which he was placing himself. Nevertheless he did have a few friends. Thomas Barry (Spranger Barry's son) and Robert Mahon, two fellow actors in the Cork company, offered to go bail for the sum of £500 each, although their offer was refused by the Court and, in spite of what must have been formidable legal opposition, he did manage to engage an attorney* to defend him.

So, in and out of jail, depending on the whim of this or that magistrate, suffering cross examination in what, despite his years in England, was a foreign language – the letters bearing his signature which were written at the time were undoubtedly 'ghosted' for him – it is little wonder that he contracted what almost certainly was pneumonia. From this he would very likely have died had not a humane Quaker physician with the initials J.F.S.** issued a certificate which gained for him a final release from prison on bail. Even out of prison the Maunsell family continued to harass him. A cousin Waller forced Thomas Barry, who was managing the Cork company, to cancel a performance of an opera which had been announced for Tenducci's benefit and to substitute *The Merchant of Venice*. The malicious attempt failed, however; 'the house was filled with the best company in the city. At the end of the first act Tenducci was called on for a song', and on the following evening he had the satisfaction of having an opera 'performed with universal applause'.[38]

The outcome of this continuous intimidation resulted in Tenducci leaving Cork for County Waterford, thereby foregoing his engagements and so losing his means of livelihood. In Waterford he stayed for a time at Lismore, later taking refuge in the home of a Mr. Parker '(a gentleman to whom he was recommended by some friends)',[39] who lived at Ballymacarbry not far from the town of Clonmel. Having recuperated there, he next left for Dublin where, according to Dorothea's letter, Spranger Barry, who had earlier engaged him for Crow Street in June, 1766, when his contract with Mossop had ended, appeared reluctant to re-engage him for the winter season of 1766/67. Thus the situation continued to drag on, with Tenducci returning to Cork to stand trial at the March assizes of 1767. Nor had it been resolved by the time Dorothea had finished writing her letter – 'From the place of our Retreat, August the 26th, 1767'.[40]

*A 'Mr. B. H—es.'

**According to the archives of the Religious Society of Friends, Dublin, he was almost certainly Joseph Fenn Sleigh, born Cork, June 19, 1733, died there, May 10, 1770.

However, on September 21, writing from Clogheen in County Tipperary, she adds the following cheerful postscript: 'Since the above letter was finished, the scene (happily for us) has been changed, and we released from the misery in which we had been so long involved. My F[ather] inspired at length by justice to commiscerate the distresses he had unjustly (from a mistaken notion of resentment) plunged us into, thought proper to withdraw all the charges which had been brought against Tenducci on my account; and in consequence thereof, general releases and discharges were signed on both sides at the beginning of the last term; and to prevent any vexatious suit in future, we have been since Married (or rather RE-married) in the parish church of ——* by virtue of a Licence obtained for that purpose.'[41]

One should like to be able to record that they now lived happily ever after, and that all their early tribulations had been worthwhile. Regretfully that sort of happy ending is confined to the works of lady novelists of the period under discussion. Instead, sad to relate, the romance finally ended in 1776 when on February 28 there 'came to be heard before Dr. John Bettesworth, at Doctors-Commons, a cause brought by Mrs. Tenducci against her husband, a singer at the Opera-House, for nullity of marriage; when, after hearing all matters, the Judge declared the marriage void from the beginning'.[42]

*The word 'Limerick', like many others in this narrative, is written in ink in contemporary hand-writing into a blank space occurring in the printed text. In *Grove's Dictionary of Music and Musicians,* Third Edition, Vol. V, p. 304, Dr. Grattan-Flood writes: 'On July 4, 1767 the marriage was legalised in the parish church of Shaurahan, Co. Tipperary.' This contradicts the church at Limerick noted above and is inconsistent when compared with Dorothea's letter which places the date of the marriage sometime between August 26 and September 21. Nevertheless, these facts do not necessarily invalidate Dr. Grattan-Flood's information. One cannot be sure that Dorothea wrote this narrative herself, although its style suggests that she did. A more likely cause for error is that she may not have written it by August, 1767, but at a later time - it was published in London in 1768 - and that the dates she gives were written from memory. Consequently neither the names of the churches nor the dates can unreservedly be accepted as correct. The Maunsells' insistence on a second marriage in a Protestant church was due not only to religious prejudice. As an Italian, Tenducci had almost certainly been baptised a Roman Catholic. On May 1, 1746, an Act relating to mixed marriages had come into force in Ireland decreeing that such marriages if celebrated by a Roman Catholic priest 'shall be null and void to all intents and purposes, without any process, judgement, or sentence of law whatsoever'. Tenducci and his wife were consequently not legally married until the second ceremony had taken place.

One other factor must be mentioned in fairness to Thomas Maunsell who had some justification for describing Dorothea as 'an infatuated unhappy daughter'.[43] A most contentious topic between the Maunsells and Tenducci was that he might permit, perhaps even encourage, Dorothea to appear on the stage. To allay their fears, Tenducci offered any security that they should demand that this would never happen. Yet Dorothea eventually became an actress, nor can any spectre of a Svengali-like Tenducci be observed hovering in the background when this occurred. Dorothea may have been infatuated with Tenducci, but her real love affair was with the bright lights of the theatre.

She was to make an early appearance in 1770 when it was announced, 'From London we learn that the lovers of music have great expectations of the celebrated Mrs. Tenducci, who arrived there a few days ago from Edinburgh, and will make her first appearance in a musical entertainment, which is to be performed for the benefit of her husband'.[44] Later during the same year she was to perform in Dublin at Crow Street Theatre, and even in Cork, where four years earlier she had encountered so much unhappiness.

After this digression, on returning to Tenducci's arrival in Dublin in 1765, we find that he was joined there on July 6 by Clementina Cremonini,[45] a soprano from the King's Theatre, London. Cremonini was no great find on Mossop's part. Horace Walpole reports that she had been 'advertised for a perfect beauty with no voice' and then continues, 'but her beauty and voice are by no means so unequally balanced: she has a pretty little small pipe, and only a pretty little small person and share of beauty, and does not act ill'.[46] Burney confirms this, explaining that 'Her voice, though a young woman was in decay, and failed on all occasions of the least difficulty; which, however, did not prevent her from attempting passages that not only required more voice, but more abilities than she could boast'.[47]

Her chief claim to notice seems to rest with her appearance as one of several artists who took part in some London concerts, one at Hickford's Great Room in Brewer Street, on May 13, 1765, 'For the Benefit of Miss Mozart of Thirteen, and Master Mozart of Eight

Years of Age, Prodigies of Nature' when 'all the Overtures [were] of this little Boy's own composition' and Cremonini sang 'The Vocal Part'.[48] Presumably she had at least patted the head of greatness.

Tenducci was an artist of a different calibre. Of the many descriptions of his singing, perhaps the one which epitomises his vocal qualities best is to be found, strangely enough, in Tobias Smollett's famous epistolary novel, *The Expedition of Humphrey Clinker*. There we read, 'At Ranelagh I heard the famous Tenducci, a thing from Italy; it looks for all the world like a man, though they say it is not. The voice to be sure is neither man's nor woman's, but it is more melodious than either, and it warbled so divinely, that the while I listened, I really thought myself in Paradise'.[49]

Mossop had brought one other artist from London to join his English opera company. This was Miss Thomas, who had made her 'first appearance on any stage'[50] as a member of Garrick's company at Drury Lane Theatre on March 1, 1753, singing Laura in Boyce's *The Chaplet*. She remained at Drury Lane until 1755, but during the following year, like Signora Passerini, her name is to be found only among the cast lists of London booths and minor theatres. However, for the 1761/62 season she reappeared at Drury Lane and sang also at Covent Garden. She seems to have ended her career at Marylebone Gardens where she was singing in burlettas in 1770 and 1771.

Good, bad and indifferent, Mossop now had a company for his opera season; he also had Peretti, and from his theatre company he was able to add singing actors such as James Wilder and Thomas Ryder, both long popular with Dublin audiences. With this cast he now commenced his season on July 18, 1765.[51]

His choice of opera was *The Royal Shepherd*, an English version of Metastasio's libretto of *Il Re Pastore* by Richard Rolt, with music by George Rush and Tenducci. Shortly before Rush had composed this opera for Drury Lane in 1764, he had returned from Italy, 'and knew the taste of that country, but wanted the judgement to adapt that taste to English ears, or rather to English hearts'.[52] Tenducci's share of the musical authorship probably consisted of additional airs for himself. The cast was as follows:

Amyntas, The Royal Shepherd	Tenducci
Alexander	Peretti
Agenor	Wilder
Thamyris	Miss Thomas
Eliza	Signora Cremonini.

The dresses and decorations were new, nobody was to be permitted behind the stage, ventilators were 'fixed in different parts of the Theatre, in order to keep the House cool'[53] and – once again – the opera was performed 'to a numerous and splendid Audience, and was received with universal Applause'.[54]

The applause on this occasion appears to have been genuine, for there were thirty performances between the opening of the season and April 14, 1766. *The Royal Shepherd* was presented alternately with a revival of Arne's *Artaxerxes* which re-entered the repertory on July 30, 1765. The cast of this opera now included Tenducci and Peretti in their original roles of Arbaces and Artaxerxes, Wilder again sang Artabanes, Jagger sang Rimenes, Miss Thomas, Semira and Signora Cremonini, Mandane. Tenducci introduced 'two Additional Songs in the Character of Arbaces'[55] and in this opera scored his greatest success with Dublin audiences. O'Keeffe relates that his singing of 'Water parted from the sea' (by Arne) 'was the great attraction'[56] and describes the Dublin street urchins singing a parody to the tune of 'Over the hills and far away' which ended with the couplet:

> 'And all the tunes that he could play
> Was "Water parted from the Say"'.[57]

On August 3 it was advertised that henceforth *Artaxerxes* would be performed on Tuesday, and *The Royal Shepherd* on Saturday, of each week. This arrangement was not adhered to after August 31, but *Artaxerxes* was to alternate with *The Royal Shepherd* for what may well have been a record run for one opera in eighteenth-century Dublin, of thirty-three performances between July and the following May 13.

Tenducci took his benefit in *The Royal Shepherd* on August 17, 1765 when, we read, 'At the end of the Opera (by particular Desire) Mr. Tenducci will sing a favourite song called "Se Piei

Felice" from the celebrated Burletta La Cascina . . Tickets to be had from Mr. Tenducci, at Finegan's, Grocer, in Mary-street'.[58] From O'Keeffe we again learn that for his benefits in Dublin, Tenducci 'had thirty, forty, and fifty guineas for a single ticket',[59] although such sums were undoubtedly the exception rather than the rule.

Between August and December, 1765, there were incidental events in connection with the performances, such as the introduction of 'the celebrated Scotch Air, called Through the Wood, Laddie . . The Musick by Mr. Michael Arne'[60] (T. A. Arne's son who would later perform in Dublin), in *The Royal Shepherd* on August 31. Cremonini took her benefit in the same opera on September 5 when tickets were to be had 'at her lodgings, at Mr. Cochran's, Taylor, in Abbey-street'.[61]

It was advertised that no opera performances would take place between Saturday, September 7, and Monday, September 16, 'as next Week will be the Time of the Curragh Races'.[62] Towards the end of September, 'Mrs. Cremonini' was 'indisposed for some days'[63] but recovered sufficiently to sing Mandane on September 24. Then, early in October, the engagement for the season of Ann Catley was announced. For her first performance on October 7[64] she took over the role of Mandane, and on October 21 appeared in *The Beggar's Opera*.

On December 12, yet another 'new English Opera, called The Revenge of Athridates'[65] was produced. Its precise identity requires investigation, for an opera 'Pharnaces Altered from The Revenge of Athridates' was to be produced by Tenducci at Crow Street Theatre during the following July. This bears a close resemblance to an opera called *Pharnaces*, with text by Thomas Hull, based on a libretto by A. M. Lucchini and with music by William Bates which had had its first performance at Drury Lane Theatre on February 15, 1765. Sonneck, however, lists a libretto – 'Pharnaces: or, The Revenge of Athridates. An English opera. As it was to have been performed* at

---

*The following note which is printed in the libretto may help to clarify the enigmatic mood of this sentence - 'As Mr. Gibson is extremely ill, the part of Athridates is obliged to be left out, and part of Pompey - and of Gilades - and all the recitatives (except Mr. Tenducci's with accompanyments) as they would be tedious to the audience'.

the Theatre Royal, Edinburgh. The music selected from the most capital composers, and adapted by Mr. Tenducci . . Three acts . . The original text presumably was Antonio Maria Lucchini's 'Farnace'. The English version is not that by Thomas Hull.'

Here, therefore, is evidence of two different libretti. Further, the advertisement for the Smock Alley production includes the comment, 'The Musick selected from the most capital Composers and adapted by Mr. Tenducci',[66] which corresponds exactly to the announcement in the Edinburgh libretto. Coincidentally, it makes no reference to William Bates. There can be little doubt therefore that the *Pharnaces* performed by Tenducci in Dublin was not the Hull-Bates version, but was a *pasticcio* with music arranged by Tenducci. But if Bates' music was not used, who then were 'the most capital composers' whom Tenducci had called upon? The following clues may provide an answer.

It is recorded that Tenducci in 1756 sang at Naples with great success in an opera called *Farnace* set to music by Perez and Piccini.[67] Three years later, when he had arrived in London, an opera *Farnace* was frequently performed at the King's Theatre between April 21, 1759, and March 24, 1760. The casts of these performances are not recorded, but on March 3, 1760, a performance was advertised for Tenducci's benefit into which he introduced three new airs,[68] so he was undoubtedly taking part. 'The favourite Songs' from this opera were published in London by John Walsh in 1759 with Davide Perez and Gioacchino Cocchi named as composers.

From this it seems possible that the libretto of the Dublin production was a new translation of the Lucchini *Farnace* and that the music employed by Tenducci was composed primarily by Perez and Cocchi with some additional numbers by himself. Alternatively it may have been a complete *pasticcio* with the music chosen by Tenducci from a number of different composers.

The cast of the Smock Alley production was made up of Tenducci, Wilder, Peretti, Ryder, Miss Thomas, Signora Cremonini, and a new artist, Miss Frances Ashmore, who was making her first appearance on the stage. According to Hitchcock, in this opera 'she sung a pleasing air of "Dearest Mother" much adapted to her powers, and in which she was well instructed by Signior Tenducci'.[69] Yet some years later we read of a performance by her in *Love in a Village*, 'It were much to be wished Miss Ashmore had more spirit in the part of Rosetta, and not attempt, by way of supplying the defect to imitate the witless buffoonery of Miss Catley whose follies are overlooked in consideration of her agreeable person and inchanting voice.' Frances Ashmore was later to marry the noted Dublin actor Richard Sparks.[70]

The exaggerated praise with which *Faulkner's Dublin Journal* greeted the first performance of *The Revenge of Athridates* arouses suspicion that on this occasion it was not entirely universal. This is to some extent borne out by the number of performances it received. In exactly four months, from December 12, 1765, to April 12, 1766, it had only fourteen.

So much activity at Smock Alley Theatre was undoubtedly causing Spranger Barry considerable concern at Crow Street where, during the same period – at least operatically – there was little opposition. On November 14, 1765, *The Maid of the Mill* was revived there with Spiletta as Fanny the gipsy.[71] This interchanging of artists between the two theatres was a frequent occurrence at this period. Spiletta and Francesco Giordani had left Smock Alley for Crow Street during the summer, Spiletta making her first appearance as Fanny on July 9. On November 23 she sang in *Love in a Village,* and on November 29 and December 2 again performed in *The Maid of the Mill*.

Some novelty was introduced into the programme on December 6 when a one-act comic opera by Isaac Bickerstaffe called *Daphne and Amintor* was performed.[72] It has been described as 'little more than "The Oracle" of Mrs. Cibber with a few songs interspersed'.[73] Mrs. Cibber's masque was in turn nothing more than a plagiarism of *L'Oracle* by G. F. Poulain de St. Foix. The cast was Amintor – Ryder, Mindora – Miss Thomas, another 'exchange' artist from Smock Alley, and Daphne – 'Miss Slack from the Theatre Royal in Drury Lane'.[74]

Miss Slack had made her *début* at Drury Lane on November 28, 1764, announced as 'a Young Gentlewoman'[75] – 'whose amiable

GIUSTO FERDINANDO TENDUCCI. CASTRATO (c. 1736–? c. 1800)
HOLDING A COPY OF THE MUSIC OF 'WATER PARTED FROM THE SEA'.

THOMAS PINTO.
VIOLINIST (1714–1783)

THOMAS RYDER.
MANAGER AND ACTOR
(1735–1791)

Figure and delicate Manner immediately engaged the Spectators in her Favour'.[76] It was considered, however, that she would succeed as an actress 'rather than as a singer' for we learn that 'her voice though really melodious is not of sufficient strength'.[77] She was another pupil of William Bates who in 1768 was to be the plaintiff in an action against Spranger Barry 'for a large sum of money due to him from the Defendant, for the performance of Miss Slack, the Plaintiff's apprentice'. 'After a short hearing'[78] Bates won his case.

A first performance of rather more interest took place at Crow Street on January 20, 1766. This was advertised as 'a new Comic Opera called, Tit for Tat or The Cadi Gull'd'.[79] No author's name is given. The cast was as follows:

Darab, the Cadi	Mahon
Selim, Prince of Bagdad	Palmer
Caled, the Aga	Hamilton
Omar, the Dyer	Vernel
Fatima, the Cadi's wife	Mrs. Hawtrey
Balkis, the Dyer's daughter	La Spiletta
Zelmira	Mrs. Mahon.

There was a second performance on January 23. W. J. Lawrence, comparing it to *Love in a Village,* which he considers to have been the first English comic opera, describes *The Cadi Gulled* as 'the first Irish comic opera'.[80]

Concerning the opera's origin, there can scarcely be a doubt that it was a translation or adaptation of Pierre Réné Lemonnier's one-act *opéra comique, Le Cadi Dupé.* This had twice been set to music in 1761, first by Monsigny at Paris and later in the year by Gluck at Vienna. Monsigny's name appears frequently among composers whose music is included in *pasticcios* at this period. For example, among the *pasticcios* which had already been performed in Dublin, he had three airs in *The Maid of the Mill* and two in *Daphne and Amintor.* It is likely therefore that at least some of his music was retained in the Dublin version of *The Cadi Gulled.* Unfortunately no evidence can be adduced to suggest that a Dublin audience would

K

also have heard some of Gluck's music for the first time among this *mélé d'ariettes*.

For further opera performances of any consequence one must now return to Smock Alley where, on January 31, 1766, Arne's *Comus* was revived.[81] Henry Mossop played Comus and 'The Vocal Characters' were:

Bacchanals	Wilder and Peretti
Female Bacchanals	Miss Catley, Miss Slack and Miss Thomas
Pastoral Nymph	Miss Slack
Euphrosyne	Miss Catley
Sabina	Mrs. Cremonini, '(being her first appearance in that Character)'[82]

Ariel Spirit 'with additional Songs in Character'[83]

Tenducci.

The cast, as can be seen, was a strong one and John O'Keeffe particularly praises Tenducci's singing. Thirteen performances were given between January 31 and May 1.

The last performance on May 1 was followed by David Garrick's farce *Miss in her Teens* when the artists included not only Miss Catley, but 'Miss Catley's sister [Mary], (being her first Appearance upon the stage)'.[84] It may equally have been her last in Dublin for, while much is recorded of her private life, little is known of her life in the theatre except that 'having a tolerable voice, and a name which could make an attracting figure in a country play bill, [she] got an engagement in a strolling company, from which time, Fame has neglected to report the incidents of her life'.[85]

On February 8 Mossop announced that at Smock Alley Theatre the curtain would in future rise at a quarter to seven, since there had been many complaints that the performances had 'begun at too late an hour'.[86] Previously, during this season, performances had commenced at half-past seven. The first opera to be presented at the earlier time was *Love in a Village*. The date was March 3 and rather surprisingly Tenducci sang the part of Young Meadows, for which role he had 'been a considerable Time preparing himself'.[87] For the performance there was also 'a new occasional Prologue & Epilogue by Mr. Tenducci with Dances incident to the Opera and the usual Decorations'.[88] It cannot have been completely successful or it may have been crowded out by new productions of other operas since by the season's end it had received only four performances, of which Tenducci took part in only three.

Two operas by Tommaso Giordani were now produced. The first, presented on April 24, having been postponed from April 21 to allow extra rehearsal time, was 'a Comic Opera, called Love in Disguise. The Story entirely new, and the Music composed for the Piece by Mr. Thomas Giordani, who will accompany it on the Harpsichord'.[89] The cast was composed of Tenducci 'for whom his Character has been particularly adapted',[90] Wilder, Edwin, Jeffreys, Mrs. Jeffreys, Miss Thomas, Mrs. Glover and Miss Catley. Concerning the performance ('universal Applause' – 'most numerous and brilliant Audience') it is reported that 'the Piece is a lively and just Comedy, ingeniously and naturally interwoven with pleasing Objects of ——* Life and pastoral Simplicity, and the whole heightened and improved with elegant Airs suitable to the Characters represented. Most of the young gentlemen of our University were pleased to honour the Performance with their Presence, dressed in their Gowns which seems to favour the Report prevailing, that the Opera is written by a young Gentleman of their Community**'.[91] A second performance of the opera was advertised for April 26 with the additional comment, 'With a compleat Band of Musick'.[92] It was performed four times only, the last performance (without Tenducci) ending the opera season at Smock Alley on the evening of June 6.[93]

For his second production Giordani chose an *opera seria*, 'the celebrated Opera of Metastasio, entitled L'Eroe Cinese . . first acted at Vienna by the present Emperor and the Princesses of the Imperial Family'.[94] This reference is to the version composed by Giuseppe Bonno, performed at Schönbrunn by 'giovani distinte dame e cavalieri'[95] in May 1752. There were two performances only of

*Word indecipherable.
**Who eludes identification.

Giordani's version during the season. The first took place on May 7, the second on May 16. The cast of the first performance included Tenducci, Peretti, Signora Cremonini and Signora Marina Giordani ('being her first Appearance on the Stage this Winter'.)[96] but for the second performance the cast list, which is given in much greater detail, was as follows:

Siveno	Tenducci
Mineto	La Spiletta
Leango	'Mr. F. Passerini'[97]
Ulania	Signora Giordani
Lisinga	Signora Cremonini.

Presumably Spiletta sang in both performances. The first advertisement, which omits her name, originally appeared on April 12 when she may still have been under contract to Barry at Crow Street, and the same advertisement could have continued in print without alteration until the performance. The re-setting of the advertisement for the second performance was almost certainly due to the replacement of Peretti by 'Mr. F. Passerini', and here for the first time we find Master Passerini of earlier years now grown to manhood. The unfortunate tragedy at Booterstown which was to end his life was still forty-three years in the future.

Both performances of this opera were for Giordani's benefit with 'Tickets to be had at Mr. Giordani's Lodgings at Mrs. Gardiner's on the Batchelor's Walk, the corner of Batchelor's Lane'.[98] where also to be had were 'Books of the Opera, with an English Translation'.[99] A notice of the first performance relates that 'The Musick of this Opera is entirely new composed by Mr. Thomas Giordani, and the general Approbation it met with, was so great, that the composer is allowed to have shewn a very masterly Genius and has acquired a very considerable Addition to his Reputation'.[100]

The opera's production in Dublin is of historic rather than artistic importance. Its significance is contained in the announcement already quoted in Chapter 2: 'It is hoped that the Lovers of Music will patronise this first Attempt of producing a serious Italian Opera on the Irish Stage'. Again one finds evidence that Italian opera was performed in Dublin for the first time during the seventeen-sixties, and that it was Giordani's *L'Eroe Cinese* and not Handel's *Rinaldo* which had the distinction of being the first *opera seria* to be staged there.

The Smock Alley season having ended, Spranger Barry now engaged Tenducci and Signora Cremonini for a theatrical venture at Crow Street. The season was both short and sparse. Arne's *King Arthur* was announced, but seemingly did not materialise. *The Royal Shepherd* had one performance for Tenducci's benefit on July 10. *Pharnaces – or The Revenge of Athridates* alone had a short run and was given six performances. The first was postponed until June 24 'on Account of Mr. Tenducci's indisposition'.[101] A performance on July 3 included the added attraction of 'several new and surprising performances on the Tight Rope by the Italian Monkey'.[102] The final performance for Signora Cremonini's benefit ended the season on July 15, 1766.[103]

I I

SEVEN YEARS OF ENGLISH
OPERA

THERE NOW FOLLOWED seven lean years – from 1770 until 1777 – when musically nothing more adventurous than English comic opera was to be performed in Dublin's theatres. True, it had been announced in 1769 'that Mr. Mossop has engaged a Sett of Italian Singers to perform Burlettas twice a week, the ensuing Winter at the Theatre in Smock Alley',[1] but by this time Mossop was in such financial difficulties that while a season may have been contemplated, it could never have materialised.

By 1767 Spranger Barry's debts had at last overwhelmed him. In the autumn of that year he let the Crow Street Theatre to his old rival Mossop and no doubt much relieved at ridding himself of so formidable a situation set out for London. Meanwhile, if Mossop had triumphed over one rival, it was no more than a Cadmus-like sowing of dragon's teeth, for almost at once up sprang another opponent who before long was to conquer him.

This was a mediocre actor-cum-country theatre manager named William Dawson who, having a brash personality combined with an astute mind, decided that this was an opportune time to enter the Dublin theatrical arena. He seems to have judged correctly that Mossop, weakened from prolonged contention with Barry, would now offer little opposition. Consequently, in association with the singing actor Robert Mahon, he took over a small theatre in Capel Street. Contemporary sources have identified this theatre with one originally built by a puppeteer called Stretch, which had been closed for a number of years prior to 1770. So successful was Dawson's venture that Mossop was obliged to surrender Crow Street Theatre in June 1770, which Dawson then leased and closed down until the following March in order to prevent competition, meanwhile transferring the title of 'Theatre Royal' to his smaller house in Capel Street. Mossop continued to fight a losing battle at Smock Alley until the spring of 1771, when his creditors became so pressing that he too was obliged to follow Barry to London. He died there at Chelsea in December 1774 with, it is said, only four pence half-penny in his possession.

Dawson began his season at the Capel Street Theatre early in 1770 – not, as has been recorded, on Wednesday, February 21 – but on the following Monday, February 26. The reason for this postponement was 'on account of several performers (who had promised to be in Dublin on Saturday last) not being yet arrived'.[2] We learn also that the theatre 'is now completely fitted up for the reception of the publick with Scenes, Cloaths, Machinery and every other decoration, entirely new, and the strictest regularity will be observed'.[3]

The first opera to be performed there, on February 26, was Charles Dibdin's *The Padlock*, with libretto by Isaac Bickerstaffe. This was not the first performance of *The Padlock* to be given in Dublin; it had earlier been produced at Smock Alley Theatre on January 9, 1769.[4] It was now announced 'with Additions and Alterations by the Author as performed in London, with entire new Scenes painted by Mr. Jolly, new Dresses and every necessary Decoration'.[5]

Poor Bickerstaffe was soon to have to flee to the continent, where he would live a hand-to-mouth existence for the remainder of his life. In 1783 he was reported to be dead, but this was immediately contradicted and instead, he was rumoured to be 'living in great distress in an obscure Baillage in the South of France'.[6] This news was again contradicted, the same source announcing, 'A correspondent says we were misinformed respecting Mr. Bickerstaff, he being at present at Milan, in Italy, where he goes by the name of Mr. Commandoni.'[7] He probably had various aliases, for in 1781 we hear of him, again in Milan, under the assumed name of 'Squire Cameron'.[8] In 1786 he was still there as 'Signor Commindoni' earning a living 'by teaching the English language'.[9]

The cast of the Dublin production consisted of:

Don Diego	Glenville
Leander	Willis
Mungo	Mahon
Ursula	Mrs. Hoskins
Leonora	Miss Ashmore.

The role of Mungo, created in the original performance at Drury Lane by Dibdin himself, is that of a West Indian slave – slavery was not abolished in England until 1807 – who seems to have been the first 'stage' black man in comic opera, and consequently lineal ancestor of the Christy Minstrels.

In honour of the occasion the Capel Street Theatre was illuminated with wax. The performances were advertised to commence 'precisely at seven o'clock', and no person would 'on any account be admitted behind the scenes'.[10] Seat prices conformed to the then existing Dublin charges of: Boxes and Lattices 5/5, Pit 3/3 and Gallery 2/2. Places for the boxes were to be taken 'of Mr. O'Neil at his house in Abbey-street'.[11]

Although Dublin theatre criticism during the eighteenth century was, as has been demonstrated, unreliable, it does appear that the orchestra at Capel Street was above average. The leader and conductor was Charles Clagget, a Waterford-born violinist who introduced a number of improvements in the construction of several instruments.

Dawson's second operatic production was another Dibdin-Bickerstaffe work, *Lionel and Clarissa, or The School for Fathers* which had its first Dublin performance at Capel Street on April 2, 1770.[12] This was an alteration of an earlier opera called *Lionel and Clarissa* which had originally come out at Drury Lane Theatre in 1768. According to Dibdin he composed 'for this piece about twenty-five things' but sales of the music produced little 'till it came out under the title of *The School for Fathers*'.[13] The cast at Capel Street included Mahon, Wilks, Herbert, Glenville, Dawson, Tyrer, Miss Ambrose, Miss Barre, Mrs. O'Neill and Miss Ashmore. Again, the house was illuminated with wax for the opening performance.

The School for Fathers was probably the most successful of the operas produced at Capel Street, having a run of twenty-six performances during the season. On the occasion of the tenth performance we learn that 'The desire of the public to see this piece exhibited at the above theatre was so great that the pit and gallery were filled in less than ten minutes and what is remarkable, the ladies insisted on being admitted into the pit, according to the custom of the theatres in London'.[14]

On May 24, Robert Mahon took his benefit in 'a new Comic Opera (never acted in this Kingdom) called Tom Jones'.[15] The cast was:

Tom Jones	Mahon
Western	Herbert
Alworthy	Dawson
Supple	Wilks
Nightingale	Glenville
Old Nightingale	Tyrer
Blisful	Walsh
Miss Western	Mrs. O'Neill
Nancy	Miss Hudson
Honour	Miss Grace
Sophia	Miss Ashmore.

The music was compiled by Samuel Arnold, who composed seven airs for it; eight others were by T. A. Arne. The libretto, taken from Fielding, was by Joseph Reed, an English dramatist born in 1729, who being a rope maker by trade described himself on the title pages of his early publications as 'a halter-maker'.[16]

To this comic opera was added 'a new Comic Farce (never performed in this Kingdom) called A Peep behind the Curtain or The New Rehearsal'[17] and, like a Chinese box, fitting one into the other, this comic farce in turn contained another, 'the Burletta of Orpheus'.[18] The following players took part: Mahon, Lewis, Wilks, Glenville, Miss Ambrose, Mrs. Barre, Mrs. Dawson and Miss Ashmore, and tickets were to be had 'of Mr. Mahon at his house in Middle Liffey-street'.[19] The music of *A Peep behind the Curtain* was composed by

François Barthélemon, a French violinist who enters this history in 1771. The libretto, an adaptation of *The Rehearsal* by George Villiers, Duke of Buckingham, was by David Garrick.

Garrick's powers as an actor are too well-known to require comment here. Much less known was his minor talent as a dramatist. Apart from his 'improvements' of a number of Shakespeare's plays to make them conform to eighteenth-century theatrical taste, he wrote or adapted over twenty stage productions ranging from tragedy to farce and from opera to interlude. The burlesque of *A Peep Behind the Curtain* is an example. A description by W. T. Parke suggests that Barthélemon anticipated Offenbach, for he relates that the most popular scene in the burletta of *Orpheus* was one 'wherein Orpheus, by the force of his lyre, made not only men but trees* and cows dance'.[20]

Dawson's first season ended successfully with a final performance of *Lionel and Clarissa or The School for Fathers* on June 30, 1770. He presented the first new opera of his second season on January 23, 1771.**

This was *The Romp or A Cure for the Spleen*, an operatic farce which Dibdin explains had been adapted from an earlier comic opera called *Love in the City* by himself and Bickerstaffe. We learn that 'The music has been compiled from the works of the most capital Italian masters, and partly new set by Mr. Dibdin, composer of The Padlock on purpose for the Capel-street Company'.[21] According to Dibdin, music composed by him which was retained in *The Romp* after its alteration from *Love in the City* consisted of 'the chorus, the quintetto, the boxing trio, and "Dear Me how I long to be Married" '.[22] The cast was Mahon, Lewis, Keeffe (John O'Keeffe, the author), Dawson, Herbert, Glenville, Mrs. Barre, Mrs. Price, Mrs. Sidney and Miss Ashmore. A notice of a performance of *The Romp* in London in 1785

---

*In the original libretto fauna only are mentioned in the stage directions. They state: 'Orpheus leads out the Shepherds in a grand Chorus of singing and dancing and the Beasts following them'. (Libretto at Trinity College Library, Dublin.)

**Reported by Professor William Smith Clark in *The Irish Stage in the County Towns, 1720–1800*. p. 320. Advertisements in the *Dublin Mercury* are rather ambiguous. The edition of January 24/26, 1771, announces a performance 'On Tuesday next' (January 29) of 'a new Comic Opera call'd The Romp, or A Cure for the Spleen' which is then postponed until February 2. Although the advertisement is headed 'Third Day this may have been the first performance.

disparagingly reports, 'In praise of the piece we can say nothing'.[23]

Charles Dibdin, who had been born at Southampton in 1745, joined Covent Garden Theatre as a singing actor about 1763. There he was befriended by John Beard, the famous English tenor, then owner and manager of the theatre. In addition to composing for Covent Garden, Dibdin was later to compose for Drury Lane Theatre, Ranelagh Gardens and Sadler's Wells.

Hogarth has recorded that his 'musical learning was far inferior to his excellence as a melodist'[24] and Dibdin himself boasted of this incompetence, relating that he had 'never learnt more of music than the gamut and the table which points out the division of the time'.[25] Explaining that the compositions of Corelli and Rameau were his only tutors, he then simplifies the theory of harmony by expounding, 'having proved theoretically by one, and practically by the other, the difference between passing and emphatic notes – the nature of supposed basses – and found by a fair trial of these matters in every point of view, that two chords comprehend the whole system of harmony, I determined fearlessly to give a loose to my fancy – to what purpose is pretty well known'.[26]

Such audacity in music befitted a man who in private life was to desert both a wife and a mistress, leaving them destitute, and who could yet find another wife content to spend her life with him. In 1789, having failed in a number of attempts to have his compositions performed in London, he decided to present on his own initiative what he announced as a series of 'table entertainments'.[27] Of these, 'he was author, composer, narrator, singer and accompanist'.[28] They were very successful and included songs such as 'Tom Bowling' (written on the death of a much loved brother), which today are nostalgically remembered from old gramophone records of tenors like Edward Lloyd and Ben Davies.

Eventually his entertainments became so successful that he built himself a small theatre in Leicester Place (just off Leicester Square) which he appropriately named *Sans Souci*. During this period he had also written several now forgotten novels, and a history of the English stage in five volumes. Whatever his transgressions, he at least cannot be accused of the sin of sloth. In 1802 he was to give his entertainments in Dublin. He died on July 25, 1814.

A new opera by a new and eccentric composer was next performed at Capel Street. This was *Cymon,* the libretto by David Garrick, based on Dryden's poem *Cymon and Iphigenia,* the music by Thomas Augustine Arne's son, Michael. The first music by Michael Arne to be heard in Dublin seems to have been his arrangement of the song 'Thro' the Wood, Laddie' which, as has been noted, was introduced into a performance of *The Royal Shepherd* in 1766. As a child he had been coached for the stage by his distinguished aunt Mrs. Cibber and as early as 1751, under his father's tuition, was appearing at Marylebone Gardens as a singer. But composition was his true *métier* and in 1767, after two luckless operatic adventures, he succeeded with *Cymon.*

Had he remained satisfied with his success all might have been well, but he now abandoned musical composition in order to take up the practice of alchemy – a profession perhaps even more unpredictable than that of opera composer. The occult philosopher's stone which he so persistently pursued retained its mystery, however, and so after a time he was obliged to return to composition. Burney records that 'he was always in debt, and often in prison; he sung his first wife to death, and starved the second, leaving her in absolute beggary'.[29]

Cymon had its first Dublin performance on March 4, 1771, although it had been announced as being in rehearsal as early as the previous May. It was described as a 'celebrated dramatic Romance . . with entire new scenery, machinery, habits and every necessary decoration. The music by Mr. Arne. The Accompaniments composed by Mr. W. Clagget. The paintings by the celebrated Mr. Carver, Mr. Campbell, Mr. Lee and others'.[30] 'Mr. W. Clagget' was Walter Clagget, a less renowned musician than his brother, Charles. The cast was:

Cymon	Mahon
Merlin	Glenville
Dorcus	Herbert
Damon	Walsh

Dorilas	Burden
First Demon of Revenge	Chaplain
Other Demons	Connor, Fawset, Lee, Beatty
Linco	O'Keeffe
Knights of the Several Orders	Lewis, Clinch, Dawson, Kane, Hollocombe, Dodd, Tyrer
Shepherds	Dawson, Day, Galway, Booth, Reynolds and Master Dawson
First Shepherdess	Mrs. Dawson
Second Shepherdess	Mrs. Price
Cupid	'a young Gentlewoman (being her first appearance on any stage)'[31]
Fatima	Miss Younge
Dorcas	Mrs. Hoskins
Urganda	Mrs. Barre
Sylvia	Miss Ashmore.

The performance would 'conclude with a grand procession of Knights of the order of chivalry and Arcadian shepherds and shepherdesses'.[32]

Over the two seasons, Robert Mahon and Frances Ashmore were the principal artists of the company. Miss Ashmore received the accolade of a newspaper address expressed in Grub-street doggerel, no doubt self-inspired and remunerated. It was poetically entitled 'On Seeing Miss Ashmore perform at the City Theatre'[33] and from it the following eulogistic couplets are quoted:

> 'Catley, no more you lead the listn'ing throng
> For here–a tuneful sister claims the song;
>
> . . . .
>
> What wond'rous grace and dignity unite
> Which fill us thus with exquisite delight.
> Oh! long may Ashmore grace Hibernia's stage,
> And please a fickle, very fickle age!'[34]

Dawson's next production of a new opera took place, not at Capel Street, but at Crow Street Theatre, which he had reopened in March,

1771. This was *A Summer's Tale* (here called *The Summer's Tale*) performed for the first time in Dublin on April 13,[35] with music composed by Arnold and T. A. Arne, and compiled from the works of twenty-two other composers. The libretto was by the British dramatist, Richard Cumberland, who at the age of twenty-nine had come to Ireland in the retinue of the Earl of Halifax when he was appointed Viceroy in 1761, and whom Richard Brinsley Sheridan was later to immortalize as Sir Fretful Plagiary in *The Critic*. Once again, Robert Mahon as Bellafont and Frances Ashmore as Maria led the cast. Others taking part were:

Frederick	Glenville
Sir Anthony Withers	Hollocombe
Henry	O'Keeffe
Shifter	Herbert
Ferdinand	Kane
Peter	Dodd
Paddy O'Connor	Dawson
Amelia	Mrs. Barre
Olivia	Mrs. Hoskins.

The arrival in Dublin of the French violinist Barthélemon on May 1, 1771, should be recalled, since his name is associated with two burletta seasons advertised to take place later in the year. As has already been briefly noted in Chapter 7, Barthélemon married the singer Polly Young in 1766. Since some minor inaccuracies concerning his birth and parentage still recur in musical dictionaries, it may be noted that he was christened not François Hippolyte but simply François.* (Hippolyte may have been his confirmation name which he began to use later.) His father was not a French government officer but a wig maker nor, as has been claimed by his daughter, was his

---

*The following is a transcript of his baptism certificate taken from the Register of the Parish Church of Saint-André, Bordeaux, now deposited at the Archives de la Ville:
'. . . du Samedi 29ᵉ Juillet 1741 à été baptisé Francois fils legitime de Emanuel Barthélemon perruquier et de Francoise Laroche paroisse St. Pierre parrain Francois Barthélemon marraine ~~Jeanne~~ Philippe Castaigna et à sa place Jeanne Barthélemon. Naquit le 27ᵉ de ce mois à 9 heures et demi du soir. Barthélemon père Barthélemon Jeanne Barthélemon. [Indecipherable initial] Marsin Curé.'

mother likely to have been 'an Irish lady of a wealthy family in the Queen's County'[36] for her name, Laroche, is far more indigenous to the Department of the Gironde than it is to the County Leix.

Barthélemon may or may not have been an officer of Berwick's Regiment in the Irish Brigade; his importance to this narrative commences with his arrival in London in 1765 where he became leader of the orchestra at the King's Theatre in the Haymarket. Apart from a number of brief visits to Paris he appears to have spent the next six years in England. In 1766 his opera *Pelopida* was produced at the King's Theatre, and during the season of 1769/70, accompanied by his wife, he joined the players at Marylebone Gardens. There he conducted a number of performances of *La Serva Padrona, or The Servant Mistress*, and also composed music for two other burlettas, *The Noble Pedlar* and *The Magic Girdle*. His wife, Polly Young, now announced as Mrs. Barthélemon, took part in all these performances.

These activities at Marylebone Gardens are of significance when related to the two following advertisements concerning burlettas in Dublin which appeared in 1771. The date of the first is October 5, and announced, 'Letters from Dublin mention that a Winter Ranelagh will be opened in that metropolis in the month of November, at which place Italian operas will be performed twice a week. Mr. and Mrs. Barthelemon are both engaged at the above place, and are to have, as we are well assured, the sum of one thousand guineas, besides two benefits for their performance there'.[37] The second, dated December 7, reports, 'A subscription is opened for 12 burlettas in the new Gardens [Rotunda] under the direction of Mr. Bartholoman [sic], which is the only entertainment we can expect, this winter, plays being out of fashion with us'.[38]

The question now is, did either of these burletta seasons take place? In considering this, it is first necessary to explain something about Ranelagh and the Rotunda. Ranelagh house and gardens in Dublin, which had originally been a bishop's residence, were opened by an organ builder named William Hollister on August 30, 1768, as 'a New Place for the Entertainment and Amusement of the Citizens in imitation of Ranelagh Gardens near London'.[39] They were situated 'a small distance beyond Northumberland-street, known at present by the name of Willibrook or Milltown Road'[40] and we learn that 'The House, with the Liberty of the Gardens, will be opened to receive Company through the Year, at any Hour after six in the Morning, for Breakfasting and in the Evening to drink Tea. A good Harpsichord and Fortepiana [sic] is provided for the Entertainment of such ladies as chuse it'.[41]

The Rotunda gardens were attached to the famous Lying-In Hospital founded by Dr. Bartholomew Mosse and were originally laid out in 1748 for the purpose of entertainment as at Ranelagh, but with the added worthy object of raising funds by concerts, balls, levees and assemblies for the maintenance of the hospital. The Round Room or Rotunda from which the hospital takes its present name had been built in 1767. An account of the gardens as they appeared between these two dates explains that 'One promenade led down to an octagonal coffee-house in the South-east corner which was used as a music room in inclement weather as well as the long room in Granby Row'.[42]

These descriptions confirm that burletta performances were at least practicable at both venues, since concert rooms existed there. In addition, John O'Keeffe relates that at Ranelagh a 'Burletta theatre was built out in the gardens: it had an orchestra, a fine band, and the favourite public singers stood or sat in the orchestra'.[43] It is unlikely, however, that it would have been used for this season. It was undoubtedly flimsily built, and *al fresco* performances during November and December would hardly have been attractive because of the cold.

Complementing these amenities there now was Barthélemon to direct, and his wife to sing, in an already rehearsed reportory from London – an opportunity for mounting a burletta season which would seem to have been ready-made. Yet no evidence whatsoever is forthcoming that either season took place. Indeed the announcement of a season of burlettas at both places following one another so closely rather suggests either some error on the part of newspapers, confusing

THE REV. SIR HENRY
BATE DUDLEY.
DRAMATIST AND
JOURNALIST
(1745–1824)

RICHARD DALY.
MANAGER AND ACTOR
(c. 1758–1813)

John O'Keeffe. Dramatist (1747–1833)

John Henry Johnstone. Tenor (1749–1826)

one venue with the other or, more likely, an attempt to establish a subscription season at the Rotunda, the season at Ranelagh having failed to materialise.

Barthélemon's name is first discovered among Dublin newspaper advertisements in June, 1771, when he was one of a number of artists who took part in a concert at the 'Great Musick-hall in Fishamble-street'.[44] Neither his name nor his wife's can be found among the artists performing at Ranelagh, though this of course does not preclude their engagement there – newspaper notices of these entertainments appeared only sporadically. Both certainly performed at the Rotunda, and productions of burlettas or operas were in fact presented at both places.

At Ranelagh, Dibdin and Bickerstaffe's burletta, *The Ephesian Matron or The Widow's Tears*, was advertised for July 23, 1771.[45] It was a suitable choice, for it had had its original performance at Ranelagh House, London, as part of a 'Jubilee Ridotto or Bal Paré'.[46] Earlier in the year it had been published 'that the Proprietor of Ranelagh at his sole Expense is putting up lamps from Ranelagh-gate to Northumberland street and will also continue to light these already erected by the spirited inhabitants from the corner of said Street to Dublin, every Concert Evening',[47] and in connection with the burletta performance it was now announced that 'The Gardens will be Illuminated'.[48] As ever, 'the Proprietor' was being put 'to a considerable Expense', and optimistically hoped 'to meet a Kind Reception from the Public'.[49] At the reasonable admission charge of 2/2, this he should have done, had his burletta not been turned into a form of farce.

The principal artists taking part were Miss Ashmore, Mrs. Hawtrey, Mr. Atkins and a Signor Fedela Rosselini. Little can be discovered of Signor Rosselini except that in April 1770, he had arrived at Ranelagh, Dublin, 'from Ranelagh House, London'.[50] He now proceeded to play Harlequin to Hollister's Pantaloon. The first indication of trouble appeared in an advertisement on July 27 which stated, 'The Proprietor of Ranelagh Gardens, is extremely concerned for the Disappointment the Company met with on Thursday Evening last, and begs leave to assure them, that it was intirely owing to the insolent Behaviour of

L

Signoir [sic] Rosselini, who refused to sing his Part in the Entertainment'.[51]

To this pronouncement Rosselini delivered an indignant denial. He declared, in convoluted English '. . as Mr. Hollister either cannot or will not tell Truth, Rosselini will take the Liberty to explain to the Public what his intentions were upon this Occasion: Mr. Hollister found it necessary, from his bad success, to change his Plan of Entertainment; and the Burletta Scheme occurred. Good singers were to be provided; he was in Possession of Rosselini, but it was expedient to make him an Actor. At first then, he was to sing, as usual with his Book in his Hand (in a language of which he was unskilled. What a villainous Design was this to ruin the Reputation of Rosselini, and what a Mockery of the Town!)'.[52] The result of this discord was the postponement of the opening performance of *The Ephesian Matron* until August 1, 1771, when, *sans* Rosselini, it 'met with universal pprobation'.[53]

At the Rotunda,September on 11, 'a new set of Concerts'[54] had commenced, and on November 7 a series of twenty-one winter concerts, 'one each Week on Thursday evening',[55] was inaugurated. Once again, reports of these concerts appear only infrequently, but neither Mr. nor Mrs. Barthélemon's name is to be found among them. However, on March 24, 1772, the following announcement at last proves that opera was performed at the Rotunda. It states, 'For the Benefit of the Lying-in-Hospital . . the celebrated opera of Artaxerxes will be presented at the Theatre in Smock Alley, on Thursday evening next, conducted in the same manner, *as it was performed at the Rotunda.** The Dresses, which are of the manufacture of Ireland, are allowed to be the most elegant of the Kind ever exhibited in this Kingdom. The Tickets of the Subscribers to the Rotunda Concerts will be admitted to any Part of the House'.[56] And, in a notice of this performance at Smock Alley on March 26, the Barthélemons' names at last appear in opera. 'Mrs. Bartlemon' [sic], we learn, 'was clear and excelled in her songs; and Mr. Bartlemon discovered upon this, as

*The italics are the writer's.

upon every other occasion, a Taste and Execution on the Violin, that proves him one of the first Performers in the World, on that Instrument'.[57]

A lapse of almost two years now occurred before the next English opera to have a vogue was produced in Dublin. This was an adaptation of Monsigny's *Le Déserteur* by Charles Dibdin. Musically it had been much altered from the original. From a list of fifteen airs and an overture, five airs only were by Monsigny, two by Philidor and five by Dibdin. A literal translation of Sedaine's original text had been sent to Dibdin by 'the Hon. Mr. Debourg, a gentleman whose taste in elegance and the arts was equal to the courage which so honourably distinguished him in America[58]* and from it Dibdin fashioned his libretto.

The Deserter was first performed at Smock Alley Theatre (then under the management of the actor, Thomas Ryder, 'the Roscius of Dublin'[59]) on February 10, 1774. It was advertised with 'entire new Scenery, Machinery, Dresses and Decorations'.[60] The cast was:

Henry	Mahon
Russet	Wilder
Simkin	Miell
Skirmish	Vandermere
Flint	Jackson
Soldiers	Glenville, Chaplain, Baker, Crosby
Jenny	Mrs. Miell
Margaret	Mrs. Hoskins
Louisa	Miss Ashmore, now Mrs. Richard Sparks.

'The music' was 'conducted'[61] by the violinist Thomas Pinto who had arrived in Dublin the previous year accompanied by his wife, *née*

---

*The heroic gentleman remains unidentified, but was he a Mr. Du Bourg who in 1785 held 'a public Exhibition of his celebrated collection of Cork Models of Roman and English Antiquities at the Great Room, Spring Gardens'† London? When, alas, the Great Room caught fire, intrepid as ever, 'the first object of that meritorious artist's attention was to save "Windsor Castle." His Loyalty was that of an honest Englishman, to think of the model of his Sovereign's residence, in preference to all other considerations.'‡ Or was he Jacques Barbeu-Dubourg, translator, historian, physician, botanist, and French disciple of Benjamin Franklin?

†*Morning Herald* (London), February 28, 1785.

‡*Morning Herald* (London), May 3, 1785.

Charlotte Brent, and daughter – by his former marriage to Sybilla Gronamann. It will be remembered that both these ladies had already sung in Dublin, Gronamann in 1743, Brent in 1755. Of this second visit, John O'Keeffe, who had heard Charlotte Brent when she first sang Mandane in 1762, laconically remarks, 'it was then autumn with her'.[62]

Thomas Pinto was born in London in 1714. Almost sixty years later a theatrical speculation at Marylebone Gardens in which he had been associated with Dr. Arnold having failed, he took refuge in Ireland to escape his creditors.

In Dublin he was appointed leader of the orchestra at Smock Alley Theatre, retaining the post from 1773 until 1779. O'Keeffe remembers him as being 'very capital' but 'rather absent in mind'[63] and his description of his conducting gives an excellent assessment of orchestral performance in Dublin at this time. He relates that 'When the person, whose office it was to prepare and supply the performers who composed the band with their respective parts, and have them ready laid in their places in the orchestra, as his duty required, would ask Pinto what pieces he chose to have played such and such a night, he was generally answered with "Pho! pho! lay the parts all along in the orchestra, that's enough." And without any previous practice or trial of the band, at the proper time Pinto would step into the orchestra, take up his violin, just throw a glance on the bit of music paper before him, give three taps of his bow on the desk, and off set the whole concert in full and complete harmony'.[64] O'Keeffe then continues, 'When the opera of the Deserter was first got over to Dublin, he looked at the overture of it, and touched a few of the notes. I was standing near him, and never saw a man in greater rapture, or more delighted, than he was with the beauties of that composition: and well did he play it, and had it played, managing the pianos, fortes and crescendos with most effective skill'.[65] Greater virtuosity was never demonstrated, not even by Sir Thomas Beecham!

Pinto was to die in Dublin in 1783, leaving his wife penniless. On May 2 of that year we read '. . Poor Pinto's widow, the quondam most popular singer of Covent Garden – Miss Brent – is now condescending to accept an eleemosynary concert at the Exhibition Room in William-street. And this concert it is thought expedient to buckram up with a ball'.[66] The following October, 'a meeting was held of the Society of Musicians at the Feather's Tavern, in the Strand, to take into consideration the distressed situation of Mrs. Pinto, the once celebrated Miss Brent, and grant such relief as with propriety could be allowed of, she having lost her claim to that charity from Mr. Pinto's having neglected his contributions to it'.[67] On March 15, 1785, she was announced to play Polly in *The Beggar's Opera* at the Theatre Royal, Haymarket, 'Being her last Appearance on the Stage'.[68] She did, however, make one further appearance when, about five weeks later, on April 22 at Covent Garden, she sang the air 'Sweet Echo' in a performance of *Comus* which, W. T. Parke sympathetically recalls, 'she sung with an unexpected degree of excellence and was loudly applauded'.[69] She died in the habitual poverty which besets most aged singers, at London in 1802.

Among her roles at Smock Alley Theatre had been Urganda in Michael Arne's *Cymon,* and in a performance of this opera announced for April 23, 1774, she was joined by Michael Arne's wife, who sang the role of Sylvia, 'being her first Appearance in this Kingdom'.[70] This was Michael Arne's second wife, and late pupil, Ann Venables, who had made her first appearance at Drury Lane Theatre on November 12, 1772, as Philadel in *King Arthur*. A notice of her performance records that 'her figure is small, but pleasing; her features are marking, and well calculated for creating the necessary effect the stage often requires. At present, no great compliment can be paid her as a singer; she appears to be the unfinished scholar of an able Master. How polished and perfect she may be rendered by good instructions, and much practice, cannot be foreseen; but there certainly is great room for improvement'.[71]

In August, 1774, the Pinto family had a benefit performance at Crow Street Theatre for which they chose *Artaxerxes*. It was notable for presenting Miss Pinto as Arbaces, 'her first appearance on any Stage',[72] and for a *contretemps* which led to the postponement of the opera from August 23 to August 30. This was 'on account of the Key of the Pit Door being mislaid', for which mishap Mr. Pinto hastened to beg 'Leave to assure his Friends and the Public, that they need be under no Apprehensions of another Disappointment, as the Doors will be opened punctually at 6 o'clock, and the performance being precisely at 7'.[73]

The year 1775 brought a second opera by Michael Arne to Dublin, for what would to-day be extravagantly described as a world *première*. This was *The Maid of the Vale*, the libretto 'translated and altered'[74] from Goldoni's *La Buona Figliuola* by Thomas Holcroft. (Holcroft had been prompter at the Capel Street Theatre under Dawson for a season, but by 1775 he had returned to England.) The first perform-ance took place at Smock Alley Theatre on February 15, with the following cast:

Lord Lovewell	Mahon
Sir John Lofty	Glenville
Kriegsman	Wilder
Robin	Vandermere
Lady Lucy	Mrs. Lee
Fanny	Mrs. Arne
Phillis	Mrs. Sparks
Susan	Mrs. Tisdall
An old woman, nurse to Fanny	N.N.
Sportsmen, Servants, Ruffians.[75]	

'Entire new scenery, new Dresses and other Decorations' were assured, 'With an additional Orchestra conducted by Mr. Arne'.[76] The production was well received and we learn that 'Mr. Arne in his Composition of the Musick of The Maid in [sic] the Vale, has given the Publick another striking Proof of his excellence in that way'.[77] It was to have six performances during the season, the last, for Arne's benefit, taking place on March 29. On March 14, Mrs. Arne had taken her benefit as Polly 'for the first Time'[78] in *The Beggar's Opera*.

The following intriguing notice was next published on August 7, 1775. 'A gentleman just arrived from Dubl'n informs us, that half a dozen Irish noblemen, at the head of whom is the musical Lord M-g-l-n, have taken Crow Street house from Mr. Barry, for the purpose of having Italian Operas there next winter, and that a subscription has been opened, and near one thousand pounds already subscribed'.[79] Nothing came of it, however; it was just one of a number of seasons which were provisionally planned during these years but which never reached the stage. The head of the half dozen Irish noblemen referred to can probably be deciphered correctly as Lord Mornington. This distinguished peer, who may be punctiliously described as an amateur musician of professional standard, achieved the double distinction of being the father of the Duke of Wellington and the first Professor of Music at Dublin University.

On November 17, 1775, at Smock Alley Theatre, a Dublin audience could at last applaud an opera composed by a Dublin musician. This was *The Rival Candidates* by Charles Thomas Carter, which for good measure had a librettist with Irish associations, the Reverend Sir Henry Bate Dudley. The principal roles were taken by Robson (?Robinson), Willis, Vandermere, Jackson, Wilder, Glenville, Tyrell, Mrs. Wilson and Miss Jameson, and we read that 'The scenery, which has been a considerable Time preparing at a great Expense, is entirely new and painted by Mr. Whitmore'.[80]

Little news of the opera can be found in the Dublin papers except that it had been 'acted Thirty Nights successively'[81] at Drury Lane Theatre during the previous season, and that five songs from it would be published by 'John Lee at No. 64 Dame-street'.[82] Of the original Drury Lane production, we learn that 'Upon the whole the author has fully answered the end he proposed of introducing a deserving young composer whose name it seems is Carter to the public, and who more than promises to be a composer of taste and genius'.[83]

The author was undoubtedly the principal partner in this undertaking, a matter of no surprise when one learns something about the life and times of the Reverend Sir Henry Bate Dudley. Originally known to his acquaintances as Parson Bate – he was to assume the additional name of Dudley in 1784 to comply with the will of a relative – it was said of him that he 'was more calculated to wield the sword than the crosier'.[84] Having taken Holy Orders, he succeeded to the rectory of North Fambridge in Essex but spent most of his time in London, leading a highly fashionable life.

In 1773, an affray at Vauxhall Gardens gained him considerable notoriety, whereupon he became curate to James Townley, vicar of Hendon and author of the celebrated farce, *High life below stairs*. The association of pulpit and stage had evidently proved irresistible to both reverend gentlemen. Bate next became editor of *The Morning Post,* where the vindictiveness of his articles provoked frequent duels and earned him the nickname of the 'Fighting Parson'. In 1781 he was committed to King's Bench prison for a libel on the Duke of Richmond, and a short time later was banished to Ireland.

Through the influence of the Lord Lieutenant, the Earl of Carlisle, he was there appointed to a rectory in the diocese of Ferns. After some delay, due to a natural reluctance on the part of his bishop to institute him, he was appointed prebend of the parish of Kilscoran in County Wexford, eventually becoming chancellor of the diocese. He was a friend of Garrick and his circle, played the 'cello and was a connoisseur of talented young opera composers for, as well as Carter, he was to discover William Shield.

Much less is known of Carter than of Bate Dudley and what is known is complicated by what in certain quarters will undoubtedly be considered to be typical Irish perversity, for in a land of so few composers, during the latter part of the eighteenth century there were three with the same name. Some distinction can be made between them since the musician who concerns us was christened Charles Thomas, though later he was familiarly known as 'Tom'; the second was named plain Thomas, and the third can be traced to 1809 which was after Charles Thomas's death.

The date of his birth is uncertain. In was certainly after 1734, the year usually given, if he can still be described as a 'deserving young composer' as late as 1775. O'Keeffe relates that, as a boy, Carter had been in the choir of Christ Church Cathedral and was later appointed organist at St. Werburgh's Church, a post he held until 1769.

According to Dr. Grattan-Flood, he then married a Miss Margaret May, and set off for London. It is here that ambiguity arises between the two names.

It was probably Charles Thomas who, in 1785, described as 'Poor Carter', was announced as making 'an unsuccessful attempt in the musical line at Windsor from which he hoped to have attracted Royal favour. He has composed an anthem for the chapel there in which there is such an injudicious mixture of antient melody and modern bass, that it has been forbidden to be again performed'.[85] Yet one cannot be certain, for two years later we learn, 'It is not Mr. Carter, who is candidate for the Organist place at St. George's, but Carter, the Piano Forte performer, and composer of the Rival Candidates'.[86] The *Dictionary of National Biography* pithily sums up the situation when, having explained that Thomas Carter had died of a liver complaint in 1800, it then continues , 'The Dictionary of Musicians (1827) and Georgian Era (iv 526) have transferred the younger Carter's age, liver, widow and children to the elder musician, thus creating a remarkable confusion'. Between 1775 and 1792, Charles Thomas was to compose a number of operas for Drury Lane and Covent Garden Theatres. These included *The Milesians, The Fair American* and *Just in Time*. He died in London on October 12, 1804.

Among the artists taking part in the Dublin production of *The Rival Candidates*, Miss Jameson, lately arrived from London, was to have a successful career on the Dublin stage. She was a pupil of T. A. Arne and made her first London stage appearance at Covent Garden Theatre as Rosetta in *Love in a Village* on September 29, 1773. The *Westminster Magazine* considered that 'Her musical powers were not extraordinary; her acting powers still worse'.[87]

An extract from a Dublin letter published in London on January 1, 1776, which reported that 'Crow-street is to be opened about the middle of January by a company of Italians, and some very capital singers'[88] is merely a prolongation of the news published during the previous August, and equally unreliable. This inaccurate news was supplemented on January 9 by the information that 'An Irish

paper says, that Mr. Ross and Mrs. Fitzhenry* are the managers of
the company that are to open Crow-street theatre, and that they have
engaged some very capital Italian singers for the purpose of entertaining the town twice a week with operas'.[89]

Faulty press information was, of course, not unusual at this period.
Nevertheless these London announcements are exceptional since at
precisely the same time the Dublin newspapers were releasing
completely contrary and, in the outcome, accurate news. For example,
on January 4, 1776, the following notice was published by *The
Freeman's Journal*. 'Mr. Arne. Deeply impressed with a most grateful
sense of the generous encouragement wherewith he had hitherto
been honoured by the Nobility and Gentry of this Kingdom, and
being therefore ambitious to establish himself here, under their
Favour and Protection, has undertaken the Conduct of English
Operas, both Serious and Comic; Burlettas and all musical performances, to be represented alternately on every Monday and Thursday evening during the remainder of the season. He has for this
purpose engaged the Theatre in Crow Street, together with the
compleat Company of Vocal and Instrumental Performers; flattering
himself that by his assiduous endeavours 'he cannot fail to render
this pleasing species of entertainment satisfactory to the Public'.[90]

Michael Arne's season opened on January 18 with his opera *Cymon*.
Among those taking part were Miss Pinto as Urganda and Mrs. Arne
as Sylvia. *Faulkner's Dublin Journal* was eulogistic, declaring that
'The Performance from first to last (with the Addition of a noble
Band, conducted by Mr. Arne, and led by Mr. Pinto) was chaste,
just and elegant, and the Characters were supported with the greatest
Spirit and Propriety of Action'.[91] Such praise was not universal, the
above notice provoking the following ironic response: 'A correspondent deeply impressed with gratitude, for Mr. Arne's acknowledged
humble endeavours to please in a new manner by inexperienced

---

*Elizabeth Fitzhenry was a noted Dublin actress who had first appeared at Smock Alley in
1754. Ross was probably David Ross, a minor singing actor who had performed at Smock Alley
Theatre under Thomas Sheridan's management. In a performance of *The Beggar's Opera* in
1749, Macheath was announced to be attempted by Mr. Ross'. (Reported by Esther K. Sheldon
in *Thomas Sheridan of Smock Alley*. p. 400.)

performers declares he totally agrees with that classical paragraph which stiled the first night's performance at Crow Street Opera House: "Chaste," because Shakespeare has said "as chaste as ice" and there is no doubt an equal degree of coldness was maintained'.[92] The season continued until April. Among other operas, *Artaxerxes* was presented, with Ann Catley as Mandane, Francis Passerini as Artaxerxes and Miss Pinto as Arbaces.

Catley seems to have been the only attraction – if the London newspapers can be believed – the *Morning Chronicle* announcing that she had been engaged 'at the enormous salary of *eighty guineas* per week: – when she plays, the house overflows; on other nights it has a very poverty-smitten aspect indeed'.[93] At her fee, *The Gazette* was to marvel, 'This is equal to the salary paid the most celebrated Italian singer ever engaged in this Kingdom' and then admonish the insouciant Irish with the following comment: 'If such a salary can be paid to a performer in a public amusement, none can pretend to say that that country where such is given can be in ruinous condition. Certainly the people must be either in a most flourishing state, or deprived of their senses.'[94] Whether due to Ann Catley's extravagant salary, or the 'poverty-smitten' houses on the nights when she did not perform, the result was disaster for Arne, and on April 20 we read, of his 'unfortunate Failure, in the Management of Crow-street Theatre'.[95]

During 1776, two other operas which are of interest were performed, one at Smock Alley, the second at Crow Street. The Smock Alley production on January 11 was *Artaxerxes* and introduced Signora Salvagni as Arbaces, 'being her 2nd appearance upon any stage'.[96] Her first may have taken place at the King's Theatre in London on March 17, 1774, where she sang Cecchina in Piccini's *La Buona Figliuola*. Primarily, however, she was a concert singer appearing in concerts at the Pantheon during the same period. She first appeared in Dublin in May, 1774, where she had been engaged for concerts at the Rotunda Gardens. There, her programmes frequently included a duet from *La Buona Figliuola*.

The second opera, at Crow Street, which was performed almost a year later on December 4, was of more importance and was the first production in Dublin of Dibdin's *The Waterman, or The First of August* with Robert Owenson in the role of Tom Tug.

Owenson was a Connaught man from County Mayo who had anglicised his name from the original Gaelic Mac Eoghan. He was born in 1744 and as a boy had little formal education. He did have the talents of a good ear and a fine natural voice which enabled him to acquire a repertory of old Gaelic songs. He also had the good fortune to be befriended by a wealthy patron, a Mr. Blake, who had returned to his Irish estates from the West Indies. Blake brought him to London where he arranged for T. A. Arne to hear him sing. Arne declared Owenson's voice 'to be one of the finest baritones he had ever heard, and particularly susceptible to that quality of intonation . . the falsetto'.[97] In London he became friendly with Oliver Goldsmith – a distant relation – and had singing lessons and a certain amount of elementary education. At singing classes a fellow pupil was Mrs. Weichsel, mother of the subsequently celebrated Elizabeth Billington. In her *Memoirs,* Owenson's daughter, Lady Morgan, applauds an affair which developed between her father and Mrs. Weichsel, but Mr. Blake held more puritanical views and peremptorily dismissed him from his patronage with, however, a not ungenerous golden handshake of a banker's order for £300. Owenson turned at once to his kinsman, Goldsmith, who introduced him to David Garrick and so he made the theatre his career.

He had a good appearance, stood six feet tall, and in time was to acquire a commanding stage presence. He became renowned for his performance of Irish character parts, but his London schooling seems to have caused him to fall, dramatically, between two stools. It was said that 'In the higher class of Irish characters (old officers &c) he looked well, but did not exhibit sufficient dignity; and in the *lowest,* his humour was scarcely quaint and original enough; but in what might be termed the *middle class of Paddies,* no man ever combined the look and manner with such felicity'.[98] He in fact seems to have been what one would today consider an entirely natural actor, for the above commentator in a mildly critical vein adds, 'he acted as if he had not received too much schooling, and sang like a man whom nobody had instructed'.[99] The distinguishing characteristic which he brought to the Irish stage, where both in Dublin and the provinces his career was to run from 1776 to 1798, was his unique ability to sing old Irish songs in the original Gaelic. O'Keeffe describes this capacity as having 'great effect with the admirers of our national melody'.[100] He 'grew old without growing rich'[101] and was to die in Dublin in 1812.

The cast of the Dublin production of *The Waterman* also included John O'Keeffe as Mr. Bundle, Kennedy 'Jun'. as Robin (the Gardener), Miss Potter as Wilhelmina and Mrs. Thompson as Mrs. Bundle.[102]

Mrs. Thompson, a recent arrival from London, had previously been married to Joseph Vernon, the singing actor, whom she had divorced in favour of a 'linen-draper of some consequence in the city'.[103] His consequence in the marriage unfortunately did not endure, and soon Mrs. Thompson was having an affair with Charles Bannister of Drury Lane Theatre. This provoked the following acerbic quatrain from George Colman, manager of the Haymarket Theatre, on being informed that she could not attend a rehearsal of *Thomas and Sally* due to having fallen down stairs.

'So, Madam Dorcas, in your airs,
You send us word you cannot stir,
Because you've tumbled down the stairs,
And *fell* against a Bannister'.[104]

She was undoubtedly an accomplished singing actress, upon whom, it was said, 'the critic may repose his eye, his ear, and his judgement, with satisfaction, nor venture to wish for an amendment'.[105]

The libretto of *The Waterman* was by Charles Dibdin, the music partly composed and partly selected by him. The entertainment had been devised from a selection of ballads originally composed for Ranelagh and the theatres, and which had 'been but little heard'.[106] Dibdin explains, 'I thought I could not better employ my leisure time than in furnishing, upon some familiar plan, the dialogue necessary to work up these materials into a ballad farce'.[107] It was leisure time well spent, for even during the eighteenth century this little opera was to travel abroad for production as far as Jamaica and the United States, while as late as 1911 it was still being performed at Covent Garden, as a farewell benefit matinée for Sir Charles Stanley. No report of the first Dublin performance can be discovered, but the libretto of the opera and some airs from it were published at the time by John Beatty of 32 Skinner Row.[108]

Meanwhile, during November, 1776, the following announcement was published by three discontented players who were seceding from Thomas Ryder's company, taking others with them. 'Messrs. Vandermere, Waddy and Sparks present their humblest Respects to the Public, and beg leave to inform them, that they have contracted with Mr. William Gibson, Proprietor of the Music Hall in Fishamble-street for the furnishing of an Elegant Theatre which will be ready in a few weeks.'[109] Ryder had taken a lease on the Crow Street Theatre during the previous May and, having renovated and decorated it, had transferred his company there, meanwhile closing down Smock Alley.

The Fishamble Street Theatre, having been 'fitted up in the most elegant Manner',[110] opened its doors on January 27, 1777.[111] The season's productions included a number of popular comic operas already performed in Dublin such as *The Deserter, Lionel and Clarissa, The Padlock, The Jovial Crew, Love in a Village* and *Daphne and Amintor*.

There were also performances of two operas new to Dublin. The first of these, a noteworthy production at Fishamble Street, was *The Duenna, or The Double Elopement* by Richard Brinsley Sheridan and Thomas Linley. A dilemma arises in deciding exactly when this opera did have its first Dublin performance. The problem is due to the perpetual competition existing between the rival theatres, for a comic opera called *The Governess* which was a pirated version of *The Duenna* was produced by Thomas Ryder at Crow Street on February 1, 1777.[112] Just how far removed from the original this production was it is impossible to say, but since the names of the characters were altered–for example Isaac Mendoza became Enoch Issachar, Donna

Louisa and Donna Clara became Flora and Sophia–and the production was described, admittedly in an announcement advertising the subsequent Fishamble Street performances, as 'curtailed, altered' and having 'two Characters confusedly blended in one',[113] it is difficult to accept Ryder's achievement as the authentic first performance. The performance at Fishamble Street was declared to 'be represented in the Manner it first came out, and was so universally admired on the English Stage'. Added to this, the correspondent comments, 'the band of Music at Fishamble Theatre, being so vastly superior to any other in this City and the Songs being rehearsed under the Direction of Mr. Arne, cannot fail to make this opera to be capitally performed'.[114]

Capitally performed it undoubtedly was on its original production at Drury Lane in 1775. As has been quoted many times, Tom Moore, in his *Memoirs of the Life of Sheridan,* records, 'Sixty-three nights was the career of the *Beggar's Opera,* but the *Duenna* was acted no less than seventy-five times during the season, the only intermissions being a few weeks at Christmas, and the Fridays on every week; – the latter on account of Leoni, [the Don Carlos] who, being a Jew could not act on those nights'.[115] A century and a half later it was just as viable, when it had a London run of one hundred and forty-one nights at the Lyric Theatre, Hammersmith.

Of Richard Brinsley Sheridan, the librettist, it need only be recollected in passing that he was Thomas Sheridan's son, born in Dublin in 1751, and the author of the best eighteenth-century comedy in the English language – *The School for Scandal.*

'The Music partly New and partly selected from the most Eminent Composers'[116] was arranged by Thomas Linley, Sheridan's father-in-law. Linley, who was born in 1733, first established himself as a singing master at Bath. In 1776 he purchased a part share in Drury Lane Theatre, where he became musical arranger.

Various letters passing between them testify that their collaboration in *The Duenna* was a happy one. Sheridan begs his father-in-law to come to London from Bath to superintend the musical rehearsals, and asks, 'Could not you leave Tom [Linley's son] to superintend the concert for a few days?'[117] while a postscript from Sheridan's wife adds, 'Dearest father, I shall have no spirits or hopes of the opera, unless we see you'.[118] Sheridan also whimsically writes, 'I shall profit by your proposed alterations but I'd have you to know that we are much too chaste in London to admit such strains as your Bath spring inspires. We dare not propose a peep beyond the ankle on any account, for the critics in the pit at a new play are much greater prudes than the ladies in the boxes'.[119] Since Linley either could not or would not come to London, their correspondence is valuable in identifying some of the music employed in the *pasticcio*. It also reveals that Sheridan took a very active interest in the selection of the music and demonstrates his sure theatrical instinct in its arrangement throughout the opera.

He writes to Linley that he has received the songs 'Banna's banks' and 'De'il take the wars' which he 'had words for before they arrived, which answer excessively well'.[120] 'Banna's banks' is now much better known as 'The Harp that once through Tara's Halls'. In Act 1 of the opera it became 'Had I a heart for falsehood framed', while 'De'il take the wars' was transformed into 'When sable night, each drooping plant restoring'. He sends in return 'another for Miss Brown'[121] – Donna Clara. This is undoubtedly the bravura air 'Adieu, thou dreary pile' from Act 3, for we read that she 'sings hers in a joyful mood; we want her to show in it as much execution as she is capable of, which is pretty well; and, for variety, we want Mr. Simpson's hautboy to cut a figure, with replying passages, &c . . to abet which, I have lugged in "Echo", who is always allowed to play her part'.[122] 'Dr. Harrington's Catch'[123] which he had decided upon as a trio between Don Antonio, Isaac Mendoza and Father Paul, seems to have been deleted early – if it was ever performed – for it does not appear in a vocal score published about 1790/1800 by Broderip and Wilkinson. The air, 'Wind, gentle Evergreen' became the catch ending Act 2, sung to the words, 'Soft pity never leaves the gentle breast', and the songs 'Let's drink and let's sing' and 'How merrily we live' became the jolly chorus in six-eight time, 'The bottle's the sun of our table' and 'Let mirth and glee abound!' in Act 3. These choruses, Sheridan advises, are to be 'sung by a company of *friars* over their wine. The words will be parodied, and the chief effect must arise from their being *known*; for the joke will be much less for these jolly fellows to sing anything new, than to give what the audience are used to annex the idea of jollity to'.[124] Of the 'comic' song, 'O the days when I was young' sung by Don Jerome at the beginning of Act 3, he tells Linley, 'I have written it to your tune . . I think it will do vastly well for the words: Don Jerome sings them when he is in particular spirits . . We have mislaid the notes, but Tom remembers it'.[125]

The overture and five other pieces were by Linley's son, Thomas. These were a simple ballad in two-four time, 'Could I each fault remember' and a more elaborate song, 'Friendship is the bond of reason', both occurring in Act 1. He also composed a trio beginning 'Never may'st thou happy be' which ended the finale to this act. For the complete finale, Sheridan* had earlier sent precise instructions to Linley senior as to what was required, down to a 'flourish' in an air for Leoni since 'he never gets so much applause as when he makes a cadence'.[126] The younger Linley also composed a little duet, 'Turn thee round I pray thee' and a song 'Sharp is the woe' of which Sheridan had written, 'I could wish to be a broken, passionate affair, and the first two lines may be recitative, [which they are] or what you please, uncommon'.[127]

Thomas Linley junior was born at Bath in 1756. He showed decided musical precociousness as a child and in 1770 was sent to Florence for further tuition. There he became friendly with the young Mozart, who was just four months older. Like Mozart, his life too was short – much shorter – for he was to drown in a boating accident at the age of twenty-two.

The Dublin production at Fishamble Street Theatre attracted considerable attention from the newspapers. Undoubtedly the opera's fame had preceded it from London. Undoubtedly, too, competition between the two Dublin theatres, each performing the same opera in one or other version, was intense. The first performance

*See *The Rise of English Opera* by Eric Walter White. London 1951. pp. 71/73, where this letter is extensively quoted.

M

took place on February 21, 1777 – three weeks exactly after *The Governess* – and the following unusually detailed notice appeared three days later:

'The Author of this opera has most happily hit the Genius and Disposition of the Audience; the Language is familiar, elegant and pure; the Similies most ingeniously adapted to the Characters, and the Characters finely contrasted; every Incident is new, and without the least Similitude to each other. The Jew, the old Man and the Duenna kept the House in a Roar; their Sarcasm on each other, and the manner in which they expose their own Foibles are highly entertaining, and what gives much Honour to the Author, and Reputation of a Piece, it is devoid of Buffoonery, Ribaldry and Obsenity.

'The Performers have very judiciously fell into the idea of their Author which they support with great Propriety in their Performance. The converted Jew appears as a cunning, scheming, immoral, vain Knave, who falls a Sacrifice to his own Machinations, and Mr. Vandermere performed it with that Propriety and genuine Humour, which has ranked him high in the comic line of this Age. The old Man (Don Jerome) was finely played by Mr. Moss; he supported the firm old Buck with great Spirit, and sung with so much Humour, that he was encored thrice in one Song. Jerome should not be represented as a debilitated old Man, the Author has drawn him a hale, merry old Fellow, full of Glee and good Nature, but avaricious and testy. It would be hard to determine, whether Glenville in Father Paul, or Doyle in the starved Lay-brother was best supported, the Contrast was highly laughable, and Mr. Glenville did great Justice to the Wit of his Author, as did the Rest of his Brethren to the "Bottles" which lay before them, and the Glee they sung. Mr. Waddy was obliged to play one of the Lovers, and an Apology informed the Audience that he undertook it at 4 hours' Notice; he acted the part well, and if he has musical Talents, should continue in it. Johnson, who played the Lover, is much improved, he was excellent in the singing Parts, and executed them with greater vivacity than usual. Mrs. Arne and Miss Jameson spoke and sung the Parts of Louisa and Clara with Justness and Taste, they were repeatedly encored, and the latter's Voice was so exquisite in singing 'Adieu thou dreary Pile' that the Audience seemed enraptured, they not only encored her, but after she had left the Stage, gave her three several Plaudits. Mrs. Remington played old Margaret, the Duenna, and in Appearance and Playing, was far superior to Mrs. Green, who played it originally, with the highest Reputation. Her Humour and Figure were inimitably supported and finished, and those who have seen the Opera in London, acknowledged that in the Love Scene between Isaac and Margaret, Vandermere and Mrs. Remington far exceeded the original Performance.

'Much of the Merit of this Exhibition is undoubtedly due to the Labour, Skill and Taste of Mr. Arne; the Band was excellent, and the Accompanyments gave universal Satisfaction. But the Duenna has not, as yet, been perfectly performed, there were a few Inaccuracies, which Rehearsals only can mend, and a Spectator only can point out. Isaac should be more deform'd, Clara should appear as a Nun during the last Scene. Don Jerome should be more emphatical in pronouncing his last Speeches, and the Songs should be sung nearer the Audience, for the Benefit of those in the Gallery. The last Scene of Mrs. Cornelli's Recesses was extremely pretty, there were other Scenes wanting; but it is not doubted that the Managers will pay a due Attention to these Matters, and that on this, and the future Nights, the Public will have a highly perfect Representation.'[128]

Such commendation should have guaranteed the opera's success, but in the *ambiance* of the theatre, comedy can quickly change to drama, or to melodrama. A whiff of drama was wafted on stage in mid-March when it was announced 'that a Bill is fyled in the Court of Chancery by the Managers of the Theatre Royal, Covent Garden, for an injunction to stop the representation of the Comic Opera of "The Duenna" at the New Theatre in Fishamble-street'.[129] By mid-April, the scene had changed to the Court of Chancery and melodrama with patriotic overtones – inherent in all good melodramas – was being performed.

'The great question concerning literary property', we are informed, 'received yesterday a final decision in the Court of Chancery. The matter in debate was conversant about a favourite Opera called the "Duenna" which the Managers of Covent Garden alleged they had purchased from Richard Brinsley Sheridan, Esq., the author, for a certain stipulated sum. Under this assignment the English Managers, alleging a sole and exclusive property in the piece, entitled the "Duenna", complained against *John Byron Vandermere* and his partners, adventurers in a new Theatre in Fishamble-street, for having exhibited on their Stage the said piece, called "The Duenna", and prayed that they might be restrained and injoined from printing, publishing or acting said piece. After hearing the debates on this question by the advocates on both sides, the Lord Chancellor gave his sentiments on the whole, viz, that the injunction sought by the plaintiffs to restrain the acting or exhibiting the piece ought not to be granted. He confined himself merely to the matter of acting, as he imagined that to be the only object relied on, in the case. By this decision, an arbitrary restraint by English despots can no longer prevent this oppressed country from being a little entertained, as a consolation in times when they are greatly taxed'.[130] What makes this particular blow struck for Ireland unique is that it was in defence of opera!

The second new opera, which was performed on March 7, 1777, was *A Christmas Tale,* the libretto by David Garrick, the music by the ubiquitous Charles Dibdin. The text was an adaptation of C. S. Favart's libretto, *La Fée Urgèle ou Ce qui plait aux Dames,* which had been set to music by Duni in 1765. Of the first production at Drury Lane it was stated, 'This piece was written by Mr. G. which he wrote in a hurry and on purpose to Shew some fine Scenes which were designed by Mons. De Loutherberg particularly a Burning Palace &c which was extremely fine and Novel' – and, as a rapier-like afterthought, 'The Music by Mr. Dibdin, the worst he Compos'd!'[131] W. T. Parke confirms that it 'was got up with great splendour'. De Loutherbourg's scenery was lit by 'his newly-invented transparent shades, so much admired afterwards in his popular exhibition called "The Eidophusicon" which by shedding on them a vast body and brilliancy of colour, produced an almost enchanting effect'.[132]

The production in Dublin, too, appears to have been unusually lavish, and we read of a 'grand Prospect of Camila's Garden and the Enchanted Laurel – A View of Bonora's Cell and the Destruction of Nigromant, the Enchanter's Castle – with a View of the Fiery Lake'.[133] The opera was conducted by Michael Arne and the cast consisted of Vandermere, Johnson, Gaudry, Kelly, Mrs. Remington, Miss Pope, Mrs. Osborn, Mrs. White and Mrs. Arne. We read that 'The House will be illuminated with wax' and – an innovation – 'Proper Persons are appointed to conduct the Company to the different parts of the Theatre'.[134] A notice of the performance reports that it 'had its Applause, and indeed meritoriously, for the music is well adapted and in the part of Tycho, Vandermere was so inimitable as to keep the House in continual Laughter. The Scenery is something which far surpasses both in Beauty and Taste, anything we have seen since the time of Carver'.[135]

At Crow Street Theatre during the same period there was one other opera produced which deserves scrutiny. This was a performance of *The Shamrock, or Saint Patrick's Day,* which took place on April 15, 1777.

It was announced as 'Mrs. O'Keeffe's Night . . (for that Night only) a new Comedy of two Acts, never performed here, called the Shamrock; or Saint Patrick's Day as it is now acting at the Theatres in London with universal Applause. Written by the Author of a certain much admired Comic Opera. The principal Characters by Mr. Clinch, Mr. O'Keeffe, Mr. Owenson, Mr. Kennedy, junr., Mr. G. Dawson, Mr. Parker, Miss Potter, with the original Song, and Mrs. Heaphy. After the Farce will be exhibited a grand emblematical Festive Choral Procession and Pagent; consisting of Kings of Leinster, Ulster, Munster and Connaught; Strangbow [sic] Earl of Pembroke, De Courcy, Baron of Kingsale; Sitric King of the Danes, Hibernia in a triumphal Car; each attended with their respective Arms, Achievements Ensignia and Appendages, Druids, Bards, Games, Banshees, Leporehauns, [sic] Hibernians in their original and present State, Peace, Fame, Hospitality, Industry, &c. &c. To conclude with a Song by Carrolan, [sic] the ancient Irish Bard and grand Chorus of all the Characters, Carrolan Mr. Owenson'.[136]

The Shamrock, or The Anniversary of St. Patrick, later to be altered to *The Poor Soldier,* was an extremely popular opera written by John O'Keeffe to music arranged and composed by William Shield. The author's name is omitted from the above advertisement but since it was 'Mrs. O'Keeffe's Night' and since O'Keeffe was one of the cast, there can be no doubt that this was John O'Keeffe's libretto. It may also be noted that the entertainment is styled a comedy, and not a comic opera or pastoral romance, as it was later to be described.

There has always been some doubt concerning the date of the first performance of this opera; Stockwell alone gives it correctly. Sonneck records: Dublin, Smock Alley, March 28, 1783, and London, Covent Garden, April 7, 1783. Loewenberg omits the Dublin date but confirms the London date of April 7, 1783. But at what London theatres was it being acted with universal applause in 1777, or was this merely theatrical promotion? O'Keeffe confuses the matter further when he relates, 'In 1783 I brought out my little opera of "The Shamrock" . . having chosen the subject from a wish of contributing my small share of honours to the installation of the Order of St. Patrick . . The piece was made up of Irish characters and customs, pipers, and fairies, foot-ball players, and gay hurlers'.[137] Lord Temple, as Lord Lieutenant, created the Order of Saint Patrick in February, 1783, but the Irish characters mentioned do not appear in *The Poor Soldier.* They may however correspond to the various kings, druids, bards, banshees and leprechauns of which we read above.

One cannot of course be sure that the performance presented in 1777 was in fact an opera and not a straight play; yet, there is some evidence that it was an opera. For example, there is 'Miss Potter with the original Song'. There is also the information from O'Keeffe that 'My piece of "The Shamrock" having been only a temporary subject, and the occasion gone by, Mr. Harris [Manager of Covent Garden Theatre] regretted that the fine Irish airs of Carolan, which I had selected, and which had been taken down from my voice by the composer,* (airs never before heard by an English public), should

---

*Presumably Shield. In a Dublin performance the Irish airs would have been familiar to the players - and to the public.

be lost; on which I suggested to him the idea of my working at it again, and bringing it out at his theatre in another shape. I did so, and completed my "Poor Soldier", Shield did the accompaniments to the airs of Carolan, which I had chosen, and those of his own original composition'.[138] From this it seems probable that old Irish airs without any arrangement by a musician were sung in ballad form at the first performance – Robert Owenson in the role of Carolan makes this almost a certainty – and that a number of these old airs remained, harmonised in Shield's score of *The Poor Soldier*.

What presumably occurred was that O'Keeffe 'tried out' *The Shamrock* as a novelty for his wife's benefit. At the time it did not meet with success, and this one performance on April 15, 1777 soon slipped from memory, but the creation of the Order of St. Patrick in 1783 provided a topical platform from which to relaunch it.

12

THE ITALIAN OPERA

IN THE SAME way that we owe our knowledge of the first performance of Mozart's *Le Nozze di Figaro* to the Irish tenor Michael Kelly, so are we indebted to him for a description of the first season of total Italian opera in Dublin – total in that each evening's entertainment consisted of an opera only without an added play, farce or afterpiece. Unfortunately, details in Kelly's *Reminiscences* are inaccurate; his main error arises from telescoping two consecutive seasons into one. His story, however, sets the scene. It now remains to present authentically the players.

The first contemporary newspaper account of the season appears on January 8, 1777, when, we read, 'A great Number of the Nobility and Gentry having often express'd a Desire to establish a Comic Italian Opera in this City, two Gentlemen undertook to send to Italy for Performers, who are actually engaged. As this Undertaking must necessarily be attended with a heavy Expense, they offer the following Proposal of a Subscription to the consideration of the Lovers of this species of elegant Entertainment. Each person subscribing five guineas will be entitled to two transferrable Tickets for fifteen Nights: said Subscription money not be paid until the Arrival of the Company and delivery of the Tickets, which will be within two Months. Those who intend favouring this Undertaking with their Patronage, are requested to send their Names to the Printer hereof, in order that they may be waited on by a proper Person with a Subscription Book'.[1]

'Two Gentlemen' are here described as having undertaken the engagement of the artists, and neither in this season nor in the one immediately following is any announcement to be found of a mysterious impresario whom Kelly describes as 'a Portuguese, who called himself Il Cavaliero Don Pedro Martini'.[2] This entrepreneur, he relates, 'played the Spanish guitar delightfully, and succeeded in ingratiating himself with the Duke of Leinster, Earl of Westmeath, Lord Belmont and most of the leading people'.[3] There certainly was a 'Manager of the Italian Opera'[4] who later was to become the target of some sinister extra-operatic activity, but except by Kelly his name is not published. Kelly also states that Martini defaulted on the artists, who thereupon left Dublin, but neither in 1777 nor 1778 is there any evidence that the season ended precipitously or before the appointed time.

Pinto was engaged to lead the orchestra and a Signor St. Giorgio, a key-board player and singer who had made his first Dublin appearance at the Rotunda Gardens in 1774, was engaged to conduct the operas from the harpsichord. For a time he had been Kelly's singing teacher and Kelly recalls that 'his voice was not powerful, but he possessed exquisite taste'.[5] Kelly also relates that as a child his choice of a musical career had been influenced by seeing St. Giorgio enter a shop and prodigally buy and eat some expensive fruit. 'While my mouth watered', he records, 'I asked myself, why, if I assiduously studied music, I should not be able to earn money enough to lounge about in fruit-shops, and eat peaches and pineapples as well as Signor St. Giorgio'.[6]

The opera season was presented at 'the New Theatre, Fishamble-street'[7] and the opening performance took place on April 12, 1777, having been postponed from April 8 'on Account of some necessary Preparations'.[8] The first opera to be produced was Giuseppe Gazzaniga's *L'Isola d'Alcina,* with libretto by Giovanni Bertati. It was cast as follows:

Alcina, a fairy	Signora Cardarelli
Lesb a ⎫ Alcina's	Miss Jameson
Clizia ⎭ Waiting-women	Miss Pinto
La Rose, a Frenchman	Pinetti
Don Lopez, a Spaniard	Peretti
James, an Englishman ⎫ Baron Brickbrack, a German⎭	Cardarelli
Brunoro, an Italian	Passerini.[9]

Miss Pinto had replaced a Signora Teresina whose name appeared in some of the earlier advertisements but who did not take part in the season. Choruses are announced in the libretto but they appear to have been nothing more than concerted numbers sung by the principal performers.

In an attempt to create a sense of occasion, 'a large Room, adjoining the Box Room, lighted with Wax' was 'opened for the Accomodation of the Nobility and Gentry with Tea and Coffee during the Performance. Admission, one Shilling'.[10] Theatre prices had evidently been raised although this is not made clear by the advertisements, for on April 19 it was announced, 'the Proprietor of the Italian Opera, willing to accomodate the Public in General, thinks proper to leave the Gallery and Pit at the usual Price'.[11] The libretto of the opera 'translated into English with the Italian opposite'[12] was published and could be purchased from R. Moncrieffe, 16 Capel Street, M. Mills, 135 Capel Street 'opposite to Abbey-street',[13] L. Flin, 15 Castle Street, and D. Chamberlaine, 5 College Green, 'Price a British shilling'.[14]

Members of the cast new to Dublin were Pinetti, Cardarelli, and Signora Cardarelli. Nothing can be discovered of Cardarelli but Signora Cardarelli, presumably his wife, had appeared at the King's Theatre, Haymarket during the 1775/76 season as *seconda buffa* where on March 28, 1776 she had already sung in *L'Isola d'Alcina*. In Dublin she was to be promoted to *prima buffa*.

Pinetti, according to Kelly, was a Venetian and 'a most excellent actor'.[15] Giuseppe Antonio Pinetti certainly sang in many operas at Venice between 1762 and 1781. Towards the end of his career, however, he was reduced to singing in 'An Attic Entertainment' at the 'Freemason's Hall, Great Queen-street', London, where he was announced as having 'generously engaged to exhibit his most select performances without gratuity . . The whole to conclude with a Ball'.[16]

Isola d'Alcina was one of Giuseppe Gazzaniga's most popular operas. Gazzaniga was the composer whom Michael Kelly once heard denounced by an outraged member of an audience with – 'the curse of God light on him who first put a pen into your hand to write music'.[17] He claims attention principally as the composer of the opera *Don Giovanni Tenorio o sia il Convitata di Pietra,* which was the immediate source of Lorenzo Da Ponte's text for Mozart's *Don Giovanni.* Da Ponte inconsequentially dismisses Gazzaniga as 'a composer of some merit, but of a style no longer in vogue'.[18] He also heartily disliked Giovanni Bertati, the librettist of *Don Giovanni Tenorio* as well as *L'Isola d'Alcina,* presumably because Bertati had succeeded him as poet to the Imperial Theatres at Vienna and declared 'that in every respect the signor poet Bertati was nothing more nor less than a bag of wind'.[19]

In Dublin, *L'Isola d'Alcina* received what are commonly called mixed notices. Comment in the *Hibernian Journal* was enthusiastic and proclaimed that 'The Italian Opera was a third Time performed on Saturday last, at the New Theatre in Fishamble-street, and met as usual with universal Applause. The story of the Piece is simple, but the amazing powers of Signior Pinetti, both as an Actor and a Singer, the sweet toned voice of Signora Cardarelli, her Elegance, Beauty and comic Abilities and the seraphic Notes of Miss Jameson – accompanied by one of the best and most harmonious Bands of Music that ever sat in an Orchestra, have made this Opera so greatly superior in point of vocal and instrumental Music to any Thing of the Kind ever performed in Ireland, that it diffuses the most delightful Sensations among the Audience and gains Approbation and Applause from every Person present. It is almost needless to add, that the Boxes are filled every Night of Representation with such brilliant Company of the Nobility and the first People of Fashion in Ireland, as has been seldom seen at one and the same Time in any Theatre in this City'.[20]

Criticism in the *Freeman's Journal* was devastating. 'Comical enough, egad!' it scoffs, '– advanced prices for squeaking and skipping, for masked mummeries and patch-work pantomimes – and at the Home Manufacture Hotel* in Fishamble-street too! But it would

---

*A comment on propaganda to encourage the wearing of Irish-made cloth which was then active. An extract from a Dublin letter appearing in *The Public Advertiser* (London) of July 19, 1784, reports, 'The Mob of this City seem determined to prevent the wearing of any English

not do. No company! Pit and boxes almost laid waste, with gaping boxes soon made them lower their top-sail prices. The whole rare[e] show may now, for a few nights, (some think the 15 will not be spun out before an ever-lasting farewell shall be given) be seen at common rates. Crowd, therefore, ye citizens, have your money or passes ready that no delay may happen at the doors, as great overflowings are expected, and will afterwards be puffed off'.[21]

That even more malevolent influences were active can be discerned from the following announcement. 'The Manager of the Italian Opera thinks it incumbent on him to inform his Friends and the Subscribers that having met with an unexpected Accident on the fourth Night of Representation [April 22] and which Accident he has Reason to suppose, was premeditatidly calculated to put a stop to the Performance of the Operas in the Infancy of the Undertaking, he is apprehensive that in his present Situation, persecuted and confined it will be impossible for him to put his original intention into Execution. He will gladly however contribute every Endeavour in his Power to continue to the Public the Performance he has promised. But should his [word indecipherable] prove ineffectual, feeling more for his company than for himself, he has only humbly to beg leave to Recommend them to the Protection of the Nobility . .'[22]*

Withal, the manager's original intention of having fifteen subscription performances was in due course realised. Also, instead of opera performances at 'common rates', it was on the contrary found necessary once again to increase prices, and by mid-May we read, 'The Nobility and Gentlemen, Subscribers to the Italian Opera, having inspected into the Receipts and Disbursements of the Opera, have found that the Receipts are inadequate to the Disbursements and, of course, that there is an absolute Necessity of advancing the Prices of Entrance, viz. Gallery 3s. and the Pit, Boxes and Lattices 7s. 6d. but the Regulation not to take place until the 17th of May,

---

Manufactures. . . I could hardly get my Hat brushed by an Irish Domestic because the Felt was English'. The Fishamble Street Theatre frequently advertised that their costumes were of Irish manufacture.

*Some words were excised from the last line when the newspaper file was being bound.

when the new Opera will be brought on. And in order that the Subscribers shall bear a Proportion of the Advance, it is resolved, that all Subscription Tickets, from the 17th forward, are to pay 2s. 6d. each Night'.[23]

The new opera which was in preparation was *La Buona Figliuola,* the libretto by Carlo Goldoni, based on Samuel Richardson's radical novel *Pamela, or Virtue Rewarded,* the music by Nicola Piccinni. Born in the Kingdom of Naples in 1728, Piccinni is the opera composer whose name is best remembered by the furore created on his arrival in Paris where a feud between his followers and the admirers of Gluck caused greater discord than the *Guerre de Bouffons* of twenty-six years earlier. *La Cecchina, ossia la Buona Figliuola* was his most successful opera and is still occasionally performed.

Hogarth records – 'The enthusiasm which it excited in Rome, where it was first performed, amounted to extravagance. It was immediately performed all over Italy, even in the smallest country theatres, and everywhere received with the same admiration. All classes from the highest to the lowest, crowded to see it. New fashions in dress were named from it; and shops and taverns took *La Cecchina* for their sign . . The airs were sung by ladies and gentlemen in their domestic circles, by artisans at their labour, by country people in the fields, by itinerant musicians in the streets and highways'.[24] Musically, the finales which ended the three acts – although the concerted opera finale was not Piccinni's invention – were considered an innovation.

The libretto of *La Buona Figliuola* was published in Dublin by Henry McKenly, 23 Skinner's Row, on May 10, and the opera was first performed there on May 17, 1777.[25] The cast was Pinetti, Cardarelli, Peretti, Passerini, Signora Cardarelli, Miss Jameson, Miss Pinto and 'The Character of Armedoro, a young Gentleman, being his first Appearance on any Stage'.[26]

The 'young Gentleman' was Michael Kelly, who relates that *La Buona Figliuola* had been 'put into rehearsal at the express desire of some of the old cognoscenti who had seen it performed in London . . when a circumstance occurred which threatened its being laid aside;

namely, the severe illness of Signor Savoy, who was to have performed the Count'.[27] Instead, the shadowy 'Portuguese' offered the role to Kelly – with a generous fee to his father. Both were eagerly accepted.

A correction is required here. Although Gasparo Savoi, a castrato singer well-known in London, had sung in Dublin at the Rotunda Garden concerts during 1769 and 1770, he was not a member of the opera company that performed at Fishamble Street Theatre in 1777, nor did he appear elsewhere in Dublin during that year.

Another enigma: in the opera of *La Buona Figliuola* there are roles for four male singers only – the Marchese della Conchiglia (presumably Pinetti in this production), Mengotto (perhaps Cardarelli), Tagliaferro and Armidoro. From the advertisements the remaining two roles would have been taken by Peretti and Passerini. How then was room found for Michael Kelly in the cast? Obviously by temporarily deposing either Peretti or Passerini. The reason for this seems equally obvious – whatever Kelly may relate. It was a pre-arranged manoeuvre almost certainly initiated by Kelly senior to allow his son, then thirteen to fifteen years old, to make his *début* in Italian opera. Following the first performance on May 17, Kelly was to sing in two others on May 20 and 24. Unfortunately no notice of any performance appears to be extant.

There were seventeen performances in all during the season, twelve of *L'Isola d'Alcina* and five of *La Buona Figliuola*. Two of these were benefit performances, for Pinetti and Signora Cardarelli, which were exclusive of the subscription series. The subscription season of 'fifteen Nights' Representation'[28] originally promised was therefore completed. Performances were held on Tuesday and Saturday evenings and the final performance took place on Saturday, June 21.

Benefit performances were taken as follows: May 24, 'Proprietor's Night'*,[29] *La Buona Figliuola*, May 27, *L'Isola d'Alcina* – 'to which will be added some new favourite songs'.[30] This was Pinetti's benefit and tickets were to be had at 'his lodgings No. 12 Winetavern-street'.[31] Signora Cardarelli took her benefit in *La Buona Figliuola* on June 3, when tickets could be had at 'No. 18 Exchange-street'.[32]

*The proprietor was William Gibson. See Chapter 11, p 174.

Signor St. Giorgio chose *L'Isola d'Alcina* on June 7 and 'added New Songs, Trios & Glees, in order to render the Entertainments as elegant and pleasing as possible'.[33] He lived at 'No. 7 Moore-street'.[34]

While Pinetti's benefit was advertised at the regular advanced prices of 7/6 and 3/-, Signora Cardarelli and Signor St. Giorgio accepted the lower prices of 5/- and 2/-, Signora Cardarelli especially 'being studious for the accomodation of the Public'.[35] The result was satisfactory and Signora Cardarelli made metaphorical obeisance, acknowledging 'with heart-felt Gratitude . . the generous patronage of the Nobility and Gentry of this Kingdom'.[36]

Plans for the following season were announced as early as July 25, 1777, when we learn that performances would be held at Smock Alley Theatre and not at Fishamble Street as in the previous season. 'The Committee',[37] headed by the Duke of Leinster, the Earls of Charlemont and Louth, Lord Southwell and David Latouche, Esq., had engaged their artists with discernment for, besides Pinetti and Signora Cardarelli, they included two important singers, Vincenzo Fochetti, and Giovanna Sestini. Pinetti retained his position of 'first man' from the previous season, Fochetti was 'second man', while Sestini and Cardarelli assumed their King's Theatre rank of 'first' and 'second' women. Peretti, Passerini and Mrs. Thompson were also members of the company, the last appearing as 'Third Woman'.[38]

Once again St. Giorgio conducted from the harpsichord but Pinto had been replaced as leader of the orchestra by Signor Giorgi. The similarity of these two names has created the impression that St. Giorgio and Giorgi were the one musician. This is incorrect. As has already been noted St. Giorgio was a singer and a key-board player while 'W. Giorgi',[39]* who was to die in Dublin in late April or early May, 1798, was a violinist.

With the 'Bank of David Latouche Esq.'[40] acting as treasurer for the

---

*Burney, in *The Present State of Music in Germany, the Netherlands and United Provinces*, mentions a 'Signor Giorgi' whom he describes as 'a scholar of Tartini' (Vol. I. p. 280) and a 'Signor Giorgio' who appears to have been a keyboard-instrument teacher, both of whom he had met in Vienna in 1772. They may have been the same artists.

subscribers, a much more imposing season could be anticipated. Paisiello's *La Frascatana* was advertised as the inaugural opera for November 29, but once again there was an apology that 'The Committee for conducting the Italian operas desirous of exhibiting those species of entertainments as compleat as possible find it absolutely necessary to postpone the first entertainment'.[41] So it took place instead on December 3.

As Smock Alley Theatre had been closed for some time, it was also reassuringly announced that 'The Theatre is perfectly well aired, for Stoves are being placed in different Parts of the House for that purpose, and will be continued to the Day of Representation'.[42] The cast was composed of Pinetti, Fochetti, Peretti, Passerini, and the Signore Sestini and Cardarelli. Sestini and Pinetti sang the roles of Violante and Nardone.[43]

Vincenzo Fochetti was born at Modena and ended his days there singing in the choir of the ducal chapel. His name is first discovered singing at Venice between 1769 and 1773. He was engaged at the King's Theatre, London, for the 1773/74 season and continued to sing there each year until his arrival in Dublin in 1777. He had already sung in the first London production of *La Frascatana* in 1776 when, it was despondently announced, he 'appears to have a rattle in his throat'.[44] Consequently, it is probable that his voice was in decline by the time he reached Dublin. Three years earlier on his arrival in London it had been said of him, 'This Actor would do Honour to any stage; he has an admirable Voice, is natural yet spirited, comic without the least Mixture of Farce'.[45] Michael Kelly relates that while travelling through Italy he met Fochetti at Modena 'who', he writes, 'had performed with me when I was so much younger in Dublin'.[46] Once again, Kelly's memory is at fault. He did not take part in the 1777/78 opera season, the only one in which Fochetti sang.

Giovanna Sestini was the attraction of the company, comparable with La Spiletta of earlier years. She had appeared in London as *prima buffa* at the King's Theatre during the 1774/75 season and was to return there each year almost without a break until 1791. A Vincenzo

Sestini, presumably her husband, had joined the company with her as 'last man' but subsequently little was heard of him. Much, however, was heard of Giovanna. She appears to have had two vocations, singing in opera and bearing children. She is announced as having been 'brought to bed' in 1775, 1779, 1781 and 1782. On the last occasion she cut things rather fine by performing less than forty-eight hours before, when it was remarked that 'seeing her beautiful figure, none could imagine that she was in such a situation'.[47] It is little wonder that in an appeal for her benefit in 1783 it was announced, 'In her private character, she is entitled to every consideration, and we are informed that she has eight children all alive and she is their only support, and of her old mother'.[48] But where, one wonders, was 'last man' Vincenzo?

During her years in London she performed continually and with considerable success. In February 1775 she appeared in *La Buona Figliuola* when it was reported, 'Her voice is so delightful, her figure so pleasing, her delivery so full of sensibility and grace, that every note she sings, every word she utters commands the plaudits of the whole audience; the most surprising is, the justness of her action, considering that Italian singers are most generally very bad actors'.[49] The following October at a 'grand concert at the Queen's Palace' attended by the Royal Family, 'most of the foreign ambassadors and a great Number of the Nobility', we learn that 'his Majesty was so pleased with her voice that he encored her in some of her capital songs. Notwithstanding the concert lasted between three and four hours, no person sat down during the entertainment, the Royal family excepted'.[50] The inevitable vocal decline then set in and in November, 1776, it was noted 'Signora Sestini is very much altered for the worse. We were exceedingly sorry to observe, that she was very often out of tune'.[51] By 1786 her voice was gone. We read, 'A correspondent recommends to Signora Sestini to tour to Spa or to Montpellier, where she may, perhaps, recover her vocal powers, which, at present, are in a *sad* condition indeed'.[52]

Her status as a singer is perhaps best portrayed by Lord Mount Edgcumbe who wrote, 'At her first coming over [she] was handsome,

N

sprightly, and a good actress, if great exuberance of gesticulation, activity of motion, and affected Italian *smorfie* could make her one; but her voice was gritty and sharp (something like singing through a comb) and she was nothing of a singer, except for lively comic airs. Yet she was much liked at first, and long a favourite with the mass of the public though not with the *connoisseurs*. She was first woman for many years, then, in the decline of her voice, became second; sung at intervals at Covent Garden and the little theatre in the Haymarket; in short, condescended to everything to keep herself from starving, and constantly remaining in England, died here at last in great poverty'.[53]

La Frascatana, with libretto by Filippo Livigni, was one of Paisiello's most successful operas, yet it was not universally acclaimed when it was first performed in London in November, 1776. The *New Morning Post* declared, 'There never was an Opera more heavy and tedious than "*La Fraschetana*". The subject of the piece presents no meaning at all, and the music does nothing but roar and thunder; it makes a noise to no purpose'.[54] This London production was probably a *pasticcio* by Paisiello, Perez and Anfossi, for a score of *La Frascatana* containing music by these composers was published by R. Brenner in London in 1777. Probably the same version was presented in Dublin, to which Tommaso Giordani was to add a 'Favourite Rondo',[55] *Non dubitare bell' idol mio* for Sestini.

Giovanni Paisiello was born at Taranto in 1740 and died at Naples in 1816. His music may now sound effete and colourless yet judged against its own period it has an expressive charm and gaiety. *Il Barbiere di Siviglia* remains his best known opera, less for its musical merit than for the furore created when the young Rossini had the audacity to set the same comedy. Paisiello was said to be jealous of his fellow composers. In the beginning of his career he had a rival in Piccinni, while towards the end he had to suffer a second in Cimarosa.

Concerning the production of *La Frascatana* in Dublin, Michael Kelly's fallibility is again evident. Describing a day spent at Frascati he records, 'I was delighted with this village, the scene of Paisiello's beautiful comic opera, called La Frascatana, particularly as it was the first Italian opera I had ever seen in Dublin'.[56] It seems most unlikely that Kelly did not see *L'Isola d'Alcina* in Dublin in April 1777. He must have seen *La Buona Figliuola* in May since he took part in it. *La Frascatana* did not receive its first Dublin performance until the following December.

That the present opera season had greater social pretensions is demonstrated by the number of performances commanded by the Lord Lieutenant, Lord Buckinghamshire, of whom it was said 'though he saw much company, could never divest himself of a formality little agreeable to the gaiety of the Irish'.[57] These began on December 6 and 13 and continued right through the season. Their snob *cachet* automatically resulted in the nobility and gentry being 'respectfully entreated to give positive Orders, to their Servants, to set down with their Horses' Heads towards Fishamble-street and to take up with their Horses' Heads towards Essex-street'.[58] They were further advised that 'The old Pit Door will be opened every Opera Night for Chairs only'.[59]

A description of the performance by Michael Kelly enlivens the occasion. He relates that 'The etiquette was, that the band in the orchestra, as well as the company in the boxes and pit, should be fully dressed. Bags and swords were then the order of the day: the prices were, boxes and pit, half-a-guinea; first gallery, five shillings; and the upper one, three shillings'.[60]

Arthur Young, who was then visiting Dublin, tells a different story. He records: 'An ill-judged and unsuccessful attempt was made to establish the Italian Opera, which existed but with scarcely any life for this one winter; of course they could rise no higher than a comic one. La Buona Figliuola, La Frascatana and Il Geloso in Cimento, were repeatedly performed, or rather murdered, except the parts of Sestini. The house was generally empty and miserably cold.'[61]

Which to believe? Whatever else, Kelly had his prices wrong. They remained as they had been for the previous season, Boxes and Pit, 7/6, Middle Gallery, 3/- and Upper Gallery 2/-.

Performances of *La Frascatana* continued although there were some cancellations – on December 20 'on account of the indisposition of Signora Sestini',[62] and again on December 24 'on account of the continuance of Signora Sestini's indisposition'.[63] By December 26 she had recovered, when it was announced that 'she will certainly perform tomorrow evening'[64] but on January 7, 1778, her 'indisposition' caused a further cancellation. The Lord Lieutenant again commanded the opera on January 10.

On January 14 *La Buona Figliuola* 'with new dresses and decorations',[65] originally announced for January 10 but postponed, was performed. The cast was made up of Pinetti, Fochetti, Peretti, Passerini, Signora Sestini, Signora Cardarelli, Mrs. Thompson and Miss Pope.

The newcomer, Jane Pope, had previously sung in English opera at Fishamble Street Theatre during the previous year. She had made her first appearance at Drury Lane Theatre in 1759 and before long succeeded Kitty Clive as the principal London performer of hoydens and servant-maids. She created many roles, including Mrs. Candour in *The School for Scandal* and Tilburnia in *The Critic*. She was obviously more actress than singer for of her performance in *The Beggar's Opera* we read, 'what the managers could mean in casting *Lucy* for Miss Pope is extraordinary, as she sung, or indeed rather squalled every song so much out of tune, that it was impossible for the music to accompany her'.[66]

Performances of *La Frascatana* and *La Buona Figliuola* now alternated, the Lord Lieutenant commanding the latter for Saturday, January 24. A performance of *La Buona Figliuola* had to be cancelled on February 7 'on account of the indisposition'[67] – this time – of Pinetti. This led to the postponement of a new opera, *Il Geloso in Cimento* by Pasquale Anfossi, until February 18, as Pinetti had 'not sufficiently recovered from his indisposition to perform a new character'.[68] We are assured that 'no expense has been spared in the purchasing of new and elegant dresses, scenes, etc. to render it worthy the attention of the subscribers and public in general'.[69]

Anfossi was born near Naples in 1727 and, like most of his contemporaries, studied there. He was a pupil of Piccinni and Sacchini. He remains a footnote in the history of opera because of his setting of *La Finta Giardiniera* in 1774. Mozart's composition of the same opera in the following year has dethroned the Anfossi version, but since the Mozart recitatives to Act 1 have been lost, Anfossi's recitatives for this act are frequently used in revivals of the Mozart work.

The cast of *Il Geloso in Cimento* was as follows:

Signor Fabio	Pinetti
Don Perichetto	Fochetti
Signor Rosbif	Passerini
Donna Flavia	Signora Sestini
Modesta	Signora Cardarelli
Paterio	Peretti
Vittorina	Mrs. Thompson.[70]

The libretto was printed by 'James Parker and Co. (No. 28) Temple-Bar' with an aria *Ah per me non v'e piu bene* by Tommaso Giordani interpolated for Sestini.

Between February 18 and March 3 *Il Geloso in Cimento* was performed twice weekly. Then on March 7 Sestini took her benefit in *La Frascatana*, with 'two new favourite songs'[71] added. Tickets, 'at the usual Prices of the Opera' were to be had from her address 'at No. 11 Mary-street'.[72] It was later reported that receipts for the performance had reached the very handsome sum of 'five hundred and sixty-two pounds'.[73] Afterwards she considered it 'her duty to return the most humble thanks to the Nobility, Gentry and the public who honoured her benefit with their numerous company; and to assure them, at the same time that wherever her profession may call her, she shall ever retain the most grateful remembrance of their kind indulgence and matchless generosity'.[74] Sestini was once again indisposed for a performance of *Il Geloso in Cimento* on March 18, and on March 28 'Their Excellencies'[75] commanded yet another performance of *La Frascatana*.

Pinetti then fixed his benefit for April 4. It consisted of a galli-maufry combining Act 1 of *La Frascatana* 'in which (by particular desire) will be introduced the favourite song Non Dubitare by Signora Sestini',[76] Act 2 of *Il Geloso in Cimento* and Act 3 of *La Buona Figliuola* 'in which will be introduced the Song Viva Paris* by Signor Pinetti'.[77] It was announced that the different acts would be 'preceded by their Symphonies' and 'In each Act, the Dresses, Scenery, Decorations will be suited to the respective piece'.[78] Pinetti had returned to his lodgings of the previous season, for tickets were again to be had at 'No. 12 Winetavern-street'.[79]

Tragedy occurred during the performance for, we read, 'Saturday night a riot happened at the opera in Smock-alley, between the gentlemen's servants and the soldiers, in which the latter were compelled to fire, when James Martin (a poor industrious chairman who has left a wife and four children) was killed on the spot, and three others wounded, one of whom, we hear, is since dead'.[80] The incident passed unnoticed by Pinetti who 'with equal gratitude and respect',[81] acknowledged the generous patronage accorded by the nobility and gentry. At the same time he was 'extremely concerned for the disappointment they met with in respect to the lights, Mr. Pinetti's agreement being that the house should be illuminated in the usual manner'.[82]

Signora Cardarelli probably took her benefit in *Il Geloso in Cimento* on April 8—the advertisements are ambiguous. William Dawson, late of Capel Street Theatre, engaged both Smock Alley Theatre and the Italian artists for a benefit on the evening of April 22. This was because a benefit performance arranged by him at Crow Street Theatre about a month earlier had failed, when 'many ladies and gentlemen who intended honouring Mr. Dawson with their presence . . were prevented by the fatigue of the masquerade which was on the evening before, and the Oratorio for the Benefit of Mercer's Hospital appointed for the same evening'.[83] He also chose *Il Geloso in Cimento* with 'an English farce and entertainments of dancing'.[84]

Signor St. Giorgio arranged another *pasticcio* for his benefit on April 29. It was made up of Acts 1 and 2 of *La Frascatana* and Act 3

*'Viva Paris' was published as an aria from Gazzaniga's *L'Isola d'Alcina* by Anne Lee in Dublin circa 1780. (See *The British Union Catalogue of English Music*. Vol. I. p. 548.)

of *Il Geloso in Cimento*, 'preceeded by a new Symphony of Signor Sacchini' and ending with 'all the favourite songs, Chorus and the Duet from the celebrated opera of L'Isola d'Alcina',[85] The presentation of acts from different operas to make up the evening's entertainment continued. Fochetti and a Signor Gerna had a joint benefit consisting of a comedy and some musical interludes on May 11.

Signor Gerna, whose name has not previously appeared, was the translator of the Italian opera libretti into English. In an advertisement he also took 'the liberty of offering his Services to the Nobility for reading the Italian Authors and teaching that Language so as to converse politely – to be sent for to No. 1 Paradise-Row, corner of Dorset-Street'.[86] Polite conversation seems to have paid off, either for Signor Gerna or a member of his family, for in 1793 a 'Catalogue des Livres Français, Italien, &c.'[87] listing over two thousand volumes, was issued by an Antoine Gerna who was in business at 'No. 31 College-Green, à Côté de la grande Poste aux lettres'.[88]

The last performance of the official season took place on May 16, when *La Frascatana* was performed, but there was a further performance of the same opera on May 23: 'The Italian Company having proposed a Play without any payment, for the Benefit of the poor distressed Manufacturers of this City.'[89] It was hoped 'no lady will have an Assembly on that Night'[90] but with the Ladies Antrim, Moira, Bective, Charlemont, Ely, de Vesey and Kingsborough and Mesdames Pery, Gardiner and Adderly, all distributing tickets, such a request seems superfluous – there can hardly have been any other ladies left in Dublin.

Excluding performances of miscellaneous acts, there were thirty-eight opera performances during the season, sixteen of *La Frascatana*, fifteen of *Il Geloso in Cimento* and seven of *La Buona Figliuola*. Performances were held on Wednesday and Saturday evenings each week, with one exception, when a performance was held on Tuesday, March 3, due to Ash Wednesday falling on March 4.

13

THOUGH IN A FOREIGN
LANGUAGE

FOLLOWING THE SEASON of 1778, a break now occurred in the production of Italian operas which lasted for three and a half years. Meanwhile on March 23, 1781, a new English comic opera, *The Lord of the Manor*, was performed for the first time in Dublin at Crow Street Theatre. The cast consisted of Ryder, George Dawson, O'Keeffe, Glenville, Stephens, Bowles, Richards, Barnshaw, King, Johnstone, Mrs. Richards, Miss Francis and Mrs. Johnstone.[1] Thomas Ryder, then manager of Crow Street, had a year or so previously been forced to relinquish control of Smock Alley Theatre to a new and flamboyant rival, Richard Daly. In June, 1781, he was to lose control of Crow Street to Daly as well, but he remained as an actor in Daly's company at Smock Alley.

On taking over Smock Alley, Daly had managed to induce most of Ryder's best players to join him. Obviously he had also decided on a policy of direct competition, for on April 2 he mounted a second production of *The Lord of the Manor*.[2]

This opera was composed by William Jackson of Exeter who, Burney relates, had adhered to a style of his own, 'formed upon the melodies of our best old English masters'.[3] Surprisingly, he was an eclectic painter as well, and was the friend and biographer of Gainsborough, whose paintings he copied. The libretto of the opera was written by one of the most colourful personalities ever to combine the professions of stage and sword. This was General John Burgoyne, dupe and loser of the battle of Saratoga in the American War of Independence, immortalised by Bernard Shaw as 'Gentlemanly

Johnny' in *The Devil's Disciple*. Known to Dublin in 1781 as a celebrated author, in 1782 he was attending the Phoenix Park to review 'the regiments of horse and foot in the garrison preparatory to their being reviewed by his grace the Lord-Lieutenant'.[4] Of much more importance than *The Lord of the Manor* is his preface to it. This deals with the development of opera, particularly English opera, and contains passages which express insight and judgment rare for their time, and still apt and perceptive today almost two hundred years later.

At length, on October 17, 1781, a new season of Italian opera was announced, troubled, it would appear, by a social *contretemps*. We read that 'Messrs. St. Giorgio and Carnevale present their humble respects to the Ladies Patronesses and Subscribers to the Italian Opera, and, as they understand that some of the Subscribers are displeased that the operas should commence before Christmas without the subscribers Tickets being admitted, they are directed by the Lady Patronesses now in Town, to give the following Information, viz. – that if any Subscriber shall choose to have their Subscription commence before Christmas, by writing a Letter and paying their Subscription to Messrs. St. Giorgio & Carnevale, No. 7 Moorestreet, they shall receive a transferable Ticket, which shall be entitled to Admission for 30 successive Representations only, commencing from the first Opera Night'.[5] From this announcement we also discover that the season was intended to run for thirty performances and that Signor St. Giorgio had found a new partner.

Signor Carnevale seems to have come to Dublin as a viola player (tenor violinist) for in May, 1779, he is advertised as performing on that instrument at a Rotunda concert. Subsequently he was to settle in London where he enjoyed a moderately successful career. His name appears as tenor violinist among the numerous instrumentalists who took part in the great Handel commemoration concerts at Westminster Abbey in June, 1784.[6] In September, 1785, he was appointed stage manager at the King's Theatre in the Haymarket, and eighteen months later on returning from Paris, where he had been engaging dancers, he is described as 'Deputy-Manager at the King's

Theatre'.[7] During the opera season in Dublin his address is given as
'at Mrs. Rhames, No. 16, Exchange-street'.[8]

The theatre engaged for the opera season was Smock Alley. It had
been 'fitted up in a most elegant Manner' and with 'the acknowledged
rising Merit of Mr. Daly' was said to bid 'fair to be the favourite
Scene of Amusement the ensuing Winter'.[9] Daly's 'merit' was
indeed rising. Like Thomas Sheridan and Henry Mossop, he had
been a student at Trinity College, entering at the age of fifteen in
1773. He later trained as an actor under Charles Macklin, but having
made an unsuccessful *début* as Othello at Covent Garden in 1779, he
returned to Ireland. In the same year he was engaged by Thomas
Ryder for his Crow Street company and, as has been noted, was soon
to supplant Ryder – it is said, in a not entirely honourable manner –
as manager of both theatres. A short time previously he had married
a widow, Mrs. Lyster, *née* Jane Barsanti, a popular Dublin singing
actress, who – of importance to Daly's future – was reputed to have
been 'possessed of considerable property'.[10] He has been described
as 'a very fine-looking young fellow, but with such a squint that it
was totally impossible to say what he looked at, except his nose, of
which he never lost sight'.[11]

On or off-stage, Daly indulged in theatricality. It is recorded that
in his youth he 'had the greatest predilection for single combat' and
'had fought sixteen duels in the space of two years'.[12] For one such
event, which took place at Donnybrook at seven o'clock on a cold
March morning, he arrived dressed in 'a pea-green coat; a large tucker
with a diamond brooch stuck in it; a three-cocked hat with a gold
button-loop and tassels; and silk stockings; and a *couteau-de-chasse*
hung gracefully dangling from his thigh'.[13] His reputation with the
more attractive female members of his company was notorious.

The opera season at his theatre commenced on November 3, 1781,
with Paisiello's *L'Innocente Fortunata*. The performance was announced as 'a new Comic Opera, with Dances',[14] for a ballet company
had also been engaged. The ballet did not form part of the opera,
but helped to extend the evening's entertainment, and dances were
a constant feature of each performance throughout the season.

The opera was advertised to be conducted by St. Giorgio and Carnevale – the latter acting as leader of the orchestra – and the cast was as follows:

Brettone	Urbani
Don Trippone	Fortunati
Don Gusmano	Ferrari
Geppino	Viscardino
Bettina	Signora Castini
Lilletta	Signora Giovanelli
Trippone	Signora Bartolini.[15]

The ballet master was Monsieur Laurent and the principal dancers, including him, were Messieurs Fleury, and Obry (? Aubry)* and the Signore Rossignoli, Melongini, and Romanini. 'Figure Dancers' taking part were Monsieur Felix, Madame Laurent, the Signori Greco, Sala and Sala junior and the Signore Sala, Ullenghi and Urbani. 'The Dresses [were] invented by Signor Sestini and executed by Mr. Campbell.'[16] The entire opera and ballet company is included in the above list. The Signore Castini, Giovanelli and Bartolini are described as first, second, and third woman respectively. Urbani was first tenor, and Ferrari, first *buffo caricato*.[17] Among the dancers, Laurent is described as leader – 'from the King's Opera at Paris, where he acted the above character last Winter with universal Applause'.[18] Laurent and Fleury appear to have been engaged independently by Daly prior to the arrival of the other dancers.

As was customary, the theatre was 'illuminated with Wax'[19] for the first performance. The libretto of the opera was on sale at the 'Box-door'[20] and the usual requests were made to the nobility and gentry concerning the direction of their horses' heads 'in order to make Room for those that come after'.[21]** Instruction was adamant con-

---

*The dancers' names are spelled differently in the various advertisements and libretti (Obry/Ofry, Melongini/Meloncini, Romanini/Romanina, etc.), indicating either careless proof reading or illegible manuscript copy for the printers.

**This information is not recorded as an example of period whimsy. Each age has its own traffic problems. Dublin's theatre traffic in the late 18th century is exemplified by the following letter from 'A Frequenter of the Theatre':

'To Richard Daly Esq, Theatre-Royal, Smock-Alley. Sir . . 'tis requested by many of your well

cerning 'No Person to be admitted behind the Scenes upon any Account whatsoever'.[22] Prices of admission conformed more with what Michael Kelly had earlier recorded, for boxes and pit were half-a-guinea, middle gallery was 4/– and upper gallery 2/–.[23] A significant patriotic announcement was – 'Dresses for the aforesaid, and all succeeding Operas, entirely new and solely of Irish Manufacture'.[24]

According to the *Hibernian Journal, L'Innocente Fortunata* was well received and 'though in a foreign Language, was represented in a Manner so forcibly expressive, as to render it intelligible to all the Audience. The parts were well cast, and admirably supported. Signora Castini, in the Character of Bettina, displayed such abilities as a singer, such Elegance as an Actress, as excited the admiration, and most marked Applause from every part of the House. The Harmony of Signor Urbani's Voice, and the Powers of Signor Ferrari's as also the great performance of Signor Dell'Oca, a mere Youth, on the Violoncello, were particularly admired. The infinite Variety and inimitable Performance of the Dancers, were such as extorted the loudest and most uninterrupted Applause. Mons. Laurent's Performance was so inexpressibly great and so universally acknowledged by every Spectator, that we are not at all surprised he was the Admiration of the Parisian Audience, last Winter. Signora Rossignoli, the Principal Dancer, acquitted herself to the Satisfaction and Admiration of all the Audience. The Dresses were allowed to display Taste and Propriety'.[25]

Further performances followed – on November 8, 'By Command of his Excellency, the Lord Lieutenant, and Countess of Carlisle'.[26]

---

wishers that you would follow the London mode in regard to the carriages waiting at the Box-door. The passage to the Theatre is exceedingly inconvenient, and is rendered still more so by the insolence of the coachmen, and inattention of their employers, who either are not ready or do not chuse to depart when their vehicles are prepared to receive them. At the London Theatres, each carriage is allowed to stand a sufficient length of time and a person is placed at the box door, on purpose to warn the person of its being ready, and after calling three times, without further notice is ordered to drive off, and the next in rotation to draw up. The efficacy of this mode may not have struck you till conveyed through the medium of a news-paper; but dont disregard a hint so well calculated to free the Public from the many inconveniences which necessarily arise, in not being obliged to wait about in a state of suffocation from the smell of Oil, Flambeaux, and disappointment of not being able to get to their carriages.'

Carlisle had lately arrived in Dublin where he was hailed as 'Taciturn to a degree of disgust and was neither remarkable for his munificence or affability of manners'.[27] Later performances took place on November 10, 14, 17 and 21, and on November 28, once again by the Lord Lieutenant's command.

Gazzaniga's *L'Isola d'Alcina* was next revived – from four years earlier – on November 24. The cast was:

Alcina	Signora Castini
Lesbia	Signora Giovanelli
Clizia	Signora Bartolini
La Rose	Urbani
James	Ferrari
Baron Brickbrack	
Brunero	Fortunati
Don Lopez	Viscardino.[28]

Significantly there was some reduction in admission prices. 'Boxes & Part of the Pit railed in' remained at 10/6, but the 'Remainder of the Pit' was now reduced to 5/– and the middle gallery to 3/–.[29] Once again the *Hibernian Journal* reports that the opening performance was attended by 'an undoubtedly polite and discerning Audience'.[30] Three further performances followed on December 1, 5 and 8.

Then on December 12 *La Contadina in Corte* by Antonio Sacchini, with libretto possibly by Gasparo Gozzi, brother of the celebrated Carlo, was performed. Sacchini, born in 1734, and described by Burney as 'This graceful, elegant, and judicious composer'[31] was yet another Neapolitan. By 1788 he could tell Burney that he had composed seventy-eight dramatic works 'of which he had forgot even the names of two'.[32] He first came to London in 1772 riding high on his continental reputation, but jealousy and theatrical intrigue, dissolute living and at last illness led to misfortune. An announcement in the newspapers which charged him with having Venanzio Rauzzini compose some of the music for his operas proved to be a catalyst which induced him to leave for Paris. There he composed his principal opera, and the only one to be performed in recent times, *Oedipe à Colone*.

At Dublin *La Contadina in Corte* was cast as follows:

Sandrina	Signora Castini
Tancia	Signora Giovanelli
Ruggiero	Urbani
Berto	Ferrari
Pancrazio	Viscardino.[33]

Two dances were again added by the ballet company and the audience was advised to purchase their libretti 'from the several Door-keepers [as] those sold by the Hawkers outside the Doors are Spurious'.[34] Of the performance we read, 'Nothing could exceed the Applause, universally testified by the Audience; an Audience as polite and consequently as discerning as ever graced any of our Theatres'.[35] Performances continued on December 15, 19 and 22 – the last 'At the Desire of several Lady Patronesses'.[36]

The next opera to be performed was *L'Avaro,* 'the favourite Production of the celebrated Signor Anfossi never performed in these Kingdoms'. 'Two new ballets', we read, 'are also in Rehearsal'.[37] *L'Avaro* had its first Dublin performance on January 23, 1782, with the following cast:

Laurina	Signora Castini
Rosalinda	Signora Giovanelli
Tortura	Signora Bartolini
Stefanello	Urbani
Orgasino	Ferrari
Felicino	Fortunati
Macobrio	Viscardino.[38]

It was repeated on January 26 and 30 and on February 2, 6, 9 and 12. A social mishap is reported from the performance on January 30 when several ladies complained of the theatre being very cold. This was found to be due to a window having been left open 'owing to the Neglect of one of the Underlings whose Business it is to superintend these Matters'.[39] The public was reassured that no such inconvenience would occur again.

L'Isola d'Alcina was repeated on February 16 and 20, and the first of the benefit performances took place on February 23 when Signor Carnevale chose *La Contadina in Corte*. This opera was again performed on February 27.

'The Favourite Comic Opera of L'Amor Artigiano. The music by the celebrated Signor Gusman [sic]'[40], the libretto by Goldoni, was performed on March 2. The cast was:

Rosina	Signora Castini
Angiolina	Signora Giovanelli
Countess Costanza	Signora Bartolini
Giannino	Urbani
Giro	Ferrari
Tarra	Fortunati
Bernardo	Viscardino.[41]

When first performed in London four years earlier it was noted that 'However favourably the composition may have been received at Vienna . . one hazards little in saying, that its intrinsic merit would not recommend it to any very capital distinction'.[42]

The composer Florian Gassmann was born in Bohemia in 1729 but trained as a musician in Italy, first at Bologna under Padre Martini and later at Venice. He was appointed Court Kapellmeister at Vienna in 1772 but did nothing to influence the advance of musical form there during that fruitful period.

His opera had additional performances in Dublin on March 7, and on March 13, when also announced was 'a new species of Ballet Entertainment, usually called in foreign Countries "un divertissement" '.[43]

Signor St. Giorgio took his benefit in *L'Innocente Fortunata* on March 9. Afterwards, 'penetrated with the deepest sentiments of true gratitude to the Nobility and Gentry of Ireland, for the indulgent protection wherewith they have been pleased to favour him during his Seven Years Residence* in this Metropolis' he humbly took the

*This period of residence disposes of the possibility of identifying him with the famous Chevalier de Saint Georges from Guadeloupe, distinguished as violinist, swordsman, composer and soldier of fortune.

'Opportunity of returning his sincerely thankful Acknowledgements'.[44] A miscellany of performances then followed – *L'Amore Artigiano* on March 16 and April 6, *L'Avaro* on March 20, and *La Contadina in Corte* on March 23.

Then, on April 10, Sacchini's *L'Amore Soldato* was produced. The librettist of this opera was Antonio Andrei, a hack writer who arranged a number of operas for the King's Theatre, London, between 1778 and 1784. The season continued with repeat performances of all the operas. These had originally taken place each Wednesday and Saturday, as they had during the 1777–78 season, until April 17, when they were announced for Tuesday and Saturday 'on Account of the Rotunda Concerts interfering on Wednesdays'.[45]

On June 1, 1782, an opera by Domenico Cimarosa was performed in Dublin for the first time. This was *L'Italiana in Londra* which, strangely enough, was not to reach London for another five and a half years. Its early Dublin production was prompted by Signor Ferrari who had chosen it for his benefit. He announced that 'The extraordinary Expense incurred . . as well in the Purchase, as the several Preparations for its public Representation obliges him respectfully to inform the Public, in the most positive Manner, that this Performance will not be repeated this Season'.[46]

It was, of course, repeated, the new Lord Lieutenant, Lord Portland, commanding it a week later. Portland, who had replaced Carlisle, was to redeem the bad impression created by his predecessor, entertaining 'with the splendor of royalty and [receiving] every one around him with that degree of amiable politeness which constitutes the real ornament of Nobility'.[47]

Cimarosa – yet another Neapolitan – was born in 1749, just six years before Mozart. His best known opera *Il Matrimonio Segreto,* although composed at the time of Mozart's death, exists in the opera domain as the link connecting the innumerable effete eighteenth-century compositions with Mozart's masterpieces. As a composer, fame and success brought him from the court of the Empress Catherine of Russia to the post of Kapellmeister at Vienna. His latter days alone were unhappy, due not to music but politics, for he had backed the

French when they entered Naples in 1799. He died in exile in Venice in 1801.

His librettist for *L'Italiana in Londra* was the Abbé Giuseppe Petrosellini, a Roman by birth and one of the most prolific librettists of his time. When the opera was first produced in London in 1788 under the title of *La Locandiera*, Dr. Burney was not impressed. He relates, 'I was much disappointed in its effect, after all that I had heard and read of its prodigious favour in Italy . . Much of the Music seemed feeble, common, and not of the newest taste. The symphony, however, of one movement only, and the duet in the second act, taken from another opera, were very good'.[48]

The casts of the Dublin productions of *L'Amore Soldato* and *L'Italiana in Londra* so far remain undiscovered.

On Thursday, June 6 – 'the [King's] Birth-Night interfering on Tuesday the 4th'[49] – *L'Amore Soldato* was performed, followed by *La Contadina in Corte* on June 15. A performance for June 18 was postponed, 'several of the Opera Performers being ill of the Influenza'.[50] The Lord Lieutenant paid St. Giorgio and Carnevalle the compliment of commanding their joint benefit performance of *L'Amore Soldato* on June 22, and on June 29 '(positively the last Time of the Italian Company's performing this Season)'[51] there was a final performance of *L'Italiana in Londra* 'with additional Songs. End of the 1st Act – I Cacciatori. End of the 2nd Act – Annette and Lubin'.[52]

In presentation, this season seems to have lacked the social *éclat* of the previous one in 1778. Yet it was by no means unsuccessful, for the thirty performances promised were almost doubled, the final number totalling fifty-two. It may be noted that while 'choruses' were recorded once again in the libretti, they were undoubtedly *tutti* ensembles by the principals, and chorus members were not mentioned.

The principal singers were not a particularly distinguished lot. Three only can be identified. Ferrari was almost certainly Giuseppe Ferrari who was singing at the Teatro San Cassiano in Venice during 1779/80. He was then described as 'primo buffo in carattere'[53] which

o

corresponds with the description given to him in Dublin. During his visit he lodged at 'No. 18 Exchange-street'.[54]

Pietro Urbani was a Milanese who had lived in London prior to his Dublin engagement. Concurrently with his Dublin stage appearances, he announced to the nobility and gentry that he would 'receive their commands with the due Acknowledgment, for teaching to Sing, the Violin and Composition'.[55] Subsequently he lived in Edinburgh where Michael Kelly was to hear him and report that 'like his countryman, David Rizzio, [he was] very partial to Scotch melodies, some of which he sang very pleasingly, though in a falsetto voice'.[56] He returned to Dublin about 1804 and died there in poverty in 1816. His wife was a 'figure dancer' in the *corps de ballet.*

Signora Castini, whose Dublin address is given as 20 Mary Street, was the most interesting artist in the company – at least socially. She excites curiosity from an announcement on February 28, 1782, which reports a clandestine affair between her and 'our *little* celebrated parliamentary *hero,* Mr. —— who we are informed is now closely soliciting her smiles and her graces'.[57] The following September, a London newspaper augments this gossip, reporting from Dublin that 'An incident of *beau ton* has for some days past kept the circles of the *beau-monde* here in high spirits: Mr. G. —— who has for some time carried on an amorous correspondence with Signora Castini. After bestowing pecuniary favours upon her with a hand of liberality, on his departure for Spa, gave her an unlimited credit upon different tradesmen, and an order to receive ten guineas per week. No soon [sic] had the patriot left his country, than the lady opened accounts with the tradesmen, and gave her hand to a countryman of her own, Signor Carnevalli. A Signor Peretti, qualified in every respect to officiate as groom to a lady's bed chamber, directed the marriage, and informed a friend of Mr. G. ——, who immediately stopped the fair Syren's credit with the tradesmen, but not till she had raised a very comfortable portion to bestow upon her spouse'.[58] Further news occurs in a Dublin letter of October 26 when we learn that 'C-st-ni is singing at present at the Hague. It is whispered that her decampment from Ireland, a little previous to the arrival of the *Spa-Patriot,* was a measure effected by his friends, lest the *Syren* should engage too much of his attention, and charm away too many of the 50,000 pounds. It is asserted nevertheless, that a *Cameo-Head* has been forwarded to her, to console her for the loss of the *Adonis*-original'.[59]

Without a doubt the '*little* celebrated parliamentary *hero*' was Henry Grattan. However groundless the gossip, it was certainly Grattan who was being lampooned, for we know that he was small in stature, that in 1782 he had been voted a parliamentary grant of £50,000 by a grateful nation, and that he spent the months of August and September of that year at the resort of Spa in Belgium.[60]

Castini as Signora Carnevale had a short career at the King's Theatre, London. She made her first appearance there on January 7, 1783, when it was reported 'that both as a Singer and Performer she stood at a great Distance from Perfection'.[61] She apparently acquiesced in this critical opinion and, 'ambitious to Court the Favour of the Public, put herself under the Tuition of Signor Anfossi'.[62]

Few of the dancers can be identified. Teresa Rossignoli was a member of the Teatro San Cassiano company in Venice during 1776/77. Signora Sala was to appear at the King's Theatre, London, in 1782. Her husband's or son's name occurs among the dancers there in 1786, and both a Signor and a Signora Sala were dancers at the Royal Circus, St. George's Fields, in a burletta during the same year. Signora Sala's distinction as a ballet dancer was at least individual. We read that she 'pretends not to be more than a Second Rate; and she does very decently what she pretends to do. Considering the Weight she carries, for she has something more about her than the En-bon-point Charmant, she is very alert.'.[63]

The rest of the company was made up of the costume designer, Signor Sestini, who was probably Signora Sestini's son and who later became a wellknown costume designer at the King's Theatre, London. During the 1795/96 season there, he is described as 'tailor'[64] with a salary of £200 or £250. The tailor for the Dublin season was a Mr. Campbell.[65] The remaining member of the company was a Mr. Kennedy, translator of the operas 'and Teacher of the Italian Language'.[66]

Consequently it seemed a routine season, at least musically – but socially a cabal had been organised by a section of the press against St. Giorgio and Carnevalle which for invective and malice was remarkable even in a period when libel was accepted not as a hazard but as a commonplace of public life. The first inkling of the situation appeared in the *Hibernian Journal* almost immediately after the season had begun. This was an announcement by St. Giorgio and Carnevalle 'that the Reason of the Virulence of a certain Newspaper against them is their not choosing to pay for their Advertisements *eight* Times the Price always agreed for, besides a *modest* Demand of *four* Tickets every Night of Performance'.[67]

True or distorted as the accusation may be, the newspaper involved was the *Freeman's Journal* which had reported as follows on November 10, 1781: 'A disappointed musical connoisseur says, that had not their Excellencies commanded the Italian Opera, on Thursday evening last, Carnevalle's wretched troop would have probably played to an empty house. As it was, but one spectator was in the pit, and but five in the lettices. Carnevalle's first woman singer is by no means to be compared to Sestini, nor would she get a third place at the Opera house in London. His third woman singer, being hissed the first night, did not sing on Thursday night. – Our correspondent thinks, they must in general been picked up in Italy from strolling opera companies; and that his dancers, excepting Laurent and Fleury, who were got by mere chance, are by no means equal to those of our own Theatres. Thompson far exceeds any female dancer imported by the *worthy* Mr. Carnevalle; who seems to have thought that any singers and dancers, so they were Italians, would be good enough for an Irish audience'.[68]*

This tirade was quickly followed by a second in which, the musical connoisseur exults, 'It must be a considerable satisfaction to a discerning public (who wish to encourage native theatrical merit, as well as home manufactures) to be informed, that last night appeared the first sure symptom of a speedy dissolution to the Italian Opera –

---

*This last sentence has a familiar ring about it and has been reiterated in Dublin over the past two hundred years.

the pit and galleries being opened at under prices to what were at first advertised. This is exactly in the stile of the exhibiters of giants, dwarfs, wild beasts and raree shews; with this difference, however, that such exhibiters generally stay till the last moment before they lower their terms; whereas Carnevalle and St. Giorgio, from downright want of encouragement, or rather, from the just judgement of the town, are necessitated on the commencement of the season, to shew their Squalinis, Castratos, and dancing Buffoons at half price'.[69]

Abuse of this kind persisted in almost every issue of the paper, culminating on November 27 in the following personal attack on Carnevalle who seems continually to have been the principal target. 'It is a common and true observation says a correspondent, that an upstart, when he arrives at power, generally exercises it to a degree of insolence intolerable. This was verified the other night between Mons. Laurent, a man, it must be allowed of the first abilities as ballet master, &c. and Carnevalle, who, but a few years since, was a common strolling fidler in Italy, then a smuggler, and at length came to Ireland in a very menial musical capacity, in the service of a respectable family. This upstart had the impudence to interfere with Mr. Laurent concerning the propriety of Mr. Fleury's dress, and told Laurent, that he had him now on Irish ground, and would make him know his master'.[70]

Nor did the persecution stop at acrimony in the press. More drastic action was launched in December. Continuing the saga of the unfortunate 'conductors of the Italian Opera' we now learn that 'The renowned *Peg,* who by their order was turned out of the Theatre on Wednesday night last, intends to go there this evening with pistols, declaring that she is determined to give a brace of bullets to any Italian who wants *jewels* or *pebbles,* and who dares to deny her admittance. *Peg* swears, the Theatre is open and free, on payment, to all – that her half guinea is as good and chaste as that of the purest virgin'.[71] The 'renowned Peg' was undoubtedly a well-known prostitute sent to the theatre as an *agent provocateur* both to create a disturbance and to discourage the ostensibly respectable patrons from attending.

She at least achieved a disturbance for in the next edition of the paper we read: 'On Saturday night last Signior Carnevalle, and two of the box-room keepers on Opera nights, were committed to Newgate, on a charge of Mrs. Peg Plunket, for grossly assaulting and abusing her the Wednesday evening before, and despoiling her of some ornaments during the scuffle of turning her away from the the Opera. After remaining in jail for some hours, they were released at the earnest application of some gentlemen of distinction to the Sheriffs, and to the Magistrate on whose warrant they were committed; but we hear the affair will be finally determined in a court of judicature'.[72]

If the story be true we can only ask in wonder – with whose connivance was this injustice contrived? Could it have been the notorious Francis Higgins – the 'Sham Squire ' – government informer and betrayer of Lord Edward Fitzgerald, who commenced to write for the *Freeman's Journal* in 1780,[73] becoming its owner about 1787? Higgins was associated with Richard Daly, and at the same time that the opera season was being damned, Daly's productions at Smock Alley were being lavishly praised.

The reason for the diatribe is not easy to understand but may have been due to personal spite against Carnevale. Sarcastically the obloquy in the *Freeman's Journal* continued. We find it 'reported that Lady *Macbeth* ordered her family physician to attend Carnevalle on Sunday morning last, as his confinement overnight in Newgate, and his horrors at the sight of a pair of bolts that were about to be put on him, had such a violent affect on his nerves, that alarming consequences are dreaded. We have the happiness however to inform the public that he is in a fair way of recovery, and will in all likelihood be well enough to appear to-morrow evening in the Orchestra. It is feared nevertheless that should Mrs. Peg Plunket be present, the sight of her will endanger a relapse'.[74] This was followed by the news that 'Signor Carnivalle has offered Mrs. Margaret Plunket ten tickets for admission to the opera, during the remainder of the season, for herself and sisterhood, provided that she will drop her intended prosecution; and that she returned the following verbal answer, it being *inconvenient* to Peg to write "Tell the torturer of catgut that I and my virgins will never become Lady Patronesses of his outlandish lingo – that we love true Shilelah music.'[75]

With commendable restraint Carnevale and St. Giorgio answered all criticisms six months later when in the *Hibernian Journal* of June 21 they were able, at least, to have the last word.

'Opera Intelligence', they write. 'Whereas amongst many false Reports circulated to injure the Managers of the Opera, it has been rumoured about by ill-minded Persons, with persevering Malice and Assiduity, that whilst they were making ample Fortunes by the Opera, their Performers were not paid their Salaries, and thereby were reduced to Want; Messrs. St. Giorgio and Carnavale think it incumbent on them to refute so unmerited an Aspersion on their Character, by declaring, that upon the last Quarterly Day of Payment (the stipulated Mode on the Italian Stage) they discharged their several Engagements with their Performers to the last Farthing, nay advanced Money to some, and went Security for others – they are challenged to deny it in the public Papers if they can.

'As to the ample Fortunes made by the Opera, the Reverse is literally the Fact. The Expenses of each Night's Performance, including the Travelling Charges of thirty-two Performers from a distant Country, and in War Time, included, have exceeded the Opera Receipts, Subscriptions included, by no less a Sum on an Average, than thirty Pounds per Night. – In Consequence thereof the Managers are at this Moment fourteen Hundred Pounds out of Pocket, a Deficiency which they have made good, by a Sacrifice of their own private Property, the Fruits of many Years' Industry. Moreover they are now at the close of the Season (the latter End of this Month) when a further Sum of eight Hundred Pounds will be necessary to answer their Quarterly Engagements with Performers, &c. without any probable Prospect of making Half that Sum by three Nights yet to come. Hence the Italian Managers may state their Losses this Season in no less a Sum than Two Thousand Pounds at least, not to mention their Loss of Time, and the immense Trouble unavoidably attending the Management of Musical Performances. What a melancholy Truth!'[76]

So ended what for St. Giorgio and Carnevalle must have been a melancholy season. History makes some reparation to their memory by according them the honour of being the last to present a season of Italian opera in Dublin during the eighteenth century.

Two other events took place in 1782 which deserve reference. One concerns Anna Maria Phillips, 'pupil to Mr. Linley',[77] later the renowned Mrs. Crouch, who made her first appearance in Dublin at Smock Alley Theatre on June 13, 1782, and not in 1783 as is frequently quoted. She performed Polly in *The Beggar's Opera* 'and was received with extraordinary marks of approbation'.[78]

The second event is of much more importance. An entertainment at Smock Alley on June 7 'for the Benefit of Poor Insolvent Debtors confined in the Marshalsea'[79] included the production of 'a French Comedy, called Le Barbier de Seville'.[80] The cast, headed by 'Le Sieur Fleury' as Figaro – our ballet dancer? – was, with one exception, entirely French. To the play was 'added the comic Opera, called Annette and Lubin'[81] later to be included with the last Italian opera performance. The cast was as follows:

Lubin	Le Sieur Fleury
Le Seigneur	Le Sieur Aubry (Another dancer, Obry?)
Le Bailie	Le Sieur Levasseur
Annette	Miss Hitchcock – who also played Rosina in *Le Barbier de Seville*.

Le Sieur Levasseur, who was also the Don Basile of *Le Barbier,* seems to have been the organiser of the performance, for he considered 'himself bound publicly to acknowledge the humane assistance of the Manager, Mr. Daly, who charitably declined the usual fees paid on those occasions, and accepted barely of the necessary expenses of the house'.[82]

The importance of this simple afterpiece, *Annette et Lubin,* is that it was the first and, as far as can be discovered, the only production of a French opera (in French) to be performed in Dublin during the eighteenth century. It was an important little pastoral which was to become a world success. The libretto was by the Favarts and J. B.

Lourdet de Santerre, the music by Benoit Blaise, a bassoonist and composer at the *Comédie Italienne* for thirty-five years. It is impossible to assess the standard of the Dublin performance, but of Miss Hitchcock it was recorded on another occasion that she 'sings somewhat out of tune, and walks as if her little legs were tyed together'.[83]

14

NOT A WORD OF ITALIAN

T HE FIRST DUBLIN performance of Charles Thomas Carter's *The Fair American* on New Year's eve, 1782, makes an opportune occasion to introduce the Irish tenor, John Henry Johnstone. Sir Jonah Barrington remembers Johnstone's mother calling at his grand-mother's house 'to sell raw muslins, &c. which she carried about her hips in great wallets, passing them off for a hoop'.[1] Conflicting accounts exist of everything about him, from his date and place of birth to his personality. There is of course the usual deluge of salacious theatrical gossip concerning his private life.

The weight of evidence suggests that he was born at Kilkenny on August 1, 1749, where his father was then stationed as quarter-master in a dragoon regiment. He had a good natural tenor voice and on his discharge from the army, for which various reasons have been given, he was engaged by Thomas Ryder for Smock Alley at four guineas a week. He made his first appearance there in 1775 as Lionel in *Lionel and Clarissa*.

In 1783 he was engaged by Thomas Harris, manager of Covent Garden Theatre, at a weekly salary of £16. In time he became famous for his performance of Irish – or, to be more explicit, 'Oirish' roles, and was soon known as 'Irish Johnstone'. In appearance he was 'about five feet nine inches in height, with a handsome face'.[2] He had a laughing brightness, too, which played about his countenance, and won you before he spoke'.[3] His voice was a clear melodious tenor, with a sweet, though somewhat disproportionate falsetto; and he sang in a plain and pleasing style, without the slightest affectation or mixture of the foreign graces in music'.[4]

On his Covent Garden *début*, once again in *Lionel and Clarissa*, his voice and singing were praised and, it was remarked, 'His manner of speaking is, as to its Tone, to be more commended even than his Singing – it is as harmonious as old Barry's, and as it struck our Ear last Night, very much like him.'[5] Comparison at a first performance with his distinguished fellow-countryman Spranger Barry was praise indeed. His voice is said to have deteriorated early – undoubtedly due to too much singing combined with too much good living. He took his last benefit performance at Covent Garden in 1820 when 'The first two rows of the pit were filled by his countrymen with shamrocks in their hats [and] his appearance as Dennis Brulgruddery was the signal for unanimous shouts.'[6] He died in London on December 26, 1826, and is buried in St. Paul's Churchyard, Covent Garden.

Some confusion also exists concerning the identity of Johnstone's wife, *née* Maria Ann Poitier. She was probably 'the daughter of Colonel Poitier, governor of Kilmainham gaol, an accomplished lady'[7] who joined Crow Street Theatre as a singing actress in 1776. She taught Johnstone music and performed in many operas with him in Dublin. She was also engaged with him for Covent Garden Theatre. There she made her *début* as Rosetta in *Love in a Village*, when it was reported that she 'sings prettily and pleasingly, if not capitally'.[8] A month later she won equal praise in the far more exacting role of Mandane 'unless in the Air of "Monster, away!" – in which she was twice most abominably out of Tune'.[9] But it was an unlucky change of theatres. Johnstone soon deserted her for a Mrs. Wilson and within a year or so she was dead.

Both took part in the first performance of *The Fair American* at Smock Alley Theatre on December 31, 1782, Johnstone playing Admiral Dreadnought, his wife, the role of Angelica. The remainder of the cast consisted of:

Colonel Mountford	Graham
Summers	Butler
Carbine	O'Reilly
Boreas	Kane

Bale	Wilder
Charlotte	Miss Jarrett
Rachel	Mrs. Hitchcock
Miss Kitty Dreadnought	Mrs. Heaphy.[10]

A report of a subsequent performance records that 'This Opera does not give an opportunity for an advantageous display of the abilities of the several very principal Performers who appeared in it. The part of Admiral Dreadnought seems the only character in the piece, in which any performer can possibly shine. Mr. Johnstone did it full justice, and executed his Songs with a force of expression worthy his first rate abilities'.[11] At its *première* at Drury Lane Theatre much the same opinion had been expressed though rather more pungently. It is, we read, 'an opera of that species, which for the left-handed *credit* of our theatre, but too generally prevails at present – the species of mediocrity! It is neither excellent nor execrable'.[12] Carter's music also disappointed, 'and rather exhibited a judicious prettiness, certain of not displeasing, than a bold originality capable of demanding animated applause'.[13]

The librettist of *The Fair American* was Frederick Pilon, a rather eccentric Corkman born in 1750. Having been educated in his native city, he set off for Edinburgh University to study medicine, but evidently soon decided to exchange his scalpel for the stage. His first attempt as an actor was made at Edinburgh, but failed, and he then joined a second-rate strolling company. In 1770 he returned to his native Cork where he was announced as 'a young gentleman who has had an university education, and who is also possessed of every other accomplishment necessary to form a capital Actor'.[14] Seemingly he lacked the only accomplishment he really needed – acting ability, for his initial performance revealed 'poor voice, and deportment'.[15] Michael Kelly describes him as 'a thoughtless extravagant hair-brained fellow'[16] and Boaden perceptively relates, 'He was one of the large class, who, feeling in themselves the indications of mental power, disdain the fetters of any regular profession, and determine to instruct or amuse the world by their wisdom or their wit . . He lived a life of embarrassment and died [in 1788] within a year, after his union with an amiable woman and the arrangement of his affairs began to brighten the prospect before him'.[17]

The next new opera to be performed, which in course of time was to become universally popular, was *The Castle of Andalusia*. In December it had been announced 'that the spirited Manager of Smock-alley Theatre, has purchased the copy of the Castle of Andalusia, the words, music, with all the original accompaniments, models of the scenes, clothes, &c. from the Manager of Covent-Garden, at the capital sum of Two Hundred Guineas'.[18] On January 2, 1783, expectation was heightened by information that the 'new scenes, decorations, dresses, etc., necessary to the piece, are in great forwardness; and no cost will be spared that they may be executed with the greatest taste, splendor and magnificence'.[19] The first performance took place on January 13, 1783. Like practically all operas of its type it was a *pasticcio* with 'Airs from Handel, Vento, Giordani, Bertoni, Giardini, Dr. Arne and Carolan, the Irish Bard. The Overture, Choruses and new Airs etc. composed by Dr. Arnold. With all the original Accompaniments and an additional Band'.[20] Those taking part included Ryder, Johnstone, Fotteral, Owens, Kane, Screven, Bennet, Lynch, Palmer, Butler, Wilder, O'Reilly, Mrs. Johnstone, Mrs. Melmoth, Mrs. Hitchcock, Mrs. Heaphy and Miss Jarrett.

The librettist was John O'Keeffe, a dramatist and artist born in Dublin in 1747, 'his father . . a native of King's County, and his mother (an O'Connor) of Wexford'.[21] He was a prolific writer for the stage and in the eighty-six years of his life – the last forty of which he lived a blind man – he wrote, according to his own reckoning, sixty-eight dramatic pieces. Like most dramatists and actors of his time he also wrote his *memoirs,* a kaleidoscope of people and events. Even towards the end, old and infirm, his sight completely gone, he still wrote with a dauntless sense of humour; as a man of theatre he was still on stage, the curtain had not yet come down. Eventually, it did. In 1800, Thomas Harris gave him Covent Garden Theatre for a performance – 'that night being for the benefit of the "unfortunate" author: upon which abject and ill-chosen word,' he explains, 'I seriously remonstrated'.[22] But a show of pity was required in order to attract an audience and so his friend William Lewis, the actor, urged him to speak an address from the stage, 'and have this intention put in the playbills. I shuddered at this now to me awful proposal,' he continues, 'but consented, and said I would write it myself, and that he Lewis must bring me on and fetch me off'.[23]

He still had many years to live and to the eternal credit of George IV, whose unmotivated kindly acts were few, one at least should be recorded. In 1826 a letter written by him – or by a compassionate secretary – enquires 'into the distressed circumstances of poor old O'Keeffe, now ninety years of age, and stone blind, whom I knew a little of formerly, having occasionally met him at parties of my juvenile recreation and hilarity to which he then contributed not a little'.[24] The King offered his help so that O'Keeffe might 'close his hitherto long life in comfort'.[25] As it happened O'Keeffe, though poor, was not destitute but, as he recalls, 'On Sunday the 22nd of January, 1826, my humble cabin was cheered by the presence of the Lord Bishop of Chichester, who, with the joy of benevolence, came to inform me of an accumulation of honour from the King, and a most welcome and happy addition to my means'.[26] He was to enjoy his king's bounty for seven years, until his death on February 4, 1833.

The Castle of Andalusia was first produced at Covent Garden Theatre as *The Banditti, or Love's Labyrinth,* in which form it failed completely. According to O'Keeffe, ' The audience seemed to take offence at lightning flashing outside of the house through the windows of a dark room'[27] and to have disliked one of the characters, 'a good-natured talkative old nurse'.[28] He then rewrote the opera, introducing a new role 'of a Lady Abbess' – for Ann Catley! – 'with a song and chorus of Nuns, to the tune of Stony Batter'[29] and under its new title 'its success was decisive'.[30]

In Dublin, too, it had a triumph. Daly wrote an enthusiastic letter to O'Keeffe describing its success and other newspapers re-echoed the following review which appeared in the *Freeman's Journal*: 'The uncommon reputation of Mr. O'Keeffe's celebrated opera of the Castle of Andalusia, announced yesterday evening, for the first time in this Kingdom, at the Theatre Royal, Smock-alley, drew prodigious crowds to its representation; there was soon an overflow from every part of the house. Great as the expectations of the public were raised, yet on this occasion they were amply gratified, nay, exceeded; we may venture to say, there never was a piece better got up, better performed through the whole, or better received than the Castle of Andalusia yesterday evening: the continued roar of applause, from the beginning of the opera to the end, could scarcely be paralleled, and at the dropping of the curtain, when it was given out again for Thursday next, the marks of satisfaction were astonishing'.[31]

Once again, however, as so often happened on the Dublin theatrical horizon, clouds of dissension were rising in a seemingly clear sky. The first indication of discord appeared in a newspaper announcement on January 11. 'The Public', it declares, 'is cautioned against being imposed on by a spurious copy of the Opera of the Castle of Andalusia that is about to be stole out from the most illiberal, envious, and malevolent purposes. A mangled copy having been procured in London, with an intention of being performed in Dublin, and the Managers not being able to get it up, have no other method of attempting to injure the very capital representation of it, that is to take place on Monday next, at the Theatre Royal, Smock-alley, but to insult the town with an imperfect and spurious publication'.[32]

The 'mangled copy' was intended for Crow Street Theatre* and there, despite all protests, including a published letter from O'Keeffe acknowledging Daly's sole right to the opera, it was announced for performance. With complete disdain for an author's right to his property, 'the proprietors' admitted that though they 'have not purchased their copy from the managers of Covent Garden, yet they beg leave to assure the public, that theirs is a *genuine* one, as they hope

*Originally both theatres seem to have entered into fair and open competition for the Dublin production of the opera. The *Morning Herald* (London) of November 21, 1782, reports: 'The contention is hot between the Dublin Managers for Mr. O'Keeffe's "Castle of Andalusia" and the offers run high for a copy of this excellent performance. Mr. Daly, it is supposed will carry it, as Mrs. Daly, formerly Miss Barsanti, is capital in Italian imitations, and her performance of Signora Sestini's part must render this opera a valuable acquisition to the Irish stage.' In the event, Daly in his letter to O'Keeffe regretfully had to explain, 'A very severe cold prevented Mrs. Daly the happiness of playing Lorenza. . . Miss Jarret played the part at a very short notice, and sung the songs with great applause'. (O'Keeffe. *Recollections*. Vol. II. p. 41.)

the representation will testify'.[33] Their testimony seems to have gone awry for subsequently we learn 'that low and vulgar as is [sic] Mr. O'Keeffe's comic productions in general, his "Castle of Andalusia" appeared much more so from the manner in which it was performed at Crow-street Theatre, on Tuesday night last. The parts were duplicated, and the piece so abominably mutilated, jumbled, and patched, that the elegant songs . . could not excite a smile'.[34]

Charles Thomas Carter had yet another opera, *The Milesian,* performed in Dublin on February 25,[35] this time at Crow Street for Robert Owenson's benefit. The librettist was Isaac Jackman, a Dublin journalist and dramatist born about the middle of the century. No report of the production which was described as 'a new musical farce' can be discovered.

On the same evening that *The Milesian* was being performed at Crow Street, much more important events were taking place at Smock Alley, for at that theatre was advertised 'the divine opera of Artaxerxes, in which the very celebrated Tenducci makes his first appearance, after many years absence from this Kingdom'.[36] So he did, singing the role of Arbaces, the remainder of the cast consisting of:

Artabanes	Wilder
Rimenes	Palmer
Artaxerxes	Johnstone
Semira	Mrs. Palmer
Mandane	Miss Jameson '(her first

appearance on this Stage these two years).'[37]

Tenducci had originally been engaged by Daly for six nights, but this period was to be extended. After the initial performance of *Artaxerxes* on February 25, during which he '(laboured under so heavy a cold . . that it was with great difficulty that he could in any manner get through his character)',[38] he sang again in the same opera on March 8 and 15, and on April 10.

On March 29 he appeared in 'a new English opera called Amintas; or the Princely Shepherd'.[39] The plot, we learn, 'is nearly the same as that of the Royal Shepherd, performed here some years, since; but the dialogue differs'.[40] The music, which had been selected by Tenducci, was principally 'the composition of Signor [Matteo] Rauzzini'[41] (then living in Dublin), with other airs by Giordani, Bach (Johann Christian and not his distinguished father, the great Johann Sebastian), Sacchini, Arnold and Rizzio and was 'entirely new, set by Giordani and Rauzzini'.[42] The inclusion of music claimed to have been by David Rizzio, Mary Queen of Scots' musician, is interesting although it is unlikely to have been composed by him. William Thomson published a number of airs traditionally attributed to Rizzio in his *Orpheus Caledonius* in 1725 and it may have been one of these. The cast included Tenducci as Amintas – 'The other principal characters by Signor Urbani (his first appearance this season), Mr. Wilder and Miss Jameson'.[43] Miss Jarrett was also advertised to take part. The opera was repeated on April 5 and 12.

There had been a pause in Tenducci's season on March 18 for the first Dublin performance of the comic opera *Rosina, or Love in a Cottage* which was presented as an 'afterpiece'. The librettist was Frances Brooke, a literary lady of high moral tone who also wrote dull novels.

The composer was William Shield, who was born in County Durham in 1748. His father was a singing teacher who taught him music from the age of six. He was later apprenticed to a boat builder, probably due to his father's early death, but soon returned to music, eventually becoming principal violinist at the theatre in Scarborough. In 1772 he set out for London where he found employment as violinist and viola player. His first comic opera, *The Flitch of Bacon,* was produced at the Haymarket Theatre in 1778. Its success led to his engagement as composer to Covent Garden where *Rosina* was first performed in 1782. In 1817 he had the honour of being appointed Master of the King's Musick. Today, one song only, 'The Ploughboy', from his and John O'Keeffe's opera *The Farmer*, often considered to be a folksong, retains his name and place in the repertory. He died in 1827 and is buried in Westminster Abbey.

Hogarth assessed Shield's music fairly when he wrote: It 'is not marked by force or energy, but it is perfectly suited to the subjects

P

of the pieces, which are sweet and simple pictures of rural life. His melodies in style, character, and adaptation to the accents of our native speech, are perfectly English; though, in their smoothness, grace, and refinement, they bear marks of the composer's intimate acquaintance with the Italian school'.[44]

In Dublin a preliminary notice of the opera's production stated that 'There has not been a piece performed for several years so much the fashion . . Their Majesties have repeatedly commanded it, and so much is it the topic in London, that not to have seen Rosina implies a want of taste'.[45] The artists who took part in the performance were Johnstone, Butler, Wilder, Fotteral, Owens, Palmer, Mrs. Hitchcock, Mrs. Heaphy and Miss Jarrett.[46]

Returning to Tenducci: on May 8 'a new English opera called Pharnaces'[47] was announced for his benefit. There was undoubtedly some similarity between this opera and *Pharnaces, or the Revenge of Athridates,* originally performed in Dublin during December 1765 and July 1766. There was, however, considerable difference in the music employed. This, we find, was 'selected by Mr. Tenducci' from 'Bach, Dr. Arne, Paisiello, Cimarosa, Galuppi, Cocchi, Vento, David Rizzio, Rauzzini &c . . The Overture, first and last, by Alexandri [?Felice Alessandri] and the middle Movement by Hayden'.[48] He also introduced seven airs of his own composition, an air by the Neapolitan composer, di Majo (?Giovanni Francesco), and a chorus by the Dublin organist, Richard Woodward. The libretto was also altered, an 'ingenious author' having 'composed most of the stanzas for the airs'.[49]

The 'ingenious author' turned out to be Robert Houlton, a graduate of Oxford University who had arrived in Dublin in 1767 or 1768 with a new form of inoculation against small-pox. In Dublin he was admitted to an *ad eundem* M.A. of Trinity College and subsequently, it is said, to an M.B., but the conferring of the latter degree is doubtful as no evidence of it can be found. He was, however, usually described as 'Doctor'.* He seems to have been a kindly man for

---

*The *Freeman's Journal,* July 30/August 1, 1789, published an announcement from 'Doctor Houlton' concerning an alleged libel in which he claims 'that he bears very respectable Degrees in the Universities of Oxford and Dublin'.

finding the poet Thomas Dermody destitute, he took him to live in his house. (The house at the time was being ostentatiously decorated by a Smock Alley scene-painter.) He certainly was one of the many flamboyant figures who lived in a Dublin *demi-monde* of the theatre, law, medicine, politics and spying for the English government toward the end of the eighteenth century.

In 1770 the Dublin newspapers had published a scurrilous correspondence between him and an apothecary in Capel Street named John Clark. Such expressions as 'the living picture of Shakespeare's beggarly apothecary' and 'fastidious fugitive empyrical quack'[50] were freely exchanged. As a 'medical practitioner' he seems to have succeeded for a time. For example, in May 1770 we read, 'Mr. Houlton, having been engaged for some Time to attend the Inoculation of several Families in the Baronies of Tyrawly and Hollymount, in the County of Mayo, he cannot receive any more Applications in Dublin until his Return, of which he will give Notice in the Papers'.[51] Later, evidently, his practice declined and so, like a poor man's Oliver Goldsmith, he turned his talents to writing for the stage, and to journalism, as a literary associate of Francis Higgins.

The cast of *Pharnaces* was as follows:

Pharnaces	Tenducci
Athridates	Wilder
Gilades	Palmer
Mithrenes	Master Gemea
Pompey	Urbani
Selinda	Miss Jarrett
Aspasia	Miss Jameson.[52]

The success of the production seemed assured, for we read: 'On account of the extraordinary demand for places (all the Boxes being already taken) Mr. Tenducci begs the indulgence of the Public, to grant him leave to accomodate the Ladies and Gentlemen who have desired places, in the Pit'.[53] That success was achieved is confirmed by a report that 'The opera of Pharnaces, performed on Thursday night to a most numerous and brilliant audience, contains much of the most capital music that ever captivated the ear of a most splendid and judicious audience. Mr. Tenducci's vocal powers and execution won him the loudest peals of applause. Miss Jameson gained much credit. She was always allowed to have a sweet and excellent voice, but since she has evidently received great improvement in point of taste, from Tenducci's manner, she may be said to be one of the first singers on any stage. The rest of the performers supported their characters, and executed their airs with considerable force and approbation. The words of many of the songs, in this opera, were exceedingly admired; and though in general set to Italian music, must have had a far more pleasing effect, than the nonsensical jargon in general of those Operas which were performed here, last winter, in the Italian language.'[54]

The season continued with a second performance of *Pharnaces* on May 17. *Artaxerxes,* for Urbani's benefit, was advertised to take place on May 31, but the performance seems to have been cancelled. This opera was, however, performed for the last time that season on June 17. Tenducci, Wilder, Palmer and Mrs. Palmer retained their roles, but Urbani took over Artaxerxes from Johnstone and Anna Maria Phillips sang Mandane, 'being her first appearance this season'.[55] She was to continue the season in pastoral and comic operas.

At this point it is necessary to go back in time to notice Robert Houlton's first successful effort for the Dublin stage, not for his libretto, but because of his musical colleagues. It was a comic opera named *The Contract* and it had had its first performance, the only one that season, at Smock Alley Theatre on May 14, 1782. The cast included Mitchell, Fotteral, Wood, Cornelys, Kane, Gemea, Murphy, Johnstone, Mrs. Heaphy, Mrs. Hitchcock, Miss Hitchcock, Miss Wood and Mrs. Johnstone.[56]

The composers, two young Irishmen who were later to earn renown, were Philip Cogan, whose musical reputation was merited, and John Andrew Stephenson* (later Sir John), then only twenty-two years old, whose subsequent distinction was much less justified. Stephenson was to compose about ten operas, but even in his arrangements of Moore's *Melodies,* by which he is now solely remembered,

*Later the name was usually spelled Stevenson.

he showed poor musicianship. Sir Jonah Barrington has observed that 'some of Sir John's proceedings in melodizing simplicity, remind me of the Rev. Mark Hare, who whitewashed the great rock of Cashel to give it a *genteel* appearance against the visitation'.[57] Music for *The Contract* was also composed by Monsieur Laurent (the ballet dancer) and it was announced that 'The adapted Airs are some of the most admired Compositions of Giordani, &c.'[58] On May 24, 1783, it was performed for the fifth time '(being for the Author's Benefit)'.[59]

Tenducci's winter season, which had been announced as early as the previous April 19, began on November 15 with a performance of *Artaxerxes*. The cast was the same as in the previous February except that Johnstone, now in London, had again been replaced by Urbani. On this evening, in addition to the afterpiece, there was the attraction of 'several performances on the Tight Rope by Signor Placido, with a variety of Tumbling by Signor Placido and Mr. Huntley, from the Theatre Royal, London'.[60]

The Castle of Andalusia was revived on November 19 with Tenducci as Alphonso '(with additional songs)', and Urbani as Phillipo '(being their first appearance in those characters)'.[61] The opera was repeated on November 26, December 3 and 6 (when it was commanded by the Lord Lieutenant, Lord Northington), on December 13 and 18 (a second command performance), and on January 10 and 15, 1784.

Amintas also had had a revival on November 29. The cast was announced for this performance and was as follows:

Amintas	Tenducci
Alexander	Wilder
Guards	Lynch, Murphy, Malone
Officer	Withrington
Agenor	Urbani
Thamyris	Mrs. Palmer
Eliza	Miss Jameson.

'The Dances incidental to the Opera by Mr. Ward, (his 1st appearance, this season), Monsieur Greco, Miss Andre and Signora Rossignoli.'[62]

With such activity at Smock Alley Theatre it is remarkable to find a significant operatic enterprise occurring across the Liffey in Capel Street at the same time. This came about as follows. Tommaso Giordani after twelve years' absence from Dublin had returned during the summer of 1783 to take part in a series of concerts at the Rotunda Gardens. Performing with him was the noted singer Leoni, and thus began an association, limited in its artistic design, disastrous in its financial consequences, but historically a symbol marking the first and only attempt to found a national opera house, however unsophisticated, in Dublin.

Leoni was a Jewish cantor whose real name was Myer Lyon. He was reputedly born at Frankfurt-on-Main, but this is uncertain and seemingly his birth-date cannot be traced. Even as a boy the exceptional quality of his singing carried his reputation to London, where he was promptly engaged for the synagogue in Duke's Place at Aldgate. His success there led to an introduction to David Garrick, who, impressed by his talent, obtained the permission of the elders of the synagogue to allow him to appear at Drury Lane Theatre. He made his first appearance there on December 13, 1760, when he 'was received with great applause'.[63] In a letter of October 12, 1760, Garrick refers to him as 'ye boy Leoni'[64] so he must have Italianised his name prior to his Drury Lane appearance and he cannot then have been more than fifteen or sixteen years old. He next seems to have quitted the theatre for a time and to have returned to the synagogue. However in October 1775 he was on stage again, singing Arbaces in *Artaxerxes* at Covent Garden. His most famous role was Don Carlos in *The Duenna* which he performed at the same theatre for its exceptionally long run. He was still singing in the theatres and at concerts in London as late as 1788 and possibly later. Eventually he emigrated to Kingston, Jamaica, where he was appointed 'Chazan' at the local synagogue, and where he died about 1800.

His voice, due partly perhaps to his specialised training, seems to have been unusual although in a period when florid singing was universal, this should have attracted far less notice than it would now. It may have been its quality which was displeasing to some, for we read that 'his tone of voice was that which by the cognoscenti is termed a falsetto'.[65] Today, the counter-tenor, known through one or two notable exponents, would resemble it and as such it may have sounded strange to audiences used only to castrati or tenors.

Boaden relates that 'Its effect resembled the flute part of an organ with the tremor stop upon it'.[66] Another writer records, 'The truth is, that Leoni has in reality, *no voice* at all – his tones being neither *vocal* nor *instrumental*. They have a peculiarity of sound in them that we never heard before. When he stood before us on the Stage, the voice did not seem to proceed from his lips, but fell into our ears as if it had descended from the clouds. This rendered it a matter more of curiosity than delight; and his admirers therefore, lay mostly among the female part of his audiences, who are ever well pleased when their curiosity is satisfied'.[67] When advising Thomas Linley on the composition of *The Duenna*, Sheridan wrote of Leoni, 'I should tell you that he sings nothing well, but in a plaintive or pastoral style; and his voice is such as appears to me to be hurt by much accompaniment'.[68] His abilities were perhaps most authoritatively summed up in the following review of his Arbaces: 'In the songs his taste and execution was [sic] manifest; and when it is considered he sings in a feigned voice, admiration cannot be carried too high. In the pathetic he evinced a feeling superior to any performer since Tenducci. He executed the divisions with a degree of neatness and articulation, that could not fail of giving delight to a cultivated ear . . however, the total absence of any ability as an actor rendered his recitatives tedious and insipid'.[69] We may perhaps assume that his acting was to improve with greater stage experience.

Leoni very probably made his first Dublin appearance at the Rotunda Gardens on June 13, 1777.[70] He sang there again during the following year. On September 13, 1783, the opera season arranged by him and Giordani was first announced in the following notice:
'Opera House. Messrs Giordani and Leoni with the utmost respect inform the Nobility, Gentry and Public in general, that they have

taken the New Theatre* in Capel-street, which they intend to
dedicate solely to the exhibition of English Operas, during the
ensuing Winter season. The entertainments will chiefly consist of new
Pieces. The Vocal Performers will be select, and of real Excellence; –
and every Attention will be given that the Orchestra be filled with
Proficients of the first Abilities on their respective Instruments. That
the Public may have the opportunity of judging the Merit of the
proposed Entertainments, Subscriptions are at first solicited for only
Twelve Nights, at Three Guineas the Subscription. Books for
receiving Subscriber's Names are opened at Messrs. Giordani's and
Leoni's Lodgings, No. 19, Abbey-street; at T. T. Faulkiner's Esq,
Parliament-street; and at Mr. Rice's, Jeweller, Capel-street.'[71]

This was followed by a second notice two months later which
reported that 'On account of the great and extensive preparations,
particularly in point of Scenery, which are making at the Opera
House, the Subscribers and Public in general, are most respectfully
informed, that the theatre will not open 'till about a fortnight . .
N.B. An idea having gone abroad, that Italian Operas, with Recitatives, &c. are intended to be exhibited at this Theatre, the Managers
beg leave to observe, that not a word of Italian, nor a single line of
Recitative shall be introduced in any one of the Representations'.[72]

Meanwhile, administration went ahead. The theatre was renovated.
'Subscriber's Nights' were advertised 'twice a Week, viz on Wednesdays and Saturdays, when the Pit will be opened with the Boxes at
Box Price, the Seats being stuffed, and to be elegantly covered for that
Purpose'.[73] Mr. Cullen of 5 Fownes Street had been appointed box-
keeper and from new addresses (48 Great Britain Street and 6
Ormond Quay), Giordani and Leoni requested subscribers 'to be as
speedy as possible in fixing on their Boxes and Seats; that no Mistake
may be made on the opening of the House'.[74] Postponements then
occurred: first, on December 10, 'On account of Mr. Leoni's not
arriving from England till Saturday last'[75] (December 6); then, on

---

* Not Stretch's Puppet Theatre that William Dawson had leased in 1770. This was a second
theatre which had been hastily erected by a number of disgruntled players from Smock Alley
Theatre and which was first opened on January 17, 1744/45.

December 15, 'It having been expected that some very capital pieces of scenery and machinery that are preparing . . would have been ready by Monday next, it is found they cannot be completely executed till the Thursday following'.[76] At last, on 'the Thursday following', December 18, 1783, the theatre opened.

The programme consisted of 'A New Comic Opera entitled Gibraltar. With new Dresses, new Scenery, Machinery, Decorations, &c. &c. The Music entirely new and composed by Signor Giordani. The Scenery, Machinery, &c. done from Models designed by Mr. Messink, from the Theatre-Royal of Drury-lane and Covent-Garden, and painted by Mr. Jolly. The principal Characters by Mr. Leoni (his first Appearance on Stage in this Kingdom) Mr. Barrington, Mr. T. Baker (their first Appearance in this Kingdom) Mr. Waterhouse (his first Appearance on any Stage) Mr. Glenvil; Mr. Corry (his first Appearance on any Stage) Mr. Whitmore; Mr. Murphy; Mr. Smith; Mr. Brennan; and Mr. Miell (his first Appearance these Ten Years in this Kingdom). Mrs. Melmoth (her first Appearance on this Stage) Miss Langrishe (her 1st Appearance in this Kingdom) Miss Evans (her 1st Appearance on any Stage) Miss Palmer, and Miss Wheeler, from Venice (being her first Appearance on an English Stage) . . to which will be added A Musical After-Piece (never yet performed) entitled The Haunted Castle'.[77]

The company was hardly distinguished and, from the number of first appearances, one might even add, somewhat inexperienced. Giordani, who had also composed the score of *The Haunted Castle*, was evidently depending more on his music than his players to carry off the season and in this he almost succeeded. Prices of admission were modest – Boxes 5/–, Pit 3/–, Galleries 2/– and 1/– and for the opening performance the theatre was ritually 'illuminated with wax'.[78]

The Dublin newspaper reviews all too obviously overrated these two productions – as they would others during the season. The *Freeman's Journal,* especially, published reports invariably eulogistic and mostly dull, which tell nothing of interest either about the music, production or performances. Without exception they suggest that the season was splendidly successful.

Two notices taken from London newspapers seem to be more objective and so are more informative. The first reports: 'Last night Giordani and Leoni opened their house in Capel-street for the performance of English Operas. The Opera was named "Gibraltar", the after-piece "The Haunted Castle" in both of which Miss Wheeler yclep'd the English Nightingale, and lately from Venice performed a principal part. Though her acting is rather destitute of those necessary stage requisites, ease and elegance, yet she sung most divinely; the sweetness and melody of her voice far surpassing any-thing ever heard in this country. Her songs were repeatedly encored, and she received the most unbounded applause from the audience who were people of the first fashion in Dublin, among whom was his Grace the Duke of Leinster. Leoni personated the noble veteran of the rock, from which the piece derives its name. One or two of his songs were admirable, but he did not meet with uncommon applause: his vocal powers seem much altered for the worse.'[79]

The second reports, as early as January 6, 1784, 'The Opera scheme of Giordani and Leoni, in Dublin, has already so far begun to droop, that they thought it elligible to depart from their original plan of music only, and vary their entertainments with the addition of either a play or a farce'.[80] Shorn of the praise in the Dublin reviews, this tells us that Miss Wheeler was very good, that Leoni was then beyond his best and that as a season of opera the enterprise seems to have been doomed from the start.

Miss Wheeler was without doubt the star of the company. She was one of those artists who have a meteoric career and then are heard of no more. According to John O'Keeffe she was the daughter of a Mrs. Parsloe who kept a chop-house in St. James' Street, London. She became a pupil of Venanzio Rauzzini and probably made her first stage appearance at the theatre in Bath in 1781 – not at Capel Street as stated above. After leaving Bath, she went to Italy for further study. Her engagement in Dublin was extremely successful. She was even more popular than the famous Mrs. Billington who was making her first Dublin appearance at Smock Alley at the same time. This success gained her engagements in London—at Covent Garden in

1784, where she played Celia in the first performance of O'Keeffe's opera *Fontainebleau,* and at the King's Theatre, as 'second woman' in 1786. By November 1788 she was performing in Belfast. She had then married a Mr. Molloy, but subsequently 'lost her husband in a disagreeable manner'.[81] She is said to have died in 1794.

The librettist of *Gibraltar* was Robert Houlton. Wally Chamberlain Oulton, a Dublin-born dramatist and theatre historian who was later to gain some success in London, was the author of *The Haunted Castle.* He wrote it while still a boy.

On December 31, 1783, *Gibraltar* was performed with 'a musical entertainment "The Enchantress" written by a lady, music by Signor Giordani'.[82] The lady was an Anna Maria Edwards[83] and *The Enchantress or The Happy Island* included a new artist of some importance in the cast. He was Peter Duffy, who began his adult life as a Dublin hatter, 'but declined business for the stage, having been flattered by his friends, into a high opinion of his vocal abilities'.[84] He may have been the proprietor of 'Peter Duffy, and Co. Hatters' who in 1780 had 'opened shop at No 10 College-Green within one door of Anglesea-street' and who having just returned from London assured all those who might command them that they could 'depend on having their Hats cocked in the newest and most fashionable Manner, now in Use in that Metropolis'.[85] His *début* at Capel Street was most successful and he was 'allowed by Connoiseurs to have the best natural voice of any man-performer now on the Irish or English stage'.[86] As a pupil of Giordani he succeeded well enough to be engaged for Covent Garden in 1789, but he remained there only one season, afterwards singing at Vauxhall Gardens. In 1805 *The Thespian Dictionary* reported, 'He then found it necessary to return to business, though different to his first occupation, and has been lately married'.

A 'new comic opera' called *The Happy Disguise* was then performed on January 7, 1784.[87] The librettist was again Wally Oulton, the composer, Giordani, and however eulogistic the reviews, the following appraisal of Giordani at least was deserved: 'in the four new pieces already brought out, at the opera-house, more genuine new music has been presented the town, than has been given for the last 10 years at all the theatres in Ireland'.[88] It is unlikely however that quality equalled quantity.

The season continued with a variety of performances. On January 21, *Love in a Village* was produced 'with new Finales and several new Airs composed by Signor Giordani'.[89] Duffy played Young Meadows, Miss Wheeler, Rosetta. A second actress in the company was admonished as follows: 'A frequenter of the Opera House [begged] to ask Miss Langrishe if yellow shoes and paste buckles were proper, on the last representation of "Love in a Village," in her part of the House-maid; and if last night, the cap of feathers which she wore in the opera "Gibraltar" was suitable to her, as a spirit in the "Enchantress". The frequenter of the Opera House [was] sorry also to observe, within these few days, a giggling inattention in Miss Langrishe, and negligence of dress, that render her far less pleasing than on her first appearance, at the Opera House'.[90]

The Maid of the Mill for Miss Wheeler's benefit was performed on February 2, and on February 9 Giordani had his benefit in a 'Masque' called the *Genius of Ireland* with yet again the 'music entirely new and composed'[91] by him.

On February 16 the twenty-fifth performance of *Gibraltar* took place before 'a very numerous and polite audience'.[92] Some uncertainty exists about the exact number of times *Gibraltar* was performed. On March 6 it was announced for the 'Twenty-Third Time'.[93] Should this have been *thirty*-third or had somebody anticipated the twenty-fifth performance on February 16? In either event the opera was having a most successful run which seemed to justify Giordani's belief in his compositions and in his venture. We read, for example, 'Several Families of the first Distinction having been disappointed of places on Thursday last [February 26] it is humbly hoped that the Nobility and Gentry, who wish to honour the next Representation of the Opera with their presence, will be early in their application for Seats'.[94]

On February 24, 1784, a second subscription for the 'English Opera House' was invited. Both Giordani's and Leoni's names are appended to the announcement but it is extremely unlikely that Leoni had anything to do with this second season. He took his benefit in *The Beggar's Opera* and *The Haunted Castle* on March 2, and shortly afterwards, probably after the performance of *Gibraltar* on March 6, must have set out for London. This is confirmed by a report on April 28 that 'At the desire of many Ladies and Gentlemen, Mr. Leoni has consented to appear once more in public on Saturday next, at Covent Garden Theatre, when he will sing his most approved Airs, being positively the only Night of his performing this Season'.[95]

The second subscription season continued consequently under the sole direction of the indefatigable Giordani. On Wednesday March 3 a surprising change occurred in the programme, when Handel's oratorio *Messiah* was performed, followed on Friday March 5 by *Judas Maccabaeus*. It was of course during Lent. Some ambiguity occurs in the advertisements concerning the venue of these two performances. They may have taken place at the Rotunda which would seem the more appropriate environment, but evidence in favour of the theatre is to be found in an article *Eighteenth Century Magazine Music* by W. J. Lawrence.[96] In this Mr. Lawrence gives a list of music published between 1743 and 1794 in *Exshaw's London Magazine*. From No 253, March 1784, he records 'Song in the Oratorio of "The Messiah" as sung at the Opera House, Capel Street.'

On March 4, *Love in a Village* had another performance combined with a 'Farce' called *The Musical Lady* which had 'Several new Airs composed by Signor Giordani'.[97] The libretto may have been an adaptation by a Mr. Williams of the elder George Colman's farce of the same name. On March 11, still another 'new musical Entertainment . . The Dying Indian' was performed, 'The music the entire composition of Signor Giordani with Finales, Choruses, &c. incidental to the piece'.[98] This was followed on March 25 by *The Lady of the Manor*, 'written by the late Dr. Kenrick, and never performed in this Kingdom, with alterations and new Finales written by the author of the opera of Gibraltar [Houlton had submitted *Love in a Village* to the same type of surgery] and set to music by Signor Giordani'.[99] The original composer of *The Lady of the Manor* was James Hook. The 'late Dr. Kenrick' had been a journalist and scurrilous libeller (particularly of David Garrick); he at least had the courage of his arrogance and the effrontery to record it in the following epigram:

'The wits who drink water and suck sugar candy
Impute the strong spirit of Kenrick to brandy
They are not so much out; the matter in short is
He sips *aqua-vitae,* and spits *aqua-fortis.*'[100]

Lionel and Clarissa was next presented on March 30.

Then, in June, Giordani made what appears to have been a last prodigal throw for success. This was the production of 'a tragic-comic, farcical, pantominical, burlesque opera of Orpheus and Euridice'[101] which had been first announced as early as the previous January. During January a version of Gluck's *Orfeo ed Euridice* had been profitably staged at Smock Alley Theatre, and presumably the opportunity to exploit a ready-made success was too good to miss. The extravagance of Giordani's game lay in his engagement of Elizabeth Billington, who had been the Euridice at Smock Alley, for the Capel Street company. It was here that she entered into direct competition with Miss Wheeler, and it was here – for a very short time – that Miss Wheeler was declared the winner. Such competition was undoubtedly encouraged. Even before the first performance it was asserted that 'The finest duet perhaps, that ever was sung in this Kingdom, will be executed, on Monday next in the new burlesque opera of Orpheus and Euridice . . The duet is to be sung by no less vocal performers than Mrs. Billington and Miss Wheeler, a piece of intelligence that cannot fail of being exceedingly welcome to all true lovers of harmony'[102] – nor, it might be added, 'to all true lovers' of singing as a competitive sport.

There was what seemed like desperate extravagance too in the *mise-en-scène*: eight different scenes described as 'more perhaps than ever appeared in any one Piece, and equal, if not superior, to any that ever was presented in any theatre in the three Kingdoms'.[103] In fact so elaborate was the production that, it was announced, 'From this very extraordinary number of new scenes, and the many men indispensibly required to work them, it is earnestly requested that no Person whatever, exclusive of those immediately concerned, will solicit to be admitted behind the scenes, as a refusal must be general and peremptory'.[104]

The first performance took place on June 14, when we read, 'An audience principally of the first distinction and so crowded, that notwithstanding the severity of the evening, there was an overflow from every part of the house, stamped such a sanction on this opera, by as repeated loud and continuous plaudits as ever filled a theatre, that its stability of representation is secured beyond any possibility of doubt . . Mr. Moss in the character of Orpheus had ample field for his comic powers . . but it is impossible to paint the merits of Mrs. Billington in St. Cecilia – and Miss Wheeler in Euridice. The united powers of harmony seemed centred in them. They may be truly said to have fascinated the whole audience'.[105] Ten further performances resulted, the last taking place on July 27.

Then the following doleful announcement appeared. 'English Opera House, Capel-street. On account of Mrs. Billington's indisposition which will not admit of her appearing Abroad for a short Interval, the Public are most respectfully informed, that the Opera-House is closed until Monday the 30th of next Month'.[106] But it was never to re-open under Giordani's management. Instead he joined Richard Daly at Smock Alley Theatre as composer and musical arranger when the next season began. Presumably he made some arrangement with his creditors, paid his debts and lived long enough afterwards to forget the unhappy experiment. He was to remain at Smock Alley Theatre until it closed in 1787, and in the next year he transferred to Crow Street. He had married a Dublin lady named Wilkinson and spent the remainder of his life in Dublin as a composer and music teacher. He died there at his home in Great Britain Street in February 1806.

Two unbiassed authorities, Dr. La Tourette Stockwell and Mr. W. J. Lawrence, have suggested that Giordani's venture was dramatic rather than operatic. Stockwell states unequivocally that 'The title of English Opera was misleading for the real purpose of this theatre was to produce a number of light pieces by Irish writers each with some musical embellishments by Giordani'.[107] The facts refute this.

Without attempting to divine what Giordani may or may not have had in mind when he announced his intention to 'dedicate' the season 'solely to the exhibition of English Operas', he did declare his interest in the orchestra and he did stress that 'The Vocal Performers would be select and of real Excellence'. Regarding the singers he at least kept his word. Miss Wheeler, Mrs. Billington, Leoni and Peter Duffy all had careers of greater or lesser importance in London. Also, it was these singers and not his actors and actresses who received the greater publicity and, as has been noted, it was merely in a vain attempt to bolster up 'their original plan of music only' that he and Leoni introduced 'the addition of either a play or a farce'.

Furthermore, Giordani chose 'Irish writers' not for their 'light pieces' but as indispensable providers of his libretti. As a composer with little capital or resources, he was unlikely to entice a libretto from successful authors such as John O'Keeffe or General Burgoyne and so he fell back on Houlton and the boy Wally Oulton, both of whom were at hand – physically and financially. Certainly this was no attempt to found an eighteenth-century Abbey Theatre. Giordani was not an actor like Barry, Mossop or Daly; he was a composer. Hearing some of his music now one is obliged to add, a pretty third-rate composer. Still, a grandiloquent statement which declared, 'what would demand half the life of some composers to accomplish, Giordani effects in a few weeks, so powerful are his conceptions and with such rapidity and facility does he write',[108] had some truth in it. Facile and rapid he certainly was, as his programme for the season can testify. Yet, what did he accomplish? Nothing! His dream of an English Opera House in Dublin or what, were he alive today, he would undoubtedly be promoting as Irish National Opera, seemed – at least to him – a good idea at the time. But the time was not right; nor, for Dublin and a national opera, has it come right since.

15

'ORPHEUS' AND
MRS. BILLINGTON

IF ONE HAD to list the most important years of opera in Dublin during the eighteenth century, it would be difficult to exclude 1784, for in that year Gluck's *Orfeo ed Euridice* was performed, and among the singers taking part was the soprano Elizabeth Billington – one of two prima donnas who would dominate the Dublin lyric stage for the succeeding thirteen years.

Orfeo ed Euridice was produced in an English version at Smock Alley Theatre, and in returning to Smock Alley from Capel Street one must also go back in time, for its first performance took place on January 5, 1784. The production was organised by Tenducci who, it will be remembered, was then singing at that theatre, and was advertised as follows:

'Orpheus and Euridice. An English musical Drama, in imitation of the ancient Greek Theatrical Feasts, as performed at the principal Theatres in Europe, with uncommon applause. The music principally by the Chevalier Christopher Gluck, Composer to the Emperor, with additions by the late celebrated John Christopher Bach. The Orchestra to be enlarged, and the Band conducted by Master Weichsel. The Character of Orpheus by Mr. Tenducci. Principal Shepherds, Furies and Shades of departed Heroes by Messrs Wood, Cubitt, Wilder, Powell, Palmer, Owenson, Meadows, Lynch &c. &c. Hymen – Mr. Urbani. Amore – Miss Hitchcock. Principal Shepherdesses, Furies and Shades of departed Heroines by Miss Jameson, Mrs. Hitchcock, Mrs. Taplin, Mrs. Beynon, Miss Jarret, Mrs. Palmer, Mrs. Meadows, Mrs. AEcey, &c. &c. And the Character of Euridice by Mrs. Billington (being her first appearance in this Kingdom). The

Q

Dances composed on the ancient Greek model, by Mr. D'Elpini. The principal characters by Messrs D'Elpini, Ward, Huntley, Grecco, Signora Rossignoli, Mme. Urbani, Mrs. O'Reilly and Signora Andre. The Scenes entirely new and painted by Mr. Walmsley, pupil of Mr. Loutherbourg. The machinery by Mr. Kelly. The dresses by Mr. Campbell and Miss Fox. In the course of the performance will be introduced Views of the infernal regions, the Elysian Fields and the Temple of Love.'[1]

It epitomizes the theatrical taste of the time that after this extolling of Gluck and *Orpheus,* the advertisement should end – 'to which will be added a Farce'.[2] Yet, exceptional care seems to have been taken with the production, and we learn that 'The performers are obliged to attend rehearsals twice every day. The manager has been under the necessity of giving up two nights this week and having no play, that all his attention might be directed to the grand object in view – Scene painters, carpenters, taylors, mantua makers (*it is said there are upwards of one hundred dresses for the piece*) mechanists, property-men, &c. &c. work day and night. In short, as it is allowed that Orpheus and Euridice will be the most expensive, so it is expected to be the most capital entertainment ever exhibited in this kingdom'.[3]

The approbation of the following detailed notice indicates that these unusual efforts were justified by the result. 'Yesterday evening', we read, 'the opera of Orpheus and Euridice was exhibited for the first time in this Kingdom, at the Theatre-royal, Smock-alley, to a very crowded and brilliant audience, in a style that reflected the highest credit on the manager, for the finished manner in which it was represented. The well-known story of Orpheus was first adapted to the stage, and set to music by the Chevalier Gluck,* by command of the Emperor, and brought out at Vienna, with the utmost magnificence. Its fame quickly spread thro' Europe and wherever an opera was established, Orfée ranked in the highest place. Mr. Tenducci, when in Italy had often an opportunity of performing the character; and his surprising execution of the songs, decidedly

---

*But only if one ignores compositions by Monteverdi, Luigi Rossi, Sartorio and others. (*Author.*)

fixed his character as the first singer in Europe. In London, Orpheus brought more money than any opera ever produced. Tho' it has long been wished for in this Kingdom, by the lovers of music, yet the very great expense, and the want of capital performers hitherto hindered the managers from attempting it. Mr. Daly, whose spirit in the service of the public no bounds can restrain, boldly undertook the arduous task; how he succeeded, the unbounded plaudits of the audience sufficiently testify.

'The music of "Orpheus" is acknowledged to be amongst the very first compositions; and it was executed thro' the whole with utmost correctness. Mr. Tenducci never sung or acted better. His last scene particularly was a masterpiece, and the celebrated song "What alas! shall Orpheus do?" [*Che farò senza Euridicè*] was capable of moving the most obdurate breast. Mrs. Billington was first introduced to our acquaintance in the character of Euridice, and in every respect fully answered our most sanguine expectations. Her figure is remarkably easy, elegant and interesting; her face beautiful, animated, and expressive of the passions; her voice harmonious and extensive, cultivated by the best masters, and capable of executing the most difficult passages with the greatest ease; her recitatives and several of her airs, particularly, "Forbear, forbear to sooth my griefs" were beyond description enchanting, and justly ranks her with the first singers ever in this Kingdom. Miss Hitchcock gave us a perfect idea of the heart-stealing god of love, who had just purloined his mother's smiles and graces.

'The choruses, as they were supported by the most respectable number of musical performers ever at one time in a theatre in Dublin, so they were the best executed and contributed much to the success of the piece. The band was excellent, and conducted by Master Weichsel, who gave fresh proofs, especially in the song of "Comfortless is every thought", of his surprising taste and execution. The dances were characteristic; the dresses remarkably picturesque. The scenes painted by Mr. Walmesley had great merit, and deserved the utmost praise. The whole formed the most beautiful and finished entertainment ever exhibited in this Kingdom. It was received with unbounded testimonies of approbation and there is not the least doubt but the opera of Orpheus and Euridice from its great merit, and the very capital manner in which it is exhibited, will become as great a favourite in Dublin, as hitherto it has been in any part of Europe'.[4]

When *Orfeo ed Euridice* was first produced in London in 1770, music by J. C. Bach and Pietro Guglielmi was interpolated. Not even Gluck's masterpiece was sacrosanct from that ingrained British theatrical idiosyncrasy, the *pasticcio,* and between its first London performance and a Covent Garden revival in 1792, extraneous music by at least Bach, Guglielmi, Handel, Anfossi, Sacchini, Weichsel, Reeve, Mazzinghi and Gyrowetz had been introduced into its several productions. It is necessary therefore to consider how much the opera owed its success in Dublin to Gluck, how important were the 'additions' of J. C. Bach, and if music by other composers was included.

Smock Alley was the first theatre to stage an English version of the opera. The libretto had been translated by Francis Gentleman, a Dublin actor and dramatist born in York Street in 1728. He was to have a varied and interesting but unsuccessful career and died on December 18, 1784, at George's Lane, 'having during the last seven years of his life undergone extreme sickness and want'.[5] Unfortunately Gentleman's libretto does not seem to have been published, a rather remarkable omission in view of the importance of the production. He may have been incapable of making the necessary effort at the time, for he was to die within the year.

A vocal score in English translation, but omitting the author's name, was published in London in 1792, associated with a revival of the opera then taking place at Covent Garden. The titles of the three airs mentioned in the review of the Smock Alley performance, 'What alas! shall Orpheus do?', 'Forbear, forbear to sooth my griefs' and 'Comfortless is every thought' correspond exactly with the titles in the London score, denoting that Gentleman's translation was again employed. This is confirmed by a manuscript note on a playbill advertising the Covent Garden production which reads, 'alt. from the Italian by F. Gentleman first acted in Dublin'.[6] The phraseology of part of

Gentleman's translation, however, seems to owe more to the French version of Pierre-Louis Moline than it does to the original Italian of Ranieri Calzabigi.

A comparison between the English score and an authentic Gluck score consequently should determine which music was by Gluck and which by Bach – if the English score did not describe the music as 'Composed by Gluck, Handel, Bach, Sacchini and Weichsel with additional new Music by William Reeve'.[7] Since the different airs are not headed by each composer's name, any examination short of thorough scrutiny would merely reveal which music was by Gluck and which by another composer; nor could the most thorough scrutiny confirm what had taken place in Dublin eight years earlier.

Nevertheless the Smock Alley advertisement states, 'The music principally by the Chevalier Christopher Gluck . . with additions by . . John Christopher Bach'. Having reviewed the question, one can accordingly assume that the opera was probably presented mainly as Gluck had composed it, with additional airs by Bach only, since no other composer's name is given.

The historic importance of the opera belongs not only to the musical reforms instituted by Gluck but equally to the original treatment of the situations introduced by the librettist, Calzabigi. As such, it is a oldest opera to remain firmly in the international repertory and as such, it remains a landmark in Dublin's operatic history.

Charles Weichsel, the violinist, who is described as conductor of the band, was Mrs. Billington's brother. He was born in London sometime between 1764 and 1770 and was to remain associated with his famous sister throughout much of her career. His first Dublin appearance was at Smock Alley on December 6, 1783, when, after a performance of *The Castle of Andalusia,* he played 'a solo concerto on the violin'.[8] There is evidence that his sister, accompanied by her husband and her parents, arrived in Dublin at the same time, for it was announced from London that the 'Weichsels, their new-married daughter, Billington included, are added to the musical band of Tenducci and Co.'[9] Weichsel senior was an oboist and although his name is not recorded throughout the season he may have been a member of the orchestra. His wife was a singer from Vauxhall Gardens (where, it will be recalled, Robert Owenson had sung duets with her about 1770) but, as a concert singer, she presumably would not have been engaged for stage performances.

Elizabeth Weichsel, their daughter, was born in London either in 1765 or 1768. Both she and her brother were taught music from a very early age, for they appeared as pianist and violinist at concerts in London in March 1774 and May 1777. Elizabeth first appeared as a singer at Oxford in 1782, and on October 13, 1783, while still very young, she married James Billington, a double bass player – perhaps to escape overbearing parental control. Two months later they came to Dublin. The Billingtons were undoubtedly badly off financially when they arrived and so were obliged to Richard Daly for their engagement. This in turn accorded Daly the distinction of launching Elizabeth on her triumphant career.

It has already been noted that at this period Dublin audiences preferred Miss Wheeler to Elizabeth Billington. This attitude has been interpreted by some biographers to suggest that Billington's engagement was a failure. There is absolutely nothing to sustain this opinion. On the contrary, as reported in the various newspaper reviews, her success, while not phenomenal, was extremely satisfactory – especially for a beginner.

One other fallacy concerning this engagement should be corrected. An Irish theatre historian has related that a breach occurred between Mrs. Billington and her husband 'caused by a connection she formed with Owenson, who in point of years might have been her father'[10] but the only rather negative evidence he cites to support this assumption is an announcement by her husband in *Faulkner's Dublin Journal* repudiating responsibility for her debts. Such an announcement certainly appeared on March 6, 1784, when notice was 'given to all Persons not to credit or trust Elizabeth Billington (formerly Weichsel) the wife of me James Billington, as I am determined not to pay any Debts she may contract, on any Account whatever',[11] but no relationship can be established between this incident and Owenson. Owenson indeed was old enough to have been her father but, as related earlier, there is considerably more evidence to suggest that he had had an affair with her mother.

Michael Kelly was to describe Mrs. Billington as 'an angel in beauty'[12] but she quickly lost this angelic feature – if in fact she had ever possessed it – long before Kelly came to know her. Following her Dublin engagement she travelled to Waterford to perform there at the newly opened theatre. When her second benefit performance failed to attract a full house, she went on stage and 'berated the audience like a common street-walker'[13] – let it be noted, at the tender age of not more than nineteen. Other examples of similar capricious behaviour can be quoted from Limerick and Cork in 1791.

Such stories of her arrogance lend some justification to the account of her personal behaviour as reported by that not entirely reliable historian, Mrs. Oxberry. She has recorded that on her first visit to Dublin Elizabeth had affairs with (1) a Mr. Kray, (2) Richard Daly (naturally, but why was he only second?), (3) the Duke of Rutland (the Lord Lieutenant), but the Duchess 'being universally esteemed, our heroine was rendered particularly obnoxious by this last intimacy'.[14] She thereupon transferred her affections to London. His Grace of Rutland passed her on to the Marquis of Carmarthen 'who interested himself *warmly* on her behalf, the moment he beheld her',[15] so much so, that he arranged to have her first appearance at Covent Garden commanded by their majesties, 'which the late queen is said to have subsequently much regretted'.[16] Well she might, for Elizabeth became the king's mistress. The king was then Prince of Wales (he still had a long time to wait before he became George IV) and 'The vicinity of her dwelling to the Thames, it being situate at Fulham and immediately on the banks of the river, offered many facilities to the Prince to partake of the Society of the fascinating syren, and to enjoy the delights of her musical conversaziones, which were held almost every night that her presence was not required at the theatre. The connexion of the Prince was not, however, of long duration; the coarseness of her manners soon disgusted him'.[17] And there her personal life may be allowed to rest, for as a female artist of the eighteenth-century theatre she had socially 'arrived'. But, whatever Kelly may have sentimentally believed, Elizabeth was no angel.

One episode in connection with her visit to Dublin should perhaps be recorded. There is some slight evidence that the 'indisposition' which caused her rather abrupt withdrawal from Capel Street Theatre in July 1784 was the birth of her (and Billington's) child, which did not long survive.[18]

Kelly was on surer ground when he called her 'the Saint Cecilia of song'.[19] As such, Sir Joshua Reynolds painted her portrait, and contemporary evidence suggests that she could with justice lay claim to the title.

'The compass of her voice', we learn, ' – a pure soprano, more sweet than powerful – was of extraordinary extent in its upper notes, from A to A in alt; but the lower part was very limited. Of this she was aware, and, in a bravura she would often substitute one octave for another'.[20] Burney relates that 'the natural tone of her voice is so excessively sweet, her knowledge of Music so considerable, her shake so true, her closes and embellishments so various and her expression so grateful, that nothing but envy or apathy can hear her without delight'.[21] Mount Edgcumbe adds, 'Her voice, though sweet and flexible, was not of that full nature which formed the charm of Banti's, but was rather a *voce di testa,* and in its very high tones resembled a flute or flageolet. Its agility was very great, and everything she sung was executed in the neatest manner, and with the utmost precision. Her knowledge of music enabled her to give great variety to her embellishments, which, as her taste was good, were always judicious. With all these great and undisputed excellencies something yet was wanting; for she possessed not the feeling to give touching expression, even when she sung with the utmost delicacy and consummate skill. Her face was handsome and her countenance full of good humour, but it was incapable of change, and she was no actress'.[22]

Her inability to act incurs frequent criticism. 'As an actress she has something to study: the management of her arms – and in the delivery of dialogue'[23] is an ever recurring theme. Awkward arm movements seem to have attracted the most censure. We constantly meet comments such as, 'in point of gesture, she is not distinguished for much grace, and the motion of her hands exhibits an insipid uniformity not much allied to feeling'[24] and 'Of her action we must violently disapprove. The raising both her arms at once, and then turning up both her hands, have the appearance of the prayers at an execution!'[25]

It was also said of her that she was only a *bravura* singer, so to refute this opinion she chose the pastoral role of Eliza in *The Flitch of Bacon* for a benefit performance and, as Parke relates, 'If this was her object, she attained it completely, by singing the natural and plaintive music of the part in the most chaste and beautiful style imaginable'.[26] But she did have some vocal faults. One, strangely enough, was poor pronunciation of English, which 'was not quite free from impurities, arising principally from the introduction of vowels before consonants, a habit probably acquired from the Italian custom'.[27] If so, she must have formed the habit by imitating Italian singers whom she had heard in London, for she had adopted it before she ever crossed the English Channel.

In July 1786 she was to travel to Paris to receive singing lessons from Sacchini, just before he died. Between 1794 and 1801 she sang exclusively in the principal opera houses throughout Italy – where, incidentally, she was to lose her husband, who died suddenly in Naples, and was to marry again, disastrously, a Frenchman named Felissent. She died near Venice on August 25, 1818.

If one star was rising with the Dublin production of *Orpheus,* another was setting, for although Tenducci was still highly esteemed in newspaper reports, his career as a singer was coming to a close. The first signs were evident from an advertisement on March 27 advising 'the Nobility and Gentry, and his friends, in particular, that he is resolved to settle himself in this Kingdom, and teach the art of Singing. Their commands shall be duly attended, by directing to him at No 2 Nassau-street'.[28] He may have remained there as a singing teacher until December 1784, when his return to London 'from Dublin'[29] is announced. The following year his excellent treatise on singing, *Instruction of Mr. Tenducci to his Scholars,* was published in London.

In May 1785 he appeared for the last time on the London stage, singing in Gluck's *Orfeo* (once again in *pasticcio* form) at the King's Theatre, and 'though an Atlas of former times, found his physical powers so much diminished, that he was unable to bear the pressure to the satisfaction of the public'.[30] Mount Edgcumbe is more explicit when he writes, 'But the performance of an old man, who had never been very capital, and could now have scarcely any voice left, and that too in a part in which many still remembered Guadagni, was not likely to prove very attractive'.[31] Mount Edgcumbe did not hear these performances since he was then in Italy but, he explains, 'I had heard Tenducci in concerts before I left England, but his voice was then cracked, and I did not like him'.[32]

Tenducci ended his career with the following announcement published on March 15, 1786: 'Mr. Tenducci Knowing, that a Time must arrive when every Professor ought to retire from the public Eye . . at the End of the present Musical Season . . intends to quit the Occupation of a public Singer, and engage himself entirely in Teaching'.[33] So he did, but for how long, and when or where he eventually died remain unknown.

Orpheus had ten performances at Smock Alley Theatre between January 3 and March 4. Mrs. Billington and Tenducci both took their benefits in this opera. It was originally advertised for Urbani's benefit on March 24, but the comedy of *The School for Wives* was substituted. Perhaps he could not risk the engagement of Billington and Tenducci at the fees they commanded, for the following pathetic announcement marks him as an impoverished man. 'Mr. Urbani solicits the Protection of a generous Public on that occasion, and humbly hopes his being a stranger will rather recommend than exclude him from their notice.'[34]

Other operas were revived: *Artaxerxes* with Mrs. Billington as Mandane '(being her first appearance in that character)',[35] *The Castle of Andalusia, The Padlock,* and that very tired joke 'The Beggar's Opera Reversed'[36] with Mr. Palmer as Polly and Mrs. Billington as Macheath.

There was also a new production, a comic opera called *The*

Campaign, or Love in the East Indies, 'the music selected and adapted by Mr. Tenducci'.[37] Tenducci had spread his musical net wide and into it he had collected Rauzzini, Sacchini, Galuppi, Bach, Anfossi, Rutini, Sarti, Cocchi, Paisiello, Franchi, Philidor, Rameau, Handel, Gretry, David Rizzio and 'Carolan, the Irish Bard'.[38] In contrast there was only one librettist, Robert Jephson, but to compensate, he too was a man of many parts. He was an army officer on half pay, a typical eighteenth-century 'carpet bagger' who on returning to Dublin rose in influence by clutching the coat-tails of his patron Lord Townshend. Townshend as Lord Lieutenant appointed him Master of the Horse and found him a seat in the Irish House of Commons. Jephson intrigued with the elder George Colman to have an Act passed by Parliament 'for the regulation of, and exclusive right for one Theatre only in Dublin'[39] – in other words to secure a theatrical monopoly – but the Bill was rejected. He also wrote plays.

The Campaign was first performed on January 31 and the artists taking part were: Tenducci, Ryder, Palmer, Wood, Wilder, Owenson, O'Reilly, Cubitt, Hurst, McCready, Meadows, Sparks, Withington, Miss Hitchcock, Mrs. Hitchcock and Mrs. Billington. It was subsequently produced at Covent Garden Theatre on May 12, 1785.

One other first performance had been slipped in as an afterpiece to *The School for Scandal* on January 16. This was John O'Keeffe's *The Poor Soldier,* which, as related in Chapter 11, had first seen theatrical light as *The Shamrock* in 1777. In its new form it had received its first performance at Covent Garden on November 4, 1783. O'Keeffe recounts that Richard Daly paid fifty guineas for the right to produce the opera. The cast was:

Pat, the Poor Soldier	Wood
Captain Fitzroy	Cubitt
Bagatelle	George Dawson
Dermot	Palmer
Darby	Ryder
Father Luke	O'Reilly
Norah	Miss Jarrett
Kathleen	Mrs. Hitchcock.[40]

When the theatre reopened after the summer vacation in November, 1784, Daly's company included two valuable acquisitions: Giovanna Sestini, who in 1782 had transferred from Italian to English opera in London, and Maria Teresa Romanzini, later Mrs. Bland.

Romanzini was the daughter of Jewish-Italian parents who came to London soon after she was born. According to Michael Kelly, she was first engaged at Hughes' Riding School, later the Royal Circus, 'in the spring of 1773'.[41] In 1781 she appeared at Drury Lane as Cupid in Purcell's *King Arthur,* but 'was under such Apprehensions, notwithstanding the most generous Indulgence of the House, that it would be difficult to give any opinion of her Powers'.[42] At the time of this engagement her age was said to be eighteen,[43] which would establish the year of her birth as 1763 and not 1769 as is usually claimed.

Her appearance was homely, her figure short, her face swarthy and pockmarked, but she was a clever actress with remarkably clear enunciation. She had a mezzo-soprano voice and excelled as a ballad singer. In the good old theatrical tradition she was reported to be able to 'draw tears by her impersonation of a street singer or beggar maid'.[44] In comic ballads she would interpolate a few words of speech and then revert to singing. She sang at the King's Theatre (as Mrs. Bland) during the 1798/99 season when, according to Mount Edgcumbe, she 'performed very creditably to herself and agreeably to the audience'.[45] To this he adds, 'Though Mrs. Bland was only a singer of the second class, few, if any, English singers who have appeared at the opera sung with such pure Italian taste, or equalled her in recitative and pronunciation of the language'.[46]

She made her first appearance at Smock Alley Theatre on November 2, 1784, when she played Rosetta in *Love in a Village* – with Giordani's 'capital improvements that have lately been introduced into it'.[47] Her reception was cordial. 'She supported the character . . with considerable credit, and discovered, in many parts of her performance, such an archness of manner, expression, &c. as shows her extensively to possess the true "vis comica." The force and sweetness of her vocal abilities were repeatedly acknowledged from the warmth of approbation conferred, and which must prove a valuable acquisition to the operas that are to be presented through the season.'[48]

Meanwhile, with what today would be considered a first-class public relations effort, the arrival was announced of Signora Sestini. Five different communications were released to the press covering topics ranging from her arrival 'By yesterday's packet'[49] to her recent appearances in London 'in English operas with as great consequence and éclat, as she had before shewn in those of Italian'.[50]

She had made her initial appearance in English opera at Covent Garden, as Lorenza in the first performance of *The Castle of Andalusia*, when her 'whimsical deportment, and her broken English delivery, added to her incomparable manner of singing'.[51] It was also in *The Castle of Andalusia* that she first appeared in English opera at Smock Alley Theatre on November 6, 1784. She 'was encored in every one of her songs'[52] and the opera was repeated on November 10 and 24.

She next appeared on November 13 as the fop, Jessamy, in *Lionel and Clarissa,* a 'breeches' role which she had already performed successfully at Covent Garden. At Smock Alley her success was repeated. She 'gave the character a fire, a life, a soul in fact, that won her every tribute of approbation which it was possible for an audience to confer'.[53] She was mellifluously supported by Romanzini, who sang Clarissa, and less harmoniously by 'The astonishing performance of the Celebrated Dogs from Paris under the direction of Mons. Castelli'[54] which concluded the evening's entertainment. The opera's success, or rather Sestini's success as Jessamy, led to five further performances by December 18.

On November 29, Arnold and O'Keeffe's comic opera, *Peeping Tom of Coventry,* had its first Dublin production with Romanzini in the cast. Then, on December 8, *The Maid of the Mill* was revived with Sestini as Fanny and Romanzini as Patty.

A second new opera was produced on December 13. This was *Robin Hood, or Sherwood Forest* by Leonard MacNally and William Shield 'with additional songs by Signor Giordani. The principal Characters by Messrs. Ryder, Wood, O'Reilly, Glenville, McCready, Corry, Baker, Barrington and Younge; Miss Romanzini, Mrs. Worrell (her 1st appearance in this Kingdom) Mrs. Hitchcock and Signora Sestini'.[55]

Leonard MacNally, the librettist, is too well-known as the government informer and hypocritical betrayer of Robert Emmet to require comment on his political life. Both psychologically and physically he was a bizarre figure. Barrington has described him as 'one of the strangest fellows in the world. His figure was ludicrous; he was very short, and nearly as broad as long: his legs were of unequal length, and he had a face which no washing could clean: he wanted one thumb, the absence of which gave rise to numerous expedients on his part; and he took great care to have no nails, as he regularly eat every morning the growth of the preceeding day: he never wore a glove, lest he should appear to be guilty of affectation in concealing his deformity. When in a hurry, he generally took two thumping steps with the short leg, to bring up the space made by the long one; and the bar, who never missed a favourable opportunity of nicknaming, called him accordingly "one *pound* two" . . in a word, McNally was a good-natured, hospitable, talented, dirty fellow, and had, by the latter qualification, so disgusted the circuit bar, that they refused to receive him at their mess'.[56] Was it this repulsive appearance and the ridicule of his colleagues that warped what seems to have been a clever and inventive mind? By betraying his friends to the prosecution was he not having the last paranoic laugh? His song, 'The Lass of Richmond Hill', set to music by James Hook, is still sung. He is said to have written it to his (? first) wife, a Miss Janson, 'daughter to a very rich attorney'.[57]

Boaden has described *Robin Hood* as 'a rather pleasing *pasticcio*, enforced with Goldsmith's Edwin and Angelina, and other excrescences',[58] and notes that 'Shield supplied seventeen new airs in this opera and adapted twelve old ones'.[59] The Dublin production was well received. 'Sestini displayed new abilities, which possibly she does not herself know she possesses; but which, from cultivation and experience must indisputably succeed. Sestini, in short, seems a gem, whose lustre appears the greater, the more it is brought forward. Romanzini never shone to so great advantage . . her character admitted of some degree of vivacity, (which, with humour, is evidently her forte), and sung her different airs with an energy, spirit and excellence'.[60]

The season continued with performances of *The Maid of the Mill, Lionel and Clarissa* and *Robin Hood*. But it was chiefly Sestini's season, mainly because of her performance of Jessamy, since for *Lionel and Clarissa* we learn there existed 'as great a demand for places, as was ever known almost on any of Mrs. Siddon's nights'.[61] It was surely this season Lady Morgan had in mind when she recounted how Sestini 'lisped her Italian airs in broken English, which had a peculiar charm for the capricious amateurs of the day'.[62]

On January 21, 1785, Elizabeth Billington made a grand re-entry into Smock Alley Theatre as Annette in *The Lord of the Manor*. 'To Mrs. Billington's vocal abilities', it was declared, ''tis needless to offer panegyric; but it was with much pleasure we perceived that she is greatly improved as an actress, and seems to display many qualifications to shine in the comic line'.[63] Eight days later, on January 29, she was to scintillate in Shield and O'Keeffe's comic opera *Fontainebleau, or Our Way in France*. 'Never acted in this Kingdom . . With new Finales and additional Airs, the Words by the Author of Gibraltar, the music composed by Signor Giordani.'[64] The performance was cast from strength. Those taking part were:

Lackland	Daly
Colonel Epaulet	Signora Sestini
Sir Shenkinap Griffin	O'Reilly
Sir John Bull	Moss
Captain Henry	Wood
Lord Winlove	Waterhouse
French landlord	Baker
La Poche	Ryder
Celia	Miss Romanzini
Miss Bull	Miss Hitchcock
*Nannette	Mrs. Hitchcock

*There may have been a change of cast in the actual performance, with Mrs. Sparks (Frances Ashmore) taking over Nannette. Alternatively she may have sung a role not listed here, but recorded in the London performances as 'Mrs. Casey'.

Lady Bull   Mrs. Hannam
Rosa   Mrs. Billington.

One Dublin newspaper was somewhat critical of the work 'which', it commented, 'we think the author ought to have stiled a "Comedy with Songs" rather than an "Opera." Mr. Daly in the character of Lackland, deserves our warmest approbation, and he both dressed and performed the Chevalier de Industrie to absolute perfection; had the author written up to the actor, this part would have stood the test of criticism, but O'Keeffe in this, as in all his dramatic writings, only sketches an outline, but never finishes the picture . . Sestini wears the breeches so perfectly that her Irish friends are inclined to wish she would doff the petticoat entirely, in the theatre . . Mrs. Billington, Miss Hitchcock and the rest of the Dramatis Personae, were extremely perfect in their respective Characters'.[65]

Charles Dibdin's musical entertainment, *Poor Vulcan,** was presented on February 23, with Sestini as Adonis (another 'breeches' role), and Mrs. Billington as Venus. *The Lady of the Manor* followed on March 1, Mrs. Billington playing Lady Lucy, and Romanzini, Mrs. Townly. On March 8, Sestini once again performed the favourite role of Jessamy, and on April 11 Mrs. Billington appeared in *The Beggar's Opera.*

This was a gala occasion with the Lord Lieutenant, the Duke of Rutland and the Duchess present. 'Their Graces', we are informed, 'were accompanied by their beautiful offspring, the young Marquis of Granby, and their two eldest daughters, a circumstance which impressed the minds of the auditory with the strongest emotions of joy, and a similar instance to which does not live within our memories. The children entered the box appropriated for their Graces, first, amidst the united and most forcible acclamations; her Grace immediately followed, who experienced a repetition of congratulatory applause. The Duchess being seated, his Grace entered, when a renewal, and, if possible, more general expression of joy was resounded

---

*First produced in Dublin at Crow Street Theatre on December 21, 1780. 'The Music by Mr. Dibdin, Dr. Arnold and the late Dr. Arne.' (*Hibernian Journal,* December 18/20, 1780).

ELIZABETH BILLINGTON. SOPRANO (c. 1765–1818)

MRS. CROUCH *née* ANNA MARIA PHILLIPS. SOPRANO (1763–1805).
AS ROSETTA IN *Love in a Village*.

MICHAEL KELLY. TENOR (c. 1762–1826)

from every part of the Theatre'.[66] Ryder was the Macheath, Mrs. Billington sang Polly, and Mrs. Hitchcock, Lucy.

Poor Vulcan was revived on April 28 and, as part of a 'Dramatic Olio' for Robert Houlton's benefit, *Gibraltar* was performed on May 10, with Mrs. Billington as Donna Almeida and Sestini as Count Toilet, 'a part as much in the stile of playing of this excellent actress as the character of Jessamy'.[67] Mrs. Billington's benefit performance took place on May 12. She chose Clorinda in *Robin Hood* 'being her first appearance in that character' and at the 'End of the Opera, by particular desire' played 'a celebrated Concerto of Schroeter's on the Grand Piano Forte'.[68]

Performances continued during the summer. On July 28, *Comus* was performed for Richard Daly's benefit, with Miss Jarrett as Euphrosyne, John Henry Johnstone (briefly returned from London) as the principal Bacchanal, and 'the Song of Sweet Echo by Mrs. Billington'.[69] Giordani's burlesque of *Orpheus and Euridice* was also in rehearsal with Mrs. Billington and Miss Wheeler for production on August 15, with an announcement that 'The trial of "Orpheus" in the infernal regions before Rhadamanthus is a scene of such true and exquisite humour . . that one of the Judges of our Four Courts attended the representation no less than 6 nights successively, during its exhibition, last summer'.[70]

Shortly afterwards the theatre closed for the summer vacation, during which time Richard Daly had to suffer a disapproving press. The previous March it had been pointed out that 'Mr. Daly should know that in a town like Dublin, which scarce produces (as alleged by the play-going people) more than an audience and a half – that a Manager cannot conduct a Theatre with emolument to himself – if novelty is not presented to the town, each season he opens his campaign. 'Tis reckoned in London, that strangers and visitors alone fill each night half their Theatres – this advantage our capital never can have; insular situation prevents an influx of travellers. A wise manager should therefore push his real object by tempting the resident inhabitant to sport his money at the Theatre, and break up those Knots at evening whist, which the old "tabbies" so indefatigably promote'.[71]

R

In September a London newspaper put the matter more forcibly. 'Nothing can be more wretched', it declares, 'than the state of the stage in Dublin at present. Smock Alley Theatre, from local situation obscure and inaccessible but through dirty streets and stinking alleys, in the course of the past winter, has presented a scene of stage exhibition unworthy of the primitive players. The interior of the house during that period, wore a constant face of distress; and the habits of the performers, generally speaking, would have disgraced the cart of Thespis. The Manager is an enterprising man, and endeavours to deserve the publick patronage; but when the reader is informed that the press is under the Manager's control, and that there is no such thing as a newspaper in Dublin, in which the free animadversions of uninterested writers on theatrical performances is admitted; he will not wonder at the miserable condition of the Irish Theatre'.[72]

Whatever the condition of the theatre, and certainly without any attempt at novelty, the new season opened on October 24, 1785, with *Love in a Village*. The Rosetta was Mrs. Billington, 'who not only delivered the dialogue with the greatest propriety, but executed the songs allotted to that character in the most finished and delightful stile'.[73] The Young Meadows was Peter Duffy, who was making his first appearance at Smock Alley.

Certain new productions were, however, 'getting up',[74] among them the comic opera *Two to One* by Samuel Arnold and George Colman junior. It had its first Dublin performance on November 5 with a cast consisting of Ryder, Cornelys, Paulet, George Dawson, Wood, Moss, Mrs. Hitchcock and Mrs. Billington.

Two to One was the younger Colman's first work for the stage and was originally produced with a prologue written by the author's father at his Little Theatre in the Haymarket. The success of its London run was repeated in Dublin where, we learn, 'Notwithstanding the continual rain of Saturday last, it could not prevent a very numerous and polite audience from attending the 1st representation, in this Kingdom, of the new Comic Opera of Two to One, written by G. Colman, junior and set to music by Dr. Arnold. In point of dialogue, this production is a happy medium between the sentimental

gravity of "Cumberland" and the extreme farce or burlesque of
O'Keeffe, and therefore the more likely to win the approbation of the
judicious part of an audience, who neither wish to doze over heavy
moralising reflections, nor to be kept constantly on the broad grin . .
The music, for the most part, particularly the overture,* is masterly;
and several of the songs, some of them very humorous, deservedly met
an encore. It is but just here to mention, that the new accompaniments
to the music of this opera, are by young Weichsel and do much credit
to his extraordinary abilities'.[75]

Between November and the end of 1785 there were further revivals
of *Comus,* the burlesque of *Orpheus and Euridice, Love in a Village* and
Fountainebleau.

A comic opera of little artistic consequence, though of some
individual interest, was produced at Smock Alley on April 17, 1786.
This was Charles Dibdin's *The Match for a Widow, or the Frolicks of
Fancy* which he composed for Dublin and for which, if we can believe
his *memoirs,* Daly paid him only one hundred and forty pounds out
of an agreed fee of six hundred.[76] The score is said to include the old
French air *Ah! Vous dirai-je, maman* made familiar by the Mozart-
Adam variations. The author of the opera (adapted from Patrat's
L'Heureux Erreur) was Joseph Atkinson, another Irish-born English
army officer turned dramatist. He was to write a second libretto, *Love
in a Blaze,* which in 1799 was set to music by Sir John Stevenson and
produced at Crow Street Theatre. The artists who took part in the
first performance of *The Match for a Widow* were Duffy, Ryder,
Cornelys, Moss, Wilder Owenson, Glenville, G. King, Wood, Miss
Hitchcock, Mrs. Hitchcock, Mrs. Heaphy, Miss Langrishe, and Mrs.
Melmoth.[77] It was the only new opera of any significance to be
produced in Dublin during 1786.

*Composed by Charles Weichsel.

16

MICHAEL KELLY AND
MRS. CROUCH

O N NOVEMBER 25, 1786, Richard Daly was appointed
'Master of the Revels and Masques'[1] for a period of fourteen
years at a salary of £300 a year – so perpetuating for a while
longer the sinecure recorded in Chapter 1 as being first granted to
John Ogilby in February 1637/38. More important was a patent
granted to Daly[2] at the same time which gave him the sole right to
produce public dramatic performances in Dublin for a similar period.
Concerning this appointment a London newspaper had acidly
commented, 'The moment that Daly is established in the patent, his
first provision must be a wardrobe. The apparatus at present under
that name would disgrace a barn'.[3]

With the first performance in Dublin of Grétry's *Richard Coeur de
Lion* which took place on March 2, 1787, he seems at least to have
taken trouble, prompted perhaps by the motive that it was for his
benefit. Originally performed in Paris in 1784, two versions of the
opera had had rival London productions in English during 1786. The
first, at Covent Garden, was a *pasticcio* arranged by Shield with a
libretto by Leonard MacNally which 'produced no effect at all'.[4] The
second had the music arranged by Thomas Linley, and the libretto
adapted (from the original of J. M. Sedaine) by General Burgoyne,
'whose taste and skill rendered the afterpiece at Drury Lane a
permanent property of the theatre. By throwing the interest of
Blondel into the character of Matilda, the translator made a provision
for the gratification of the ladies, which the original author, had
neglected; or imagined too strong a deviation from Millot's narrative

of Roland's captivity'.[5] Incorporating the role of Blondel with the new role of Matilda meant that Blondel had to forfeit all his music. Most of it, including the favourite air, *O Richard, ô mon roi,* passed to Matilda and so in Burgoyne's translation Blondel became little more than an acting role.

It was this version that was produced in Dublin at Smock Alley Theatre with the following cast:

Richard	Paulet
Antonio	Chambers
Blondel	Duffy
Florestan	Owenson
Sir Owen	Brett
Guillot	Corry
Matthew	Wilder
Pilgrim	Smith
Seneschal	King
Peasants, Soldiers, Cavaliers	{ Glenville, Lynch, Barret, Smith, E. King, Malone
Matilda	Miss Wheeler
Laurette	Miss Hitchcock
Julie	Miss Wood
Colette	Mrs. Hitchcock
Dorcas	Mrs. Heaphy
Country Girls	{ Mrs. Hannam, Mrs. Wood, Mrs. Gemea, Mrs. Barret.

'The Dances by Mme. Julian, Mr. Holland, and Miss André'.[6]

The reviews were good and we read that 'Richard Coeur de Lion bids fair to rank foremost amongst our most favourite Operas – when we consider its first representation, the intricacy of its business, and its numerous and interesting incidents, we shall not be less pleased than surprised, at the great éclat with which it went off on Friday night: as to the merits of the music, the encomiums universally bestowed on it, places the musical abilities of Mr. Grétry, very high in our opinion; the performers were particularly well adapted to their different songs, and captivated with the most soft and mellifluous strains every auditor: the audience, numerous and brilliant, bore testimony of their powers, and the extraordinary merit of this beautiful Historical Romance, which was warmly evinced by those loud and unceasing plaudits which issued from every part of the Theatre'.[7] 'The Duke of Rutland honoured the house with his presence' on March 10, when the entertainment consisted of *Richard Coeur de Lion* combined with *The Beggar's Opera,* 'but the indisposition of her Grace, which was sincerely lamented, prevented her from adding to the dignity of the scene'.[8]

Although it won good reviews, the opera was never to become a favourite in Dublin. A reason for this may be found in the novelty of the music, for contrary to the extensive changes which Burgoyne had made in the text, Grétry's score was performed virtually without alteration. Apart from a ballad introduced at the beginning of Act 3 instead of the original trio, and some essential transposing down of Richard's music for John Philip Kemble (the Drury Lane portrayer of the role – a celebrated actor but no singer), the music remained almost note for note as Grétry had composed it. Sensibly and artistically, all Linley seems to have done, according to his published vocal score, is to have added suitable accompaniments.

The opportunity of hearing an opera by a foreign composer as it had been composed and not as a *pasticcio* was most unusual for a Dublin audience; remarkable also that it should have been by so important a composer of *opéra comique* as Grétry, and surely unique that Dublin should be hearing contemporary French opera, even in English translation, for *Richard Coeur de Lion* was being performed at Smock Alley Theatre less than three and a half years after its initial production in Paris.

The composer, André E. M. Grétry, was not French but Belgian, and was born at Liège on February 8, 1741. His father was a violinist and Grétry was taught music from an early age, yet never seems to have mastered harmony and counterpoint thoroughly. Probably the most important early influence on his career was hearing burlettas of

Pergolesi, Galuppi and Jommelli sung by a company of Italians (such as had performed in Dublin), which had inspired him to become an opera composer. He studied in Rome for over seven years and then set out for Paris, spending a year in Geneva on the way. On arriving in Paris, according to Burney who was writing in Grétry's lifetime, he 'brought with him all the taste of Italy, which, however, in compliance with the language and national taste of France, he has been frequently obliged to sacrifice, in order to please his protectors and judges'.[9] Burney concedes, however, that 'He has, at least, improved the French taste as much as they have corrupted his'.[10] Grétry had his first Paris triumph with an opera called *Le Huron* – yes, a romantic tale about a North American Indian, a noble savage, whose nobility, it ultimately transpires, is due to his being half French. His next outstanding success was *Zemir et Azor,* produced in 1771, and still occasionally performed. *Richard Coeur de Lion* was his finest work.

Just over three months after the production of *Richard Coeur de Lion,* Michael Kelly, having won fame and some little fortune on the continent and in London, returned to Dublin and Smock Alley Theatre where he had made his first stage appearance ten years before. It may be noted once again that Kelly's *Reminiscences* are extremely unreliable, particularly when he quotes dates. They were not written by Kelly, but compiled by Theodore Hook, a contemporary author and journalist, from material supplied by Kelly in his old age. Inaccuracies are consequently inevitable and in recounting details of Kelly's life, little reliance can be placed on what he says unless there is confirmation from other sources.

For example, until Kelly's baptismal entry is discovered, the date of his birth must remain indefinite, although it was probably sometime between 1762 and 1764. In 1801 we are informed that 'At eleven he had attained to such a degree of excellence in the science, [of music] as to be employed in some of the first private concerts, in which he soon attracted general attention by his admirable execution on the harpsichord'[11] which, if correct, would establish his involvement in the musical life of Dublin about 1773 to 1775. His statement that he became a singing pupil 'under Signor St. Giorgio, who was engaged at the Rotunda'[12] can be accepted as accurate. There was nothing to be gained by naming such an indifferent musician as one of his teachers. We know that St. Giorgio was in Dublin during the autumn of 1774 when, with Signora Salvagni, he sang in concerts at the Rotunda Gardens. What we do not know is the identity of 'a young Gentleman'[13] who sang with them. There is no evidence that it was Kelly, but further information coupled with this announcement may perhaps someday reveal that it was.

An advertisement in 1769 addressed 'To the Nobility and Gentry' confirms that his father was 'Mr. Thomas Kelly, of Mary-street, Dancing-Master' who, having been informed 'that some designing Persons have intimated, for their own Purposes, that he had quitted his Profession; he therefore thinks proper to give this public Notice, that he will give the strictest Attendance and Care, and will attend three Evenings in the Week at his House, to teach Minuets and Cotillons, where he has built a large and elegant Room for that Purpose'.[14]

It seems quite definite that if Kelly sailed from Dublin for the continent as he relates, 'On the first of May 1779',[15] then he did not take his farewell in a performance of *Lionel and Clarissa* shortly before. John O'Keeffe lends credence to Kelly's date by recalling that 'It was in the spring of 1779 I returned to Dublin . . [when] many ladies of the highest rank, who patronised the youthful Michael Kelly, now asked me to step out on the boards of Crow-street, and play Beau Jessamy for the benefit of their young favourite, Master Lionel who was just preparing for his voyage to Italy'.[16] But doubt arises when he continues, 'and here, at present, in the year 1826, I take occasion to say that I have a due sense of the well-meant, and indeed happy mention of me by my highly endowed and kind townsman, Mr. Michael Kelly, in his well-written, entertaining "Reminiscences" '.[17] In plain words, John O'Keeffe, another old man, in writing his recollections, was using Kelly's reminiscences as an *aide-mémoire*.

To refute this date it must first be pointed out that while O'Keeffe's name appears among the cast lists at Crow Street Theatre between

January and June, 1779, Michael Kelly's does not. Neither does Michael Arne's, and in his *Reminiscences* Kelly explains at some length that he had performed the roles of Cymon and Lionel as a member of Arne's company, with Mrs. Arne as principal soprano. Arne, Mrs. Arne, Kelly and O'Keeffe were however all present in June 1777. On May 29 of that year we first find an advertisement for a performance of *Artaxerxes* to take place at Crow Street Theatre on June 7, 'For the Benefit of Master Kelly'.[18] The cast is given as follows: Arbaces '(for the 1st time)'[19] – Kelly, Artaxerxes – F. Passerini, Rimenes – Owenson, Artabanes – Webster, Semira – Mrs. Webster,* Mandane – Miss Jameson.

The Italian opera company was then performing in Dublin and in a subsequent edition of the newspaper Passerini and Miss Jameson explain that they had been engaged to perform for St. Giorgio's benefit at Fishamble Street on that particular evening, but that they 'would most willingly perform for Master Kelly, at any Time in their Power'.[20] A long communication from Master Kelly followed. In it he announced the cancellation of *Artaxerxes* owing to 'Mr. Webster's State of Health obliging him to decline the Part of Artabanes'; the opera was consequently changed to *Lionel and Clarissa* with 'Lionel, for the first Time, by Master Kelly, Jessamy Mr. O'Keeffe' and 'Clarissa Mrs. Arne'. The names of the remainder of the cast were also given. The opera was conducted by Michael Arne and tickets for the performance could be 'had of Mr. Faulkner, Parliament-street; at No. 6 Lower Ormond Quay; No. 38 Dorset Street; and of Mr. Cullen, at the Theatre'.[21]

The announcement is significant for two reasons. Firstly, the addresses from which tickets could be bought do not include Kelly's home in Mary Street. Had the family come to live at another address or had the young Michael Kelly been indentured to Michael Arne, who we know was one of his teachers and who presumably would have been entitled to his apprentice's earnings? Secondly, the cast which Kelly has recorded in his *Reminiscences* for the performance said to

---

*As Kelly relates (*Reminiscences*. Vol. I. p. 13), she was really the wife of Jonathan Bathishill the composer, and had eloped with Webster to Dublin.

have taken place in 1779 corresponds almost exactly with the cast recorded in 1777. Differences occur among the names of artists performing four of the roles, but these could be explained by last minute cast changes or merely that in compiling the names for his *Reminiscences* Kelly was still writing from memory. In either event, the casts resemble one another so closely that, coupled with Mr. and Mrs. Arne's and Kelly's absence from Dublin in 1779, whatever the date of his departure may have been, the 1777 performance was the one Kelly remembered as 'Being the last night of his appearing on the stage previous to his going to Italy'.[22] The unanswered question that remains is – did Kelly in fact leave for the Continent as early as 1777 or, as he has related, not until 1779?

His many adventures there, including his singing in the first performance of *Le Nozze di Figaro* at Vienna, are not part of this story. As far as London and Dublin are concerned, he does not reappear until April 20, 1787, when he made his *début* at Drury Lane. Meanwhile his voice had developed from the unbroken treble of Master Kelly to become a tenor.

Hogarth observes that 'As a singer, his powers were by no means great, but his intelligence, experience, and knowledge of the stage, rendered him very useful'.[23] An anonymous critic states, 'His voice is dreadfully wanting in sweetness, and melody of tone and may altogether be considered deficient of every necessary requisite that constitutes a good one'.[24] Even Mount Edgcumbe, who had earlier heard him in Vienna, where he describes him as one of 'a most excellent set of singers',[25] was disappointed when he heard him sing in Italian opera at the King's Theatre on his return to London. He describes him as 'a good musician, and not a bad singer, having been long in Italy', but adds, 'yet he had retained, or regained so much of the English vulgarity of manner, that he was never greatly liked at this theatre'.[26]

Boaden alone is enthusiastic, although he admits to prejudice, declaring that 'I owe it to an intimacy of more than 30 years to say something beyond a common notice of a very kind and friendly man, and a very able and scientific singer. It often happens in music, that the sweetest organ leads to nothing brilliant, and that truth of tone and flexibility, and compass, achieve perfection in the art. Something like this was true of Kelly. His voice had amazing power and steadiness; his compass was extraordinary. In vigorous passages he never cheated the ear with the feeble wailings of falsetto, but sprung upon the ascending fifth with a sustaining energy, that often electrified an audience'.[27]

In appraising Kelly's voice today, one must remember that Mozart, who knew its quality well, composed only *comprimario* roles in *Le Nozze di Figaro* for him and, as a very famous singer once remarked 'What the public pays for, is timbre'. Measured against these standards, Kelly seems to have been a second-rate singer.

When Michael Kelly returned to Dublin, he brought with him Anna Maria Phillips, now Mrs. Rollings Edward Crouch. This joint engagement was not just a coincidence, for on the first evening of his arrival in London from the continent, Kelly visited Drury Lane Theatre, saw Mrs. Crouch play Laurette in *Richard Coeur de Lion* and fell irrevocably in love. Simply, almost poetically, he relates, 'I was struck with admiration of her wonderful beauty, and delighted to hear that she was to be my prima donna in the opera in which I was to perform. She seemed to me to aggregate in herself, like the Venus of Apelles, all that was exquisite and charming'.[28]

Anna Maria Phillips was born in London on April 20, 1763, the daughter of Peregrine Phillips, an unsuccessful lawyer and author. Her first music teacher was an organist named Wafer, but in 1779 her father articled her to Thomas Linley. She made her *début* at Drury Lane on November 11, 1780, as Mandane in *Artaxerxes* – not very successfully. Nor was she entirely successful in her second opera there, *Lionel and Clarissa*, although it was agreed that 'the situations of delicate embarrassment, in which Clarissa is involved, received a natural coloring from the apprehensive timidity which Miss Philips still feels very strongly, and which had an interesting and engaging effect'.[29] Boaden confirms that 'She was always timid upon the stage, and really needed all the indulgence that she experienced'.[30] Success, in fact, came only with her Dublin engagement when 'In public she was followed and admired; in private she was courted, esteemed, and invited into the politest circles'.[31]

In Dublin in 1782 she was also involved with John Philip Kemble in the first of a number of romantic episodes. During 1783, there was a second admirer who 'to prove the fervour of his attachment threatened to shoot her if she declined his suit, saying he would go into the theatre for the purpose'.[32] As he was seen sitting in the second row of the pit on the following night, with some justification 'He was taken into custody, but no weapons being found upon him, he was liberated'.[33] A more serious affair was soon to follow, recorded as follows: 'Mr. Loftus, son of Sir Thomas Loftus, a gentleman of the first connections in Ireland, having fixed his affections on Miss Phillips, and paid his addresses to her sometime gave her a matrimonial contract. After having taken every legal step in order to have their marriage solemnized, they could not get any divine in all the parishes they visited, for an extent of upwards of thirty miles to administer the ceremony. The objection was that Sir Thomas Loftus being related to the Primate of Ireland had influence enough to effect their ruin if they acted in opposition to his will, which they had learned was adverse to the alliance. Sir Thomas having heard where his son had taken up his residence, had him seized by a party of his tenants, and conveyed home to his seat, where he is said to be detained under strict watch.'[34]

Shortly afterwards, Anna Maria became attracted to 'Mr. Crouch, a lieutenant in his Majesty's navy',[35] whom she married in 1785. The marriage was a failure, and with an economy of language worthy of a young James Joyce, Kelly records in 1791, 'It was in this year that Mr. and Mrs. Crouch separated by mutual consent, he never appreciating the gem which he possessed'.[36] Kelly had formed a *ménage à trois* with them as early as 1787, when he went to live at their house in Titchfield Street near Cavendish Square. In due course the Prince of Wales would also briefly join the household—at about the same time that his brother, the Duke of Clarence, was taking the Irish actress Mrs. Jordan to bed. But what could a poor actress do when advancement in her profession depended on such honours? Mrs.

Crouch was merely succeeding Mrs. Billington. While she did not have Billington's temperament, she did share her good looks, and was described as 'the personification of innocent loveliness'.[37]

At the commencement of her career her voice was said to be 'a high counter-tenor, [which] is heard to more advantage in the comic than in serious opera; the tone is more natural, and has less of that instrumental sound, which is the effect of labour, in a task that is yet too arduous for her musical experience'.[38] Hogarth adds, 'Her vocal powers were not highly cultivated, nor was her musical knowledge great; but she possessed a voice of exquisite sweetness, much flexibility and considerable extent'.[39] Later she was involved in a coach accident, when a heavy dressing case fell on her larynx, permanently injuring her voice. Like the 'First Gentleman' he was, the Prince sent 'the first medical men to her assistance' but 'her voice never recovered its pristine power; and she was frequently obliged to apply leeches to her throat in a morning, previous to singing at night'.[40]

Mrs. Crouch also had her detractors. Mrs. Oxberry records that when she retired to Brighton for her health in 1804, 'she actually drank to excess'.[41] She also seems to have suffered from attacks of manic depressive insanity. She died at Brighton on October 2, 1805, with the loyal and warm-hearted Kelly by her bedside. Kelly's relationship with her was ambiguous and has never been clearly defined, but it can at least be said that he cherished her till the end, and shortly before he died, over twenty years later, he would still say of her, 'she was a sweet creature'.[42]

Together they returned to Smock Alley Theatre on June 16, 1787, in *Lionel and Clarissa*. Kelly, who played Lionel, was introduced with consummate inaccuracy as '(from the Theatre-Royal, Drury Lane, being his first appearance in this Kingdom)'[43] – in the same role of the same opera and at the same theatre in which he had given his farewell performance ten years before. But Kelly in his *Reminiscences* is equally unreliable. He states, for example, that Richard Daly had offered him and Mrs. Crouch an engagement for twelve performances. According to the news reports, it was for six – with the usual benefits added. He gives the date of their arrival in Dublin as June 12, and of their initial performance there as June 22. A contemporary newspaper reports the former on June 10;[44] the latter, we know, took place on June 16. He relates that the Lord Lieutenant commanded two performances when in fact he commanded only one, and he includes a production of *Comus* which did not take place until a return visit in 1789. He also recalls (correctly) that he stayed at his 'father's house in Abbey Street',[45]* a street running parallel to Mary Street, so Thomas Kelly must have changed from his old address. 'Mr. and Mrs. Crouch', he explains, 'went to lodgings taken for them in College Green'.[46]

Both artists were well received in the opening performance of *Lionel and Clarissa,* their reputations having 'assembled a very great audience',[47] but Mrs. Crouch was clearly the favourite. 'Mr. Kelly in Lionel', it was announced, 'was something above mediocrity. He possesses an excellent voice and has a more perfect command of it than most public singers we recollect to have heard. His person is not the most prepossessing, but his execution makes ample amends for it. If his action possessed a little less of that studied uniformity, which looks like affectation it would more recommend him to a Dublin audience – a sameness in anything is tiresome, but it is peculiarly so in acting. Of Mrs. Crouch, in Clarissa, we hesitate not to declare, she fully answered the expectation that had been formed of her. To the most pleasing voice and execution, she added a propriety and gracefulness of action, and to distinguish any one of the songs as better executed, would convey a species of negative censure on the rest, which they be no means merited. In short, through the whole of her part, she displayed much superior execution, taste and judgment. We cannot say much for the other performers, and save Wilder, the less that is said of them, the better'.[48]

Love in a Village was the next opera performed, on June 18, with Kelly as Young Meadows and Mrs. Crouch as Rosetta. There followed a double-bill on June 23 of *The Beggar's Opera* and *The Poor Soldier,* Kelly playing Macheath, Mrs. Crouch, Polly and Norah. Once again Kelly records incorrectly, both for time and place: 'In April 1789, I

*It was No. 33. See *Dublin Evening Post.* July 2, 1787.

played Macheath for the first time, for my benefit [at Drury Lane] Mrs. Crouch, Polly'.[49]

The success in this role which he remembered having achieved two years later in London, had eluded him in Dublin. It was the command performance already mentioned, and 'On his Grace's entrance, he was received with the plaudits of the house, which he returned by bowing with the most graceful condescension. Not the smallest noise or interruption took place during the whole performance. Kelly acted the part of Macheath, and Crouch that of Polly. Mrs. Crouch in acting and singing was all that we could wish – but justice will not permit us to say the same of Kelly. His voice and action appeared to be at open variance. His action was something à la mode à Paris, and his voice in many parts favoured of what might be termed Vulgar; accompanied in the singing by a most uncouth aspiration; Flower and Hour, he caused to undergo a most ungraceful metamorphosis . . sounding them . . Flowher and Howher. It is to be hoped, he will not again repeat what he may think an improvement of the language, but which we conceive to be a species of barbarism'.[50] Nor, according to this report, was the Lord Lieutenant 'accompanied to the theatre by his Duchess, a most beautiful woman'[51] as Kelly has related. Artistically and socially, the performance must have been a sad disappointment to him.

For the fourth performance on June 26, there was a repetition of *Love in a Village* with *The Padlock* added. Kelly received much better reviews for this performance: 'the character of Young Meadows', we are assured, 'sat vastly easier on him than that of Macheath'.[52] We read that 'his execution is very great; his shake is capital; and his stile of singing is Italian; his Duet with Mrs. Crouch was most capital'.[53] He was much applauded for a new song which he had introduced and which 'seemed composed entirely for his voice'.[54] This was probably an aria by Gluck 'to which', he relates, 'Mrs. Sheridan did me the honour to write English words, "Love, thou maddening power" '[55] and which he had introduced into the opera when he first performed in it at Drury Lane Theatre the previous May. The duet was probably another interpolation entitled 'Each joy in thee possessing'.

It was Mrs. Crouch, however, who again won the public. Not only was her singing extravagantly praised but her appearance was equally admired. 'Her dress', we learn, 'was exceedingly neat in the first act; she was neither obliged to the balloon before, nor millinary protuberances behind. In short she was elegance unadorned', while 'in the 3rd Act [she] looked divinely, and the Gods from the upper regions gave her a peal of hands on her entry; the dress she changed to was a loose robe or sack of white gauze or muslin (tied round the waist by a silver cord, with selvage tassels pendant); the sleeves were loose, something like a Chemise à la Reine, but did not come down to the wrists, and she wore a blue hat with white feathers edged with blue. She was enchanting in Leonora, in the entertainment [The Padlock] and she was encored in "Sweet Robin" which she delightfully sung; the bird on her finger seemed enchanted in gazing upon her, and chirped to her singing, his tribute of praise'.[56] Mrs. Crouch sang again in *The Padlock* on June 30. This was a special performance, as an afterpiece to Shakespeare's *Romeo and Juliet,* and was not included in her contract with Daly.

The '5th Night'[57] of the engagement took place on July 3, the evening's entertainment consisting of *The Maid of the Mill* followed by *Rosina.* Kelly was the Lord Aimworth, Mrs. Crouch the Patty and Rosina.

In *The Maid of the Mill*, Sir Harry Sycamore was performed by William O'Reilly, a popular member of the Smock Alley company since 1782. He may have been jealous of young Kelly's return to Dublin in principal roles. Alternatively he may just have been a practical joker on stage. Whatever the reason, he decided to guy Kelly's performance. We read that 'The "Squallini Thrill" [sic] and the Italian attitude of O'Reilly were so risible a few nights since, in the finale of the "Maid of the Mill," that no gravity could resist them, and everyone of the audience joined in an immoderate peal of laughter. The testy "Sir Harry" feeling much hurt at being left in the background among the rest of the characters, by "Lord Aimworth" leading his "Patty" to the verge of the orchestra – in his turn singled out "Lady Sycamore" and figured away to the amusement of all

MICHAEL KELLY. TENOR (c. 1762–1826)
AS LIONEL IN *Lionel and Clarissa*.

LEONI. COUNTER-TENOR
(c. 1745–c. 1800)
AS DON CARLOS IN
The Duenna.

GERTRUDE ELIZABETH MARA. SOPRANO
(1749–1833)

CHARLES INCLEDON.
TENOR (1763–1826)

parties, save his Lordship, who seemed dejected at seeing himself so ably mimicked – and was absolutely cast down on hearing it encored by the audience'.[58]

Evidently Kelly was being treated as a prophet without honour in his country, for this report suggests that the audience, if not hostile was, at least, prepared to laugh at his discomfiture. There is certainly no demonstration of a triumphal return to his native city, having performed before many of the crowned heads of Europe.

He took his benefit on July 7 in *Lionel and Clarissa,* followed by *The Deserter.* In the latter opera he played Henry, Mrs. Crouch played Louisa. At the end of the performance, she introduced 'the favourite song of "Gramachree Molly" ' and 'by very particular desire' both sang 'The Duet composed by Mr. Kelly'.[59] This may have been the duet composed for his *début* at Drury Lane, of which he recounts, 'I composed the melody, and Stephen Storace put the instrumental parts to it. This duet was his first introduction to Drury Lane theatre'.[60] The same duet was introduced into Mrs. Crouch's benefit performance of *Artaxerxes* on July 5, which was 'very decently performed to a brilliant and crowded audience'.[61]

The sixth and last performance of the season took place on July 10 when *Love in a Village* and *Rosina* were repeated. According to his *Reminiscences,* Kelly and Mrs. Crouch then left Dublin for Holyhead *en route* for York where they had been engaged for a short season.

On December 5, 1787, *Inkle and Yarico,* a comic opera by Arnold and the younger Colman, had its first Dublin performance at Smock Alley Theatre. The cast included:

Inkle	Marshall
Sir Christopher Curry	O'Reilly
Trudge	Cherry
Yarico	Mrs. Marshall.[62]

Parke describes the music as 'natural, pleasing, and characteristic'.[63] At Smock Alley the opera created its greatest effect in the auditorium, for on December 13, we read, 'A disturbance in the upper gallery of the Theatre was kept up, last night, prior to the commencement of the comic opera of Inkle and Yarico, which very much annoyed the audience. It was said to have arisen from the circumstances of the Manager having discharged the greater part of the musicians employed in the orchestra, for some misbehaviour, and his having employed a band from London in their room. Through the exertions of Mr. Daly however, order was shortly restored, and a very crowded and brilliant audience were suffered to enjoy their evening's entertainment without further molestation, or having their ears wounded by indelicacies, more savage than the war-hoop [sic] of the Indians whom the piece presented'.[64]

It was the last opera of any kind to have its initial Dublin performance at Smock Alley, for from the previous July Richard Daly had been rebuilding and renovating Crow Street Theatre, whereto he would now transfer his company and his theatrical fortunes. With his departure from Smock Alley, the theatre gradually fell into disuse. In 1789 it became a warehouse. Then in 1815 the old building was razed and the present church of SS. Michael and John was built on the site. After considerable alteration, Crow Street Theatre, which had been closed since early 1783, reopened for Daly's first season on January 18, 1788. It was to Crow Street Theatre, therefore, that Kelly and Mrs. Crouch returned for their next Dublin season on July 7, 1789.

Once again the opening opera was *Lionel and Clarissa* followed the same evening on this occasion by the masque of *Comus*. 'The Kelly and Crouch', we read, 'were divine, and charmed beyond expression'.[65] In *Comus,* Kelly sang the role of the principal Bacchanal, Mrs. Crouch, Euphrosyne, in which part Kelly tells us, she looked 'as lovely as if she had been bathed in the fountain of the Graces'.[66] It was into this production that Kelly introduced the duet by Martin y Solar, *Pace, cara mia sposa* translated as 'Oh, thou wert born to please me' which remained a favourite in Dublin for many years. *Love in a Village* was presented on July 11 and *Inkle and Yarico* on July 14, in which opera Mrs. Crouch sang the air 'Hush every breeze' by James Hook which was 'given in a capital stile of excellence and deservedly encored'.[67] On July 16, *Artaxerxes* was performed and on July 20, *The Maid of the Mill* and *The Padlock*.

The sixth night of their engagement was on July 22, when Kelly sang Don Carlos, and Mrs. Crouch Donna Clara in *The Duenna,* followed by the first Dublin performance of *The Doctor and Apothecary*.[68] This was a translation by James Cobb of von Dittersdorf's and Stephanie's opera, *Doktor und Apotheker*. Cobb was an official in the East India Company and a well known author of over twenty plays and opera libretti. When the manuscript of one of his plays was lost in the Drury Lane fire of 1809, Genest is said to have cynically commented that had the remainder been burned, 'the loss would not have been very great'.[69]

Karl Ditters von Dittersdorf, or Ditters (his original name) was born in Vienna in 1739. He could be – in fact, he has been – described as the Grétry of Germany. He was originally a violinist, playing in the church orchestras at St. Stephen's and the Schottenkirche. Eventually he became one of the leading violinists in Europe. Like most musicians of his time, he travelled continually through Europe from one princely Court to another, seeking employment. For a time he became musician to the Prince Bishop of Breslau, who was then living in dishonourable retirement at Johannisberg in northern Poland. He arranged musical entertainments to alleviate his patron's loneliness, and in return received a patent of nobility which permitted the addition of von Dittersdorf to his name. He also joined his peers, Gluck and Mozart, on being created a Papal Knight of the Golden Spur. His last position was at the castle of Count von Stillfried near Neuhäusel in what is now Czechoslovakia. He died there in 1799. He composed almost thirty operas among which *Doktor und Apotheker* alone still holds the stage.

Unfortunately, when arranged for the English stage, his opera did not receive the artistic musical treatment accorded to *Richard Coeur de Lion*. Kelly explains the circumstances: 'Cobb was adapting, with Storace, Baron Dittersdorf's "Doctor and Apothecary," for Drury Lane; they wished to consult me upon the kind of songs I should wish to be written for me'.[70] Yet the main plan of Stephanie's libretto and much of von Dittersdorf's music remained intact.

Stephen Storace was a son of the double-bass player who had been one of the lessees of Crow Street Music Hall in 1751. He received his first music lessons from his father, and at the age of twelve was sent to his father's native city of Naples where he studied at the *Conservatorio* of St. Onofrio. Kelly first met Stephen Storace and his sister Nancy through an amusing incident at Leghorn in Italy, and has recorded that they 'continued through life the warmest and most attached of my friends'.[71] They were together in Vienna where Stephen had two operas performed, and all three returned to London together in 1787. *The Doctor and Apothecary* was Storace's first adaptation for the English stage. In Dublin the cast was as follows:

Don Carlos	Kelly
Don Juan	Palmer
Signior Tomaso	O'Reilly
Sturmwold	Cherry
Don Guzman	Duffy
Doctor Bilioso	Simpson
Anna	Mrs. Crouch
Isabella	Mrs. Mountain
Teresa	Mrs. Dawson.[72]

The production was received with 'uncommon applause'[73] and was repeated on July 25 as an afterpiece to *Robin Hood*. Another error must be noted here in Kelly's chronology. He has recorded that 'In the summer of 1789' Mrs. Crouch and he 'performed "The Haunted Tower" in Dublin with complete success',[74] but corrects his mistake when he notes that the first performance of *The Haunted Tower* took place at Drury Lane only on 'Nov 24th 1789'.[75] He had confused this opera with *The Doctor and Apothecary*. Both singers had been engaged in the original production of *The Haunted Tower*, but they would not take part in a Dublin performance until 1793.

The last performance of the season, for Kelly's benefit, took place on August 1. The programme consisted of *The Beggar's Opera* followed by 'The Celebrated Italian Burletta in one Act called L'Gli Amanti Gelossi;* [sic] Or, The Jealous Lovers, As performed at the Theatre-Royal of Naples, Venice, Vienna and London, with universal approbation'.[76] *The Padlock* was added as an afterpiece. Kelly and Mrs. Crouch took part in the three operas.

This was the last time an Italian opera would be performed in Dublin until the early nineteenth century. With this single performance the wheel had turned almost full circle, for *Gli Amanti Gelosi* was the first burletta to be presented in Dublin by the Giordani family twenty-five years previously. It had not been performed since that one season, and had now been disinterred probably at Giordani's insistence. He presumably saw in Kelly's knowledge of Italian opera an opportunity for its revival. Alternatively it may have been at Kelly's suggestion, as a friendly gesture to a fellow-musician. Whatever prompted the event, it brought little honour either to Kelly or Giordani. One performance of a burletta, reduced from three acts to one, was truly ending eighteenth-century Italian opera in Dublin with a whimper.

*For some reason advertised in the *Hibernian Journal,* August 1, 1789, as '*L'Enamorata osia la Gelosia.*'

17

THE ARRIVAL OF
MADAME MARA

THE OPERAS OF Stephen Storace now had a vogue in Dublin. Shortly after his return to London in 1787 Storace was engaged by Linley for Drury Lane, and by Gallini to superintend the operas at the King's Theatre; his opera *Le Cameriere astute* was produced there on March 4, 1788.[1]

His music and orchestration were naturally influenced by Mozart and the Italians whose compositions he had heard in Vienna and Italy. He indulged his sister Nancy and Michael Kelly by writing elaborate arias which enabled them to display their Italian technique in London. He was among the first English composers who developed the finales of their operas by combining the concerted music with the action of the scene* – another continental innovation. He also composed in the ballad opera style; an example is the song, 'The Pretty Creature' – much recorded in early gramophone days by the baritone, David Bispham – from his opera *The Pirates*. Hogarth relates that he had united 'pure Italian melody to the prosody and accent of English poetry with a felicity which has never been excelled by any other composer'.[2] This Boaden confirms. When writing of him, he states, 'The composers of that time cultivated a pure and flowing melody like Paisiello; they had nothing of the flight, hurry and almost excessive brilliancy of Rossini'.[3]

His first opera to be performed in Dublin, *The Haunted Tower,* was his first English opera for London. Of the London production Parke reports, 'The success of this opera was almost unbounded. The copy-

---

*Charles Dibdin was probably the first English composer to introduce this musical form, as a quintet, into *The Quaker* (1777) but one cannot be dogmatic about such innovations.

278

right of its music, which was uncommonly effective and universally admired, was sold for the sum of five hundred pounds!'[4] This music had been much compiled from Pleyel, Paisiello, Sarti, Linley, and Martin y Solar, and adapted from Welsh and French tunes. The libretto was by James Cobb and the Dublin production, which took place at Crow Street Theatre on February 18, 1790, had 'new Accompaniments by Signor Giordani'.[5] The cast was as follows:

Lord William	Palmer
Edward	Cherry
Lord de Courcy	Hamerton
Robert	J. Brown
Hugo	Duncan
Adela	Miss Brett
Cicely	Miss Hitchcock
Maud	Mrs. Heaphy
Lady Eleanor	Miss Reynolds.[6]

We read that the opera 'was got up with great propriety and much expense to the manager, and it was done ample justice to, by the performers . . The music is really charming in the true Italian style though the airs are not much different from some of our original native musick . . The scene in the "haunted tower" had a wonderful effect'.[7]

There was little of operatic interest during the remainder of the year until November, when Elizabeth Billington returned to Dublin, Richard Daly 'having concluded an Agreement with her for that Purpose, by which she is to receive the capital Sum of Fifty Pounds English for each Night of her Performance'.[8] She began her season on November 8 as Rosetta in *Love in a Village* with Joseph Kelly as Young Meadows.[9]

It seems probable that Joseph was Michael Kelly's brother although nowhere does Michael describe him as a singer or actor. But he did have a brother of that name who brought Tom Moore to visit him at Mrs. Crouch's cottage in the King's Road, Chelsea, in 1801[10] and, speaking of Michael, *The Thespian Dictionary* relates, 'His brother is on the stage and has performed in Dublin, &c. with some success'.[11] Related or not, Joe Kelly had first appeared at Crow Street Theatre in 1789 and remained highly popular with Dublin audiences for many years. He performed leading roles with Mrs. Billington throughout the season, in repeat performances of *Love in a Village* on November 26, December 7 and 14, in *The Duenna* on November 11, 22 and December 17, in *Inkle and Yarico* on November 19 and December 3, in *The Maid of the Mill* on December 10, in *Lionel and Clarissa* on December 20, and in *Robin Hood* on December 22.

The performance of *The Duenna* on November 22 had been commanded by the Lord Lieutenant, then the tenth Earl of Westmoreland, who in a very direct manner had some influence on opera. His first wife, the only daughter and heiress of Robert Child, the London banker, had eloped with him in 1782. Their son, Lord Burghersh, later the eleventh earl, was not only a distinguished soldier and diplomatist, but a composer as well, who wrote six Italian operas. His principal claim to musical distinction, however, is that through his energy and influence, the Royal Academy of Music was established in London in 1822.

The season also included two performances of *The Beggar's Opera,* on November 16, ('semi-reversed' with Miss Brett as Macheath) and on November 30. Mrs. Billington sang Polly on both occasions. Lucy was sung by a putative rival named Miss George who 'had a voice of such extent that she sang up to B in alto perfectly clear and in tune'[12] and, as the following incident makes clear, was in no way cowed by her more illustrious colleague.

During one of the performances, Parke tells us, 'Miss George, who performed the part of Lucy, (an uphill singing part), perceiving she had little chance of dividing the applause with the great magnet of the night, had recourse to the following stratagem: when the dialogue duet in the second act, "Why, how now, Madame Flirt," came on, Mrs. Billington gave her verse with great sweetness and characteristic expression, and was much applauded. Miss George in reply, availing herself of her extraordinary compass of voice, and setting propriety at defiance, sang the whole of her verse an octave higher, her tones having the effect of the high notes of a sweet and brilliant flute: the audience, taken by surprise, bestowed on her such loud applause as almost shook the walls of the theatre, and an unanimous *encore* was the result'.[13] This rivalry was to persist during the following year, where at Cork it was reported that their relationship on stage 'could compare them to nothing but St. George and the Dragon'.[14]

The performance of *Lionel and Clarissa* on December 20 was for Mrs. Billington's benefit, to which she added a performance of *Rosina. Robin Hood,* performed on December 22, was for Richard Daly, and had the first performance in Dublin of the comic opera *Marian* appended as an afterpiece.[15] In this opera Billington played Marian, a role she had created at Covent Garden; Joseph Kelly played Sir Henry. We read, 'The music of this piece, by Shield, is almost the sweetest he ever composed'.[16] The libretto was by Mrs. Brooke.

Daly then announced that he had 'renewed his Engagement with Mrs. Billington for a few Nights longer'[17] but these few nights were to be extended to the end of January 1791. The only interesting episode of this continued engagement which consisted of staple works was Billington's assumption of the role of Ophelia in *Hamlet.* Her motive for performing the part is explained by the announcement: 'in which character she will introduce the celebrated Song of "mad Bess" composed by Purcell'.[18] This song by Henry Purcell was at the time, over a hundred years after its composition, becoming fashionable with sopranos as a showpiece, and may be considered a forerunner of nineteenth-century operatic mad-scenes such as occur in *I Puritani* and *Lucia di Lammermoor.* As an interpolation in the role of Ophelia, 'Bess of Bedlam' was perfectly in character. The song commences:

> 'From silent shades, and the Elysian Groves,
> Where sad departed Spirits mourn their loves.
>
> . . . .
>
> poor senseless Bess cloath'd in her rags & folly
> is come to cure her love sick melancholly'.

Bright Cynthia, Queen Mab, and Oberon are 'gayly' introduced, and then she sings:

> 'In yonder Cowslip lies my dear
> . . . each day I'll water it with a tear'.

Musically the song passes through a variety of moods – the quietly melancholic opening of Bess's entrance, proceeding by recitative, *arioso* and song to a bright lively ending when madness having freed her from sorrow she cheerfully sings:

> 'And Bess in her straw
> Whilst free from the law
> In her thoughts is as great as a king'.

On January 26, 1791, Billington took her benefit in *The Castle of Andalusia*, and *Robin Hood*, introducing into the programme, 'the favourite Song of Auld Robin Gray . . an additional Song by Anfossi, and the celebrated Song of "Sweet Bird" from "L'Allegro e il Penseroso" by Handel, accompanied on the violin by Mr. Weichsel'.[19] 'Positively the last Night of Mrs. Billington performing in this Kingdom'[20] was then advertised for January 28 when she made a final appearance for this engagement in *Love in a Village*. The address of her lodgings was 10 Henry Street.

On February 24 a second opera by Stephen Storace, *No Song no Supper*, was performed for the first time in Dublin[21] for Daly's benefit. The libretto was by Prince Hoare* who was born in 1755 at Bath (a flourishing centre of the arts during the second half of the eighteenth century) and who was known equally as painter and dramatist. The cast was as follows:

Frederick	(Joseph) Kelly
Crop	Palmer
Robin	Cherry
William	Brown
Endless	O'Reilly

*Wrongly attributed in *Faulkner's Dublin Journal* of February 17/19, 1791, to 'Mr. Cobbe'.

Louisa	Miss Brett
Dorothy	Mrs. Hitchcock
Nelly	Mrs. Dawson
Margaretta	Miss George.[22]

For the original production of this opera in London, Storace had annexed a trio and a sextet from his opera *Gli Equivoci* (performed at Vienna in 1786) and had also included some music by Grétry. It was extremely successful and Kelly and Parke praise especially the finale of the first act, which both describe as 'masterly'.[23]

Dublin's hospitality to Mrs. Billington seems to have been un-limited, for she was back once more at Crow Street Theatre on June 6, beginning a new season in what appears to have been her (or the audience's) favourite opera, *Love in a Village*.[24] The orchestra, led by Weichsel, was augmented for her performances and it was announced that 'Servants as in the London Theatres will not be allowed to keep places after the first Act'.[25]

For the opening performance, 'A Mr. Pearce was introduced to the public as Hawthorn and justly received the warmest applause throughout his character'.[26] He was reported as 'from the Theatre Royal, Drury Lane',[27] but Genest in *Some Account of the English Stage* does not mention anyone of that name performing there between 1789 and 1792. A William Pearce wrote opera libretti for Covent Garden Theatre in 1793 and 1794. It is possible that he was the same artist.

Miss George and Joseph Kelly were also members of the company and the season proceeded with performances of the familiar *Lionel and Clarissa*, *The Beggar's Opera*, *The Duenna*, *Rosina*, *The Haunted Tower*, *The Doctor and Apothecary*, *Robin Hood* and *Inkle and Yarico*.

Some interest was introduced, firstly by performances of *Orpheus and Euridice* with Mrs. Billington on June 10 and 17, and then by a performance of *Love in a Village* on June 22. The latter opera intro-duced the English tenor, Charles Incledon who, we learn, 'charmed as Young Meadows – his figure, voice, taste, judgement and expression, are the subject of universal praise'.[28] Two evenings later, on June 24th, he repeated his success in *Orpheus and Euridice* when he 'gave to

Orpheus a colour, character and expression, which afforded universal satisfaction; it was in every respect a masterly performance'.[29] It was, coincidentally, the first time this role is recorded as having been sung by a tenor in Dublin, although Pearce had almost certainly sung it in the two earlier performances.

Charles Incledon was a doctor's son, born in Cornwall in 1763, who received his first music lessons as a choirboy at Exeter Cathedral. In 1779 he went to sea in a man-of-war, where his voice, which had become a fine tenor, attracted the attention of some naval officers. On his return to London these gentlemen gave him letters of introduction both to Sheridan and the elder Colman, but neither manager had the perspicacity to engage him. He was obliged consequently to begin his stage career in the provinces, but between 1786 and 1790 he sang each summer at Vauxhall Gardens, and during the winter performed at Bath, where he had gained Venanzio Rauzzini's patronage. His first stage appearance in London was made in 1790 at Covent Garden when he played Dermot in *The Poor Soldier,* and for the next thirty years he was to become one of the most popular singers in England.

Hogarth writes of him, 'As a musician he was almost uneducated, having spent a considerable part of his youth at sea; but he possessed a tenor voice,* of unrivalled beauty and power, and a genius which, with cultivation, would have raised him above every other English singer . . The style in which he excelled was the English ballad, and his favourite characters were those of the operas in that style, such as *Macheath, Young Meadows, Belville,* &c. His action was clumsy and

---

Grove's Dictionary of Music and Musicians (Fifth Edition. Vol. IV. p. 454) gives the following contemporary account of his voice which is of technical interest not only in relation to Incledon, but as a description of tenor voices of this period:

'He had a voice of uncommon power, both in the natural and falsette. The former was from A to g', a compass of about fourteen notes; the latter he could use from d' to e" or f", or about ten notes. His natural voice was full and open, neither partaking of the reed nor the string, and sent forth without the smallest artifice; and such was its ductility that when he sang pianissimo it retained its original quality. His falsette was rich, sweet and brilliant, but totally unlike the other. He took it without preparation, according to circumstances either about d', e' or f', or ascending an octave, which was his most frequent custom; he could use it with facility, and execute ornaments of a certain class with volubility and sweetness. His shake was good, and his intonation much more correct than is common to singers so imperfectly educated.' (Reported from *Dictionary of Musicians*. London 1822/27.)

awkward, and his elocution coarse and vulgar; but, in singing, the effect produced by his voice, energy and feeling, was irresistible'.[30]

He specialised in sea-songs such as 'All's Well', 'Heaving the lead', 'Black-eyed Susan' and 'Our Country is our ship'. A dramatic story is told that once, when returning to England from Dublin, his ship was wrecked and several passengers were lost, but 'he saved himself by climbing to the roundtop, with his wife lashed to him, in which perilous condition he was several hours, till at length delivered by some fishermen who saw their distress from shore'.[31] On his next visit to Dublin, he commemorated the event by adding another song to his repertoire, singing it in character as a sailor, called 'The Storm'.

A performance of *Orpheus and Euridice* on July 11 with Billington, Incledon, Joseph Kelly (Hymen) and Miss Brett (Cupid) derives interest from an advertisement declaring 'The Music principally by the Chevalier Christopher Gluck, Composer to the Emperor. With Additions by the late celebrated John Christopher Bach'.[32] This repeats word for word the announcement identifying the composers when the opera was first produced in Dublin in 1784, even to the extent of ignoring that Gluck had died meanwhile in 1787, and augments the evidence that the music of the initial production, and of the present one, was by Gluck and J. C. Bach alone.

Richard Daly's position as manager allowed him to introduce the first new opera of the season for his benefit on July 15. This was *The Woodman*, which had a libretto by the Reverend Sir Henry Bate Dudley who, 'judiciously availing himself of the rage for archery which then prevailed, even amongst the ladies, introduced a scene of that description in the third act'.[33] 'The Music with a few Exceptions, [was] composed entirely new by Mr. Shield.'[34] The cast was:

Wilfred	Incledon
Sir Walter	Cherry
Fairlop	Pearce
Medley	Palmer
Bob	Gaudry
Captain O'Donnell	(Joseph) Kelly

Dolly	Miss George
Miss De Clackit	Mrs. Dawson
Polly	Miss Duncan
Female Archers	Mrs. Hitchcock, Mrs. Kelly,
	Mrs. Cotrell, Mrs. Barrett
Emily	Mrs. Billington.[35]

Benefit performances for the artists then followed: first *Fontaine-bleau* and *The Deserter* on July 18 for Mrs. Billington. Among additional airs which she introduced was 'a favourite Obligato Song for Violin, Tenor [viola] and Flute, composed by Signor Giordani and accompanied by Mr. Weichsel, Mr. Fitzgerald and Mr. Ashe'.[36] Miss George chose 'a favourite Opera and a new Farce'[37] – titles not given – for July 21, and on the following evening Incledon selected *The Woodman,* including, among other airs, 'Oft on a plat of rising ground' from Handel's *L'Allegro,* and ending his programme with *The Flitch of Bacon.** Charles Weichsel, Pearce and Joseph Kelly next took their benefits, but the most remarkable benefit of all was one advertised to take place on August 3 for William Dawson. This performance, like Dawson's earlier endeavour recorded in 1778, was predestined to fail. The opera chosen was *Artaxerxes,* with Billington as Mandane and Incledon as Arbaces, but the result was disastrous, as Dawson explains in the following report:

'About three o'clock on Wednesday Afternoon, Mr. Incledon being suddenly seized at the Theatre with so violent an illness as to deprive all hope of his being able to perform on that Night, which his Physician is ready upon oath to attest, Mr. Dawson was reduced to the unavoidable Necessity of changing the Opera of Artaxerxes to Lionel and Clarissa, and adopted the only possible Means of communicating the sudden Alteration to the Public, by causing a Thousand Hand Bills to be immediately printed and distributed at the Doors and Offices of the Theatre. Notwithstanding these Precautions,

---

The Flitch of Bacon, William Shield's first opera, libretto by Bate Dudley, had had its initial Dublin performance at Crow Street Theatre on December 2, 1779. The cast included Wilder, Johnstone, Owenson, Fotteral, Whitmore, Lloyd, O'Keeffe, Mrs. George Dawson, Hester Francis and Mrs. Johnstone. (*Freeman's Journal* November 30/December 2, 1779.)

the Performance was, through the Clamour of a few Individuals, and contrary to the general sense of the Audience, not suffered to proceed, though attempted at intervals six different Times, and the Money repeatedly offered to be returned to those who disapproved of the change'.[38]

Unrest during performances was a frequent occurrence at the time and, in the same newspaper, we read: 'The late disturbances at the Theatre, particularly that of Wednesday evening, [August 3], reflect great discredit on the metropolis. Better to have no places of public amusement, than to have them thus disgraced by indecency and tumult. We cannot help thinking that the more respectable part of the audience are much to blame for their passiveness on these occasions. If they were more forward to interpose their authority, the galleries, but particularly the second one, could not presume to disturb the Theatre as they have lately done, with their noise and impertinence. Nine tenths of the audience on Wednesday night last, at the Theatre Royal, were so decidedly in favour of the night's performance going on and so thoroughly satisfied with the apology made in the numerous hand bills distributed, respecting Mr. Incledon's illness, that nothing but the most reprehensible and shameful continuance of clamor, from a small part of the house, could have obstructed the entertainment of the night; welcome, therefore, must be the intelligence to every friend to public decorum and amusement, that the most determined and legal steps will be taken against the instigators of so scandalous a riot. On this occasion, the admirers of the Drama are highly indebted to the ready attendance, and very laudable and active exertions of Alderman Carleton and Sheriff Williams, whose addresses to the audience most essentially contributed to suppress the alarming tumult'.[39]

Towards the end of 1791, on December 14, Stephen Storace and James Cobb had yet another success with the first Dublin production of *The Siege of Belgrade, or The Turkish Overthrow,* 'with new Accompaniments composed by Signor Giordani and a new Grand Martial Overture'.[40] The cast was numerous, consisting of opposing teams of Christians and Muslims. The Christians were as follows:

Colonel Cohonberg	Hamerton
Peter	Simpson
Anselm	Duncan
Michael	G. King
Austrian Officer	Gaudry
Austrian Soldiers	Lee, Murray
Servian Villagers	Barret, Dawson
Leopold	Palmer
Catherine	Miss Rose Ryder
Ohita	Mrs. Hitchcock
Lilla	Miss Brett
The Turks were:	
The Seraskier	(Joseph) Kelly
Ismael	Owenson
Turkish Officer	E. King
Turkish Soldiers	Callan, L. Kelly
Mutes	Brett, Dowling
Yuseph	Moss
Turkish Ladies	Mesdames Castelli, Dynan, Murray
Fatima	Miss Harcourt.[41]

The lavishness of the production can be judged from the following description of the ballet and settings: 'In Act I. A Turkish Dance by Mons. Jocasta, Sig. Bartholomichi and the two Signoras de Caros. In Act III The Storming of Belgrade, with a View of the City and the Turkish Camp. With new Dresses, Decorations, Trophies, Banners etc. The Scenery entirely new, designed and executed by Signor Marinari, principal Painter to the Opera House, London, particularly a Distant View of Belgrade and the Encampment of the Austrian Army, the Seraskier's Tent, a Turkish Seraglio's Tent, a Turkish Burying Ground, a Turkish Fortification, etc.'[42]

Well might Parke write of *The Siege of Belgrade's* first performance at Drury Lane, 'This opera presented a marked instance of the rapid transition which the English opera had made, from the simplicity of the ballad farce to the captivating splendours of the Italian drama. The music, which was excellent throughout, procured the author for his copy-right one thousand pounds'.[43] If it did, then the composer Martin y Solar, frequently called Martini, was being cheated. The published vocal score consists of eighty-one pages of music. Forty-nine are composed by Storace, three by Paisiello, one by Salieri, one by Michael Kelly (a serenade sung by him in his original role of the Seraskier), eight by 'Martini and Storace'[44](?) and *nineteen* by Martin y Solar.

The Dublin production seemingly equalled its London triumph, for we read, 'The exhibition of yesterday evening was one of the most correct, animated, beautifully picturesque performances we ever beheld. The pains, the expence, the time bestowed on producing the elegant Opera of the Siege of Belgrade, adds highly to the Manager's reputation. If the public voice is the criterion of our judgment, no direction of our national amusements ever stood so high in general opinion as the present. The appearance of the Theatre last night was a pleasing confirmation of this truth. We never saw a more elegant assemblage of beauty, rank and fashion'.[45]

Opera continued uneventfully in Dublin during the first half of 1792, the spirit of the period, in fact the spirit of the entire eighteenth century, being fully expressed in the following passage: 'The serious opera has never yet found many admirers in this capital; but her jocund sister with the smiling face has always been here frequented, patronised and cherished. Her gladsome sports suit best the native sprightliness of the country'.[46]

Yet, exactly four weeks later, there was a complete *volte face* of this approved comic opera policy, with a special production of *Artaxerxes,* and with, coincidentally, a eulogy for Richard Daly. 'The Manager's engagement, this day announced', we read, 'of the celebrated Madam Mara, confessedly the first singer in Europe, is an exertion to amuse the public that does his official station the greatest credit, and calls for the most decided patronage of a liberal people. No other person, however high in station, dignified by character, or generous in proposal, has hitherto been able to induce that inimitable performer

T

to visit this capital. It was reserved for Daly – whose endeavours to entertain the town know no limits of effort or expense, – to prevail on her by a salary of unexampled magnitude in Ireland (we hear from good authority *"a hundred pounds"* a night) to display her matchless abilities to a Dublin audience'.[47]

It would be satisfying to be able to confirm a report appearing in the London *Morning Chronicle* of November 10, 1785, that 'Madame Mara, who now cuts so distinguished a figure in England, was born in the county of Waterford'. More reliable authorities record that Gertrude Elizabeth Mara, *née* Schmeling, was born at Cassel in Germany, on February 23, 1749. Her mother died shortly afterwards, and she was reared by her father, a struggling musician.

As a young child she began to pick out tunes unaided on the violin, and was then given some lessons by her father. By the age of six she was proficient enough to be presented at Frankfurt, and from there set out on a long tour through Holland to Vienna, and eventually, to London. While she was in England – about 1762* – it was discovered that she had a promising voice, and she had some vocal training from Pietro Paradisi, a pupil of Porpora in London. Shortly afterwards, she returned to Cassel. About 1766 she proceeded to Leipzig, where she had further singing lessons from the composer J. A. Hiller, and at length reached the Court of the musician-king, Frederick the Great of Prussia. Frederick had earlier exclaimed, 'A German singer? I should as soon expect to receive pleasure from the neighing of my horse'.[48] Obviously she assuaged his prejudice for she was to remain at Berlin until 1780, enduring a turbulent artistic existence under her royal patron.

She also married Giovanni Battista Mara, a mediocre cellist in the Court orchestra, whose actions while playing 'gave one the idea of a coachman on his box, in the act of driving'.[49] He turned out to be a brute, a spendthrift, and an alchoholic who in time drank himself to death.

Frederick was a jealous patron who allowed his artists, particularly

*The time that she first visited Dublin, as Miss Schmeling.

Mara, little freedom and so she was obliged to escape from Berlin by a ruse. For the next four years she lived first in Vienna and Munich, and then in Paris. She arrived in London in 1784 to sing at concerts in the Pantheon, where she made her first appearance on March 29.

While she was still young, in appearance, we are told, 'She is short, and not handsome, but is far from having anything disagreeable in her countenance; on the contrary, there is a strong expression of good nature impressed upon it, which renders her address very engaging. Her teeth are irregular, and project too much, yet, altogether, her youth and smiles taken into the account, she is rather agreeable in face and figure'.[50]

Her manner, however, was capricious, and almost immediately on her arrival in London she was in trouble both with critics and audiences. For example, during the performance of a cantata, it was observed that 'the bustle she made in her tour to the orchestra, during Miss Abrams' cadence is not to the credit either of her feelings or understanding'.[51] This *hauteur* towards her audiences and fellow artists created contentious friction and during a concert at Oxford her 'aude behaviour in leaving the orchestra as soon as she had sung her songs, and refusing to stand up with the other performers during the chorusses, gave much offence to the whole audience, and to the young gentlemen of the University in particular, and she was repeatedly hissed for it'.[52] It was even ironically advertised that 'Madam Mara's treaty with the Managers of the Opera House, we understand, is at an end, she having insisted to be indulged with an *arm chair,* or a *sofa,* during the intervals of her songs'.[53]

Mara replied 'to the various Calumnies, by which her enemies have endeavoured to injure her Reputation' by explaining that she 'has only retired (an Allowance always extended to her by the Directors of Ancient Music) because she finds by repeated Experience, that the overpowering Effect of the Chorusses round her would too far operate on her Health and Spirits, to enable her to execute the Remainder of her Performance with that Degree of Force which she has perhaps exhibited on other Occasions, and which she is always anxious to display; this Circumstance, connected with the Necessity of the standing Posture which for this Account is peculiarly distressing to her, and which has been pronounced very injurious to her Constitution has been the only Foundation of that Malice which has been directed with so much Virulence against her'.[54]

Vocally, she seems to have been supreme in her time, and *Grove's Dictionary* describes her explicitly as 'one of the greatest singers of the 18th century'.[55] In a letter to Charles Burney, a correspondent from Germany declared, 'I never knew a voice so powerful and so sweet, at the same time: she could do with it just what she pleased. She sings from G to E *in altissimo,* with the greatest ease and force, and both her *portamento di voce,* and her volubility are, in my opinion, unrivalled'.[56]

Shortly afterwards Burney visited her in Berlin. She sang an *aria di bravura* by Traetta for him and he recounts: 'She sung it admirably, and fully answered the great ideas which I had formed of her abilities, in everything but her voice, which was a little cloudy, and not quite so powerful as I expected. However, she had a slight cold and cough, and complained of indisposition: but with all this, her voice was sweetly toned, and she sung perfectly well in tune. She has an excellent shake, a good expression, and facility of executing and articulating rapid and difficult divisions, that is astonishing. Her second song was a *Larghetto,* by Schwanenberg, of Brunswick, which was very pretty in itself; but she made it truly delightful by her taste and expression: she was by no means lavish of graces, but those she used, were perfectly suited to the style of the music, and idea of the poet.'[57]

Mount Edgcumbe's opinion was that 'Mara's talents as a singer (for she was no actress, and had a bad person for the stage) were of the very first order. Her voice clear, sweet, distinct, and sufficiently powerful, though rather thin, and its agility and flexibility rendered her a most excellent bravura singer, in which style she was unrivalled; but she succeeded equally well in some of Handel's most solemn and pathetic songs, though there appeared to be a want of that feeling in herself, which, nevertheless, she could communicate to her hearers'.[58]

To the charge of not being an actress she made a pertinent prima donna retort, 'What! am I to sing with my hands and legs? I am a singer; what I cannot do with my voice I will not do at all'.[59] Her greatest disadvantage in England seems not to have been her inability to act, but her inability to sing in English. Whatever amount of the language she had picked up during her childhood there, she had either forgotten or had never properly mastered. A review of a performance of Handel's *Esther* in which she and Tenducci took part peremptorily states, 'Madam Mara must excuse us if we say that we wish never to hear her again in English oratorios . . We should be deficient in filial duty, were we to suffer such murders to be committed on our mother tongue, without publick reprehension, for reprehension is due somewhere'.[60] There was also the clairvoyant-like observation, 'Let her avoid, as much as possible, English airs'.[61]

Like the mink coat to most women, Mara's arrival in Dublin came too late. She was then forty-three, and while her career in ballad operas, concerts and oratorios was to continue for many more years, her voice had lost much of its original freshness and her Italian opera career had almost ended. Nevertheless she was a star, and so she attracted the attention which stars will, even when they are fading. Consequently her first Dublin performance on July 18, 1792, was greeted with the following panegyric – however biassed and inaccurate.

'Last night the celebrated Mme Mara graced, for the first time, the Irish stage, by appearing in the character of Mandane in Artaxerxes, and was received with the most marked distinction which the liberality of a polished people is wont to bestow on such commanding merit as hers. Her person is about the middle size, her eyes sparkling and uncommonly fine, her hair beautiful and luxuriant, and her action most just and expressive: but no pen can do justice to the exquisite powers of her voice. Matchless in sweetness, powerful in body, mellow in tone: and each note melting into its successor with an harmonized melody not to be conceived without hearing: and all these made under the direction of extensive science and the correctest judgment. She possesses in the highest degree those qualities that constitute, in our opinion, the highest merit of a vocal performer:

accurate execution united with the justest taste and the utmost simplicity of manner. Three of her songs were *encored* with the loudest plaudits that ever shook a theatre. These were "Fly soft ideas", "The soldier tired" and a song she introduced from the Opera of Idalide [by Giuseppe Sarti] which was accompanied on the pedal harp, a new exhibition here of striking effect.'[62] Others taking part in the opera were:

Arbaces	Incledon
Artabanes	Palmer
Artaxerxes	(Joseph) Kelly
Rimenes	Mrs. Stewart
Semira	Mrs. Murray.[63]

We also learn that 'The band was considerably increased, but much more in merit than in number, by the addition of Mr. Mara, on the violincello, Mr. Florio, on the flute, and Mr. Myers on the pedal harp'.[64] (Also present were Dr. Cogan, the regular theatre harpsichordist, and Mr. Fitzgerald, violinist and leader of the orchestra.) Mara was, of course, Elizabeth's husband. Florio was later to play a very personal role in her life and Myers, the harp virtuoso, was Philip Jacob Meyer junior, a member of the orchestra at the King's Theatre, London, during the 1798/99 season.

With this one opera, *Artaxerxes,* between July 18 and August 8, Mara attracted overflow audiences to the theatre for ten performances. If reports are to be believed, and hyperbole does not seem to have been needed to stimulate interest on this occasion, at no time did enthusiasm falter. We read in different newspaper reports that 'The unrivalled excellence of Mme. Mara seems daily to grow on the public mind, and to increase in the public favour'[65] and that as her 'engagement with Mr. Daly approaches towards a conclusion, the eager avidity of the public to hear her admirable performance evidently appears to increase'.[66] She took her benefit performance on August 1, when 'her very superior merit and deserved favour with the public, crowded the house with an assemblage of all rank or fashion, the capital or its environs could, at present, supply; whilst those parts of the house, where places could not be kept, were speedily overflowed. As if anxious, on this occasion, to gratify her friends to the utmost, her performance even exceeded her former exhibitions in fancy ever new, and in exquisite execution'.[67] Even her final performance for Meyer's benefit on August 8, 'which concluded the theatrical campaign of this season, was graced with a house uncommonly full, considering the time of the year'.[68]

During her visit to Dublin Mara stayed at 'No. 97 Grafton-street'.[69] When the season ended she went on a short tour with Daly's company to Cork and Limerick, then, on September 6,[70] she triumphantly set sail once more for England.

18

THE END OF AN ERA

FROM 1792 ONWARDS, the history of opera in Dublin until the end of the century becomes a story of steady decline. As is customary with declining theatrical ventures, Daly tried to stay the tide by relying on programmes of popular operas and return visits of popular artists. Such an artist, Elizabeth Billington, revisited Dublin in November of that year, and for fifteen evenings until December 22 performed in a schedule of operas which included *Lionel and Clarissa, The Duenna, The Beggar's Opera, Artaxerxes, Love in a Village, The Haunted Tower, No Song No Supper, Robin Hood* and *Inkle and Yarico.*

The orchestra for her performances was led by Charles Weichsel, with the 'Accompanier on the Pianoforte, the Baron de Grifft'.[1](?) The principal tenor of the season was Peter Duffy who for his benefit performance on December 22 chose *The Beggar's Opera* and *The Poor Soldier,* introducing 'In the course of the Entertainment . . the much admired Song of mad Tom, in character'.[2] This was an extension of the male 'Polly Peachum in petticoats' jape and indicates the popularity of Purcell's 'mad Bess' that it, too, could be parodied.

Billington's first appearance for the season was in *Love in a Village* on November 12, when she was welcomed back 'with every respect the public could pay to such extraordinary abilities. The house was uncommonly crowded – almost every person of fashion in town were present. Never did this charming singer exhibit such proofs of unrivalled excellence – and never were an audience so enraptured'.[3] Evidently Billington was still both vocally excellent and charming in appearance, though by 1802 she 'had prodigiously increased in bulk'.[4]

Since she and Mara were now in direct competition, comparison of their voices was unavoidable. Mount Edgcumbe records that they 'were in most respects . . similar'.[5] However, an anonymous critic writing in 1807 appraises them in more detail and notes certain dissimilarities: 'Mrs. Billington, in compass of voice and rapidity of execution', he declares, 'stands unrivalled. Yet her defects are many and great. Though possessed of great facility of modulation, she scarcely ever varies her cadenzas upon a repetition. The lower notes of her voice are not so firm as those of Mara, who is inferior to her in the strength and sweetness of the higher. It is perhaps the bad taste of the day which induces her to dwell so long and so frequently upon a shake, to the utter disgust of every admirer of genuine ornament. In pathetic music she seldom shows sensibility, and consequently seldom excites it . . Songs of the same character with the "Soldier tired of war's alarms", or bravuras, as they have been termed, which would by no means suit Madam Mara, serve to place Mrs. Billington's powers in their proper light. In fine she may be characterised as a brilliant and astonishing singer, who never touches the finer feelings, who has contributed in no small degree to pervert the public taste, and who, compared with Mara, appears as inferior as the lowest species of Lyric poetry is to the Epos'.[6]

Billington's performances during her engagement were greeted with overflowing audiences: 'Nor was it merely an overflow of ordinary citizens – some of the most fashionable and splendid company in town found it impossible to get admission'.[7] Yet there is a sharp rebuke to the Earl of Westmoreland who seems to have been neglecting the social responsibilities of his vice-regal position. 'Invidious comparisons', we read, 'have sometimes been made between the state of theatric entertainments in this country – and England, and between the exertions of the respective managers in both countries, but let candour be consulted whether the manager of a London theatre would be able to keep the character of his house in a higher degree of estimation than that in which the Irish theatre has stood for some years – did he meet no greater encouragement from the Court than Irish managers have done from the niggard representatives of Royalty by whom this country has been disgraced? The presence of the

Monarch frequently graces the English stage – and draws thither those immense crowds which always follow in the trail of Royalty . . When do we see the "little great" ones who preside in this country, give to our theatre that little éclat which might result from their presence; whole seasons have passed over, and the Representative of Majesty, immersed in solitude, has not once "condescended" to visit the theatre!'[8]

The years 1793 and 1794 merit comment only for the return of Michael Kelly and Mrs. Crouch. They appeared at Crow Street Theatre in *Lionel and Clarissa* on November 27, 1793, their 'first appearance these four years'.[9] It was a lavish season in the number and variety of operas performed, although no new opera was introduced. Performances took place, on twenty evenings, of the following recurrently played works: *Lionel and Clarissa*, *Love in a Village*, *The Siege of Belgrade*, *The Haunted Tower*, *The Duenna*, *Richard Coeur de Lion*, *Inkle and Yarico*, *The Maid of the Mill*, *The Beggar's Opera*, *Comus*, *The Deserter*, *No Song No Supper*, *Fontainebleau* and *The Doctor and Apothecary*.

Tickets for Mrs. Crouch's benefit were to be had 'at Mr. Jewster's, hatter, Dame-street'.[10] The performance consisted of *The Beggar's Opera* and *Comus*, and took place on January 9, 1794. For Kelly's benefit on January 23,[11] when he performed in *Fontainebleau* and *The Doctor and Apothecary*, Mrs. Crouch introduced the air 'No flower that blows' from Grétry's *Zemire et Azor* and joined with him in a duet from Francesco Bianchi's opera, *La Villanella Rapita*.

Kelly's *Reminiscences* again need correction concerning two minor incidents said to have occurred during this engagement. He states that 'At this period, the Beggar's Opera was prohibited by the Irish Government from being acted'[12] and explains how he sought the influence of Mrs. Jefferies, sister of Lord Clare, the notoriously illiberal Lord Chancellor, to have the ban removed. But, as has been noted, *The Beggar's Opera* was performed as late as November 1792 during Billington's season, and probably in the intervening months prior to Kelly and Crouch's visit. Their season ended on January 29, 1794.

He then relates that they were prevailed upon to remain for the first performance in Dublin of *The Mountaineers* (an opera by Arnold and Colman junior), which he describes as 'a discredit to any barn. But blessed are the ways of Providence', he continues, 'had not my apparently idle curiosity induced us to remain, most certain it is that we should have met a watery grave; the Liverpool packet, in which we were to have sailed, foundered on the Welsh coast, and every soul on board perished'.[13] There is no reason to doubt Kelly's statement that the Liverpool packet went down, but 'most certain it is' that whatever production detained them in Dublin, it was not *The Mountaineers,* which was not performed there until the following autumn. It is more likely that the opera was *The Children in the Wood,* also by Arnold, which was in production at Crow Street Theatre at this time.

On June 29, 1795, Charles Incledon returned, bringing with him a new soprano, Miss Poole. They commenced their season in *Love in a Village* when, it was announced, 'Never did we behold an audience more enraptured than last night . . Miss Poole is, in the most extended sense, a delightful singer; with a sweetness of voice, rare to be found, she possesses the most exquisite taste and judgement: – Her Bravura Song [by Giordani] displayed infinite execution and finish'.[14]

Maria Poole, later Mrs. Dickons, was born in London about 1770, and became yet another pupil of the fashionable singing teacher Venanzio Rauzzini. She made her *début* at Covent Garden in 1791 as Emily in *The Woodman.*[15] In 1800 she married and, for a time, retired from the stage, but 'her husband having sustained losses in trade',[16] she resumed her career. She was one of several English singers who had careers of greater or lesser importance on the continent. In 1816 she was engaged at the Théâtre-Italien, Paris, but failed there, and so went on to Italy where she was successful, especially at Venice. It is recorded that her voice was 'powerful and mellifluous', that she possessed 'a sensible and impressive intonation and highly polished taste', and that in singing sacred music, 'religion seemed to breathe from every note'.[17]

The operas performed during the season were predictable and

included, with *Love in a Village, The Beggar's Opera, The Duenna, Rosina, Lionel and Clarissa, Hartford Bridge,* Robin Hood, The Deserter, The Castle of Andalusia, The Son-in-Law,** Fontainebleau, No Song No Supper, Inkle and Yarico, Artaxerxes, The Poor Soldier, The Woodman, The Quaker,†* and *Cymon.*

Miss Poole took her benefit on July 15 in *Fontainebleau* and *No Song No Supper,* 'an opportunity', it was announced, 'which we are certain the public will eagerly embrace, of paying a just and grateful compliment to the taste, science and distinguished ability of our musical favourite . . whose thrilling notes have so oft this season charmed and delighted her auditors'.[18] Incledon had two benefit performances, the first on July 13[19] in *The Castle of Andalusia,* followed by *The-Son-in-Law,* and a second on July 27,[20] the last night of the season. The latter consisted of 'A Grand Selection of Sacred Music. Chiefly from the Works of Handel',[21] and was an innovation. This form of oratorial entertainment, then having a passing vogue in London, was being imitated in Dublin and was being 'presented for the first Time at this Theatre (at Playhouse Prices)'.[22]

The year 1796 opened with a new comic opera, *My Grandmother,* performed '(for the 1st time in this Kingdom)'[23] on January 2. The librettist was Prince Hoare, 'the original music composed by Storace; with new accompaniments by Mr. Bianchi'.[24]

Once again we arrive at a problem of identity, this time of deciding just who Mr. Bianchi was. It will be remembered that Kelly and Mrs. Crouch had introduced a duet from Francesco Bianchi's opera *La Villanella Rapita,* during their 1793/94 season. According to *Grove's Dictionary,* this composer was born at Cremona in 1752 and in 1775 was appointed *maestro al cembalo* to the Théâtre-Italien, Paris, where he also had his first operas produced. In 1780 he was in Florence, in 1783 at La Scala in Milan, and from 1785 to 1791 he was second organist at St. Mark's in Venice. It is said that the Emperor Joseph

---

*By William Shield, libretto by William Pearce. First performed in Dublin at Crow Street Theatre, February 26, 1793. (*Faulkner's Dublin Journal.* February 26, 1793.)

**An operatic farce by Samuel Arnold and John O'Keeffe. First performed in Dublin 1779/1781.

†A comic opera, music and libretto by Charles Dibdin. First performed in Dublin 1778/1779.

II intended to bring Bianchi to Vienna, but he died in 1790 without accomplishing his intention. It was Bianchi's association with Vienna, however, which in a left-handed fashion has perpetuated his name, for on November 28, 1785, *La Villanella Rapita* had its first performance at the Burg Theatre, when a trio, *Mandina amabile* and a quartet, *Dite almeno, in che mancai* by Mozart were substituted in the first and third acts. His opera *Semiramide; La Vendetta di Nino*, which introduced the famous soprano Brigitta Banti to London, proved so successful that he was engaged at the King's Theatre as composer from the 1794/95 season until 1797.[25]

He is announced as having appeared in Ireland between 1796 and 1801, but on these visits he is invariably described as composer and violinist.[26] The *Hibernian Journal* of April 11, 1796, also refers to 'a Concerto on the Violin, by Mr. Bianchi' and later we read that among those whom Daly had engaged 'for the ensuing After-Season' was 'Leader of the Band, Mr. Bianchi'.[27] Surprising, therefore, that *Grove's Dictionary* should describe him as a harpsichordist or organist. It is perhaps even more significant that while he was at the King's Theatre he acted as composer only, the orchestra leaders being either Viotti or Giornovichi,[28] both excellent violinists.

Were there then two Bianchis? Francesco could of course have been proficient both as a violinist and as a keyboard player; many musicians were in those days – still, a doubt persists. Finally, to create further confusion, in 1782 a London newspaper reports, 'Sacchini confined by Illness to a Sick Room, deputes his Harpsichord to Bianchi'.[29] Was this Francesco Bianchi on a hitherto unrecorded visit from the continent, or yet a third musician with the same surname?

In July, 1796, we learn that 'On Thursday [14th instant] the fascinating Mara makes her entrée in Artaxerxes* and resumes her undisputed empire over the human heart'.[30] On July 12, she and Florio had 'arrived in the packet from Holyhead'[31] and, it was announced, 'from every circumstance we are led to expect, that the Mara will be as much the rage as she was on her first visit to Ireland'.[32]

*A later advertisement suggests that the first night was postponed to July 19.

On this occasion Florio had accompanied her to Dublin not as a flautist but as a singer. He was the Arbaces in the production of *Artaxerxes*. As with Bianchi, one might distrust Florio's identity, but the London *Monthly Mirror* places the matter beyond doubt by recording that 'Florio . . lays aside his flute to warble in a first stage attempt'.[33] He remains an excellent example of the versatile eighteenth century musician. Reputedly born in England, of foreign parents, he was both composer and flautist, though his music is said to 'have done the composer but little credit'.[34] Although some twenty years younger than Mara, he was one of her many lovers. Even as late as 1802, when she was fifty-three, Mara must have retained some peculiar fascination since, as Mount Edgcumbe has recounted, 'she suddenly quitted the country, in no very creditable manner: for in the maturity of charms, which had never been great, she eloped from her husband . . and went off with the young flute-player Florio. With him she fled to the uttermost parts of Europe, and lived for several years in Russia'.[35]

In Dublin, Florio was introduced as 'first singer at the Hanover Square Concert'[36] but his reception seems to have been cool, for an apologetic announcement records, 'As this night is only the fourth of Mr. Florio's appearance on any Theatre, it is hoped that the liberality of an Irish audience will prevail over any combination of his own profession to prejudice him in the public mind, but that every person will judge him for himself'.[37] Coincidentally there was also an 'uncommon coolness of the season',[38] which, we are informed, 'luckily prevents any fears of inconvenience from the usual heat of a full house'.[39]

Mara, who performed in *Artaxerxes* on July 19, 21, 26 and 28, was indeed attracting very full houses and it was predicted that when she 'quits Dublin, the Sun of Harmony will be set; and if any persons of taste should permit other avocations to deprive them of the ecstatic pleasure of hearing her, they will have real cause to regret their loss'.[40]

On August 2 'A Grand Concert of Vocal & Instrumental Music',[41] was advertised as giving 'to the public a Concert of the summit of Harmony, and at the usual price of plays'.[42] So successful was the concert that it was repeated on August 4. Then, on August 5, there was a fifth performance of *Artaxerxes*, this time '(Compressed into two acts)'.[43]

On August 9 Mara took her benefit – and probably, her audience by surprise – by performing Lorenza in *The Castle of Andalusia*, 'her first appearance in that character, and in which she will introduce most favourite Italian Rondeaus'.[44] This was followed on the same evening by 'the favourite Musical Opera of Marian . . being her first appearance in that character and in which she will introduce a new Song and Duetto'.[45] It was observed that 'Such marks of her respect for the public, such display of novelty and variety, cannot fail to fill her House'.[46] The Italian *rondos* which she included were by Anfossi and Andreozzi; the song in *Marian* was 'composed by herself'.[47] Her address during this season was 'No. 37 Molesworth-street'.[48] Dublin city was expanding, for theatrical lodgings, from the streets about the theatres to a later-developed and more fashionable district. On August 11, 'Positively Madame Mara's last performance in this city'[49] was announced for Florio's benefit. *The Castle of Andalusia* and *Marian* were again performed and the entertainment also included 'Mad Bess'.

The summer season ended and Crow Street Theatre, having been redecorated by Signor 'Philippo Zafforini',[50] reopened its doors on November 7, 1796, 'with a brilliancy and éclat that did honour to the manager's judicious and liberal conduct; it is now', we learn, 'decidedly one of the most commodious and beautiful theatres in Europe'.[51] Then, on November 11, it was announced, 'To the numerous proofs of the Manager's unceasing exertions to entertain the Public, the Dramatic bill of fare for tomorrow evening adds a striking instance for he presents to the town their favourite object, the divine Mara'.[52] And so he did, in yet another performance of *Artaxerxes*, when 'the universal opinion, [was] that she never looked or sung better'.[53]

For this season, Florio, significantly, did not re-appear as a singer, nor can his name be found anywhere as flautist. Mara had also changed the style of her repertoire almost entirely to English comic opera. This descent from her pre-eminent position as a serious singer was justified as follows: 'Her appearance in English Operas the London Managers have long wished for, in vain – it gives them a force and consequence beyond any other musical object'.[54] The truth was, however, that Mara was getting beyond singing in anything but simple English operas. Her acting in these essentially acting roles must have been quaintly ludicrous. As Mount Edgcumbe has observed, 'She could not sing ill, but was not exactly suited for the *pretty Polly* of the Beggar's Opera'.[55] On November 14 she appeared as Donna Clara in *The Duenna* and followed this on November 18 with Lorenza in *The Castle of Andalusia,* including in the programme 'a number of bravura songs which her talents only can execute – and her Mad Bess, one of the first pieces of acting as well as singing the stage can boast of'.[56]

An advertisement then appeared proclaiming that 'The principal object of dramatic curiosity at present in the fashionable world, is the New Opera of "The Cottage Festival or A Day in Wales," announced for Monday next, November 28th'.[57] The 'Overtures and Music'[58] were composed by Giordani. The librettist, who is cryptically described as 'an eminent Barrister whose talents have been equally successful in the Courts of Parnassus as in those of Law and Justice',[59] and whose 'popularity and numerous connections will produce as crowded boxes as have ever been known',[60] turns out to have been Leonard MacNally.[61] The cast, a long one, was made up entirely from members of the theatre's stock company with the exception of Mara who played the part of Margaret.

Reviews of the production are contradictory. The *Dublin Evening Post* reports: 'from its extraordinary merit and flattering reception, [it] promises to be as great a favourite as any piece ever produced on the Irish stage'.[62] *Faulkner's Dublin Journal,* portentiously declares, however: 'It is – and has been – matter of doubt, whether an Opera requires a plot: the Author seems to have decided the question in the negative, and his play in this instance, completely defies the power of criticism, as it is impossible to censure a plot which has no existence. A chain of snapping dialogue, connected by a few songs, may be sufficient to sustain the title of a Comic Opera – and to such merit may this be entitled, but if the songs are guiltless of any concern with the Piece, they ought also to be inoffensive to the feelings of the audience. In this instance, however, the Author has erred – for in one particular song, so malignant (though in truth so dull) an attack is made upon the present glorious ardour of the Nation in the cause of Loyalty and Honour, that we were truly surprized at the good-humoured patience of the Audience, not a few of whom were distinguished by Volunteer uniforms. One character, which we suppose was intended to sustain the *comic* title of the play, under the name of Fifa, retailed to us all the low jokes of the Tholsel Court, and several learned Readings upon Crown Law, accompanied by some practical observations upon Murder. A Scene of pantomimic effect and an Harlequin attitude, produced by the appearance of two loaded blunderbusses, wonderfully well calculated for a catastrophe, concluded the Play.'[63]

The political implications of this review are far more intriguing than the dramatic. 'The present glorious ardour of the Nation in the cause of Loyalty and Honour' and those members of the audience who 'were distinguished by Volunteer uniforms' are unquestionably references to the organisation of the District Corps, better known as 'the Yeomanry' then being formed under an Act which had just received the Royal Assent. Since the author was Leonard MacNally, was this attack on the government the duplicity of an *agent provocateur?* Was it in truth a small effort on his part to provoke the predestined rebellion of 1798? Whether the purpose of the opera was pastime or politics, it had four performances, the last for MacNally's benefit on December 16.

Mara continued her antic performances; as Rosetta in *Love in a Village* and 'Mad Bess' on December 19. Next, on January 2, 1797, she played Polly Peachum '(first time)'[64] in *The Beggar's Opera* with a shortened two-act version of *Artaxerxes,* the same programme being repeated on January 11. On January 4 there was another performance of *Love in a Village* and a two-act version of *Robin Hood.* Then on January 7, 'Mr. Daly having generously offered his Theatre, free of all expenses, for the purpose of raising a fund to be applied in

U

necessaries for the comfort of the soldiers employed in H.M. Service at this inclement season',[65] she appeared in *The Castle of Andalusia,* including in the opera 'Love's soft Illusion – a Bravura Song composed by Signor Caruso' and 'A favourite Rondo – by Paisiello'.[66] So successful was this charitable performance that 'the Rt. Hon. the Lord Mayor & the Gentlemen of the Committee'[67] who had organised it advertised a second one, this time a production of *The Duenna,* on January 9. Into this performance she introduced 'the much admired song of "Whither my Love" ' and 'A favourite air composed by Giordanello'.[68] The evening ended with a loyal paean consisting of 'God save the King', 'Rule Britannia' and 'Britons strike Home'.[69] A performance of *The Lord of the Manor* with 'Mad Bess' followed on January 13, and finally, after a lapse of some weeks, she took her benefit on January 31 in *Lionel and Clarissa* and a shortened version of *The Beggar's Opera.* Her address was then 'No. 6 Dawson-street'.[70]

Mara was now 'beginning to decline in voice and favour, as she advanced in age'.[71] A while later, as already recorded, she eloped to the continent with Florio. Subsequently she settled in Moscow but lost both her home and possessions when the city was burned in 1812. She made one further melancholy visit to London, according to Fetis in 1819, though Mount Edgcumbe places the date earlier. Whatever the year, her voice was then in ruins. We learn, 'She must then have been at least seventy; but it was said that her voice had miraculously returned, and was again as fine as ever. But when she displayed these wonderfully revived powers, they proved, as might be expected, lamentably deficient, and the tones she produced were compared to those of a *penny trumpet'.*[72] She then returned to Russia, to Reval (now Talinn, about two hundred miles from Leningrad), where she taught singing, wrote her *memoirs* and received visits of homage from younger artists passing on their way to and from St. Petersburg. She died there at the great age of eighty-four on January 20, 1833.

So the *diva* Gertrude Elizabeth Mara sang in Dublin for the last time in 1797 and in the same year Richard Daly was to end his reign as theatrical monarch. His popularity was then fast declining and he was losing control of the Dublin stage. The situation is exemplified in an advertisement for an opera by Shield and O'Keeffe called *The Wicklow Mountains, or The Lad of the Hills*. It was being produced for Daly's benefit on February 6, 1797, and was announced '(for the first Time)'[73] but this was not correct since it had had an earlier Dublin performance at Astley's Theatre in Peter Street on November 28, 1796.[74] Philip Astley had originally opened his theatre as a circus about 1788, but nine years later it had become the fashionable place of entertainment.

W. T. Parke the oboist (and memoirist), who was engaged for Crow Street Theatre in 1796, has recorded that he composed the finale to the second act of *The Wicklow Mountains,* and that Shield set O'Keeffe's songs to old Irish airs, noting that 'certainly none of his contemporaries were so happy in giving accompaniments to the beautiful but wild melodies of Ireland'.[75] O'Keeffe tells us that he got the idea of his opera from 'A gold mine discovered in the mountains of Wicklow'[76] and that he 'founded the story' on 'Ned of the Hills, as he is called in the old legend'.[77] This is the legend of the seventeenth century outlaw Eamonn an Chnuic and, almost certainly, the charming old Irish air which commemorates him was included in the opera. The cast of the Crow Street production was as follows:

Sullivan	Callan
Franklin	King
Donnybrook	Lee
Felix	Dunne
Redmond O'Hanlon	Richardson
Billy O'Rourke	Stewart
Rosa	Mrs. Mahon
Helen	Miss Duncan.

'With a variety of new Scenery, particularly A View of the Wicklow Gold Mines, painted by Signor Philippo Zafforini and Mr. Coyle.'[78]

The playbill for the evening also advertised 'a celebrated new comic opera called Abroad and at Home'[79] by William Shield, the libretto by Joseph G. Holman, an actor and dramatist who had first

performed at Smock Alley Theatre in 1785. The new opera served to
introduce 'Mrs. Second, from the Theatre-Royal, Covent Garden . .
now esteemed the best English singer next to Mrs. Billington'.[80] Mrs.
Second was hardly so renowned, and in fact was primarily an oratorio
singer* and not a stage artist. She sang in the first performances of
Haydn's *The Creation* and Mozart's *Requiem* in London. Parke speaks
very highly of her singing, asserting that her 'voice was rich and
powerful, and of great compass. She sang up to F natural in alto with
ease, and her style was of a superior order'.[81]

The production of *Abroad and at Home* was also the last performance of any opera to be initially staged in Dublin by Richard
Daly. Operas continued to be produced under his management for a
while longer, and Charles Incledon returned to Crow Street Theatre
on June 22, commencing his season with *Love in a Village* and *Rosina*.

He brought with him as his leading lady Mrs. Clendinning, of whom
it was noted: 'Notwithstanding she laboured under a severe indisposition, occasioned by her journey and voyage, yet she displayed
such powers of voice, taste, and sweetness of expression as sufficiently
justifies the general opinion of her taking the lead in Covent Garden
Theatre'.[82] Her name is first found among the Covent Garden cast
lists in 1792, and in 1796 she had played Helen in the first performance
of *The Wicklow Mountains*** there. She remained a regular Covent
Garden performer until 1798. It seems that she was Irish, for Kelly
relates that she 'had a very good voice, and was a favourite with the
town, in spite of a most implacable Irish brogue'.[83]

Operas performed during this season also included *The Beggar's
Opera, The Woodman, Lionel and Clarissa, The Wicklow Mountains,
The Duenna, The Flitch of Bacon, Abroad and at Home, The Waterman*
(this nautical one certainly for Incledon), *Inkle and Yarico, The
Castle of Andalusia, The Quaker,* and *The Poor Soldier.*

---

*Grattan Flood has recorded that she sang in oratorio in Dublin in 1791. (*Introductory
Sketch of Irish Musical History,* p. 62). He states that her maiden name was Ambrose, but
Parke (*Musical Memoirs.* Vol. I. p. 238) calls her 'Mrs. Second, late Miss Mahon'.

**Originally entitled *The Lad of the Hills, or The Wicklow Gold Mine* during its first season
of performance.

The Beggar's Opera and *Inkle and Yarico,* performed on August 1, 1797,[84] made up the final programme of operas to be presented at Crow Street Theatre under Richard Daly's management. It was appropriate that *The Beggar's Opera,* the ballad opera which had inaugurated this form of entertainment in Dublin (as it had in London) in the early part of the eighteenth century, should also bring the century to a close, for with Daly's retirement the history of eighteenth century opera (and drama) in Dublin ended. The two remaining years until 1800 belong to the incoming lessee, Frederick Jones, and the beginning of the nineteenth century.

Daly retired with *panache* as the following letter testifies:

'To the Public

After seventeen Years of public Life in which Mr. Daly has met with much individual as well as general Kindness, from the inhabitants of this City, he would deem himself wanting towards them, if he now retired to a private Situation without expressing his Sense of such their often experienced Favour and Protection. Mr. Daly ventured on the arduous Task of conducting the Dublin Theatre with a strong Feeling of his Insufficiency, but with a proportionally zealous Determination to make up in Activity and Industry what he might want in Ability: He has had the satisfaction to see his Endeavours rewarded by uniform and long continued Approbation; and while, with unfeigned Gratitude, he now pours forth his Thanks to the public for their liberal Acceptance of his Service, he is proud to say, that however the Gentleman who has obtained his Situation may exceed him in the Means and Power of discharging the Duties of it, he can never in Wish and Zeal to contribute in the best Manner to their Amusement, nor in the indelible Attachment with which he now begs Leave to subscribe himself the Public's obliged and devoted Servant.

Richard Daly.

Harcourt-street
18th August 1797.'[85]

In dramatic appeal the letter approaches a patriotic speech from the dock. It also denotes Daly's instinct for survival. Thomas Sheridan had left Dublin a disillusioned man. Henry Woodward had returned to London having lost most of his savings. Spranger Barry, 'Ruined and harassed in mind and body',[86] had yielded Crow Street Theatre to Henry Mossop, and Mossop in turn had died of pulmonary tuberculosis, literally almost penniless. His successor, Thomas Ryder, had squandered a fortune though, let it be said, more in extravagant living than on his theatre, and then had changed places in his company with one of his actors – Richard Daly. Of all the managers, Daly was the only one with sufficient judgement to know that, like the wise gambler who leaves the green baize table while he is winning, the time had come for him to leave the green baize of his eighteenth-century theatre.

EPILOGUE

IN THE NORTH aisle of the Church of Santa Maria Novella in Florence, a flag-stone bears the inscription, 'Qui giace Jacopo Peri Creatore del melodrama 1561–1633', and the city of Florence is where opera began in 1597. Two hundred years later, in 1797, to what extent had the seed been propagated in Dublin?

Statistics can make unreliable aids, especially when used as a drunken man will use lamp-posts, not for illumination but support. Yet statistics unencumbered by interpretation can present facts, and the basic facts of opera in Dublin during the eighteenth century are that, among all its forms, less than one hundred different operas of any significance were produced. When this number is analysed,* the following details emerge:

English ballad and comic operas	41
Opera buffa and burlettas	24
T. A. Arne: Operas and masques	8
Handel: Stage oratorios and a masque	7
Purcell: Operas	3
English dramatic operas and masques by other composers	7 to 9
Gluck: Opera – in English translation	1
Opéra – in English translation	1
Opéra comique – in French	1
– in English translation	1
Opera seria	1
Singspiel – in English translation	1
	——
	Total 98

*See Appendix C.

311

From these figures it is obvious that English ballad and comic opera easily led the field, followed at a distance by Italian *opera buffa*. Consequently it can at least be concluded that theatre audiences preferred comic or pastoral operas to serious and dramatic ones. Between 1761 and 1789, the only time in the eighteenth century that opera in a foreign language was performed in Dublin, there was a total of 172 performances of *opera buffa* or Italian burlettas, two performances of *opera seria* and two performances of *opéra comique*,* but between 1728 and 1797 there must have been thirty to fifty times that number of performances of English ballad and comic opera. Consequently it is not difficult to imagine opera in Dublin during this period as little more than an appendage to the comic drama with music added. The only factor which occasionally raised it above the routine was the engagement of first-class singers, and the appearance of Nicolini, Guadagni, Tenducci, Billington and Mara demonstrated the importance of singing above everything else. These artists were the operatic shoots which would come to full flower amidst the vocal exuberance of the mid-nineteenth century, and which would leave a love of great singing inherent in Dublin for evermore. Today, two hundred years later, Dublin opera-goers are still agreed that the human voice is the loveliest instrument in the world.

*See Appendix D.

APPENDIX A

THE

SIGNIOR IN FASHION:

OR THE

FAIR MAID'S CONVENIENCY.

A

POEM

ON

NICOLINIS's Musick-Meeting.

Humbly Dedicated to the Subscribers.

Ridentem dicere verum
Quid vetat?

Printed in the Year 1711.

*The same printer's device is to be found on the two following pamphlets:

The CHURCH in True Light,
above
Romish SUBTILTIES
By R. Farrar, A. M. Sometime Fellow of
University College, Oxon.
Dublin: Printed for, and Sold by E. Waters at
the New Post-Office – Printing-House in Essex-
street at the Corner of Sycamore-Alley, 1711.

Discourse on Publick Prayer
by W. Irwin.
Dublin: Printed and Sold by E. Waters.

(Pamphlets 1–7. Dublin 1711.   The National Library, Dublin.)

THE

SIGNIOR In Fashion, &c.

ALL Hail ye soft Mysterious Pow'rs, which charm
The coldest Breast, and all our Passions warm.
Sweet Thieves, which like Great Nature's Master-Key,
Thro' the pleas'd Ear, direct your secret way,
Unlock the Heart, and steal our Souls away.
See at your Call Obsequious Tories meet,
Melt for the Church, and by Subscription sweat:
The dripping Fair, distills from ev'ry Pore,
gods, 'Tis too much! she cryes, and I can hear no more,
How sweet's his Voice, how tender is his Air?
But oh! They cost th' Unhappy Youth too dear.
The gentle Beau, that Ever-dying Swain,
Beats the slow time, and Sighs with pleasing Pain;
And lisps the tender Accents back again.
Ev'n the rough Soldiers mov'd, the dusty Field,
And the big War to softer Pleasures yield;
Such is the Force of the enchanting Strains,
Where Caesar listens, but Grimaldi Reigns.

When the fam'd Greek to native Shoars design'd,
Had left in Flames unhappy Troy behind,
T'unbend his Mind the sweetest Syrens fail'd,
His Nobler Arts o'er all their Pow'rs prevail'd;
Had sweeter Nic. been in the Syren's Place,
And fond of Conquest shone in ev'ry Grace,
Th' unguarded chief had on his Accents hung,
And fall'n the noblest Triumph of his Song;
His Eyes no more, had seen the Graecian Coast,
But tristful Pen had mourn'd her Hero lost.

Mankind destroy'd, to former Vigour sprung,
From Stones which Pirrha and Ducalion slung,

Such was the way as witty Ovid taught,
Strange was the Miracle, and odd the Thought;
Tho' Nic. wants PEBLES for a Work so course,
His Voice alone had shewn a nobler Force,
A stranger Species from his Notes had sprung,
A tuneful Race, and ready cut for Song,
Whose airy Forms had Warbled in a Paste,
More soft than Man's, and more than Woman's chaste.

Lament ye Beaus, and Sigh ye powder'd Swains,
Curse your dull Snuff, and hurl away your Canes;
Tear, Tear your Wigs which could of Conquest boast;
They could alas! but now their Empire's lost,
Fair Cloe's Heart a mightier Rival charms,
Cold to the kneeling World, to Him she warms,
Her Nicolini is the moving Theme,
He, happy He, who softens every Dream,
Ah the Plump, Tender Thing, there's Musick in his Name!
Her once lov'd Poll now mourns his abject Fate,
His Noise grows dull, and idle is his Prate,
And Prince the darling of her Soul before,
Half Famish'd lies neglected on the Floor,
Pensive he shakes his Ears, and cocks his Tail no more.

Ye blooming Nymphs who warily begin
To dread the Censure, but to love the Sin,
Who with false Fears from your Pursuers run,
And filthy Nudities in Picture shun,
From Scandal free, this pretty PLAY-THING meet,
Cool as May Dew, and as it's Butter sweet,
Such is the YOUTH, Resist him if ye can,
This Foreign Curiosity of Man;
Who gently leaning on the Fair Ones Breast,
May sooth her Griefs, and lull her into Rest,
And should He, should He like her Squirril creep

To her soft Bosome when she's fall'n asleep;
Ev'n then she's safe, nor need she fear Him more
Than those kind Aids which eas'd her Heart before.

All Hail Hibernia, ever Brisk and Young!
Oh Nymph most Heav'nly wife, and worthy of my Song!
Quick to comply with ev'ry Lover's Call,
Fond to be Jilted, and Enjoy'd by All,
Proud to submit, and easie to become
The Statesman's Fiddle, or the Soldier's Drum,
Curst with the Fate of ev'ry common Whore,
Still to be wondrous Gay, and wondrous Poor.

So have I seen in melancholly State
The wretched Lunatick lament her Fate,
Vow that she's wrong'd, which all her Neighbours know,
Then name the cruel Authors of her Woe;
Thus whilst she raves, the merry Fit returns,
Now for the Park, or for the Ring she burns,
Pins, Straws and Paint are on the Table spread,
And gawdy Frippery adorns her Head:
Then if she hears a brisk Crowdero's Strains,
Lightly she bounds from Earth, forgets her Pains,
Sings in her Rags, and Dances in her Chains.

FINIS

APPENDIX B

THE CASE OF MR. ANTHONY MINELLI.

THAT a Letter was wrote to London, to Mr. Minelli, to know if he would undertake to engage a Company with himself, to perform an Italian Opera, or Burletta, with Dancers, &c., in Dublin; which he did, and immediately wrote to Germany, Holland, and France, for such Persons; and Mr. Dominick De Amicis came to said Minelli, to London, and said Minelli agreed to give said Amicis a thousand Pounds, English, and a Benefit, clear of all Charges, for the Performance of him and his Company, for forty Nights; but with Liberty for some Time to come to Ireland, to settle Matters.

THAT, thereupon Mr. Minelli came to Ireland, and Mr. Mossop being in London; said Minelli was encouraged in Dublin, and told he would get large Subscriptions,* to defray all the Expences he could possibly be at: Accordingly said Minelli, with Mr. Tioli. returned to London, and agreed with Mr. Mossop for the Theatre,

THAT said Minelli promised Mr. Mossop to do all in his Power to provide two Dancers, for him, to perform once a Week; and said Minelli engaged for that Purpose, in London, Mr. and Mrs. Tarrot, and gave them seventeen Guineas, in order to defray their Expences to Chester, sent with them several Trunks, with Cloaths, and Dresses

---

*The season had been arranged on a subscription basis as the following advertisement establishes:
'By Subscription, Proposals for performing Burlettas or Italian Comic Operas at the Theatre in Smock-Alley for the ensuing Season – That there shall be forty Representations during the Season – That each Subscriber, on payment of five Guineas, shall have two Tickets for Twelve Nights for either Pit, Boxes, or Lattices (which Places are to be all of the same Price); each Ticket to admit two Persons to the Gallery. As these Entertainments are undertaken under the Patronage of a Number of Gentlemen, and the Conditions of this Subscription under their Regulation, it is further proposed by them, as an Encouragement of the Subscription (without which this Undertaking cannot possibly be carried on) that no Person shall be allowed to have Places kept for them in either Boxes, Pit, or Lattices but such as are Subscribers.' (*Dublin Courier*, 18 December 1761.)

for Dancers, which they run away with; by which Means the said
Minelli was a great Sufferer to oblige said Mossop.

THAT said Minelli gave said De Amicis three hundred and fifty
Guineas in London, part of said one thousand Pounds, and paid all
said Amicis Expences on the Road coming to Dublin, which was
twenty Guineas.

THAT said Minelli, on his Arrival in Dublin, found great difficulties, as the Theatre was not ready; by Means whereof the said
Minelli lost three Weeks time, as the Burlettas were to begin in
October, and did not till December; said Minelli lost six Nights which
probably would have produced more than would pay said De Amicis
whole Demand.

THAT on Monday the twenty fifth of January, instant, and not
before, said De Amicis demanded from said Minelli the sum of one
hundred and five Pounds, which he insisted was to have been paid
him on the fifteenth day of January; though in reality it was not due,
as he the said De Amicis did not begin to Perform till December, and
had, beside three hundred and fifty Guineas, received more than he
was intitled to for the twelve Nights he Performed; but, to prevent
any Disputes, said Minelli, before credible Witnesses, offered said
De Amicis to take all the Money of the next Burlettas, only paying
the Charge of the House, and all the Subscriptions, to secure himself;
or, if that was not sufficient, that said Minelli was willing to give up
the whole, provided said De Amicis and Mossop would pay him what
it Cost him out of pocket; all which said De Amicis refused, and
would do nothing with said Minelli, without he would give him
Security, which he well knew was not in his Power, in a strange
Country; and, that Evening advertised that the Agreement was off,
and that he intended carrying on the Burlettas under the Management
of Mr. Mossop, without taking any Notice of said Minelli, who was
at all the Expence and Trouble in bringing all the Company here;
or, without taking in the Dancers, who came for that Purpose, in
order to oblige said Minelli, or to pay them.

THAT said Minelli has contracted for three thousand five hundred
Pounds and upwards, on said Account; and it is therefore hoped that

the Gentlemen and Ladies of this City, will prevent said Fraud, by discouraging and discountenancing such abuse; otherwise the said Minelli and his Family, will be utterly ruined and undone.

THAT said De Amicis, finding that said Burlettas had Success, in order to distress and ruin said Minelli, who has expended upwards of three hundred Pounds more than the twelve Burlettas amounted to, besides his own Trouble, as by a Schedule hereunto annexed appears.

A Schedule to which the annexed Case refers, being a particular Account of the Money paid by said Minelli.

	English Money.
Paid Mr. De Amicis	£367 10 0
Paid for Ditto's Expences on the Road	21 11 0
Paid Mrs. Harris's Rent of a Lodging that was taken for Ditto, and by his Order	21 0 0
Paid Mr. Lucci	48 6 0
Paid St. Lapis and Dunlap	45 14 4
Paid Mr. Tioli, and Master Goodwin	65 0 0
Paid Mr. Genovini	24 14 2
Paid Mr. Ricchi	4 4 0
Paid Mr. Tarriot	*17 7 0
Paid Mr. Zingoni for correcting two Operas *La Cassina* & *Finta Sposa*	8 8 0
Paid Mr. Phillips for copying the Musick for the Violins	3 0 0
Paid to the Figure Dancers and Servants twelve Nights	23 0 0
Paid for the Dancers Dresses	12 0 0
Paid for translating *La Cassina Finta Sposa* and the Song, Printer, Paper, Charges for *Marcato Malmentillo,* and the Books unsold	29 0 0
Paid the Door-keepers for Twelve Nights	5 6 6
Paid for a Set of Dresses for the new Dance begun and not finished	14 0 0

*A number of discrepancies occur in the printing of this broadsheet: for example, Tarrot/ Tarriot and the seventeen guineas recorded earlier here becomes £17–7–0; nor is Mr. Minelli's book-keeping completely accurate as can be discovered if one adds up his figures.

	£	s	d
Paid the Man that delivered the Subscribers Tickets	1	4	0
Paid to printed Tickets for the House . .	1	19	0
Paid for the Copy of the Dances and Paper .	2	15	0
Paid to the Players of the Dances . .	2	5	0
Paid several Charges on the Stage, for the Opera Dances, &c.	6	12	5
Paid for Mr. Minelli's Expences with Mr. Tioli from London to Dublin, and from Dublin to London	42	0	0
Paid the like a second Time for his Maintenance in Dublin for seven Weeks and Return to London	48	0	0
Paid Coach-hire in London, for the Business of the Company	1	6	7
Paid further Expences coming to Dublin with the Company	7	0	0
Paid for my Maintenance and Lodging in Dublin, from the 1st of December, 1761, to the 27th of January, 1762	20	0	0
Paid for Dresses for the first Dancers bought in London	21	0	0
Paid Lodging due the 1st of December . .	10	0	0
Paid for Mr. Tioli's Expences for his Journey from London to Dublin	17	17	0
Paid the Poet for amending two Opera's, and several Writings, such as Contracts, Agreements, &c. and other Affairs	25	4	0
Paid for mending and altering the Men and Women's Dresses	1	0	0
Paid Mr. Mossop for twelve Nights Performance for the House, at 45 £. each Night . .	497	0	0
Remains in Mr. Mossop's Hands, about 90 £. English	90	0	0

English   £1505 14 5

All which makes in Irish Money £1631 16 5 Half.

An account of all the Money received from the Subscribers, and the twelve Burlettas, and the Number of Tickets each Night, not in the Agreement with Mr. Mossop.

1761 19th Dec.	To one hundred and six Subscription Tickets at five Guineas each . .	602	17	6
	To the first Burletta *La Cascina*, in Cash in the Play House . . .	91	2	2
	To nineteen Silver, Copper, and Brass Tickets			
21st	To the second Burletta *La Cascina*, Cash	50	16	2
	To twenty-five Silver, Copper, and Brass Tickets			
22nd	To the third Burletta *La Cascina*, Cash	52	1	1
	To thirty-six Silver, Copper, and Brass Tickets			
26th	To the fourth Burletta *La Cascina*, Cash	54	3	4
	To thirty-nine Silver, Copper, and Brass Tickets			
29th	To the fifth Burletta *La Cascina*, Cash .	69	16	5
	To the thirty-nine Silver, Copper, and Brass Tickets			
1762 Jan 2nd.	To the sixth Burletta *La Cascina*, Cash	49	10	2
	To forty-four Silver, Copper, and Brass Tickets			
5th	To the seventh Burletta *La Finta Sposa*, Cash	68	5	0
	To forty-six Silver, Copper, and Brass Tickets			
9th	To the eighth Burletta *La Finta Sposa*, Cash	52	10	10
	To thirty-seven Silver, Copper, and Brass Tickets			
12th	To the ninth Burletta *La Finta Sposa*, Cash	70	11	7
	To forty-three Silver, Copper, and Brass Tickets			

w

16th	To the tenth Burletta *La Cascina*, Cash	51	5	11
	To thirty-eight Silver, Copper, and Brass Tickets			
19th	To the eleventh Burletta *La Cascina*, Cash	51	8	1
	To forty-two Silver, Copper, and Brass Tickets			
23rd	To the twelfth Burletta *La Finta Sposa*, Cash	39	5	5
	To forty-seven Silver, Copper, and Brass Tickets			

Irish   £1303   13   8

Mr. Minelli expended   £1631   16   5 Halfpenny
Out of which received   £1303   13   8

Balance   .   .   £ 328   2   9 Halfpenny

Mr. Minelli is ready to produce authentic Vouchers for all the above Articles to any Gentlemen who may be pleased to be informed concerning them.

THE CASE OF MR DOMINICK DE AMICIS

MR. De Amicis being inform'd, that Mr. Minelli, has very industriously insinuated, many Things, of the Conduct of him and his Family, in Relation to their Agreement with him Mr. Minelli; Thinks it his Duty, to set this Matter in its true Light to the Public.

By Mr. De Amicis Articles with Mr. Minelli, executed before he left London, he and his Family were engaged to said Mr. Minelli, until the 15th of June, for the Sum of 1000 £. English; By this Agreement, 367£. 10s. was to be paid to Mr. De Amicis before he left London, and the Remainder being 632£. 10s. Mr. Minelli was to pay by Gales, on the first of every Month, until the said Month of June (except the first Gale of 105£. 8s. 4d.) which was to be paid on the 15th of January last;) and Mr. Minelli by said Article, agreed to lodge the remaining Sum of 632£. 10s. in the Hands of a Person of Eminence in the City of Dublin, or give such Person as a Security to Mr. De Amicis for the Payment thereof, in manner specified, before the Twelve Representations should be concluded; and in Case said Payment was not made on the Day above mentioned, and the Security given before the first Twelve Representations were concluded, the Articles wholly exonerated, and freed Mr. De Amicis and his Family from any further Contract with Mr. Minelli.

Mr. De Amicis applyed to Mr. Minelli for said first Gale, and also for the Security as stipulated, which Mr. Minelli evaded, and at length wholly declined, under these Circumstances, (tho' Mr. De Amicis was by his Agreement freed from any further Obligation, from the 15th of January) yet he went on, and performed the first Twelve Nights, lest the Public should have any Disappointment, by his private Affairs—and then discovering that Mr. Minelli's Contract with Mr. Mossop was to end on the 31st of March, (altho' he had bound Mr. De Amicis, to the 15th of June), he was justly alarmed at this Circumstance because, according to this Contract with Mr. Mossop, three Gales, of 105£. 8s. 4d. each, were not to be paid to Mr. De Amicis, until all the Representations should be finished, and by Mr. Minelli not giving any Security as he had agreed, Mr. De Amicis had no Reasource to apply to, and must patiently submit to remain from March till June, and Mr. Minelli go where he thought proper with so much of his Money.

From Mr. Minelli's whole Conduct, his not paying the first Gale at the Time he agreed by his Articles, nor giving Security as stipulated therein, and the plain Design of the Difference of Time in the Conclusion of his Agreement with Mr. Mossop and Mr. De Amicis, by which he Mr. De Amicis evidently would risque between 3 and 400£. he hopes it is obvious to the impartial Public, who will not be impos'd on by any insinuating Pretences which are propagated by Mr. Minelli with the greatest Assiduity, which he dare not openly avow, or contradict, and which can be proved by the original Contract between the said Mr. Minelli and Mr. De Amicis, which is now in

Mr. De Amicis's Hands, and to which he humbly refers. And as Mr. De Amicis left London (where he might have been much more advantageously engaged) on the Faith of Mr. Minelli, and the Expectation of such undeniable Security, and was detained there at a vast Expence above two Months, in order on his Part, fully to keep up to his Promise and Agreement, which he has punctually adhered to; and as on the Part of Mr. Minelli, not one single Point of his Contract has been fulfilled, he thinks himself sufficiently warranted from having quitted any further Obligation or Connection with him.

Mr. De Amicis has not presum'd herein to advance the least Circumstance which he cannot make plainly appear by the original Contract, and by the Evidence of many respectable Gentlemen, which he hopes will acquit him of any dishonourable or iniquitous Design with regard to Mr. Minelli, or of any Failure in his Engagements. And especially when this farther Fact is known, that Mr. D'Amicis, notwithstanding Mr. Minelli's Failures to him, for a long while offered to enter into fresh Articles, in which he engaged to pay him Mr. Minelli 100 Guineas at the Rate of 20 Guineas per Month, and to allow him a Benefit in Consideration of his continuing to act along with the rest of the Band, as before, rather than the Public should meet any Disappointment. But this Offer Mr. Minelli was pleas'd to reject in the Presence of several Gentlemen, and haughtily insisted on having the Money paid down directly to him whether he should perform or not, and upon the Liberty of appointing what Day he pleased for such Benefit, no matter how inconsistently with the general Interest of the Company, or their other Engagements, Terms every Way so unjust and unreasonable, it is humbly presum'd could not possibly be agreed to.

APPENDIX C

A list of first performances of the more important operas, masques and stage oratorios produced in Dublin between 1705 and 1797.

First Dublin Performance	Original Production	Opera	Composer
1705/6 Smock Alley	Feb. 1699 London	The Island Princess, or The Generous Portuguese	D. Purcell, Clark, Pate and Leveridge
1709 **A** Dublin Castle	Jan. 16, 1705 London	Arsinoe, Queen of Cyprus	Clayton, Haym and Dieupart
1709 **A** Dublin Castle	Mar. 4, 1707 London	Rosamond	Clayton
1709 Smock Alley	1701 London	Acis, Galatea and Polyphemus	John Eccles
Oct. 30, 1727 Dublin Castle		A 'Serenata Theatrale'*	Kusser (Cousser)
Mar.?9?14, 1728 Smock Alley	Jan. 29, 1728 London	The Beggar's Opera	arr. Pepusch
Mar. 24, 1729 Smock Alley		The Beggar's Wedding*	Anon.
June-Sept. 1729 Smock Alley	Apr. 18, 1729 London	Flora, or Hobb's Opera	Anon.
Circa Dec. 1730 Smock Alley	June 20, 1729 London	The Contrivances	Carey
Dec. 16, 1731 Smock Alley	Aug. 16, 1729 London	Damon and Phillida	Anon.
Feb. 24, 1732 Smock Alley	Aug. 6, 1731 London	The Devil to Pay, or The Wives Metamorphos'd	Anon.

325

First Dublin Performance	Original Production	Opera	Composer
May 1, 1734 Crow Street	1719 **B** Cannons, Middlesex	Acis and Galatea	Handel
Dec. 8, 1735 **C** Aungier Street	June 1690 London	The Prophetess, or The History of Dioclesian	Purcell
Dec. 13, 1735 Aungier Street	? ?	Aminta	Unknown **D**
Jan. 15, 1736 Aungier Street	July 15, 1735 London	The Wonder of the World, an Honest Yorkshireman	arr. Carey
Jan. 26, 1738 Aungier Street	May 27, 1737 London	The Dragon of Wantley	Lampe
Jan. 25, 1739 Smock Alley	Dec. 9, 1738 London	Margery, or a Worse Plague than the Dragon	Lampe
Dec. 20, 1739 Smock Alley	Jan. 1, 1732 London	The Lottery	arr. Seedo
Aug. 6, 1741 Aungier Street	Mar. 4, 1738 London	Comus	T. A. Arne
Feb. 3, 1742 **E** Fishamble Street	Feb. 23, 1732 London	Esther**	Handel
Mar. 24, 1742 Fishamble Street	Nov. 22, 1740 London	Hymen** (Imeneo)	Handel
May 25, 1742 Fishamble Street	Jan. 16, 1739 London	Saul**	Handel
May 7, 1743 Aungier Street	Mar. 7, 1733 London	Rosamond	T. A. Arne
May 7, 1743 Aungier Street	May 31, 1733 London	The Opera of Operas, or Tom Thumb the Great	T. A. Arne
Mar. 10, 1744 Aungier Street	Aug. 1, 1740 Cliveden, Bucks.	The Judgement of Paris	T. A. Arne
Mar. 10, 1744 Aungier Street	Aug. 1, 1740 Cliveden, Bucks.	Alfred	T. A. Arne
Feb. 4, 1748 Fishamble Street	Feb. 18, 1743 London	Samson**	Handel

First Dublin Performance	Original Production	Opera	Composer
Feb. 11, 1748 Fishamble Street	Apr. 1, 1747 London	Judas Maccabaeus**	Handel
?Dec. 9, 1742 **F** ?Jan. 13, 1749 Smock Alley	1695 London	The Tempest, or The Enchanted Island	Purcell
Jan. 25, 1750 Fishamble Street	Mar. 9, 1748 London	Joshua**	Handel
Feb. 16, 1750 Smock Alley	Dec. 13, 1749 London	The Chaplet	Boyce
Mar. 17, 1750 Aungier Street	May 1691 London	King Arthur, or The British Worthy	Purcell
May 4, 1750 Smock Alley	Dec. 1, 1739 London	Nancy, or the Parting Lovers	Carey
Nov. 29, 1755 Smock Alley	May 29, 1754 London	Eliza	T. A. Arne
Apr. 27, 1761 Smock Alley	Nov. 28, 1760 London	Thomas and Sally, or The Sailor's Return	T. A. Arne
Dec. 19, 1761 Smock Alley	Dec. 27, 1755 Venice	La Cascina	Scolari
Jan. 5, 1762 Smock Alley	?1755 ?Bologna	La Finta Sposa	?Latilla, ?Zingoni **G**
Jan. 22, 1762 Crow Street		Midas*	arr. Kane O'Hara
Jan. 29, 1762 Smock Alley	? ?	Gl'Intrighi per Amore	Composer unknown **H**
Feb. 20, 1762 Smock Alley	Oct. 26, 1754 Venice	Il Filosofo di Campagna, o Il Tutore Burlato	Galuppi
Feb. 27, 1762 Smock Alley	? ?	La Creanza	Zingoni
Mar. 17, 1762 Smock Alley	Dec. 26, 1757 Venice	Il Mercato di Malmantile	Fischietti
Mar. 24, 1762 Smock Alley	Aug. 17, 1733 Naples	La Serva Padrona	Pergolesi

First Dublin Performance	Original Production	Opera	Composer
May 1, 1762 Smock Alley	?1752 [I] Rome	Li Due Rivali (I Rivali Delusi)	Jommelli
July 8, 1763 Crow Street	Dec. 8, 1762 London	Love in a Village	T. A. Arne
May 3, 1764 Crow Street	June 19, 1753 Paris	La Zingara	Rinaldo di Capua
May 12, 1764 Crow Street	Oct. 25, 1734 Naples	Livietta e Tracollo	Pergolesi
May 19, 1764 Crow Street	Sept. 19, 1752 Paris	Il Maestro di Musica	Auletta and others
June 2, 1764 Crow Street	? 1748 ?Venice	Li Tre Cicisbei Rivali (?Ridicoli)	?Resta
Nov. 23, 1764 Smock Alley		Gli Amanti Gelosi(*?)	Galuppi and T. Giordani
Jan. 7, 1765 Smock Alley		Don Fulminone*	Tommaso Giordani
Feb. 22, 1765 Smock Alley	Feb. 2, 1762 London	Artaxerxes	T. A. Arne
Mar. 26, 1765 Smock Alley		The Maid of the Mill*	Tommaso Giordani
Mar. 30, 1765 Crow Street	Jan. 31, 1765 London	The Maid of the Mill	Arnold
July 18, 1765 Smock Alley	Feb. 24, 1764 London	The Royal Shepherd	Rush
Dec. 12, 1765 Smock Alley		Pharnaces, or The Revenge of Athridates*	arr. Tenducci [J]
Jan. 20, 1766 Crow Street		Tit for Tat, or The Cadi Gull'd*	Anon. [K]
May 7, 1766 Smock Alley		L'Eroe Cinese*	Tommaso Giordani
Jan. 9, 1769 Smock Alley	Oct. 3, 1768 London	The Padlock	Dibdin

First Dublin Performance	Original Production	Opera	Composer
Apr. 2, 1770 Capel Street	Feb. 8, 1770 London	Lionel and Clarissa, or The School for Fathers	Dibdin
Mar. 4, 1771 Capel Street	Jan. 2, 1767 London	Cymon	Michael Arne
Feb. 10, 1774 Smock Alley	Mar. 6, 1769 Paris Nov. 2, 1773 London	Le Déserteur†	Monsigny, (Dibdin and Philidor)
Feb. 15, 1775 Smock Alley		The Maid of the Vale*	Michael Arne
Nov. 17, 1775 Smock Alley	Feb. 1, 1775 London	The Rival Candidates	Charles Thomas Carter
Dec. 4, 1776 Crow Street	Aug. 8, 1774 London	The Waterman, or The First of August	Dibdin
Feb. 21, 1777 Fishamble Street	Nov. 21, 1775 London	The Duenna, or The Double Elopement	Thomas Linley senior and junior
Apr. 12, 1777 Fishamble Street	Carnevale 1772 Venice	L'Isola d'Alcina	Gazzaniga
May 17, 1777 Fishamble Street	Feb. 6, 1760 Rome	La Buona Figliuola	Paisiello
Dec. 3, 1777 Smock Alley	Nov. 1774 Venice	La Frascatana	Paisiello
Feb. 18, 1778 Smock Alley	May 25, 1774 Vienna	Il Geloso in Cimento	Anfossi
Dec. 2, 1779 Crow Street	Aug. 17, 1778 London	The Flitch of Bacon	Shield
Mar. 23, 1781 Crow Street	Dec. 27, 1780 London	The Lord of the Manor	Jackson
Nov. 3, 1781 Smock Alley	Dec. 26, 1772/ Jan. 1, 1773 Venice	L'Innocente Fortunata	Paisiello
Dec. 12, 1781 Smock Alley	Carnevale 1765 Rome	La Contadina in Corte	Sacchini

First Dublin Performance	Original Production	Opera	Composer
Jan. 23, 1782 Smock Alley	*Autunno* 1775 Venice	L'Avaro	Anfossi
Mar. 2, 1782 Smock Alley	Apr. 26, 1767 Vienna	L'Amore Artigiano	Gassmann
Apr. 10, 1782 Smock Alley	May 5, 1778 London	L'Amore Soldato	Sacchini
June 1, 1782 Smock Alley	Dec. 28, 1778 Rome	L'Italiana in Londra	Cimarosa
June 7, 1782 Smock Alley	Feb. 15, 1762 Paris	Annette et Lubin	Blaise
Dec. 31, 1782 Smock Alley	May 18, 1782 London	The Fair American	Charles Thomas Carter
Jan. 13, 1783 Smock Alley	Nov. 2, 1782 London	The Castle of Andalusia	Arnold
Mar. 18, 1783 Smock Alley	Dec. 31, 1782 London	Rosina	Shield
Dec. 18, 1783 Capel Street		Gibraltar*	Tommaso Giordani
Jan. 5, 1784 Smock Alley	Oct. 5, 1762 Vienna	Orfeo ed Euridice †	Gluck (and J. C. Bach)
Jan. 16, 1784 Smock Alley	Nov. 4, 1783 London	The Poor Soldier	Shield
Dec. 13, 1784 Smock Alley	Apr. 17, 1784 London	Robin Hood, or Sherwood Forest	Shield
Jan. 29, 1785 Smock Alley	Nov. 16, 1784 London	Fontainebleau, or Our Way in France	Shield
Nov. 5, 1785 Smock Alley	June 17, 1784 London	Two to One	Arnold
Apr. 17, 1786 Smock Alley		A Match for a Widow, or The Frolics of Fancy*	Dibdin
Mar. 2, 1787 Smock Alley	Oct. 21, 1784 Paris	Richard Coeur de Lion.†	Grétry

First Dublin Performance	Original Production	Opera	Composer
Dec. 5, 1787 Smock Alley	Aug. 4, 1787 London	Inkle and Yarico	Arnold
July 22, 1789 Crow Street	July 11, 1786 Vienna Oct. 25, 1788 London	Doktor und Apotheker†	von Dittersdorf (and Storace)
Feb. 18, 1790 Crow Street	Nov. 24, 1789 London	The Haunted Tower	Storace
Feb. 24, 1791 Crow Street	Apr. 16, 1790 London	No Song No Supper	Storace
July 15, 1791 Crow Street	Feb. 26, 1791 London	The Woodman	Shield
Dec. 14, 1791 Crow Street	Jan. 1, 1791 London	The Siege of Belgrade	Storace
Nov. 28, 1796 Peter Street	Apr. 13, 1796 London	The Wicklow Mountains, or The Lad of the Hills	Shield
Feb. 6, 1797 Crow Street	Nov. 19, 1796 London	Abroad and at Home	Shield

  *   These operas were first performed in Dublin.

 **   Concert performances only.

  †   In English translation.

  A   Performances not certain. See text, p. 7

  B   Private performance. First public performance, Lincoln's Inn Fields, London, 26 March, 1731.

  C   Earlier performances may have taken place. See text, p. 55.

  D   See text, p. 57 for possible composers.

  E   An earlier performance may have taken place. See *Handel's Dramatic Oratorios and Masques* by Winton Dean. London 1959, p. 631.

  F   Date of first performance not quite definite. See text, p. 75.

  G   Composer indefinite. See text, p. 96.

  H   See text, p. 97.

  I   Date of first performance of the intermezzo *I Rivali Delusi* by Niccolò Jommelli.

  J   See text, pp. 142/143.

  K   See text, pp. 145/146.

CLASSFIED LIST OF PERFORMANCES OF ITALIAN AN

AULETTA Pietro (1698–1771)	*Il Maestro di Musica*
GALUPPI Baldassare (1706–1785)	*Il Filosofo di Campagna, o il Tutor Burlato*
	Gli Amanti Gelosi
RINALDO di CAPUA (? 1706–1778)	*La Zingara*
PERGOLESI Giovanni Battista (1710–1736)	*La Serva Padrona*
	Livietta e Tracollo
LATILLA* Gaetano (1711–1791)	*La Finta Sposa*
JOMMELLI Niccolò (1714–1744)	*Li Due Rivali*
SCOLARI Giuseppe (1720–1769)	*La Cascina*
FISCHIETTI Domenico (1729–p. 1810)	*Il Mercato di Malmantile*
GIORDANI Tommaso (c. 1733–1806)	*Don Fulminone*
	L'Eroe Cinese
ZINGONI Giovanni Battista (18th Century)	*La Creanza*
RESTA† Natale (18th Century)	*Li Tre Cicisbei Rivali (? Ridicoli)*
COMPOSER UNKNOWN	*Gl' Intrighi per Amore*
ANFOSSI Pasquale (1721–1797)	*Il Geloso in Cimento*
	L'Avaro
PICCINNI Nicola (1728–1800)	*La Buona Figliuola*
GASSMANN Florian Leopold (1729–1774)	*L'Amore Artigiano*
SACCHINI Antonio Maria Gasparo (1730–1786)	*La Contadina in Corte*
	L'Amore Soldato
PAISIELLO Giovanni (1740–1816)	*La Frascatana*
	L'Innocente Fortunata
GAZZANIGA Giuseppe (1743–1818)	*L'Isola d'Alcina*
CIMAROSA Domenico (1749–1801)	*L'Italiana in Londra*
BLAISE Benôit (17...–1772)	*Annette et Lubin*
Total number of performaces for each year	

*Composer indefinite. See text p. 96
†Composer indefinite. See text p. 115
‡Other performances may have taken place
§Total number of performances 1761–1789

332

1762	—	1764	1765	1766	—	1777	1778	—	1781	1782	—	1789	Total
		1											1
7													7
		7	3									1	11
		3											3
2		2											4
		1											1
4													4
3													3
5													9
5													5
			3										3
				2									2
3													3
		1											1
10													10
							15						15
										9			9
						5	7						12
										7			7
									4	5			9
										8			8
						7	9						16
									7	3			10
						12			4	2			18
										3			3
										2‡			2
39		15	6	2		24	31		15	39		1	176§

NOTES

CHAPTER 1

That Perpetual Singing 1705-1709

1 M.S. Signet Office Docquet Books, Index 6813, March 1660/1, p. 4. Public Record Office, London. Reported in *The Early Irish Stage* by William Smith Clark. Oxford 1955.
2 *The Dublin Scuffle* by John Dunton. London 1699. p. 340.
3 *A General History of the Science and Practice of Music* by Sir John Hawkins. London 1875. Vol. II. p. 827.
4 *The Early Irish Stage* by William Smith Clark. Oxford 1955. p. 115.
5 *The Gentleman's Journal: or the Monthly Miscellany.* Edited by Pierre Motteux. January 1692. pp. 7/8.
6 *Encyclopaedia Britannica.* Chicago 1948. Vol. 15. p. 925.
7 *The Island Princess, or the Generous Portuguese* by Pierre Motteux. London 1699.
8 *The Early Irish Stage* by William Smith Clark. Oxford 1955. Appendix B. p. 201.
9 *The Island Princess, or the Generous Portuguese* by Pierre Motteux. London 1699.
10 *Ibid.* Dublin 1726.
11 *Ibid.*
12 *Ibid.*
13 *Faithful Memoirs of the Life, Amours and Performances of that justly celebrated, and most Eminent Actress of her Time, Mrs. Anne Oldfield* by William Egerton. London 1731. p. 2.
14 *An Apology for the Life of Mr. Colley Cibber, Comedian–written by Himself.* London 1740. p. 97.
15 *Ibid.*
16 *Roger North on Music.* Being a Selection from his Essays written during the years c. 1695–1728. Transcribed from the Manuscripts and edited by John Wilson. London 1959. Pt. II. p. 217.
17 *A Sketch of the Author's Life–written by Himself.* London 1730. p. 16.
18 *Ibid.*
19 *Ibid.*
20 *Faulkner's Dublin Journal.* December 2/5, 1732.
21 *The British Union Catalogue of Early Music printed before the year* 1801. Edited by Edith B. Schnapper. London 1957. Vol. II. p. 1092.
22 *Faulkner's Dublin Journal.* May 8/12, 1733.

CHAPTER 2

The Enigma of Nicolini 1711

1 *A General History of the Stage, from its Origin in Greece down to the present Time* by W. R. Chetwood. London 1749. p. 77.
2 *A History of the City of Dublin* by J. T. Gilbert. Dublin 1859. Vol. II. p. 71.

3   *A History of Irish Music* by W. H. Grattan-Flood. Dublin 1905. pp. 266/267.
4   *Introductory Sketch of Irish Musical History* by W. H. Grattan-Flood. London 1921. p. 33.
5   *Ibid.* pp. 33/34.
6   *The Daily Courant* (London). April 24, 1711.
7   Personal communication from Harry R. Beard, Esq. 1.5.1967.
8   Personal communication from Prof. Otto Erich Deutsch 5.5.1967.
9   Personal communication from Mrs. Edith Loewenberg 17.3.1967.
10 Personal communication from Messrs. MacMillan & Co. Ltd. 1.7.1967.
11 *Henry Stevens – Bibliographer and Biblioscoper* by Victor Hugo Paltsits, Litt.D. p. xxiv – in the *Recollections of James Lenox and the formation of his Library* by Henry Stevens. Revised and Elucidated by Victor Hugo Paltsits, Litt. D. New York 1951.
12 *Ibid.*
13 *Ibid.*
14 *A History of the City of Dublin* by J. T. Gilbert. Dublin 1859. Vol. II. p. 71.
15 *Introductory Sketch of Irish Musical History* by W. H. Grattan-Flood. London 1921. p. 33.
16 *A History of the City of Dublin* by J. T. Gilbert. Dublin 1859. Vol. II. p. 71.
17 *Ibid.*
18 *The Foundation of the Hospital and Free School of King Charles II, Oxmantown, Dublin, Commonly called the Blue Coat School* by The Right Hon. Sir Frederick R. Falkiner, K.C., Sometime Recorder of Dublin. Dublin 1906. p. 102.
19 *Ibid.* pp. 127/128.
20 *Wit and Mirth: or Pills To Purge Melancholy.* Vol. VI. London 1722. pp. 282/283.
21 *The Musical Miscellany: Being a Collection of Choice Songs, Set to the Violin and Flute, by the most eminent Masters.* 1729 Vol. I. pp. 161/162.
22 *The Tatler.* December 31/January 3, 1709/10.
23 *Ibid.*
24 *The Spectator.* March 6, 1711.
25 *The Castrati in Opera* by Angus Heriot. London. 1956. p. 129.
26 *The Progress of Musick in Ireland to Mira* [by Matthew Pilkington]. Dublin 1730.
27 Reported by La Tourette Stockwell in *Dublin Theatres and Theatre Customs 1637–1820.* Kingsport 1938. p. 59.
28 *Memoirs of the Musical Drama* by George Hogarth. London 1838. Vol. I. p. 464.
29 *Ibid.*
30 *A General History of Music* by Charles Burney. New York 1957. Vol. II. p. 666.

CHAPTER 3

A Masque at the Castle 1725 – 1727

1   *Dublin Weekly Journal.* November 6, 1725.
2   *A General History of Music* by Charles Burney. New York 1957. Vol. II. p. 718.
3   *The London Stage 1660–1800.* Carbondale, Illinois. 1960. Part II. Vol. I. pp. 578, 584, 651.
4   *The Theatre.* No. XXI. March 8/12, 1720.
5   *Dublin Weekly Journal.* December 11, 1725.
6   Original libretto. Copy at Trinity College Library, Dublin.
7   *Ibid.*
8   *Mrs. Delany at Court and among the Wits,* with an introduction by R. Brinley Johnson. London 1925. p. 205.

9   Original libretto. Copy at Trinity College Library, Dublin.
10   Francis Colman. MS Opera Register 1712–1734. British Museum. (Add MS. II. 258)
11   *A General History of the Science and Practice of Music* by Sir John Hawkins. London 1875. Vol. II. p. 850.
12   Original libretto. Copy at Trinity College Library, Dublin.
13   Original libretto. *Ibid.*
14   Libretto of 'Serenade' for May 28, 1725. *Ibid.*
15   Libretto of 'Serenata da Camera' for May 28, 1717. *Ibid.*
16   Libretti for years 1709–1727 (excluding 1710/13/15/16/19/20.) Copies at Trinity College and National Libraries, Dublin, Diocesan Library, Cashel, and British Museum.
17   Original Libretto. Copy at Diocesan Library, Cashel, Co. Tipperary.
18   *Ibid.*
19   *Ibid.*
20   *Ibid.*
21   *The Musical Antiquary.* London July 1911. Transcript by W. H. Grattan-Flood from the Public Record Office, Dublin.
22   *A History of the City of Dublin* by J. T. Gilbert. Dublin 1859. Vol. II. p. 68.
23   Reported in *Introductory Sketch of Irish Musical History* by W. H. Grattan-Flood. London 1921. p. 35.
24   *Faulkner's Dublin Journal.* February 19/22, 1731/32.
25   *Dublin Gazette.* October 19/23, 1714.
26   *Hibernian Journal.* April 1, 1796.
27   *Ibid.*
28   *James Belcher. An Account of Secret Service Money.* 1723. At Marsh's Library, Dublin. (Z 3 11. No. XLI, p. 183) Transcript by Dr. T. P. C. Kirkpatrick at Trinity College Library, Dublin.
29   *Ibid.*
30   Original Libretto. Copy at Trinity College Library, Dublin.
31 *Ibid.*   32 *Ibid.*   33 *Ibid.*   34 *Ibid.*   35 *Ibid.*
36   Original Libretto. Copy at Trinity College Library, Dublin.
37 *Ibid.*   38 *Ibid.*   39 *Ibid.*   40 *Ibid.*   41 *Ibid.*
42 *Ibid.*   43 *Ibid.*   44 *Ibid.*   45 *Ibid.*   46 *Ibid.*
47 *Ibid.*   48 *Ibid.*

CHAPTER 4

From Prison to Pastoral 1728–1735

1   *Anecdotes, Observations, and Characters, of Books and Men.* Collected from the Conversation of Mr. Pope, and other Eminent Persons of his Time, by the Rev. Joseph Spence. London 1820. p. 159.
2   *Ibid.*
3   *The Dublin Intelligence.* March 19, 1727/28.
4   *Ibid.* March 23, 1727/28.
5   *The Dublin Gazette.* April 9/13, 1728.
6   *The Dublin Intelligence.* December 14, 1728.
7   *Ibid.* March 22, 1728/29.

8 Original libretto. Copy at the National Library, Dublin.

9 *The Dublin Intelligence.* March 22, 1728/29.

10 *Ibid.* December 20, 1729.

11 *Faulkner's Dublin Journal.* May 16/20, 1749.

12 *Biographia Dramatica: or, A Companion to the Playhouse* by David Erskine Baker, London 1782. Vol. I. p. 93.

13 *Doctor Anthony's Advice to the Hibernian Aesop : or, An Epistle to the Author of the B——'s W——g.* Dublin 1729.

14 *Ibid.*

15 Preface to *The Beggar's Wedding* by Charles Coffey. Dublin 1729. p. IV.

16 *The Dublin Intelligence.* November 11, 1729.

17 *Ibid.* June 14, 1729.

18 *Faulkner's Dublin Journal.* September 13/16, 1729.

19 *Ibid.* October 20/24, 1729.

20 *Ibid.* April 24/27, 1730.

21 Original libretto. Copy at the National Library, Dublin.

22 *Memoirs of the Life of David Garrick* by Thomas Davies. London 1780. p. 32.

23 *Faulkner's Dublin Journal.* December 26/29, 1730.

24 Original libretto. Copy at the British Museum.

25 *Faulkner's Dublin Journal.* December 26/29, 1730.

26 *Memoirs of the Musical Drama* by George Hogarth. London 1838. Vol. II. p. 14.

27 *A General History of the Science and Practice of Music* by Sir John Hawkins. London 1875. Vol. II. p. 828.

28 *Faulkner's Dublin Journal,* May 9/13, 1731.

29 *Ibid.* November 27/30, 1731.

30 *Ibid.* September 18/21, 1731.

31 *Ibid.* December 7/11, 1731.

32 *Ibid.* September 18/21, 1731.

33 *Ibid.* October 23/26, 1731.

34 *Ibid.* November 2/6, 1731.

35 *Ibid.*

36 *Ibid.*

37 *Ibid.*

38 *Ibid.* November 30/December 4, 1731.

39 *Ibid.* May 2/6, 1732.

40 *Ibid.*

41 *Ibid.* May 9/13, 1732.

42 *Ibid.* November 30/December 4, 1731.

43 *A General History of the Science and Practice of Music* by Sir John Hawkins. London 1875. Vol. II. p. 817.

44 *A General History of Music* by Charles Burney. London 1789. Vol. IV. p. 239.

45 *Hoey's Dublin Journal.* November 30/December 4, 1731. Reported by W. H. Grattan-Flood, 'Crow St. Music Hall, Dublin from 1730 to 1754', in *Sammelbände der Internationalen Musik-Gesellschaft.* April-June 1910. Leipzig. pp. 442/446.

46 *Faulkner's Dublin Journal.* December 11/14, 1731.

47 *An Apology for the Life of Mr. Colley Cibber, Comedian – written by Himself.* London 1740. p. 141.

48 Original libretto. Copy at the National Library, Dublin.

49 *Faulkner's Dublin Journal.* February 19/22, 1731/32.

50 Original Libretto. Copy at the National Library, Dublin.
51 *Faulkner's Dublin Journal.* February 19/22, 1731/32.
52 *Ibid.* May 2/6, 1732.
53 *Ibid.*
54 *Ibid.* September 30/October 3, 1732.
55 *Ibid.* October 16/20, 1733.
56 *Ibid.*
57 *The Dublin Intelligence.* February 3, 1729/30.
58 *Faulkner's Dublin Journal.* March 9/12, 1733/34.
59 *Ibid.* October 31/November 4, 1749.
60 *A General History of the Stage; more particularly the Irish Theatre* by W. R. Chetwood. Dublin 1749. p. 71.
61 *Ibid.* p. 73.
62 *An Historical View of the Irish Stage* by Robert Hitchcock. Dublin 1788–1794. Vol. I. pp. 93/94.
63 *Ibid.* p. 89.
64 *The History of the Theatres of London and Dublin from 1730 to the Present Time* by Benjamin Victor. London 1761. Vol. I. p. 16.
65 *The Dublin Scuffle* by John Dunton. London 1699. p. 339. Reported by La Tourette Stockwell in *Dublin Theatres and Theatre Customs, 1637–1820.* Kingsport 1938.
66 *Dublin News Letter.* January 1/4, 1742/43.
67 *Faulkner's Dublin Journal.* April 9/13, 1734.
68 *Ibid.* April 27/30, 1734.
69 *Dublin Evening Post.* November 24/27, 1733.
70 *Ibid.* January 14/18, 1734/35.
71 *Ibid.* February 11/15, 1734/34.
72 *Faulkner's Dublin Journal.* November 30/December 4, 1742.
73 *The Daily Advertiser* (London). May 10, 1745.
74 *Ibid.*
75 *The Dublin Intelligence.* June 14, 1729.
76 *A General History of Music* by Charles Burney. London 1789. Vol. IV. p. 654.
77 *Faulkner's Dublin Journal.* November 30/December 4, 1742.
78 *Dublin Evening Post.* March 1/4, 1734/35.

CHAPTER 5

The Best Voices and Hands 1735–1742

1 *Dublin Evening Post.* November 4/8, 1735.
2 *An Historical View of the Irish Stage* by Robert Hitchcock. Dublin 1788–1794. Vol. I. p. 87.
3 *Ibid.* pp. 87/88.
4 *Dublin Evening Post.* December 6/9, 1735.
5 *Ibid.*
6 *A General History of Music* by Charles Burney. London 1789. Vol. IV. p. 371.
7 *Rivista Musicale Italiana.* Turin 1923. Vol. XXX. p. 399.
8 *Dublin Evening Post.* December 2/6, 1735.

9 *The Prophetess: or, the History of Dioclesian.* Written by Francis Beaumont and ohn Fletcher, with Alterations and Additions, after the Manner of an Opera. [By Thomas Betterton] London 1690. Act II. Sc. 2. p. 26.

10 *Ibid.* The Masque. p. 67.

11 *Ibid.* p. 68.

12 *Ibid.* p. 36.

13 *Dublin Evening Post.* December 2/6, 1735.

14 *Dublin Evening Post.* January 6/10, 1735/36.

15 *Dublin Evening Post.* February 14/17, 1735/36.

16 *Music at Court* by Alan Yorke-Long. London 1954. p. 76.

17 *Dublin News-Letter.* January 21/4, 1737/38.

18 *Ibid.*

19 *Dublin News-Letter.* January 1/4, 1742/43.

20 *Memoirs of the Musical Drama* by George Hogarth. London 1838. Vol. II. p. 74.

21 *Ibid.* pp. 73/74.

22 *Dublin News-Letter.* January 21/24, 1737/38.

23 *A General History of the Science and Practice of Music* by Sir John Hawkins. London 1875. Vol. II. p. 828.

24 *Biographia Dramatica: or, A Companion to the Playhouse* by D. E. Baker, Isaac Reed and Stephen Jones. London 1812. Vol. III. p. 20.

25 *Dublin Evening Post.* December 8/11, 1739.

26 *Ibid.* January 19/22, 1739/40.

27 *Faulkner's Dublin Journal.* August 1/4, 1741.

28 *Ibid.* August 4/8, 1741.

29 *Pue's Occurrences.* August 8/11, 1741.

30 *Memoirs of the Musical Drama* by George Hogarth. London 1838. Vol. II. pp. 81/82.

31 *The Dublin Intelligence.* March 8, 1730/31.

32 *Faulkner's Dublin Journal.* March 10/13, 1743/44

33 *Ibid.* November 19/22, 1743.

34 *Note Books* c. 1713–1750 by George Vertue. Reported by William Kurtz Wimsatt in *The Portraits of Alexander Pope.* New Haven and London 1965. p. 40.

35 *A General History of the Stage, more particularly the Irish Theatre* by W. R. Chetwood. Dublin 1749. p. 128.

36 *A General History of Music* by Charles Burney. London 1789. Vol. IV. p. 654.

37 *Memoirs of the Musical Drama* by George Hogarth. London 1838. Vol. II. p. 63.

38 *Memoirs of His Own Life* by Tate Wilkinson. Dublin 1791. Vol. II. p. 175.

39 *Memoirs of the Musical Drama* by George Hogarth. London 1838. Vol. II. p. 62.

40 *Pue's Occurrences.* November 17/21, 1741.

41 *Faulkner's Dublin Journal.* January 16/19, 1741/42.

42 *Dublin News-Letter.* January 20/23, 1742.

43 *Faulkner's Dublin Journal.* January 26/30, 1742.

44 *Ibid.* April 27/May 1, 1742.

45 *Ibid.* May 8/11, 1742.

46 *Ibid.* May 18/22, 1742. Reported in *An Account of the Visit of Handel to Dublin* by Horatio Townsend. Dublin 1852. p. 95.

47 *Memoirs of the Musical Drama* by George Hogarth. London 1838. Vol. II. p. 71.

48 *Sketch of the Life of Handel* which precedes *An Account of the Musical Performances in Westminster-Abbey and the Pantheon in Commemoration of Handel* by Charles Burney, London 1785. p. 51.

49 *British Education: or, The Source of the Disorders of Great Britain* by Thomas Sheridan. London 1756. p. 417.

50 *An Account of the Visit of Handel to Dublin* by Horatio Townsend. Dublin 1852. pp. 50/51.

51 *Dublin News-Letter.* August 10/14, 1742.

52 *Faulkner's Dublin Journal.* September 16/19, 1749.

CHAPTER 6

A Very Thinking Task 1742–1750

1 *Pue's Occurrences.* June 29/July 3, 1742.

2 *Faulkner's Dublin Journal.* November 27/30, 1742.

3 *A General History of the Stage; more particularly the Irish Theatre* by W. R. Chetwood. Dublin 1749. p. 225.

4 *An Historical View of the Irish Stage* by Robert Hitchcock. Dublin 1788–1794. Vol. I. p. 87.

5 *A General History of the Stage; more particularly the Irish Theatre* by W. R. Chetwood. Dublin 1749. p. 225.

6 *Faulkner's Dublin Journal.* January 4/8, 1742/43.

7 *A General History of Music* by Charles Burney. London 1789. Vol. IV. pp. 653/654.

8 *Faulkner's Dublin Journal.* April 19/23, 1743.

9 *Ibid.*

10 *Ibid.* May 24/28, 1743.

11 *Ibid.* June 4/7, 1743.

12 *A General History of Music* by Charles Burney. London 1789. Vol. IV. p. 667.

13 *Faulkner's Dublin Journal.* January 7/10, 1743/44.

14 *Ibid.* January 24/28, 1743/44.

15 *Ibid.* March 10/13, 1743/44.

16 Reported in *Thomas Sheridan of Smock-Alley* by Esther K. Sheldon. Princeton, New Jersey 1967. p. 317.

17 *Faulkner's Dublin Journal.* January 30/February 2, 1747/48.

18 *Ibid.* February 9/13, 1747/48.

19 *A Vindication of the Conduct of the late Manager of the Theatre-Royal, Humbly address'd to the Publick* by Thomas Sheridan. Dublin 1754. p. 8.

20 *Ibid.*

21 *Faulkner's Dublin Journal.* November 21/24, 1747.

22 *Dublin Courant.* October 3/7, 1749.

23 *Faulkner's Dublin Journal.* September 24/27, 1748.

24 *The Letters of David Garrick.* Edited by David M. Little and George M. Kahrl. Oxford University Press 1963. Vol. I. p. 75.

25 Reported in *Thomas Sheridan of Smock-Alley* by Esther K. Sheldon. Princeton, New Jersey 1967. p. 415.

26 *Faulkner's Dublin Journal.* January 3/7, 1748/49.

27 *Ibid.*

28 *Ibid.* January 17/21, 1748/49.

29 *Ibid.* January 14/17, 1748/49.

30 *Ibid.* November 19/22, 1748.

31 Reported in *Thomas Sheridan of Smock-Alley* by Esther K. Sheldon. Princeton, New Jersey 1967. pp. 331, 333, 339, 398, 458.

32 *Faulkner's Dublin Journal.* November 14/18, 1749.

33 *Ibid.* December 19/23, 1749.

34 *Ibid.* January 16/20, 1749/50.

35 *Ibid.* January 23/27, 1749/50.

36 *Ibid.* March 10/13, 1749/50.

37 *Ibid.*

38 *Ibid.* March 13/17, 1749/50.

CHAPTER 7

The English Taste in General 1750–1761

1 *Faulkner's Dublin Journal.* October 11/15, 1748.

2 *Ibid.* October 31/November 4, 1749.

3 *Ibid.* February 24/27, 1749/50.

4 *Ibid.* March 20/24, 1749/50.

5 *Preface to King Arthur, or The British Worthy*, addressed to the Marquess of Halifax by John Dryden. London 1691. p. 6.

6 *Original Letters, Dramatic Pieces and Poems* by Benjamin Victor. London 1776. Vol. I. p. 185.

7 *The History of the Theatres of London, from the Year 1760 to the present Time* by Benjamin Victor. London 1771. p. 63.

8 *The Autobiography and Correspondence of Mary Granville, Mrs. Delany.* Edited by the Right Honourable Lady Llanover. London 1861. Vol. III. pp. 80/81.

9 *Faulkner's Dublin Journal.* August 31/September 3, 1751.

10 *A General History of Music* by Charles Burney. London 1789. Vol. IV. p. 495.

11 *Ibid.* p. 496.

12 *Ibid.* p. 495.

13 *Ibid.* p. 496.

14 *Faulkner's Dublin Journal.* January 21/25, 1752.

15 *Ibid.* February 25/29, 1752.

16 *Ibid.* February 22/25, 1752.

17 *Ibid.* March 7/10, 1752.

18 *Ibid.* April 7/11, 1752.

19 *Musical Reminiscences* by the Earl of Mount Edgcumbe. London 1834. pp. 35, 36.

20 *Reminiscences of Michael Kelly.* London 1826. Vol. I. pp. 149/150.

21 *Faulkner's Dublin Journal.* February 6/10, 1753.

22 *Ibid.* February 27/March 3, 1753.

23 *The Autobiography and Correspondence of Mary Granville, Mrs. Delany.* Edited by the Right Honourable Lady Llanover. London 1861. Vol. III. p. 194.

24 *Faulkner's Dublin Journal.* October 21/25, 1755.

25 *Recollections of the Life of John O'Keeffe, Written by Himself.* London 1826. Vol. I. pp. 149/150.

26 *A Complete History of the Stage, Written by Mr. Dibdin.* London 1795. Vol. V. p. 369.

27 *Faulkner's Dublin Journal.* April 16/19, 1757.

28 *Ibid.*

29 *Ibid.* November 11/15, 1755.

30 *Ibid.* November 29/December 2, 1755.
31 *Memoirs of the Musical Drama* by George Hogarth. London 1838. Vol. II. p. 86.
32 *The Pasquinade with Notes Variorum. Book the First* by William Kenrick. London 1753. p. 19.
33 *Faulkner's Dublin Journal.* February 24/28, 1756.
34 *Ibid.* March 2/6, 1756.
35 *Ibid.* May 11/15, 1756.
36 *The Autobiography and Correspondence of Mary Granville, Mrs. Delany.* Edited by the Right Honourable Lady Llanover. London 1861. Vol. III. pp. 502/503.
37 *Faulkner's Dublin Journal.* April 1/4, 1758.
38 *Ibid.*
39 *Thomas Sheridan of Smock Alley* by Esther K. Sheldon. Princeton, New Jersey 1967. p. 248.
40 *Original Letters, Dramatic Pieces and Poems* by Benjamin Victor. London 1776. Vol. I. p. 290.
41 *Dublin Courier.* April 10/13, 1761.
42 *Memoirs of His Own Life* by Tate Wilkinson. Dublin 1791. Vol. II. p. 52.
43 *Recollections of the Life of John O'Keeffe, Written by Himself.* London 1826. Vol. I. pp. 49/50.
44 *Biographia Dramatica, or a Companion to the Playhouse* by David Erskine Baker. London 1782. Vol. I. p. 28.
45 *Faulkner's Dublin Journal.* April 21/25, 1761.
46 *Ibid.* April 25/28, 1761.

CHAPTER 8

A Kind of Poor Relation to an Opera 1761–1762

1 *The Rehearsal: or, Bays in Petticoats* by Mrs. C[atherine] Clive. Dublin 1753. p. 15.
2 *The Letters of Mozart and his Family* – Edited by Emily Anderson. London 1938. Vol. I. p. 325.
3 *A General History of Music* by Charles Burney. London 1789. Vol. IV. p. 481.
4 *Ibid.* p. 479.
5 *Recollections of the Life of John O'Keeffe, Written by Himself.* London 1826. Vol. I. p. 52.
6 *Ibid.* pp. 52/53.
7 *The Irish Stage in the Country Towns 1720–1800* by William Smith Clark. Oxford 1965. p. 83.
8 Original libretto. Copy at the British Museum.
9 *Ibid.*
10 *Dublin Courier.* December 18/21, 1761.
11 *An Historical View of the Irish Stage* by Robert Hitchcock. Dublin 1788–1794. Vol. II. pp. 91/92.
12 *Recollections of the Life of John O'Keeffe, Written by Himself.* London 1826. Vol. I. p. 52.
13 Original libretto. Copy at the British Museum.
14 *Ibid.*
15 See Appendix B. *The Case of Mr. Anthony Minelli.*
16 Original libretto. Copy at the British Museum.

17 *An Historical View of the Irish Stage* by Robert Hitchcock. Dublin. 1788–1794. Vol. II. p. 92.
18 *Faulkner's Dublin Journal.* January 26/30, 1762.
19 Original libretto. Copy at the British Museum.
20 *Faulkner's Dublin Journal.* January 26/30, 1762.
21 Original libretto. Copy at the British Museum.
22 *A General History of Music* by Charles Burney. London 1789. Vol. IV. p. 474.
23 *Faulkner's Dublin Journal* May 8/11, 1762.
24 Original libretto. Copy at the British Museum.
25 Original libretto. Copy at the British Museum.
26 *Ibid.*
27 Original libretto. Copy at the British Museum.
28 *A General History of Music* by Charles Burney. London 1789. Vol. IV. p. 477.
29 Original libretto. Copy at the British Museum.
30 Original libretto. Copy at the British Museum.
31 *Ibid.*
32 Original libretto. Copy at the British Museum.
33 *Ibid.*
34 *Faulkner's Dublin Journal.* May 18/22, 1762.
35 *Ibid.* May 22/25, 1762.
36 *Ibid.* December 26/30, 1749.
37 *Ibid.* January 12/16, 1762.
38 *Recollections of the Life of John O'Keeffe, Written by Himself.* London. 1826. Vol. I. p. 53.
39 *Ibid.* p. 54.
40 *Ibid.* Vol. II. p. 6.
41 *Theatrical Biography: or, Memoirs of the Principal Performers of the Three Theatres Royal.* London 1772. Vol. II. p. 146.
42 *Faulkner's Dublin Journal.* April 8/11, 1758.
43 *The Dramatic Career of Arthur Murphy* by Howard Hunter Dunbar. New York 1946. p. 143.
44 *Early Irish Ballad Opera, and Comic Opera* by W. J. Lawrence. *The Musical Quarterly,* New York. July 1922. p. 407.
45 *The Theatrical Observer.* London. June 20, 1821.
46 *Faulkner's Dublin Journal.* February 9/13, 1762.

CHAPTER 9

More Poor Relations 1763–1765

1 *Faulkner's Dublin Journal.* January 25/29, 1763.
2 *Ibid.* January 29/February 1, 1763.
3 *Ibid.* February 1/5, 1763.
4 *Ibid.* February 12/15, 1763.
5 Reported in *Memoirs of the Colman Family* by Richard Brinsley Peake. London 1841. Vol. I. p. 189.
6 *Morning Herald* (London). January 10, 1781.
7 *Recollections of the Life of John O'Keeffe, Written by Himself.* London 1826. Vol. I. p. 56.

8 *Ibid.*

9 Reported in *Handel's Dramatic Oratorios and Masques* by Winton Dean. London 1959. Appendix I. p. 657.

10 *Saunders' News-letter.* February 14, 1809.

11 *The Gentleman's Magazine.* Dublin. March, 1809. p. 279.

12 *Faulkner's Dublin Journal.* April 16/19, 1763.

13 'From the press of M. Carey (Philadelphia) March 1, 1794.' Reported in O. G. Sonneck, *Catalogue of Opera Librettos printed before 1800.* Washington 1914. Vol. I. p. 699.

14 *The Public Advertiser* (London). April 28, 1784.

15 *Faulkner's Dublin Journal.* July 2/5, 1763.

16 *Ibid.*

17 *An Apology for the Life of George Anne Bellamy.* London 1785. Vol. IV. p. 156.

18 *Faulkner's Dublin Journal.* November 1/5, 1763.

19 *Grove's Dictionary of Music and Musicians* (Fifth Edition). London 1954. Vol. II. p. 609.

20 *Faulkner's Dublin Journal.* November 1/5, 1763.

21 *Grove's Dictionary of Music and Musicians* (Fifth Edition). London 1954. Vol. II. p. 608.

22 *Freeman's Journal.* April 7/10, 1764.

23 *Ibid.* April 10/14, 1764.

24 *Faulkner's Dublin Journal.* December 3/6, 1763.

25 Press-cutting dated September 29, 1763, from an unidentified newspaper in one of Dr. Charles Burney's Notebooks at the British Museum. (Ref. 938 e 27)

26 *Faulkner's Dublin Journal.* April 21/24, 1764.

27 *Ibid.* April 24/28, 1764.

28 *Ibid.*

29 *The York Courant.* October 18, 1763.

30 *Faulkner's Dublin Journal.* April 28/May 1, 1764.

31 *A General History of Music* by Charles Burney. London 1789. Vol. IV. p. 558.

32 Dr. Burney's article on Rinaldo di Capua in *Ree's Cyclopaedia* quoted by Dr. Percy A. Scholes, editor of *Dr. Burney's Musical Tours in Europe.* London 1959. Vol. I. p. 234.

33 *Faulkner's Dublin Journal.* May 19/22, 1764.

34 *Ibid.* May 1/5, 1764.

35 *Ibid.* June 9/12, 1764.

36 *Ibid.* May 8/12, 1764.

37 *Ibid.*

38 *Ibid.* May 5/8, 1764.

39 *Annals of Opera 1597–1940* by Alfred Loewenberg. Geneva 1955. Vol. I. Cols. 187, 188.

40 *Faulkner's Dublin Journal.* May 5/8, 1764.

41 *Ibid.*

42 *The London Stage 1660–1800.* Carbondale, Illinois 1962. Part IV. Vol. II. p. 891.

43 *Faulkner's Dublin Journal.* May 19/22, 1764.

44 *Ibid.*

45 *The York Courant.* November 15, 1763.

46 *Faulkner's Dublin Journal.* May 22/26, 1764.

47 *Ibid.* May 1/5, 1764.

48 *Ibid.* May 22/26, 1764.

49 *Ibid.*

50 *Ibid.* November 6/10, 1764.

51 *Ibid.* November 13/17, 1764.

52 *Ibid.*

53 *London Chronicle.* October 27/30, 1764.
54 *Recollections of the Life of John O'Keeffe, Written by Himself.* London 1826. Vol. II. p. 34.
55 *The Letters of Horace Walpole.* Edited by Peter Cunningham. London 1857. Vol. II. p. 364.
56 *Gray's Inn Journal.* December 22, 1753.
57 *The Morning Post* (London). March 10, 1775.
58 Press-cutting dated March 1762 from an unidentified newspaper in one of Dr. Charles Burney's Notebooks at the British Museum. (Ref. 938 d 9)
59 *Hibernian Journal.* May 8/10, 1782.
60 *Ibid.*
61 *Reminiscences of Michael Kelly.* London 1826. Vol. I. p. 4.
62 *An Answer to a Scurrilous Advertisement* by Gabriel Leone. A pamphlet published in 1764, which reproduces a contract signed by Marcucci at Bologna on August 14, 1763. Copy at the British Museum.
63 *Ibid.*
64 *Freeman's Journal.* October 13/16, 1764.
65 *Lloyd's Evening Post* (London). October 29/31, 1764.
66 Original libretto. Copy at the British Museum.
67 *Ibid.*
68 *Faulkner's Dublin Journal.* November 17/20, 1764.
69 *Ibid.*
70 *Ibid.* January 12/15, 1765.
71 *Ibid.* December 15/18, 1764.
72 *Ibid.* January 1/5, 1765.
73 *Ibid.* January 5/8, 1765.
74 *Ibid.* January 12/15, 1765.
75 *Ibid.*
76 *Dublin Courier.* November 21/23, 1764.
77 *Ibid.*   78 *Ibid.*   79 *Ibid.*   80 *Ibid.*
81 *Faulkner's Dublin Journal.* December 4/8, 1764.
82 *Ibid.*   83 *Ibid.*   84 *Ibid.*   85 *Ibid.*   86 *Ibid.*
87 *Ibid.*   88 *Ibid.*   89 *Ibid.*   90 *Ibid.*   91 *Ibid.*
92 *Ibid.*   93 *Ibid.*   94 *Ibid.*   95 *Ibid.*   96 *Ibid.*

CHAPTER 10

Divisions and Difficulties 1765–1766

1. *The Life and Memoirs of the late Miss Ann Catley* by Miss Ambross. London 1790. pp. 41/42.
2 *Ibid.*
3 *Recollections of the Life of John O'Keeffe, Written by Himself.* London 1826. Vol. I. p. 123.
4 *London Courant.* February 7, 1780.
5 *Ibid.*
6 *Faulkner's Dublin Journal.* February 16/19, 1765.
7 *Ibid.*
8 *The Rise of English Opera* by Eric Walter White. London 1951. p. 61.

9   *A General History of Music* by Charles Burney. New York 1957. Vol. II. p. 1015.

10   *Ibid.*

11   *Faulkner's Dublin Journal.* February 19/23, 1765.

12   *An Historical View of the Irish Stage* by Robert Hitchcock. Dublin 1788–94. Vol. II. pp. 136/137.

13   *The Public Advertiser* (London). December 24, 1784.

14   *The Morning Post* (London). March 10, 1775.

15   *Faulkner's Dublin Journal.* March 19/23, 1765.

16   *Ibid.*

17   *Ibid.* March 30/April 2, 1765.

18   *Ibid.* March 26/30, 1765.

19   *Morning Chronicle* (London). May 24, 1783.

20   *Faulkner's Dublin Journal.* March 26/30, 1765.

21   *Ibid.*

22   *Ibid.* April 6/9, 1765.

23   *Ibid.*

24   *A Complete History of the Stage written by Mr. Dibdin.* London 1795. Vol. V. p. 226.

25   *Faulkner's Dublin Journal.* April 9/13, 1765.

26   *Ibid.* May 4/7, 1765.

27   Reported in *Catalogue of Opera Librettos printed before 1800* by O. G. Sonneck. Washington. 1914. Vol. I. p. 871. Extract taken from a libretto of the Crow Street Theatre production. Published London (J. Williams) 1767.

28   *Faulkner's Dublin Journal.* May 14/18, 1765.

29   *Ibid.* June 11/15, 1765.

30   *A True and Genuine Narrative of Mr. and Mrs. Tenducci in a Letter to a Friend at Bath.* London 1768.

31   *Faulkner's Dublin Journal.* August 30/September 2, 1766.

32   *A Genealogical and Heraldic History of the Landed Gentry of Ireland* by Sir Bernard Burke. Tenth Edition. London 1904. pp. 393/394.

33   *A True and Genuine Narrative of Mr. and Mrs. Tenducci in a Letter to a Friend at Bath.* London 1768.

34   *Music in London 1890–94* by Bernard Shaw. London 1932. Vol. III. p. 143.

35   *A True and Genuine Narrative of Mr. and Mrs. Tenducci in a Letter to a Friend at Bath.* London 1768.

36   *Faulkner's Dublin Journal.* September 2/6, 1766.

37   *A True and Genuine Narrative of Mr. and Mrs. Tenducci in a Letter to a Friend at Bath.* London 1768.

38   *Ibid.*   39   *Ibid.*   40   *Ibid.*   41   *Ibid.*

42   *The Gazetteer* (London). March 1, 1776.

43   *A True and Genuine Narrative of Mr. and Mrs. Tenducci in a Letter to a Friend at Bath.* London 1768.

44   *Dublin Mercury.* February 17/20, 1770.

45   *Faulkner's Dublin Journal.* July 6/9, 1765.

46   *The Letters of Horace Walpole.* Edited by Peter Cunningham. London 1857. Vol. IV. p. 294.

47   *A General History of Music* by Charles Burney. London 1789. Vol. IV. p. 480.

48   *The Public Advertiser.* (London). May 13, 1765.

49   *The Expedition of Humphry Clinker* by Tobias Smollett. Dublin 1771. Vol. I. p. 194.

50   *The London Stage 1660–1800.* Carbondale Illinois 1962. Part IV. Vol. I. p. 355.

51 *Faulkner's Dublin Journal.* July. 6/9, 1765.
52 *A Complete History of the Stage, written by Mr. Dibdin.* London 1795. Vol. V. p. 229.
53 *Faulkner's Dublin Journal.* July 6/9, 1765.
54 *Ibid.*
55 *Ibid.* July 27/30, 1765.
56 *Recollections of the Life of John O'Keeffe, Written by Himself.* London 1826. Vol. I. p. 139.
57 *Ibid.*
58 *Faulkner's Dublin Journal.* July 13/17, 1765.
59 *Recollections of the Life of John O'Keeffe, Written by Himself.* London 1826. Vol. I. p. 139.
60 *Faulkner's Dublin Journal.* August 27/31, 1765.
61 *Ibid.* August 31/September 3, 1765.
62 *Ibid.*
63 *Ibid.* September 21/24, 1765.
64 *Ibid.* October 1/5, 1765.
65 *Ibid.* December 7/10, 1765.
66 *Ibid.* December 14/19, 1765.
67 *The Castrati in Opera* by Angus Heriot. London 1956. p. 185.
68 *The London Stage 1660–1800.* Carbondale, Illinois 1962. Part IV. Vol. II. p. 777.
69 *An Historical View of the Irish Stage* by Robert Hitchcock. Dublin 1788–94. Vol. II. p. 145.
70 *The Hibernian Magazine.* Dublin. February, 1771. p. 31.
71 *Faulkner's Dublin Journal.* November 9/12, 1765.
72 *Ibid.* November 30/December 3, 1765.
73 *Biographia Dramatica: or, a Companion to the Playhouse* by D. E. Baker, Isaac Reed and Stephen Jones. London 1812. Vol. II. p. 152.
74 *Faulkner's Dublin Journal.* November 30/December 3, 1765.
75 *The London Stage 1660–1800.* Carbondale, Illinois 1962. Part IV. Vol. II. p. 1085.
76 *St. James' Chronicle* (London). November 27/29, 1764.
77 *The Public Advertiser* (London). December 1, 1764.
78 *Lloyd's Evening Post* (London). November 25/28, 1768.
79 *Faulkner's Dublin Journal.* January 14/18, 1766.
80 *Early Irish Ballad Opera and Comic Opera* by W. J. Lawrence. *The Musical Quarterly.* New York July 1922. p. 407.
81 *Faulkner's Dublin Journal.* January 25/28, 1766.
82 *Ibid.*
83 *Ibid.*
84 *Ibid.* April 26/29, 1766.
85 *The Life and Memoirs of the late Miss Ann Catley* by Miss Ambross. London 1790. p. 40.
86 *Faulkner's Dublin Journal.* February 4/8, 1766.
87 *Ibid.* February 25/March 1, 1766.
88 *Ibid.*
89 *Ibid.* April 19/22, 1766.
90 *Ibid.*
91 *Ibid.* April 22/26, 1766.
92 *Ibid.*
93 *Ibid.* June 3/7, 1766.
94 *Ibid.* April 8/12, 1766.
95 *Annals of Opera 1587–1940* by Alfred Loewenberg. Geneva 1955. Vol. I. Col. 216.
96 *Faulkner's Dublin Journal.* April 8/12, 1766.

97 *Ibid.* May 10/13, 1766.
98 *Ibid.* April 8/12, 1766.
99 *Ibid.* May 10/13, 1766.
100 *Ibid.*
101 *Ibid.* June 17/21, 1766.
102 *Ibid.* June 28/July 1, 1766.
103 *Ibid.* July 12/15, 1766.

CHAPTER 11

Seven Years of English Opera 1770–1777

1 *Lloyd's Evening Post* (London). October 18/20, 1769.
2 *Dublin Mercury.* February 20/22, 1770.
3 *Ibid.*
4 *Faulkner's Dublin Journal.* January 7/10, 1769.
5 *Freeman's Journal.* February 15/17, 1770.
6 *Morning Herald* (London). October 2, 1783.
7 *Ibid.* October 3, 1783.
8 *London Courant.* September 1, 1781.
9 *General Advertiser* (London). December 19, 1786.
10 *Dublin Mercury.* February 20/22, 1770.
11 *Ibid.*
12 *Ibid.* March 27/29, 1770.
13 *The Musical Tour of Mr. Dibdin* by Charles Dibdin. Sheffield 1788. p. 287.
14 *Dublin Mercury.* May 8/10, 1770.
15 *Ibid.* May 19/22, 1770.
16 *Dictionary of National Biography* under Joseph Reed.
17 *Dublin Mercury.* May 19/22, 1770.
18 *Ibid.*
19 *Ibid.*
20 *Musical Memoirs* by W. T. Parke. London 1830. Vol. I. pp. 93/94.
21 *Dublin Mercury.* January 24/26, 1771.
22 *The Musical Tour of Mr. Dibdin* by Charles Dibdin. Sheffield 1788. p. 286.
23 *London Chronicle.* November 19/22, 1785.
24 *The Songs of Charles Dibdin.* Preface by George Hogarth. London 1842. p. vi.
25 *The Musical Tour of Mr. Dibdin* by Charles Dibdin. Sheffield 1788. p. 286.
26 *Ibid.*
27 *Grove's Dictionary of Music and Musicians* (Third Edition). London 1928. Vol. II. p. 59.
28 *Ibid.*
29 *Ree's Cyclopaedia.* 1819. Vol. II. Reported in *Dictionary of National Biography* under Michael Arne.
30 *Dublin Mercury.* March 5/7, 1771.
31 *Ibid.*
32 *Ibid.*
33 *Ibid.* April 7/9, 1770.
34 *Ibid.*
35 *Ibid.* April 9/11, 1771.

36 *Francis Barthélemon* by Charles Higham. 1896.

37 *General Evening Post* (London). October 3/5, 1771.

38 Extract of a 'Letter from Dublin' from a press cutting dated December 7, 1771 (newspaper not identified but probably the *London Chronicle* or *Evening Post*) included in one of Dr. Charles Burney's Notebooks at the British Museum.

39 *Faulkner's Dublin Journal*. August 27/30, 1768.

40 *Ibid.*

41 *Ibid.*

42 *The Rotunda Hospital, its Architects and Craftsmen* by C. P. Curran. Dublin 1945. p. 30.

43 *Recollections of the Life of John O'Keeffe, Written by Himself*. Vol. I. p. 291.

44 *Dublin Mercury*. June 13/15, 1771.

45 *Freeman's Journal*. July 16/18, 1771.

46 *Annals of Opera 1597–1940* by Alfred Loewenberg. Geneva 1955. Vol. I. Col. 307.

47 *Freeman's Journal*. July 6/8, 1771.

48 *Ibid.* July 16/18, 1771.

49 *Ibid.*

50 *Ibid.* May 1/3, 1770.

51 *Ibid.* July 25/27, 1771.

52 *Ibid.* July 27/30, 1771.

53 *Ibid.* July 30/August 3, 1771.

54 *Ibid.* September 7/10, 1771.

55 *Ibid.* October 30/November 2, 1771.

56 *Ibid.* March 21/24, 1772.

57 *Ibid.* March 26/28, 1772.

58 *The Professional Life of Mr. Dibdin, Written by Himself*. London 1803. Vol. I. p. 134.

59 *The Thespian Dictionary*. London 1805. Under Thomas Ryder.

60 *Faulkner's Dublin Journal*. February 5/8, 1774.

61 *Ibid.*

62 *Recollections of the Life of John O'Keeffe, Written by Himself*. London 1826. Vol. I. p. 347.

63 *Ibid.* Vol. I. p. 346.

64 *Ibid.*

65 *Ibid.* Vol. I. pp. 346/347.

66 *Morning Chronicle* (London). May 2, 1783.

67 *Morning Herald* (London). October 28, 1783.

68 *The Public Advertiser* (London). March 15, 1785.

69 *Musical Memoirs* by W. T. Parke. London 1830. Vol. I. p. 57.

70 *Saunders' News-letter*. March 30/April 1, 1774.

71 *Morning Chronicle* (London). November 13, 1772.

72 *Saunders' News-letter*. March 30/April 1, 1774.

73 *Ibid.* August 26/29, 1774.

74 *Hibernian Journal*. February 10/13, 1775.

75 Original libretto. Copy at Trinity College Library, Dublin.

76 *Hibernian Journal*. February 10/13, 1775.

77 *Ibid.* February 17/20, 1775.

78 *Saunders' News-letter*. February 22/24, 1775.

79 *The Morning Post* (London). August 7, 1775.

80 *Hibernian Journal*. November 15/17, 1775.

81 *Ibid.*

82 *Faulkner's Dublin Journal*. November 16/18, 1775.

83 *The Westminster Magazine*. London, February 1775.

84 *Musical Memoirs* by W. T. Parke. London 1830. Vol. I. p. 16.

85 *The Gazetteer* (London). September 16, 1785.

86 *The World* (London). January 5, 1787.

87 *The London Stage 1660–1800*. Carbondale Illinois. 1962. Part IV. Vol. III. p. 1784. Reported from *The Westminster Magazine*. October 1773.

88 *The Morning Post* (London). January 1, 1776.

89 *The Gazetteer* (London). January 9, 1776.

90 *Freeman's Journal*. January 2/4, 1776.

91 *Faulkner's Dublin Journal*. January 8/10, 1776.

92 *Freeman's Journal*. January 23/25, 1776.

93 *Morning Chronicle* (London). January 27, 1776.

94 *The Gazetteer* (London). February 7, 1776.

95 *Faulkner's Dublin Journal*. April 18/20, 1776.

96 *Freeman's Journal*. January 9/11, 1776.

97 *Lady Morgan's Memoirs: Autobiography, Diaries and Correspondence*. Edited by W. Hepworth Dixon. London 1862. Vol. I. p. 50.

98 *Personal Sketches of his own Times* by Sir Jonah Barrington. London 1827. Vol. II. pp. 221/222.

99 *Ibid*. p. 222.

100 *Recollections of the Life of John O'Keeffe, Written by Himself*. London 1826. Vol. I. p. 354.

101 *Personal Sketches of his own Times* by Sir Jonah Barrington. London 1827. Vol. II. p. 222.

102 *Freeman's Journal*. November 30/December 3, 1776.

103 *Theatrical Biography: or, Memoirs of the Principal Performers of the Three Theatres Royal*. London 1772. Vol. II. p. 23.

104 *Ibid*. p. 24.

105 *Ibid*. p. 25.

106 *The Waterman*. Libretto. London (R. Baldwin) 1783. Extract from preface.

107 *Ibid*.

108 *Freeman's Journal*. January 7/11, 1777.

109 *Faulkner's Dublin Journal*. November 21/23, 1776.

110 *Hibernian Journal*. January 6/8, 1777.

111 *Dublin Mercury*. January 21/23, 1777.

112 *Freeman's Journal*. January 30/February 1, 1777.

113 *Hibernian Journal*. February 17/19, 1777.

114 *Ibid*.

115 *The Memoirs of the Right Hon. R. B. Sheridan* by Thomas Moore. London 1825. Reported by George Hogarth in *Memoirs of the Musical Drama*. London. 1838. Vol. II. p. 433.

116 Extract from playbill of the second performance at Covent Garden Theatre on November 22, 1775.

117 *The Memoirs of the Right Hon. R. B. Sheridan* by Thomas Moore. London 1825. Reported by George Hogarth in *Memoirs of the Musical Drama*. London. 1838. Vol. II. p. 429.

118 *Ibid*.

119 *Ibid*. Vol. II. p. 428.

120 *Ibid*. Vol. II. p. 431.

121 *Ibid*. Vol. II. p. 433.

122 *Ibid.*
123 *Ibid.* Vol. II. p. 432.
124 *Ibid.*
125 *Ibid.* Vol. II. p. 431.
126 *Ibid.* Vol. II. p. 430.
127 *Ibid.* Vol. II. p. 433.
128 *Hibernian Journal.* February 21/24, 1777.
129 *Freeman's Journal.* March 15/18, 1777.
130 *Ibid.* April 24/26, 1777.
131 *The London Stage 1660–1800.* Carbondale, Illinois 1962. Part IV. Vol. III. p. 1774. Reported from *William Hopkins MS Diary 1769–1776.* Folger Shakespeare Library, Washington, D.C.
132 *Musical Memoirs* by W. T. Parke. London 1830. Vol. I. pp. 2/3.
133 *Hibernian Journal.* March 5/7, 1777.
134 *Ibid.*
135 *Ibid.* March 10/12, 1777.
136 *Faulkner's Dublin Journal.* April 10/12, 1777.
137 *Recollections of the Life of John O'Keeffe, Written by Himself.* London 1826. Vol. II. p. 49.
138 *Ibid.* Vol. II. p. 70.

CHAPTER 12

The Italian Opera 1777–1778

1   *Hibernian Journal.* January 6/8, 1777.
2   *Reminiscences of Michael Kelly.* London 1826. Vol. I. p. 14.
3   *Ibid.* p. 15.
4   *Hibernian Journal.* April 25/28, 1777.
5   *Reminiscences of Michael Kelly.* London 1826. Vol. I. p. 5.
6   *Ibid.* p. 6.
7   *Faulkner's Dublin Journal.* March 22/25, 1777.
8   *Ibid.* April 5/8, 1777.
9   Original libretto. Copy at Pearse Street Library, Dublin.
10 *Faulkner's Dublin Journal.* April 10/13, 1777.
11 *Ibid.* April 17/19, 1777.
12 *Ibid.* April 3/5, 1777.
13 *Ibid.*
14 *Ibid.*
15 *Reminiscences of Michael Kelly.* London 1826. Vol. I. p. 15.
16 *The Morning Post* (London). November 24, 1784.
17 *Reminiscences of Michael Kelly.* London 1826. Vol. I. p. 64.
18 *Memoirs of Lorenzo da Ponte.* Translated by Elizabeth Abbott. New York 1967. p. 149.
19 *Ibid.*
20 *Hibernian Journal.* April 18/21, 1777.
21 *Freeman's Journal.* April 29/May 1, 1777.
22 *Hibernian Journal.* April 25/28, 1777.
23 *Ibid.* May 7/9, 1777.

24 *Memoirs of the Musical Drama* by George Hogarth. London 1838. Vol. II. pp. 134/35.
25 *Faulkner's Dublin Journal*. May 10/13, 1777.
26 *Ibid.*
27 *Reminiscences of Michael Kelly*. London 1826. Vol. I. p. 16.
28 *Faulkner's Dublin Journal*. March 22/25, 1777.
29 *Ibid.* May 10/13, 1777.
30 *Hibernian Journal*. May 21/23, 1777.
31 *Ibid.*
32 *Ibid.*
33 *Ibid.* June 4/6, 1777.
34 *Ibid.*
35 *Ibid.* May 28/30, 1777.
36 *Ibid.* June 4/6, 1777.
37 *Saunders' News-letter*. July 25, 1777.
38 *Ibid.* November 22, 1777.
39 *Minute Book of the Dublin Musical Fund,* May 7, 1798. Microfilm at the National Library, Dublin.
40 *Saunders' News-letter*. July 25, 1777.
41 *Ibid.* December 1, 1777.
42 *Hibernian Journal*. December 1/3, 1777.
43 Recorded in Sheet Music of *La Frascatana* in the Townley Hall Collection at Trinity College Library, Dublin.
44 *New Morning Post* (London). November 27, 1776.
45 *The Public Advertiser* (London). January 14, 1774.
46 *Reminiscences of Michael Kelly*. London 1826. Vol. I. p. 180.
47 *Morning Chronicle* (London). November 11, 1782.
48 *Morning Herald* (London). September 8, 1783.
49 *The Morning Post* (London). February 15, 1775.
50 *Ibid.* October 27, 1775.
51 *New Morning Post* (London). November 27, 1776.
52 *General Advertiser* (London). March 13, 1786.
53 *Musical Reminiscences* by the Earl of Mount Edgcumbe. London 1834. pp. 23/24.
54 *New Morning Post* (London). November 27, 1776.
55 Reported in *Catalogue of Library of Royal College of Music*. London 1909. Vol. III. p. 127.
56 *Reminiscences of Michael Kelly*. London 1826. Vol. I. p. 70.
57 *General Advertiser* (London). May 22, 1782.
58 *Saunders' News-letter*. December 9, 1777.
59 *Ibid.*
60 *Reminiscences of Michael Kelly*. London 1826. Vol. I. p. 15.
61 *Arthur Young's Tour in Ireland. 1776–1779.* Edited by Arthur Wollaston. London 1892. Vol. I. p. 20.
62 *Saunders' News-letter*. December 20, 1777.
63 *Ibid.* December 24, 1777.
64 *Ibid.* December 26, 1777.
65 *Ibid.* January 8, 1778.
66 *Evening Post* (London). January 11, 1770.
67 *Saunders' News-letter*. February 7, 1778.
68 *Ibid.* February 14, 1778.
69 *Ibid.* February 18, 1778.

70 Original Libretto. Copy at Pearse Street Library, Dublin.
71 *Saunders' News-letter*. March 7, 1778.
72 *Ibid.*
73 *Morning Herald* (London). January 30, 1781.
74 *Saunders' News-letter*. March 9, 1778.
75 *Ibid.* March 27, 1778.
76 *Ibid.* March 28, 1778.
77 *Ibid.*
78 *Ibid.*
79 *Ibid.* March 10, 1778.
80 *Ibid.* April 6, 1778.
81 *Ibid.*
82 *Ibid.*
83 *Ibid.* April 13, 1778.
84 *Ibid.*
85 *Ibid.* April 29, 1778.
86 Original Libretto. Copy at Pearse Street Library, Dublin.
87 Copy of catalogue at the British Museum.
88 *Ibid.*
89 *Saunders' News-letter*. May 23, 1778.
90 *Ibid.*

CHAPTER 13

Though in a Foreign Language 1781–1782

1 *Saunders' News-letter*. March 21/23, 1781.
2 *Hibernian Journal*. March 31/April 2, 1781.
3 *A General History of Music* by Charles Burney. New York 1957. Vol. II. p. 1016.
4 *Freeman's Journal*. June 25/27, 1782.
5 *Hibernian Journal*. October 15/17, 1781.
6 *Morning Chronicle* (London). June 7, 1784.
7 *General Advertiser* (London). December 19, 1786.
8 *Hibernian Journal*. February 20/22, 1782.
9 *Ibid.* October 19/22, 1781.
10 *Dictionary of National Biography* under Richard Daly.
11 *Personal Sketches of his own Times* by Sir Jonah Barrington. London 1827. Vol. II. p. 25.
12 *Ibid.* p. 22.
13 *Ibid.* pp. 25/26.
14 *Hibernian Journal*. October 24/26, 1781.
15 Original Libretto. Copy at Pearse Street Library, Dublin.
16 *Hibernian Journal*. October 31/November 2, 1781.
17 *Ibid.*   18 *Ibid.*   19 *Ibid.*   20 *Ibid.*   21 *Ibid.*
22 *Ibid.*   23 *Ibid.*   24 *Ibid.*
25 *Ibid.* November 2/5, 1781.
26 *Ibid.*
27 *General Advertiser* (London). May 22, 1782.
28 *Hibernian Journal*. November 21/23, 1781.

29 *Ibid.*

30 *Ibid.* November 23/26, 1781.

31 *A General History of Music* by Charles Burney. New York 1957. Vol. II. p. 895.

32 *Ibid.* p. 894.

33 *Hibernian Journal.* December 10/12, 1781.

34 *Ibid.*

35 *Ibid.* December 12/14, 1781.

36 *Ibid.* December 19/21, 1781.

37 *Ibid.* December 31, 1781/January 2, 1782.

38 *Ibid.* January 21/23, 1782.

39 *Ibid.* January 30/February 1, 1782.

40 *Ibid.* February 27/March 1, 1782.

41 *Ibid.*

42 *The Morning Post* (London). March 16, 1778.

43 *Hibernian Journal.* March 8/11, 1782.

44 *Ibid.*

45 *Ibid.* April 15/17, 1782.

46 *Ibid.* May 20/22, 1782.

47 *General Advertiser* (London). May 22, 1782.

48 *A General History of Music* by Charles Burney. New York 1957. Vol. II. p. 901.

49 *Hibernian Journal.* May 20/22, 1782.

50 *Ibid.* June 14/17, 1782.

51 *Ibid.* June 26/28, 1782.

52 *Ibid.*

53 *I Teatri Musicali Veneziani del Settecento* by Taddeo Wiel. Venice 1897. p. 353.

54 *Hibernian Journal.* May 20/22, 1782.

55 *Ibid.* January 21/23, 1782.

56 *Reminiscences of Michael Kelly.* London 1826. Vol. II. p. 67.

57 *Freeman's Journal.* February 26/28, 1782.

58 *General Advertiser* (London). September 12, 1782.

59 *The Morning Post* (London). November 2, 1872.

60 *Memoirs of the Life and Times of the Rt. Hon. Henry Grattan* by his son, Henry Grattan Esq., M.P. London 1839. Vol. II. pp. 372/376.

61 *The Public Advertiser* (London). January 18, 1783.

62 *Ibid.*

63 *Ibid.* November 6, 1782.

64 *The Italian Opera and Contemporary Ballet in London 1789–1820.* Compiled by William C. Smith. London 1955. p. 36.

65 *L'Amore Artigiano.* Original Libretto. Copy at Pearse Street Library, Dublin.

66 *Ibid.*

67 *Hibernian Journal.* November 16/19, 1781.

68 *Freeman's Journal.* November 8/10, 1781.

69 *Ibid.* November 13/15, 1781.

70 *Ibid.* November 24/27, 1781.

71 *Ibid.* December 13/15, 1781.

72 *Ibid.* December 15/18, 1781.

73 *A note to the Cornwallis Papers* by William John Fitzpatrick. Dublin 1859. pp. 20/21.

74 *Freeman's Journal.* December 15/18, 1781.

75 *Ibid.* December 27/29, 1781.

76 *Hibernian Journal.* June 19/21, 1782.
77 *Freeman's Journal.* June 13/15, 1782.
78 *Ibid.*
79 *Ibid.* June 4/6, 1782,
80 *Ibid.*
81 *Ibid.*
82 *Ibid.*
83 *St. James' Chronicle* (London). July 19/21, 1781.

CHAPTER 14

Not a Word of Italian 1782–1784

1   *Personal Sketches of his Own Times* by Sir Jonah Barrington. London 1827. Vol. II. p. 209.
2   *Oxberry's Dramatic Biography and Histrionic Anecdotes.* London 1826. Vol. IV. p. 82.
3   *Memoirs of the Life of John Philip Kemble* by James Boaden. London 1825. Vol. I. p. 123
4   *Ibid.* Vol. I. p. 122.
5   *The Public Advertiser* (London). October 3, 1783.
6   *Oxberry's Dramatic Biography and Histrionic Anecdotes.* London 1826. Vol IV. pp. 81/82.
7   *Dictionary of National Biography* under John Henry Johnstone.
8   *Morning Chronicle* (London). September 18, 1783.
9   *The Public Advertiser* (London). October 17, 1783.
10 *Dublin Evening Post.* December 31, 1782.
11 *Ibid.* January 9, 1783.
12 *Morning Chronicle* (London). May 20, 1782.
13 *Ibid.*
14 *Hibernian Chronicle* (Cork). August 30, 1770. Reported by William Smith Clark in *The Irish Stage in the County Towns 1720–1800.*
15 Reported by William Smith Clark. *Ibid.* p. 98.
16 *Reminiscences of Michael Kelly.* London 1826. Vol. I. p. 287.
17 *Memoirs of the Life of John Philip Kemble* by James Boaden. London 1825. Vol I. p. 341.
18 *Dublin Evening Post.* December 28, 1782.
19 *General Evening Post* (London). January 2, 1783.
20 *Freeman's Journal.* January 4/7, 1783.
21 *The Monthly Mirror.* London. December 1794.
22 *Recollections of the Life of John O'Keeffe, Written by Himself.* London 1826. Vol. II. p. 384.
23 *Ibid.*
24 *Memoirs of the Colman Family* by Richard Brinsley Peake. London 1841. Vol. II. p. 403.
25 *Ibid.*
26 *Recollections of the Life of John O'Keeffe, Written by Himself.* London 1826. Vol. II. pp. 391/392.
27 *Ibid.* Vol. II. p. 17.
28 *Ibid.* Vol. II. p. 18.
29 *Ibid.* Vol. II. p. 21.
30 *Ibid.* Vol. II. p. 40.
31 *Freeman's Journal.* January 11/14, 1783.
32 *Dublin Evening Post.* January 11, 1783.

33 *Freeman's Journal*. January 11/14, 1783.
34 *The Morning Post* (London). April 12, 1783.
35 *Dublin Evening Post*. February 22, 1783.
36 *Ibid*. February 25, 1783.
37 *Freeman's Journal*. February 22/25, 1783.
38 *Dublin Evening Post*. April 18, 1783.
39 *Freeman's Journal*. March 25/27, 1783.
40 *Ibid*. March 6/8, 1783.
41 *Ibid*. March 20/22, 1783.
42 *Ibid*. March 6/8, 1783.
43 *Ibid*. March 25/27, 1783.
44 *Memoirs of the Musical Drama* by George Hogarth. London 1838. Vol. II. pp. 441/442.
45 *Dublin Evening Post*. March 4, 1783.
46 *General Evening Post* (London). March 18, 1783.
47 *Freeman's Journal*. May 3/6, 1783.
48 Original Libretto. Copy at Trinity College Library, Dublin.
49 *Ibid*.
50 *Dublin Mercury*. March 3/6, 1770.
51 *Ibid*. May 12/15, 1770.
52 *Freeman's Journal*. May 3/6, 1783.
53 *Ibid*.
54 *Ibid*. May 8/10, 1783.
55 *Ibid*. June 14/17, 1783.
56 *Hibernian Journal*. May 8/10, 1782.
57 *Personal Sketches of his Own Times* by Sir Jonah Barrington. London 1827. Vol. II. p. 166.
58 *Hibernian Journal*. May 8/10, 1782.
59 *Freeman's Journal*. May 10/13, 1783.
60 *Ibid*. November 13/15, 1783.
61 *Ibid*. November 15/18, 1783.
62 *Ibid*. November 27/29, 1783.
63 *The London Stage 1660–1800*. Carbondale, Illinois. 1962. Part IV. Vol. II. p. 830.
64 *The Letters of David Garrick*. Edited by David M. Little and George M. Kahrl. Oxford 1963. Vol. I. p. 330.
65 *The Monthly Mirror*. London. July 1803. Footnote to article on John Braham.
66 *Memoirs of the Life of John Philip Kemble* by James Boaden. London 1825. Vol. I. p. 397.
67 *The Westminster Magazine*. London. June 1777. Critique on the Theatrical Merits of Mr. Leoni.
68 *Memoirs of the Musical Drama* by George Hogarth. London 1838. Vol. II. p. 430.
69 *General Evening Post* (London). October 17/19, 1775.
70 *Hibernian Journal*. June 11/13, 1777.
71 *Freeman's Journal*. September 11/13, 1783.
72 *Ibid*. November 11/13, 1783.
73 *Ibid*. December 5/8, 1783.
74 *Ibid*.
75 *Ibid*. December 8/10, 1783.
76 *Dublin Evening Post*. December 13, 1783.
77 *Hibernian Journal*. December 15/17, 1783.
78 *Ibid*.
79 *Morning Herald* (London). December 26, 1783.

80   *Morning Chronicle* (London). January 6, 1784.
81   *The Thespian Dictionary*. London 1805. Under Miss Wheeler.
82   *Freeman's Journal*. December 27/30, 1783.
83   Original Libretto. Copy at the British Museum.
84   *The Thespian Dictionary*. London 1805. Under Peter Duffy.
85   *Hibernian Journal*. December 11/13, 1780.
86   *Freeman's Journal*. January 1/3, 1784.
87   *Ibid*. January 3/6, 1784.
88   *Ibid*. January 10/13, 1784.
89   *Ibid*. January 17/20, 1784.
90   *Ibid*. January 27/29, 1784.
91   *Ibid*. February 5/7, 1784.
92   *Ibid*. February 14/17, 1784.
93   *Ibid*. February 28/March 2, 1784.
94   *Ibid*.
95   *The Public Advertiser* (London). April 28, 1784.
96   *The Musical Antiquary*. London. October 1911.
97   *Freeman's Journal*. February 28/March 2, 1784.
98   *Ibid*. March 6/9, 1784.
99   *Ibid*. March 16/18, 1784.
100 *Memoirs of Mrs. Siddons* by James Boaden. London 1893. p. 78.
101 *Freeman's Journal*. January 27/29, 1784.
102 *Ibid*. June 8/10, 1784.
103 *Ibid*.
104 *Ibid*.
105 *Ibid*. July 12/15, 1784.
106 *Ibid*. July 29/31, 1784.
107 *Dublin Theatres and Theatre Customs 1637–1820* by La Tourette Stockwell. Kingsport 1938. p. 153.
108 *Freeman's Journal*. January 10/13, 1784.

CHAPTER 15

'Orpheus' and Mrs. Billington 1784–1786

1   *Freeman's Journal*. January 1/3, 1784.
2   *Ibid*.
3   *Ibid*.
4   *Ibid*. January 3/6, 1784.
5   *Dictionary of National Biography* under Francis Gentleman.
6   Play-bill advertising a performance at Covent Garden Theatre, February 28, 1792. Copy at the British Museum.
7   *Orpheus and Eurydice*. Vocal Score. London 1792. Printed and Sold by Preston and Son, Strand.
8   *Freeman's Journal*. December 4/6, 1783.
9   *Morning Chronicle* (London). January 6, 1784.
10   *The Romance of the Irish Stage* by J. Fitzgerald Molloy. London 1897. Vol. II. p. 225.

11   *Faulkner's Dublin Journal.* March 4/6, 1784.

12   *Reminiscences of Michael Kelly.* London 1826. Vol. I. p. 293.

13   *Memoirs of Mrs. Billington.* London 1792. p. 22.

14   *Oxberry's Dramatic Biography and Histrionic Anecdotes.* London 1826. Vol. III. p. 57.

15   *Ibid.*

16   *Ibid.*

17   *Memoirs of George the Fourth* by R. Huish (1830). Reported by S. M. Ellis in *The Life of Michael Kelly 1762–1826.* London 1930. p. 334.

18   *Queens of Song* by Ellen Creathorne Clayton. London 1863. Vol. I. p. 256.

19   *Reminiscences of Michael Kelly.* London 1826. Vol. I. p. 293.

20   *Queens of Song* by Ellen Creathorne Clayton. London 1863. Vol. I. p. 235.

21   *A General History of Music* by Charles Burney. New York. 1957. Vol. II. p. 1021.

22   *Musical Reminiscences* by the Earl of Mount Edgcumbe. London 1834. pp. 90/91.

23   *The Public Advertiser* (London). March 23, 1786.

24   *General Advertiser* (London). February 22, 1786.

25   *The Public Advertiser* (London). March 20, 1786.

26   *Musical Memoirs* by W. T. Parke. London 1830. Vol. I. p. 127.

27   *Queens of Song* by Ellen Creathorne Clayton. London 1863. Vol. I. p. 251.

28   *Freeman's Journal.* March 25/27, 1784.

29   *The Public Advertiser* (London). December 31, 1784.

30   *Musical Memoirs* by W. T. Parke. London 1830. Vol. I. p. 49.

31   *Musical Reminiscences* by the Earl of Mount Edgcumbe. London 1834. p. 45.

32   *Ibid.*

33   *The Public Advertiser* (London). March 15, 1786.

34   *Freeman's Journal.* March 13/16, 1784.

35   *Ibid.* January 22/24, 1784.

36   *Ibid.* February 19/21, 1784.

37   *Ibid.* January 29/31, 1784.

38   *Ibid.*

39   Reported by La Tourette Stockwell in *Dublin Theatres and Theatre Customs 1637–1820.* p. 146.

40   Original Libretto. Copy at Trinity College Library, Dublin.

41   *Reminiscences of Michael Kelly.* London 1826. Vol. II. p. 72.

42   *St. James' Chronicle* (London). October 18/20, 1781.

43   *London Courant.* October 20, 1781.

44   *Grove's Dictionary of Music and Musicians* (Fifth Edition). London 1954. Vol. I. p. 753.

45   *Musical Reminiscences* by the Earl of Mount Edgcumbe. London 1834. p. 113.

46   *Ibid.*

47   *Freeman's Journal.* October 23/26, 1784.

48   *Ibid.* November 2/4, 1784.

49   *Ibid.* October 26/28, 1784.

50   *Ibid.* October 30/November 2, 1784.

51   *Morning Chronicle* (London). November 4, 1782.

52   *Freeman's Journal.* November 9/11, 1784,

53   *Ibid.* November 13/16, 1784.

54   *Ibid.* November 11/13, 1784.

55   *Ibid.* November 25/27, 1784.

56   *Personal Sketches of his Own Times* by Sir Jonah Barrington. London 1827. Vol. II. pp. 47/48.

57 *Ibid.* p. 51.
58 *Memoirs of the Life of John Philip Kemble* by James Boaden. London 1825. Vol. I. p. 158.
59 *Ibid.* p. 159.
60 *Freeman's Journal.* December 11/14, 1784.
61 *Ibid.* November 25/27, 1784.
62 *Lady Morgan's Memoirs, Autobiography, Diaries and Correspondence.* Edited by W. Hepworth Dixon. London 1862. Vol. I. p. 79.
63 *Dublin Evening Post.* January 22, 1785.
64 *Ibid.* January 29, 1785.
65 *Volunteer Evening Post.* January 29/February 1, 1785.
66 *Ibid.* April 9/12, 1785.
67 *Ibid.* May 5/7, 1785.
68 *Ibid.* May 7/10, 1785.
69 *Ibid.* July 26/28, 1785.
70 *Ibid.* August 6/9, 1785.
71 *Dublin Evening Post.* March 24, 1785.
72 *Morning Chronicle* (London). September 17, 1785.
73 *Volunteer Evening Post.* October 22/25, 1785.
74 *Ibid.* October 27/29, 1785.
75 *Ibid.* November 5/8, 1785.
76 *The Professional Life of Mr. Dibdin, written by Himself.* London 1803. Vol. II. p. 187.
77 *Hibernian Journal.* April 12/14, 1786.

CHAPTER 16

Michael Kelly and Mrs. Crouch 1787–1789

1   *Liber Munerum Publicorum Hibe rniae.* London 1824. Vol. I. Part 3. p. 109.
2   *Ibid.*
3   *Morning Chronicle* (London). September 23, 1785.
4   *Memoirs of the Life of John Philip Kemble* by James Boaden. London 1825. Vol. I. p. 336.
5   *Ibid.* p. 337.
6   *Hibernian Journal.* February 27, 1786.
7   *Ibid.* March 5, 1876.
8   *Ibid.* March 12, 1786.
9   *A General History of Music* by Charles Burney. New York 1957. Vol. II. p. 972.
10 *Ibid.* p. 977.
11 *The Monthly Mirror.* London. August 1801.
12 *Reminiscences of Michael Kelly.* London 1826. Vol. I. p. 5.
13 *Saunders' News-letter.* August 31/September 2, 1774.
14 *Faulkner's Dublin Journal.* October 24/26, 1769.
15 *Reminiscences of Michael Kelly.* London 1826. Vol. I. p. 19.
16 *Recollections of the Life of John O'Keeffe, Written by Himself.* London 1826. Vol. I. pp. 393/394.
17 *Ibid.* p. 394.
18 *Faulkner's Dublin Journal.* May 27/29, 1777.
19 *Ibid.*

20 *Ibid.* May 31/June 3, 1777.

21 *Freeman's Journal.* June 3/5, 1777.

22 *Reminiscences of Michael Kelly.* London 1826. Vol. I. p. 19.

23 *Memoirs of the Musical Drama* by George Hogarth. London 1838. Vol. II. p. 450.

24 *Candid and Impartial Strictures on artists who have appeared at Drury Lane Theatre, and Little Theatre, Haymarket, and Covent Garden Theatre.* London 1795. Under Mr. Kelly.

25 *Musical Reminiscences* by the Earl of Mount Edgcumbe. London 1834. p. 32.

26 *Ibid.* p. 74.

27 *Memoirs of the Life of John Philip Kemble* by James Boaden. London 1825. Vol. I. p. 350.

28 *Reminiscences of Michael Kelly.* London 1826. Vol. I. p. 291.

29 *The Gazetteer* (London). April 23, 1781.

30 *Memoirs of Mrs. Siddons* by James Boaden. London 1893. p. 136.

31 *The Morning Post.* (London). September 10, 1782.

32 *Queens of Song* by Ellen Creathorne Clayton. London 1863. Vol. I. p. 194.

33 *Ibid.*

34 *Morning Herald* (London). September 22, 1783.

35 *Queens of Song* by Ellen Creathorne Clayton. London 1863. Vol. I. p. 195.

36 *Reminiscences of Michael Kelly.* London 1826. Vol. II. p. 20.

37 *Memoirs* of George Frederick Cooke. Reported in *The Life of Michael Kelly 1762–1826* by S. M. Ellis. London 1930. p. 266.

38 The *Gazetteer* (London). April 23, 1781.

39 *Memoirs of the Musical Drama* by George Hogarth. London 1838. Vol. II. p. 439.

40 *Oxberry's Dramatic Biography and Histrionic Anecdotes.* London 1826. Vol. V. p. 242.

41 *Ibid.* p. 244.

42 *The Life of Michael Kelly 1762–1826* by S. M. Ellis. London 1930. p. 389.

43 *Evening Herald.* June 16, 1787.

44 *The Public Advertiser* (London). June 20, 1787.

45 *Reminiscences of Michael Kelly.* London 1826. Vol. I. p. 301.

46 *Ibid.*

47 *Dublin Evening Post.* June 21, 1787.

48 *Ibid.*

49 *Reminiscences of Michael Kelly.* London 1826. Vol. I. p. 329.

50 *Dublin Evening Post.* June 26, 1787.

51 *Reminiscences of Michael Kelly.* London 1826. Vol. I. p. 302.

52 *Dublin Evening Post.* June 28, 1787.

53 *Evening Herald.* June 27, 1787.

54 *Ibid.*

55 *Reminiscences of Michael Kelly.* London 1826. Vol. I. p. 298.

56 *Evening Herald.* June 27, 1787.

57 *Dublin Evening Post.* July 3, 1787.

58 *Ibid.* July 12, 1787.

59 *Ibid.* July 6, 1787.

60 *Reminiscences of Michael Kelly.* London 1826. Vol. I. p. 292.

61 *Dublin Evening Post.* July 7, 1787.

62 *Ibid.* December 1, 1787.

63 *Musical Memoirs* by W. T. Parke. London 1830. Vol. I. p. 100.

64 *Dublin Evening Post.* December 13, 1787.

65 *Faulkner's Dublin Journal.* July 7/9, 1789.

66 *Reminiscences of Michael Kelly*. London 1826. Vol. I. p. 302.
67 *Hibernian Journal*. July 15, 1789.
68 *Dublin Chronicle*. July 21, 1789.
69 *Dictionary of National Biography* under James Cobb.
70 *Reminiscences of Michael Kelly*. London 1826. Vol. I. p. 310.
71 *Ibid*. p. 95.
72 *Faulkner's Dublin Journal*. July 18/21, 1789.
73 *Hibernian Journal*. July 24, 1789.
74 *Reminiscences of Michael Kelly*. London 1826. Vol. I. p. 322.
75 *Ibid*. p. 319.
76 *Freeman's Journal*. July 28/30, 1789.

CHAPTER 17

The Arrival of Madame Mara 1790–1792

1   *Musical Memoirs* by W. T. Parke. London 1830. Vol. I. p. 101.
2   *Memoirs of the Musical Drama* by George Hogarth. London 1838. Vol. II. p. 445.
3   *Memoirs of the Life of John Philip Kemble* by James Boaden. London 1825. Vol. II. p. 13.
4   *Musical Memoirs* by W. T. Parke. London 1830. Vol. I. pp. 123/124.
5   *Faulkner's Dublin Journal*. February 16/18, 1790.
6   *Ibid*.
7   *Dublin Courant*. February 20, 1790.
8   *Faulkner's Dublin Journal*. October 30/November 2, 1790.
9   *Ibid*. November 4/6, 1790.
10 *Reminiscences of Michael Kelly*. London 1826. Vol. II. p. 162.
11 *The Thespian Dictionary*. London 1805. Under Michael Kelly.
12 *Musical Memoirs* by W. T. Parke. London 1830. Vol. I. p. 128.
13 *Ibid*.
14 *Hibernian Chronicle* (Cork). October 20, 1791. Reported in *The Irish Stage in the Count Towns 1720 to 1800* by William Smith Clark. Oxford. 1965.
15 *Faulkner's Dublin Journal*. December 18/21, 1790.
16 *Musical Memoirs* by W. T. Parke. London 1830. Vol. I. p. 107.
17 *Faulkner's Dublin Journal*. December 24/28, 1790.
18 *Ibid*. January 20/22, 1791.
19 *Ibid*. January 22/25, 1791.
20 *Ibid*. January 25/27, 1791.
21 *Ibid*. February 15/17, 1791.
22 *Ibid*. February 17/19, 1791.
23 *Reminiscences of Michael Kelly*. London 1826. Vol. I. p. 330 and *Musical Memoirs* by W. T. Parke. London 1830. Vol. I. p. 132.
24 *Faulkner's Dublin Journal*. June 4/7, 1791.
25 *Ibid*.   26 *Ibid*.   27 *Ibid*.
28 *Ibid*. June 21/23, 1791.
29 *Ibid*. June 23/25, 1791.
30 *Memoirs of the Musical Drama* by George Hogarth. London 1838. Vol. II. p. 449.
31 *The Thespian Dictionary*. London 1805. Under Charles Incledon.

32 *Faulkner's Dublin Journal.* July 7/9, 1791.

33 *Musical Memoirs* by W. T. Parke. London 1830. Vol. I. p. 136.

34 *Faulkner's Dublin Journal.* July 12/14, 1791.

35 *Ibid.*

36 *Ibid.*

37 *Ibid.* July 16/19, 1791.

38 *Ibid.* August 4/6, 1791.

39 *Ibid.*

40 *Ibid.* December 10/13, 1791.

41 *Ibid.*

42 *Ibid.*

43 *Musical Memoirs* by W. T. Parke. London 1830. Vol. I. p. 135.

44 *The Siege of Belgrade.* Vocal score. London. (N.D.) Published by J. Dale.

45 *Faulkner's Dublin Journal.* December 13/15, 1791.

46 *Dublin Evening Post.* June 9, 1792.

47 *Ibid.* July 7, 1792.

48 *The Present State of Music in Germany, the Netherlands and United Provinces* by Charles Burney. London 1773. Vol. II. pp. 109/110.

49 *Musical Memoirs* by W. T. Parke. London 1830. Vol. I. p. 102.

50 *The Present State of Music in Germany, the Netherlands and United Provinces* by Charles Burney. London 1773. Vol. II. p. 110.

51 *Morning Chronicle* (London). May 18, 1785.

52 *London Chronicle.* June 25/28, 1785.

53 *The Public Advertiser* (London). July 8, 1785.

54 *Ibid.* July 1, 1785.

55 *Grove's Dictionary of Music and Musicians* (Third Edition). London 1928. Vol. III. p. 311.

56 *The Present State of Music in Germany, the Netherlands and United Provinces* by Charles Burney. London 1773. Vol. II. p. 108.

57 *Ibid.* pp. 111/112.

58 *Musical Reminiscences* by the Earl of Mount Edgcumbe. London 1834. pp. 52/53.

59 *Queens of Song* by Ellen Creathorne Clayton. London 1863. Vol. I. p. 179.

60 *Morning Chronicle* (London). May 4, 1785.

61 *Ibid.* April 20, 1785.

62 *Dublin Evening Post* July 19, 1792.

63 *Ibid.* July 31, 1792.

64 *Ibid.* July 21, 1792.

65 *Ibid.* July 28, 1792.

66 *Ibid.* July 31, 1792.

67 *Ibid.* August 2, 1792.

68 *Ibid.* August 9, 1792.

69 *Ibid.* July 31, 1792.

70 *Ibid.* September 13, 1792.

CHAPTER 18

The End of an Era 1792–1797

1 *Freeman's Journal.* November 8/10, 1792.

2 *Ibid.* December 20/22, 1792.

3 *Dublin Evening Post.* November 13, 1792.

4 *Musical Memoirs* by W. T. Parke. London 1830. Vol. I. p. 304.

5 *Musical Reminiscences* by the Earl of Mount Edgcumbe. London 1834. p. 115.

6 *The Cyclopaedian Magazine and Dublin Monthly Register*. September 1807. p. 514.

7 *Dublin Evening Post*. December 4, 1792.

8 *Ibid*. December 6, 1792.

9 *Faulkner's Dublin Journal*. November 26, 1793.

10 *Ibid*. January 9, 1794.

11 *Ibid*. January 23, 1794.

12 *Reminiscences of Michael Kelly*. London 1826. Vol. II. p. 51.

13 *Ibid*. p. 53.

14 *Faulkner's Dublin Journal*. June 30, 1795.

15 *Musical Memoirs* by W. T. Parke. London 1830. Vol. I. p. 136.

16 *Dictionary of National Biography* under Maria Dickons *née* Poole.

17 *Ibid*.

18 *Faulkner's Dublin Journal*. July 14, 1795.

19 *Ibid*. July 13, 1795.

20 *Ibid*. July 27, 1795.

21 Playbill at Trinity College Library, Dublin.

22 *Ibid*.

23 *Faulkner's Dublin Journal*. January 2, 1796.

24 *Ibid*.

25 *The Italian Opera and Contemporary Ballet in London 1789–1820*. Compiled by William C. Smith. London 1955. pp. 32, 36, 42.

26 *Anglo-Irish Music 1780–1830* by Ita Margaret Hogan. Cork 1966. p. 218.

27 *Hibernian Journal*. April 27, 1796.

28 *The Italian Opera and Contemporary Ballet in London 1789–1820*. Compiled by William C. Smith. London 1955. pp. 32, 36, 42.

29 *The Public Advertiser* (London). March 7, 1782.

30 *Dublin Evening Post*. July 12, 1796.

31 *Ibid*. July 14, 1796.

32 *Ibid*.

33 *The Monthly Mirror*. London. May 1796. p. 54.

34 *The Thespian Dictionary*. London 1805. Under C. M. Florio.

35 *Musical Reminiscences* by the Earl of Mount Edgcumbe. London 1834. p. 76.

36 *Faulkner's Dublin Journal*. July 26, 1796.

37 *Ibid*. July 28, 1796.

38 *Ibid*.

39 *Ibid*.

40 *Ibid*.

41 *Ibid*. August 2, 1796.

42 *Dublin Evening Post*. August 2, 1796.

43 *Ibid*. August 4, 1796.

44 *Ibid*. August 9, 1796.

45 *Ibid*. August 4, 1796.

46 *Faulkner's Dublin Journal*. August 9, 1796.

47 *Dublin Evening Post*. August 9, 1796.

48 *Ibid*.

49 *Faulkner's Dublin Journal*. August 9, 1796.

50 *Hibernian Journal*. November 9, 1796.

51 *Dublin Evening Post.* November 8, 1796.
52 *Ibid.* November 10, 1796.
53 *Ibid.* November 12, 1796.
54 *Ibid.* November 15, 1796.
55 *Musical Reminiscences* by the Earl of Mount Edgcumbe. London 1834. p. 75.
56 *Dublin Evening Post.* November 17, 1796.
57 *Ibid.* November 26, 1796.
58 *Faulkner's Dublin Journal.* December 15, 1796.
59 *Hibernian Journal.* November 28, 1796.
60 *Ibid.*
61 *Tommaso Giordani: An Italian Composer in Ireland* by W. J. Lawrence. *The Musical Antiquary.* London. January 1911.
62 *Dublin Evening Post.* November 29, 1796.
63 *Faulkner's Dublin Journal.* November 29, 1796.
64 *Hibernian Journal.* January 2, 1797.
65 *Saunders' News-letter.* January 2, 1797.
66 *Ibid.*
67 *Ibid.* January 9, 1797.
68 *Ibid.*
69 *Ibid.*
70 *Hibernian Journal.* January 31, 1797.
71 *Musical Reminiscences* by the Earl of Mount Edgcumbe. London 1834. p. 75.
72 *Ibid.* p. 77.
73 *Hibernian Journal.* February 3, 1797.
74 *Ibid.* November 28, 1796.
75 *Musical Memoirs* by W. T. Parke. London 1830. Vol. I. p. 266.
76 *Recollections of the Life of John O'Keeffe, Written by Himself.* London 1826. Vol. II. p. 348.
77 *Ibid.*
78 *Hibernian Journal.* February 3, 1797.
79 *Ibid.*
80 *Ibid.* January 30, 1797.
81 *Musical Memoirs* by W. T. Parke. London 1830. Vol. I. p. 238.
82 *Hibernian Journal.* June 23, 1797.
83 *Reminiscences of Michael Kelly.* London 1826. Vol. II. p. 110.
84 *Hibernian Journal.* July 31, 1797.
85 *Ibid.* August 18, 1797.
86 *Dictionary of National Biography* under Spranger Barry.

BIBLIOGRAPHY

MANUSCRIPTS

Baptismal Register of the Parish Church of Saint-André, Bordeaux, now in the Archives de la
    Ville.
BELCHER, JAMES. An Account of the Secret Service Money. At Marsh's Library, Dublin (z 3 11.
    No. XLI. p. 183) Transcript by Dr. T. P. C. Kirkpatrick at Trinity College Library
    Dublin.
Blue Coat School, Dublin. Minute Book from the year 1669.
COLMAN, FRANCIS. MS Opera Register 1712–1734. Add. MS. 11. 258. British Museum.

MICROFILMS

Minute Book of the Dublin Musical Fund. The National Library, Dublin.
The York Courant. Colindale Annex, British Museum.

NEWSPAPERS

DUBLIN

Dublin Chronicle.
Dublin Courant.
Dublin Courier.
Dublin Evening Post.
Dublin Gazette.
The Dublin Intelligence.
Dublin Mercury.
Dublin News-Letter.
Dublin Weekly Journal.
Evening Herald.
Faulkner's Dublin Journal.
Freeman's Journal.
Hibernian Journal.
Hoey's Dublin Journal.
Pue's Occurrences.
Saunders' News-letter.
Volunteer Evening Post.

LONDON

The Daily Advertiser.
The Daily Courant.
Evening Post.
The Gazetteer.
General Advertiser.
General Evening Post.
Gray's Inn Journal.
Lloyd's Evening Post.
London Chronicle.
London Courant.
London Journal.
Morning Chronicle.
Morning Herald.
The Morning Post.
New Morning Post.
The Public Advertiser.
St James' Chronicle.
The World.

BOOKS AND PRINTED ARTICLES

Alumni Dublinenses 1593–1846. Ed. GEORGE DAMES BURTCHAELL and THOMAS ULICK SADLEIR London 1924.

AMBROSS, MISS. *The Life and Memoirs of the late Miss Ann Catley.* London 1790.

An Apology for the Life of George Anne Bellamy. London 1785. 6 v.

ASTON, ANTHONY. *A Sketch of the Author's Life written by Himself.* London 1730.

—— *Doctor Anthony's Advice to the Hibernian Aesop : or, An Epistle to the Author of the B——'s W—— g.* Dublin 1729.

—— *The Coy Shepherdess.* Dublin 1709.

BAKER, DAVID ERSKINE. *Biographia Dramatica : or, A Companion to the Playhouse.* London 1782. 2 v. 1812. 3 v.

BARRINGTON, SIR JONAH. *Personal Sketches of his own Times.* London 1827–32. 3 v.

BAUER, ANTON. *Opern und Operetten in Wien.* Graz—Köln 1955.

BEAUMONT, FRANCIS, and FLETCHER, JOHN. *The Prophetess : or the History of Dioclesian. With Alterations and Additions, after the Manner of an Opera* [by THOMAS BETTERTON]. London 1690.

BOADEN, JAMES. *Memoirs of the Life of John Philip Kemble.* London 1825. 2 v.

—— *Memoirs of Mrs. Siddons.* London 1893.

The British Union Catalogue of Early Music printed before the year 1801. Ed. EDITH B. SCHNAPPER. London 1957. 2 v.

BURKE, SIR BERNARD. *A Genealogical and Heraldic History of the Landed Gentry of Ireland* 10th Edition. London 1904.

BURNEY, CHARLES. *A General History of Music.* London 1776–89. 4 v. New York 1957. 2. v.

—— *An Account of the Musical Performances in Westminster Abbey and the Pantheon in Commemoration of Handel.* London 1785.

—— *Dr. Burney's Musical Tours in Europe.* Ed. PERCY A. SCHOLES. London 1959. 2 v.

—— *The Present State of Music in Germany, the Netherlands and United Provinces.* London 1772. 2 v.

Candid and Impartial Strictures on artists who have appeared at Drury Lane Theatre, the Little Theatre, Haymarket, and Covent Garden Theatre. London 1795.

CHETWOOD, WILLIAM RUFUS. *A General History of the Stage.* London 1749.

CIBBER, COLLEY. *An Apology for the Life of Mr. Colley Cibber, Comedian.* London 1740.

CLARK, WILLIAM SMITH. *The Early Irish Stage : The Beginnings to 1720.* Oxford 1955.

—— *The Irish Stage in the County Towns. 1720–1800.* Oxford 1965.

CLAYTON, ELLEN CREATHORNE. *Queens of Song.* London 1863. 2 v.

CLIVE, CATHERINE. *The Rehearsal : or, Bays in Petticoats.* Dublin 1753.

COFFEY, CHARLES. *The Beggar's Wedding.* Dublin 1729.

CURRAN, C. P. *The Rotunda Hospital, its Architects and Craftsmen.* Dublin 1945.

The Cyclopaedian Magazine and Dublin Monthly Register. Dublin 1807–09. 3 v.

DAVIES, THOMAS. *Memoirs of the Life of David Garrick.* London 1780.

DEAN, WINTON. *Handel's Dramatic Oratorios and Masques.* London 1959.

DELANY, MARY GRANVILLE. *The Autobiography and Correspondence of Mary Granville, Mrs. Delany.* Ed. LADY LLANOVER. London 1861. 3 v.

—— *Mrs. Delany at Court and among the Wits.* Intro. by R. BRINLEY JOHNSON. London 1925.

DENT, EDWARD J. *Foundations of English Opera.* Cambridge 1928.

—— *Opera.* London 1940.

DEUTSCH, OTTO ERICH. *Handel, a Documentary Biography*. London 1955.
DIBDIN, CHARLES. *A Complete History of the Stage*. London 1795. 5 v.
—— *The Musical Tour of Mr. Dibdin*. Sheffield 1788.
—— *The Songs of Charles Dibdin*. London 1842.
—— *The Professional Life of Mr. Dibdin written by Himself*. London 1803. 4 v.
Dictionary of National Biography. Oxford 1959–60.
DRYDEN, JOHN. *King Arthur, or The British Worthy*. London 1691.
DUNBAR, HOWARD HUNTER. *The Dramatic Career of Arthur Murphy*. New York 1946.
DUNTON, JOHN *The Dublin Scuffle*. London 1699.
EGERTON, WILLIAM. *Faithful Memoirs of the Life, Amours and Performances of that justly cele-brated and most Eminent Actress of her Time, Mrs. Anne Oldfield*. London 1731.
EINSTEIN, ALFRED. *Gluck*. Trans. Eric Blom. London 1964.
Enciclopedia dello Spettacolo. Rome 1954–64. 9 v.
Encyclopaedia Britannica. 14th Edition. Chicago 1948.
FALKINER. SIR FREDERICK R. *The Foundation of the Hospital and Free School of King Charles II. Oxmantown, Dublin*. Dublin 1906.
FITZPATRICK, WILLIAM JOHN. *A Note to the Cornwallis Papers*. Dublin 1859.
FLOOD, W. H. GRATTAN. *A History of Irish Music*. Dublin 1905.
—— *Introductory Sketch of Irish Musical History*. London 1921.
—— 'Dr. Arne's Visits to Dublin.' *The Musical Antiquary*. London July 1910.
—— 'Crow St. Music Hall, Dublin, from 1730 to 1754.' *Sammelbände der Internationalen Musik-Gesellschaft*. Leipzig. April-June 1910.
—— Transcript from the Public Record Office, Dublin. *The Musical Antiquary*. London July 1911.
GAGEY, EDMOND McADOO. *Ballad Opera*. New York 1937
[GARRICK, DAVID]. *The Letters of David Garrick*. Ed. DAVID M. LITTLE and GEORGE M. KAHRL. London 1963. 2 v.
GENEST, JOHN. *Some Account of the English Stage, from the Restoration in 1660 to 1830*. Bath 1832. 10 v.
The Gentleman's Magazine. Dublin 1809.
GILBERT, SIR JOHN. T. *A History of the City of Dublin*. Dublin 1854–9. 3 v.
GRATTAN, HENRY. *Memoirs of the Life and Times of the Rt. Hon. Henry Grattan*. London 1839. 2 v.
Grove's Dictionary of Music and Musicians. London. 1st Edition 1890. 4 v. 2nd Edition 1904–10. 5 v. 3rd Edition 1928. 5 v. 5th Edition 1954. 9 v.
HAWKINS, SIR JOHN. *A General History of the Science and Practice of Music*. London 1875. 3 v.
HERIOT, ANGUS. *The Castrati in Opera*. London 1956.
The Hibernian Magazine. Dublin 1771.
HIGHAM, CHARLES. *Francis Barthélemon*. 1896.
HITCHCOCK, ROBERT. *An Historical View of the Irish Stage*. Dublin 1788–94. 2 v.
HOGAN, ITA MARGARET. *Anglo-Irish Music 1780–1830*. Cork 1966.
HOGARTH, GEORGE. *Memoirs of the Musical Drama*. London 1838. 2 v.
KELLY, MICHAEL. *Reminiscences*. London 1826. 2 v.
KENRICK, WILLIAM. *The Pasquinade with Notes Variorum. Book the First*. London 1753.
LAWRENCE, W. J. 'Early Irish Ballad Opera and Comic Opera.' *Musical Quarterly*. New York July 1922.
—— 'Eighteenth Century Magazine Music.' *The Musical Antiquary*. London October 1911.

—— 'Tommaso Giordani: An Italian Composer in Ireland.' *The Musical Antiquary*. London January 1911.

LEONE, GABRIEL. *An Answer to a Scurrilous Advertisement*. London 1764.

Liber Munerum Publicorum Hiberniae. London 1824. 2 v.

LOEWENBERG, ALFRED. *Annals of Opera 1597–1940*. Geneva 1955. 2 v.

The London Stage 1660–1800. Carbondale, Illinois 1960–65. 8 v.

Memoirs of Mrs. Billington. London 1792.

MOLLOY, J. FITZGERALD. *The Romance of the Irish Stage*. London 1897. 2 v.

The Monthly Mirror. London 1796. 1797. 1801. 1803.

MOORE, ROBERT ETHERIDGE. *Henry Purcell and the Restoration Theatre*. London 1961.

MORGAN, LADY. *Memoirs, Autobiography, Diaries and Correspondence*. Ed. W. HEPWORTH DIXON London 1862. 2 v.

MOTTEUX, PIERRE ANTOINE. *The Island Princess, or the Generous Portuguese*. London 1699.

—— [Ed.] *The Gentleman's Journal : or the Monthly Miscellany*. London 1692.

MOUNT EDGCUMBE, EARL OF. *Musical Reminiscences*. London 1834.

[MOZART] *The Letters of Mozart and his Family*. Ed. EMILY ANDERSON. London 1938. 3 v.

The Musical Miscellany. London 1729. 2 v.

Die Musik in Geschichte und Gegenwart. Ed. FRIEDRICH BLUME. Kassel-Basel 1949–51. 14 v.

[NORTH, ROGER]. *Roger North on Music*. Ed. JOHN WILSON. London 1959. 2 v.

O'KEEFFE, JOHN. *Recollections of the Life of John O'Keeffe, Written by Himself*. London 1826 2 v.

O'MAHONY, CHARLES. *The Viceroys of Ireland*. London 1912.

Oxberry's Dramatic Biography and Histrionic Anecdotes. London 1826. 5 v.

PALTSITS, VICTOR HUGO. *Henry Stevens—Bibliographer and Biblioscoper*. New York 1951.

PARKE. WILLIAM THOMAS. *Musical Memoirs*. London 1830. 2 v.

PEAKE, RICHARD BRINSLEY. *Memoirs of the Colman Family*. London 1841. 2 v.

PILKINGTON, MATTHEW. Poems on Several Occasions. Dublin 1730.

DA PONTE, LORENZO. *Memoirs*. Trans. Elizabeth Abbott. New York 1967.

Rivista Musicale Italiana. Turin/Milan/Rome 1894/1955. 57 v.

ROBINSON, MICHAEL F. *Opera before Mozart*. London 1966.

Royal College of Music. Catalogue of Library. London 1909. 3 v.

SHELDON, ESTHER K. *Thomas Sheridan of Smock-Alley*. Princeton, New Jersey 1967.

SHERIDAN, THOMAS. *British Education : or, The Source of the Disorders of Great Britain*. London 1756.

—— *A Vindication of the Conduct of the late Manager of the Theatre Royal. Humbly address'd to the Publick*. Dublin 1754.

SMITH, WILLIAM C. *Concerning Handel*. London 1948.

—— [Compiled by]. *The Italian Opera and Contemporary Ballet in London 1789–1820*. London 1955.

SMITHERS, PETER. *The Life of Joseph Addison*. Oxford 1954.

SMOLLETT, TOBIAS. *The Expedition of Humphry Clinker*. Dublin 1771. 2 v.

SONNECK, O. G. *Catalogue of Opera Librettos printed before 1800*. Washington 1914. 2 v.

The Spectator. London 1711.

SPENCE, JOSEPH. *Anecdotes, Observations, and Characters of Books and Men*. London 1820.

STOCKWELL, LA TOURETTE. *Dublin Theatres and Theatre Customs 1637–1820*. Kingsport, Tennessee 1938.

STREATFEILD, R. A. *Handel*. London 1909.

The Tatler. London 1709–10.

TENDUCCI, MRS. *A True and Genuine Narrative of Mr. and Mrs. Tenducci in a Letter to a Friend at Bath.* London 1768.

The Theatre. London 1720.

Theatrical Biography: or, Memoirs of the Principal Performers of the Three Theatres Royal. London 1772. 2 v.

The Theatrical Observer. London 1821.

The Thespian Dictionary. London 1805.

TOWNSEND, HORATIO. *An Account of the Visit of Handel to Dublin.* Dublin 1852.

URFEY, THOMAS D' *Wit and Mirth* or, *Pills to purge Melancholy.* London 1722. 6 v.

VICTOR, BENJAMIN. *A History of the Theatres of London and Dublin from 1730 to the Present Time.* London 1761. 2 v.

—— *Original Letters, Dramatic Pieces and Poems.* London 1776. 2 v.

The Westminster Magazine. London 1775. 1777.

WESTRUP, J. A. *Purcell.* London 1965.

WHITE, ERIC WALTER. *The Rise of English Opera.* London 1951.

WIEL, TADDEO. *I Teatri Musicali Veneziani del Settecento.* Venice 1897.

WILKINSON, TATE. *Memoirs of His Own Life.* Dublin 1791. 3 v.

WIMSATT, WILLIAM KURTZ. *The Portraits of Alexander Pope.* London 1965.

YORKE-LONG, ALAN. *Music at Court.* London 1954.

YOUNG, ARTHUR. *A Tour in Ireland.* London 1780. 2 v.

YOUNG. M. J. *Memoirs of Mrs. Crouch.* London 1806. 2 v.

YOUNG. PERCY. M. *Handel.* London 1948.

INDEX

The Author

T. J. Walsh studied singing with Professor A. G. Viani in Dublin and broadcast frequently both as a singer and lecturer on opera from Radio Éireann during the 'thirties and early 'forties. In 1951 he founded Wexford Festival Opera, acting as its artistic director for the next sixteen years. Dublin University conferred the degree of M.A. *honoris causa* on him in recognition of this work. On several occasions he has been a member of the jury of the Concours International de Chant de Toulouse. Since 1968 he has been researching and writing the history of opera in Dublin, Paris and Monte Carlo.

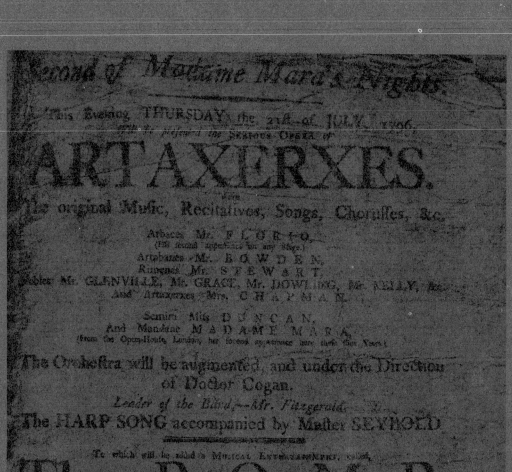

Second of Madame Mara's Nights.

This Evening THURSDAY the 21st of JULY 1796.

Will be presented the Serious Opera of

ARTAXERXES.

With the original Music, Recitatives, Songs, Chorusses, &c.

Arbaces Mr. FLORIO,
(His second appearance on any Stage.)

Artabanes Mr. BOWDEN,

Rimenes Mr. STEWART,

Nobles Mr. GLENVILLE, Mr. GRACE, Mr. DOWLING, Mr. KELLY, &c.

And Artaxerxes Mrs. CHAPMAN.

Semira Miss DUNCAN,

And Mandane MADAME MARA,
(from the Opera-House, London, her second appearance here this Season.)

The Orchestra will be augmented, and under the Direction
of Doctor Cogan.

Leader of the Band,—Mr. Fitzgerald.

The HARP SONG accompanied by Master SEYROED

To which will be added a Musical Entertainment, called,

The R O M P.

Watty Cockney Mr. STEWART,

Captain Sightly Mr. GLENVILLE,

Old Cockney Mr. BARRET,

And Barnacle Mr. GRACE.

Penelope Miss DUNCAN,

Miss Le Blond Mrs. KELLY,

Quasheba Mrs. BARRET,

And Priscilla Tomboy Mrs. CHAPMAN.

No Tickets and Places in the Boxes to be had of Mr. CHAPMAN, Bookkeeper, at the Theatre.

THE TENTH NIGHT OF

Mr. Kemble's Engagement.

To-morrow Evening, the Historical Tragedy of

CORIOLANUS.

Coriolanus Mr. KEMBLE.